ASCL STUDIES IN COMPARATIVE LAW

ASCL Studies in Comparative Law is designed to broaden theoretical and practical knowledge of the world's many legal systems. With more than sixty years' experience, the American Society of Comparative Law has been a leader in the study and analysis of comparative law. By promoting the investigation of legal problems in a comparative light, whether theoretical or empirical, as essential to the advancement of legal science, it provides an essential service to legal practitioners and those seeking reform of the law. This book series will extend these aims to the publication of monographs and comparative studies of specific legal problems.

The series has two series editors. David Gerber is Distinguished Professor of Law and Co-Director of the Program in International and Comparative Law at Chicago-Kent College of Law, Illinois Institute of Technology. He is currently President of the American Society of Comparative Law. Mortimer Sellers is Regents Professor of the University System of Maryland and Director of the Baltimore Center for International and Comparative Law. He is an Associate Member of the International Academy of Comparative Law.

Juries, Lay Judges, and Mixed Courts

A GLOBAL PERSPECTIVE

Edited by

SANJA KUTNJAK IVKOVIĆ

Michigan State University, Michigan

SHARI SEIDMAN DIAMOND

Northwestern University Pritzker School of Law and
American Bar Foundation, Illinois

VALERIE P. HANS

Cornell Law School, New York

NANCY S. MARDER

Chicago-Kent College of Law
Illinois Institute of Technology, Illinois

CAMBRIDGE
UNIVERSITY PRESS

CAMBRIDGE
UNIVERSITY PRESS

University Printing House, Cambridge CB2 8BS, United Kingdom

One Liberty Plaza, 20th Floor, New York, NY 10006, USA

477 Williamstown Road, Port Melbourne, VIC 3207, Australia

314–321, 3rd Floor, Plot 3, Splendor Forum, Jasola District Centre, New Delhi – 110025, India

79 Anson Road, #06–04/06, Singapore 079906

Cambridge University Press is part of the University of Cambridge.

It furthers the University's mission by disseminating knowledge in the pursuit of education, learning, and research at the highest international levels of excellence.

www.cambridge.org
Information on this title: www.cambridge.org/9781108483940
DOI: 10.1017/9781108669290

First published 2021

A catalogue record for this publication is available from the British Library.

ISBN 978-1-108-48394-0 Hardback

Contents

EDITORS

Sanja Kutnjak Ivković is a professor at Michigan State University, School of Criminal Justice, USA. She holds a doctorate in criminology and a doctorate in law. Her interdisciplinary, comparative, and international research on courts and policing has resulted in numerous presentations at international conferences and publications in social science journals and law reviews. In addition to her book *Lay Participation in Criminal Trials: The Case of Croatia* (1999), Professor Kutnjak Ivković has coauthored or coedited six books on police corruption and police integrity. Her book *Reclaiming Justice: The International Tribunal for the Former Yugoslavia and Local Courts* (2011), coauthored with John Hagan, won the 2014 Academy of Criminal Justice Sciences International Section Book Award. Professor Kutnjak Ivković received the 2017 Mueller Award for Distinguished Contributions to International Criminal Justice from the Academy of Criminal Justice Sciences International Section. She is currently serving as the chair of the *Division of International Criminology*, American Society of Criminology. Professor Kutnjak Ivković is the cofounder and cochair of the Law and Society Association Collaborative Research Network on Lay Participation.

Shari Seidman Diamond is the Howard J. Trienens Professor of Law at Northwestern University Pritzker School of Law and a research professor at the American Bar Foundation, USA. A lawyer and social psychologist, she has authored numerous publications in law reviews and behavioral science journals on the jury process, including research on real jury deliberations, and on legal decision-making, including the use of science by courts. Professor Diamond has been editor of the *Law & Society Review*, served as president of the American Psychology-Law Society, taught as a visiting professor at Harvard University Law School, received the 2010 Harry Kalven, Jr., Award for Contributions to Research in Law and Society, and is an elected member of the American Academy of Arts and Sciences. She has lectured to academic and judicial audiences in the United States and around the world, and her publications have been cited by US state and federal courts, including the US Supreme Court. Professor Diamond helped draft the 2005 American Bar Association's Principles for Juries and Jury Trials.

Valerie P. Hans is the Charles F. Rechlin Professor of Law at Cornell Law School, USA. Trained as a social scientist, she has carried out extensive empirical research, authored numerous articles in social science journals and law reviews, and lectured around the globe on juries and jury reforms as well as the uses of social science in law. In addition to her research on civil and criminal juries in the United States, Professor Hans is studying the introduction of juries and other forms of citizen participation in other countries, including Argentina, Japan, South Korea, Russia, Spain, and Taiwan. Her books on the jury include *Business on Trial: The Civil Jury and Corporate Responsibility* (2000); *The Jury System: Contemporary Scholarship* (2006); and two books coauthored with Neil

Vidmar: *Judging the Jury* (1986) and *American Juries: The Verdict* (2007). Associate editor or coeditor of three law and social science journals, Professor Hans has served as president of the Law and Society Association and as copresident of the Society for Empirical Legal Studies.

Nancy S. Marder is a professor of law at Chicago-Kent College of Law and director of the Justice John Paul Stevens Jury Center, USA. She is a graduate of Yale College, Cambridge University, and Yale Law School, where she was an articles editor of the *Yale Law Journal*. She clerked at every level of the US federal court system, including a two-year clerkship with Justice John Paul Stevens at the US Supreme Court. Professor Marder is currently writing a book, *The Power of the Jury: Transforming Citizens into Jurors*, and has published *The Jury Process* (2005), as well as numerous law review articles, book chapters, and essays on juries, judges, and courts. She has edited or coedited six symposia on lay participation and the courts, organized two conferences on the jury, and presented her work in the United States and abroad. In 2016, Professor Marder became a member of the American Law Institute and an academic fellow of the Pound Civil Justice Institute; in 2017, she received the inaugural Freehling Award, and in 2019, she received a Baldy Fellowship.

Contributors

Vanina G. Almeida is a lawyer in the Federal Court of Criminal Appeal, Argentina. She is secretary of the Asociación Argentina de Juicio por Jurados (AAJJ, Argentine Association of Trial by Jury).

Denise C. Bakrokar works at a criminal federal court in Argentina, and at the Delegación de Asociaciones Israelitas Argentinas (Delegation of Argentine Jewish Associations).

María Inés Bergoglio is Professor Emerita of Sociology of Law at the National University of Córdoba, Argentina, and a member of the National Academy of Law and Social Sciences.

Mariana Bilinski works at a criminal federal court in Argentina, and is a member of the board of directors of the Asociación Argentina de Juicio por Jurados.

Natali D. Chizik is a lawyer and a graduate student at the Peter A. Allard School of Law, University of British Columbia, Canada, and a member of the board of directors of the Asociación Argentina de Juicio por Jurados, Argentina.

Marie Comiskey is a senior counsel with the Public Prosecution Service of Canada and a sessional instructor in the graduate department at the Centre for Criminology and Sociolegal Studies at the University of Toronto, Canada.

Shari Seidman Diamond is the Howard J. Trienens Professor of Law at Northwestern University Pritzker School of Law and a research professor at the American Bar Foundation, USA.

Hiroshi Fukurai is a professor of sociology at the University of California, Santa Cruz, USA, and president of the Asian Law and Society Association (ALSA).

Claire M. Germain is the Clarence J. TeSelle Professor of Law (retired) at the University of Florida Levin College of Law, USA, and a professor of law (retired) at Cornell Law School, USA.

Valerie P. Hans is the Charles F. Rechlin Professor of Law at Cornell Law School, USA.

Andrés Harfuch is the chief public defender in San Martín district, Province of Buenos Aires, Argentina, and an associate professor at the Law School of Buenos Aires University, Argentina.

John D. Jackson is a professor of comparative criminal law and procedure at the School of Law, University of Nottingham, UK, and is a qualified barrister.

Mar Jimeno-Bulnes is a professor of procedural law at the University of Burgos, Spain.

Nikolai Kovalev is an associate professor of criminology at Wilfrid Laurier University, Canada, and a licensed barrister in Ontario.

Sanja Kutnjak Ivković is a professor of criminology and criminal justice at Michigan State University, School of Criminal Justice, USA.

Stefan Machura is a professor of criminology and criminal justice at Bangor University, UK.

Nancy S. Marder is a professor of law at Chicago-Kent College of Law and director of the Justice John Paul Stevens Jury Center, USA.

Giorgi Meladze is an associate professor at the Ilia State University, Georgia, and serves as the director of the Center for Constitutional Research affiliated with the law school of Ilia State University.

Sergei Nasonov is an associate professor of criminal procedure law at Kutafin Moscow State Law University, Russia, and a barrister in the Moscow City Bar Association.

Anna Offit is an assistant professor of law at Southern Methodist University, Dedman School of Law, USA.

Lilián Andrea Ortiz works at a criminal federal court in Argentina. She is a member of the board of directors of the Asociación Argentina de Juicio por Jurados, Argentina.

Jaihyun Park is a professor of psychology at Baruch College of the City University of New York, USA.

Maria Sidonie Porterie is a political scientist member of the board of directors of the Institute for Comparative Studies in Political and Social Sciences and director of the Criminal Policy Program of the same organization, Argentina.

Christoph Rennig is a presiding judge at the High Court Frankfurt am Main, Germany.

Aldana Romano is a political scientist and the executive director of the Institute for Comparative Studies in Political and Social Sciences and a consultant for the Buenos Aires City Legislature, Argentina.

Dimitri Vanoverbeke is a professor at Katholieke Universiteit (KU) Leuven, Belgium, and director of the Department of East Asian and Arabic Studies.

Acknowledgments

The editors are grateful to their spouses, Zoran Ivković, Stewart Diamond, Michael Bend, and Jeremy Eden, who have continuously provided encouragement, support, and exceptional patience as we disrupted their lives with this book. In addition, all of the editors have enjoyed the generous support of their respective institutions: for Sanja Kutnjak Ivković from Michigan State University, for Shari Seidman Diamond from Northwestern University Pritzker School of Law and the American Bar Foundation, for Valerie P. Hans from Cornell Law School (including the Milton and Eleanor Gould Research Fund and the Eisenberg Empirical Legal Studies Memorial Fund), and for Nancy S. Marder from Chicago-Kent College of Law.

The editors also wish to acknowledge the critically important support of the National Science Foundation. NSF grant number SES-1446070, Expanding Law and Social Science Research by International Research Collaboration, to Valerie P. Hans, Lawrence M. Friedman, Manuel A. Gómez, and Masayuki Murayama, provided essential travel funding for a number of the contributors whose chapters are included in this book. The Law and Society Association's financial and logistical support, and our colleagues in the International Research Collaborative on Lay Participation in Legal Decision-Making, were key factors to the success in bringing a diverse group of scholars from around the globe to annual meetings in New Orleans, Mexico City, and Washington, DC, to join in international collaborative exchanges. This book is one of the products of that collaboration.

1

Introduction

Sanja Kutnjak Ivković, Shari Seidman Diamond, Valerie P. Hans, and Nancy S. Marder

The power to convict and punish those who break the law is one of the most fundamental powers of government. In most countries, meting out justice is in the hands of legally trained judges. Remarkably, however, in many countries around the world, the government shares this awesome power with ordinary citizens. Through lay participation, citizens who have no training in the law participate in the criminal justice system and decide the guilt or innocence of their fellow citizens.

This book provides a view of the different forms of lay participation and the ways in which they are evolving across the globe. Some countries have their citizens participate as jurors on traditional juries, in which the jury reaches a verdict on its own. Other countries use a mixed tribunal or mixed court that includes lay citizens (also called lay assessors) and professional judges working together to decide the case. Still other countries use lay magistrates who can consult an adviser on questions of law, or use lay courts with lay judges who decide cases without professional input. Some countries use more than one form of lay participation.

The chapters in this book explore not only the different forms of lay participation around the world, but also how ordinary citizens bring certain advantages to the task. Lay participation incorporates community perspectives into legal decision-making and helps to provide greater legitimacy for the legal system and for verdicts. These benefits help to explain why countries in East Asia, Europe, and South America have made recent and remarkable advances toward lay decision-making, introducing for the first time traditional or advisory juries, or mixed tribunals with lay and professional judges. These benefits also help to explain why some countries have used lay participation for decades, if not centuries. Their use of lay participation is long-standing and enjoys widespread public support.

However, the use of lay participants in the criminal justice system is not without its challenges. Their use raises questions about their competence. After all, they are not trained in the law. There is also the question whether lay participants provide sufficient explanations for their decisions so that criminal defendants understand the verdict and accept it as fair. These concerns have led some countries to pull back from the use of laypersons as legal decision-makers. Yet another reason countries might retreat from lay participation is when the government or members of the judiciary want to exercise greater control over legal decision-making. In these countries, governments might restrict the kinds of cases that can be heard by lay participants, may shift from an independent jury to a mixed court of lay and professional judges, or might even abandon lay participation altogether.

The book chapters capture countries' diverse approaches to lay participation. Accordingly, we group together countries that have made advances in lay participation, countries that have enduring systems of lay participation, and countries that have responded to the challenges of lay participation by pulling back from it. The organization of this book illustrates that lay participation in a country is not fixed in stone; lay participation is being advanced, reinforced, or replaced in countries around the world. These shifting responses to lay participation also suggest the importance of stepping back and taking a global perspective, and this we do in our final section.

LEARNING FROM THE PAST

Historical accounts from Greece, England, Germany, and elsewhere document the fact that lay members of the community have long participated as decision-makers in legal disputes. For example, early accounts from England describe how propertied men from local communities formed juries that decided criminal and civil claims, determining both factual and legal issues (Constable, 1994; Green, 1985). Likewise, in Germany, free men from the community determined the outcomes of legal controversies. German practice evolved from including all free men from a community in the decision-making body, to a subgroup of free men, and by the eighth century to landowners and other prominent men who would serve permanently as lay judges (Kutnjak Ivković, 1999). In other countries, indigenous courts and tribal courts, presided over by community leaders, decided legal disputes. Community members were thus in an ideal position to decide cases in line with local knowledge, norms, and values.

The development of the legal profession in these countries, however, led to a gradual but marked shift in the role of lay participants. In England, for example, law-trained judges began to distinguish between "law" and "facts," appropriating the former to themselves and the latter to lay jurors, thus constricting the jury's law-interpreting role. In Germany, the complexities of Roman law, which increasingly dominated German courts, required legal knowledge and expertise, and thus legally trained judges joined lay judges to determine the outcomes of German cases.

As the legal profession continued to develop over the centuries, and the number of lawyers and law-trained judges increased (Abel & Lewis, 1995), many countries shifted substantial responsibility for legal fact-finding to legally trained experts. As these shifts occurred, people debated the appropriate roles and tasks of legal professionals versus lay members of the community. However, as we see in the chapters in this volume, this debate continues today. As the chapters reveal, continuing tensions persist as countries assess the optimal nature and scope of lay participation in their legal systems.

ADVANCES IN LAY PARTICIPATION

Substantial advances in lay participation have occurred around the globe in the past 25 years. Each of the chapters in Part I describes one of those recently implemented systems. Although these countries that are new to lay participation come from different cultural and legal traditions in South America, East Asia, and Europe, several consistent themes appear in the conditions that laid the foundation for lay participation and the concerns that influenced the design of these systems. Nonetheless, these countries chose different approaches, and they invite comparisons now and in the future as more cases are tried in these still-new systems.

In the modern world, legal systems typically are controlled by a cadre of professional judges and lawyers. What then leads a country to give laypersons a decision-making role in a setting previously characterized by professional control? In each instance, the proposal to include laypersons arose in a democracy in response to dissatisfaction with the professionally run legal system and mistrust of the judiciary. Stimulated by popular perceptions of judicial incompetence or corruption, skepticism about the ability of the criminal justice system to provide security, or the belief that the judiciary was responsible for wrongful convictions, movements arose to address public discontent by introducing direct community participation. In each instance, the call for lay participation received support from important elites, including both judges and scholars. But the introduction and adoption of lay participation was neither hasty nor sudden. In each country, the move was preceded by intense debate, and in some instances, by public mock trials and an experimental period.

The form of lay participation chosen in each country responded to common concerns, but the ways used to address those concerns differed. Thus, some legal professionals in each of these countries worried that by giving up substantial control to laypersons, the resulting decisions would be punitive or arbitrary, and untethered to the relevant law. To address that concern, some systems retained direct participation of professional judges in decision-making through mixed tribunals (Japan and the province of Córdoba in Argentina) while others included legal advisors (Spain) or made the all-lay jury's verdict advisory (South Korea). The newest systems in Argentina, however, took the full step toward lay participation, creating classic all-lay jury systems and focusing on jury instructions to provide legal guidance.

The choices in design did not end there and are still evolving. How many laypersons should participate in each trial? What offenses should laypersons decide? Should they also participate in sentencing? Should the decision rule require unanimity? If not, what majority? On a mixed tribunal, can laypersons outvote the professional judges? What form should the verdict take, a general verdict or a verdict accompanied by reasons? And how final is the verdict? As these systems mature, they will present opportunities to compare the effects of the different choices made by each country in designing the features of its system. Part I presents a first look.

Argentina has the newest institutions in Part I that have implemented lay participation. Nine authors wrote "The Rise of the Jury in Argentina: Evolution in Real Time" (Chapter 2): Vanina G. Almeida, Denise C. Bakrokar, Mariana Bilinski, Natali D. Chizik, Andrés Harfuch, Lilián Andrea Ortiz, Maria Sidonie Porterie, Aldana Romano, and Shari Seidman Diamond. They characterize their chapter as "evolution in real time" because the development of the jury in Argentina has spread and is evolving very quickly in the modern era. Most of this chapter's authors have been directly involved in educational and legislative efforts to bring trial by jury to Argentina.

Although the country's 1853 federal constitution promised jury trials, jury systems in Argentina took more than 150 years to emerge. Scholars, judges, and reformers in recent years argued that jury systems could address widespread distrust in the legal system. In the face of resistance, the constitution provided support for the change. Although no federal jury law has yet been passed, the provinces have taken up the mantle of fulfilling that constitutional promise. In the past decade, 8 of the country's 23 provinces have passed all-lay jury laws, the most recent in 2019. Others are currently considering jury legislation. Against the backdrop of a civil-law context, with its inquisitorial traditions, the move toward jury trials has been accompanied by the introduction of adversarial procedures and a shift to oral, public trials, bringing increases in transparency and decreases in the delay that previously characterized criminal justice proceedings. Thus, the jury has been operating as a Trojan horse to produce structural changes beyond the introduction of lay participation. Early research on the reception to jury trials has found support from both the jurors and the legal professionals who have participated in them. It has also highlighted the need for more professional training to deal with these new procedural demands. One future trend to watch is whether the early interest in Argentina's lay activity from its neighbors will lead to expansion of lay participation in other countries in South America.

In designing its new jury trials, Argentina has instituted features not typically seen in other jury systems. For example, all of Argentina's juries are required to have equal gender representation. But the Argentine provinces also vary in the procedural features they have included in their jury systems. In Mendoza, where the jury is required to reach a unanimous verdict, if the jury cannot agree and a second trial also results in a hung jury, the defendant will be acquitted rather than eligible for another trial. In Chaco, a province with a substantial indigenous population, half the jurors in a trial with an indigenous community member as victim and defendant must be members of the indigenous community. In 2019, the Supreme Court of Argentina explicitly endorsed the right of each province to design its own jury procedures, so innovative versions of the jury are likely to continue to develop in Argentina and perhaps influence lay systems elsewhere.

María Inés Bergoglio's chapter, "Twelve Years of Mixed Tribunals in Argentina" (Chapter 3), describes the experience in the province of Córdoba, which implemented the first system of lay participation in Argentina over a decade ago. In 2004, it introduced mixed tribunals. Unlike the all-lay juries that have been introduced more recently in other provinces, Córdoba's mixed tribunals sit in panels of eight laypersons and three professional judges. The members of the panel include a presiding judge who only votes if the other 10 are equally divided. A majority determines the verdict, so in principle the laypersons can outvote the professionals on the tribunal, although they almost never do so. Bergoglio was able to examine the final vote distributions for the 721 defendants tried by the mixed tribunals between 2005 and 2017. Concurrence on final votes between judges and jurors was lower than in other countries with mixed tribunals, but higher than the level of judge–jury agreement found when juries deliberate alone.

As in other countries, and despite surveys indicating increased support for being tough on crime, when citizens and professional judges on the tribunals disagreed, the laypersons tended to favor acquittals or convictions on lesser offenses. Although surveys and interviews indicated that most laypersons on the mixed tribunals were satisfied with their experience, interviews revealed some instances in which laypersons reported having been pressured by the professional judges. In 2017, the Supreme Court of Córdoba specified that the laypersons should deliberate amongst themselves before the professional judges join them, which was a change expected to empower the laypersons.

The hope among advocates of the mixed tribunals was that they would increase legitimacy and trust in the justice system. Surveys comparing attitudes in 1993 and 2011 showed that modest increases in perceived legitimacy had occurred, but it was still early in the life of the new system. Further surveys are needed to assess its full impact.

Dimitri Vanoverbeke and Hiroshi Fukurai's chapter, "Lay Participation in the Criminal Trial in Japan: A Decade of Activity and Its Sociopolitical Consequences" (Chapter 4), describes *Saiban'in seido*, a system of mixed tribunals that was introduced in Japan in 2009, after a five-year period of preparation. The intent was to promote citizen understanding of the judicial system as a way to raise citizens' confidence in it, and to address discontent with some high-profile instances of innocent defendants who had been executed.

Saiban'in seido consists of six laypersons and three professional judges who deliberate together to determine the verdict and sentence (if the defendant is convicted). Decisions are made by a majority vote, although the majority must include at least one professional judge. During its first decade, the *Saiban'in* tried over 12,000 defendants. The authors show that the nearly 100% conviction rate in these trials has never dropped below 98%. They also identify changes that have occurred in these trials over the decade. Trials and deliberations have become longer, the number of trials has dropped, and defendants are less likely to confess. The mystery is why acquittals remain so rare. Prosecutors may have changed the approach they take to charging decisions by bringing only extremely strong cases to trial. Another possibility is that the laypersons have had little influence on the verdicts.

The *Saiban'in* system, however, appears to have had important sociopolitical effects not measured directly by trial verdicts. The participation of laypersons in the justice system has been welcomed on the island of Okinawa because it has given the islanders jurisdiction over American military personnel stationed there. In addition, throughout Japan, former *Saiban'in* have organized associations and actively participated in policy debates on the death penalty and the push to videotape interrogations as a way to reduce the likelihood of a wrongful conviction. This post-*Saiban'in* activity highlights the important role that lay participation can play in enhancing civic engagement.

Jaihyun Park's chapter, "The Korean Jury System: The First Decade" (Chapter 5), provides an analysis of Korea's decade-long experience with its advisory jury system. A compromise between the all-citizen jury and the mixed tribunal, the jury's verdict in Korea is not binding. A constitutional provision giving defendants the right to trial by a judge has been used to justify having judges retain the final decision on the verdict, but early questions about juror competence also contributed to hesitation about giving laypersons complete responsibility for the verdict. To address questions about jury competence, a five-year monitoring program was implemented. Although the favorable evaluation included a recommendation to presumptively accept the jury's verdict, the Korean jury remains advisory.

Another distinctive feature of the Korean jury system is that if the jurors cannot reach unanimity, they must consult with the presiding judge and may then decide by a majority vote. Unanimous votes are ultimately reached in about 80% of cases, but we cannot tell how often judicial consultation occurred. Thus, although judge–jury agreement rates in Korea appear to be quite high, it is difficult to assess the independence of the Korean jury. Where the judge and jury disagree, the pattern of disagreement mirrors the greater relative leniency of the jurors seen in other countries, and also appears in the sentencing recommendations that Korean jurors are permitted to give.

Support for the Korean jury system has emerged not only from the Korean jurors, but also from the *Daebeobwon* (Supreme Court of Korea), which emphasized that jury decisions need to be respected. This support may lay the groundwork for future changes that will further strengthen the Korean jury.

Spain is the oldest of the lay participation systems discussed in Part I. Mar Jimeno-Bulnes's chapter, "The Twenty-Fifth Anniversary of the Spanish Jury" (Chapter 6), describes a jury system that was designed to incorporate elements from the common law in a country with a civil-law tradition, but with a variation on common-law practice that provides for greater legal control. The Spanish jury trial is an adversarial procedure in which the jurors are instructed on the law by the judge, but can be assisted by a legally qualified court clerk who might provide legal advice or assist in writing a "reasoned" verdict that gives explanations for the jury's decision. In the early years of the Spanish jury, growing pains were evident, as judges found the jury's reasons insufficient in nearly half the cases. The court clerk is in a position to help the jury with stating its reasons, but how much the court clerk does or should assist is the subject of some discussion.

Several changes have occurred over time in the types of offenses heard by juries, and there has been a general increase in plea bargaining and a drop in jury trials. These changes make it difficult to assess whether conviction probabilities have changed, but the percentage of convictions is higher in recent years than it had been in the early years.

The reaction to several high-profile jury verdicts in Spain points to an important and controversial role for media coverage of these trials when lay participation is not a deeply rooted feature of the criminal justice system. An unpopular verdict may raise questions about the viability of the institution, and in Spain it appeared to contribute to a drop in popular support for the jury. Nonetheless, despite such threats posed by these high-profile cases in Spain, Mar Jimeno-Bulnes reports that the jury trial at 25 years appears to have achieved social and legal acceptance in Spain.

In all of the systems described in Part I, the first jury or mixed court trials were heralded as important democratic experiments and covered extensively in the media. These initial trials were monitored carefully. Although some verdicts received mixed reactions, favorable reports emerged on the diligence and contributions of the lay participants. The legal professionals reported approvingly, sometimes with surprise, on the changes. In surveys of the lay participants in all of these systems, a large majority of respondents consistently expressed positive reactions to their service on the trials, although in some cases lay participants raised objections to particular procedures or rules. Overall, all five chapters provide evidence that, although some procedural adjustments may be required, the systems have promising futures for both decision-making and the legitimacy of lay participation in these countries.

ENDURING SYSTEMS OF LAY PARTICIPATION

The chapters on lay participation in England and Wales, Germany, and Canada describe enduring systems of lay participation. The forms of lay participation in these countries differ – with magistrates in England and Wales, lay assessors in Germany, and jurors in Canada – yet these forms of lay participation are well accepted and have endured for centuries. One benefit to countries with a long-standing tradition of lay participation is that they have found a way to introduce community values into their legal decision-making. In addition, they can serve as models for other countries interested in introducing lay participation into their legal decision-making in order to make their legal decision-making more accessible to the citizenry. Another benefit is that these countries can learn from each other in order to make improvements in their own forms of lay participation. Finally, countries such as England and Wales, Germany, and Canada, with their long-standing tradition of lay participation, can help to shed light on the question: What enables a country to sustain its form of lay participation over time?

Stefan Machura's chapter, "'… And My Right': The Magistrates' Courts in England and Wales" (Chapter 7), describes the practice of magistrates' courts in England and Wales. These courts trace their lineage back to the fourteenth century. The courts make use of lay participants who serve as magistrates, sometimes sitting as single decision-makers and sometimes sitting in panels of two or three, to decide criminal cases. The magistrates are not professionals, but are assisted by a legal adviser who is trained in the law. When the magistrates sit as a panel, the senior chairperson presides. The hearing is adversarial, with the prosecutor presenting the case and the defendant usually represented by counsel. The panel of magistrates deliberates together, but can invite the legal adviser into the deliberation room to answer questions of law. The magistrates decide whether the defendant is guilty or not guilty, and if guilty, then the magistrates determine the sentence as well. The magistrates also take care in explaining their verdict and sentence to the defendant so that he or she understands both.

The magistrates' court has several striking features. One is that the position of magistrate is well-regarded in England and Wales, and although it requires a significant time commitment, it is viewed as an honor. Another feature is that the magistrates take more time than the professional judges to hear a case, to learn about the defendant, and to issue an appropriate sentence that they explain carefully to the defendant. The youth court in England and Wales, which is a special section of the magistrates' courts, works even harder than the general magistrates' courts to engage the young defendant, to hear his or her perspective, and to explain its decision in a way that the young defendant will understand. Thus, the magistrates' court works hard to make the legal system understandable to those who are brought before it, and having lay participants as magistrates helps to ensure that the case will be presented and explained in terms that a layperson can understand.

Although magistrates are not as common around the world as other forms of lay participation such as jurors and lay assessors, they do offer other countries a model that has several advantages. Magistrates introduce community values into the legal decision-making process. They are also well suited as laypeople to make the law accessible to those who appear before them. They are able to explain their decisions so that an ordinary citizen will understand them. Of course, no system is perfect, and magistrates' courts raise questions about how representative magistrates are of the general population and how independent they can be as a legal decision-maker if they have to rely on legal advisers for questions of law. However, magistrates' courts are well regarded in England and Wales. Perhaps this is because they are so deeply rooted in the countries' history. Other potential explanations are that they continue to be a way of ensuring that community values play an integral role in deciding criminal cases and that the decisions reached by magistrate courts are well explained to the parties affected by them.

Stefan Machura and Christoph Rennig's chapter, "'In the Name of the People': Lay Assessors in Germany" (Chapter 8), describes the role of lay assessors who serve on mixed tribunals in Germany alongside professional judges. Lay assessors are ordinary citizens who sit with professional judges on a variety of courts, including the criminal courts, which is the focus of this chapter. Lay participation in criminal trials in Germany dates back to the nationwide unification of the judiciary code in 1869 and has been widely accepted since then.

The proceedings and the trial are investigatory in nature, and the professional judges perform the work during the preparatory phase, which means the professional judges acquire background about the case that the lay assessors lack. Indeed, only the professional judges have access to the case dossier, which the public prosecutor has prepared. The lay assessors participate only during the oral and public trial, but they have the same responsibilities as the professional judges. All of the judges – professional and lay judges alike – have to decide the factual and legal questions. The challenge for lay assessors is to make sure that they participate during the trial and deliberations and to avoid being deferential to the professional judges, who after all have legal training, access to the dossier before the trial, and a greater preliminary role to play than the lay assessors. The voting rule helps to ensure that the lay assessors remain relevant; the verdict and sentence require a two-thirds majority by all participating judges (both professional judges and lay assessors) by the mixed tribunal, typically featuring the majority of lay judges.

Interestingly, the lay assessors and professional judges who sit on a mixed tribunal together strive to reach a consensual decision. In other words, they try to reach agreement and to avoid a vote. Machura and Rennig explain that the German court strongly encourages cooperation and consensus and that there is also a culture of consensus in the judges' chambers where the lay assessors and professional judges deliberate together.

Lay assessors, like jurors in the United States, usually regard their experience in a positive light. They report that professional judges treat them well and respect them, and these favorable perceptions add to their overall positive experience and sense that the tribunal has reached a just result. The lay assessors, like magistrates in England and Wales, introduce community values into legal decision-making in criminal cases. The professional judges, and in particular the presiding judge, like the chairperson on the magistrates' court, need to set a tone in which all the judges on the mixed tribunal, including the lay assessors, feel that they can speak and their views are valued. Of course, the system depends on the presiding judge treating lay assessors fairly. Although Machura and Rennig recommend adequate training for lay assessors, perhaps presiding judges should also receive adequate training so that they will work well with the lay assessors.

With lay assessors in Germany, as with magistrates in England and Wales, the form of lay participation is much respected. One reason might be because the history of lay assessors in Germany runs very deep. Another reason might be because lay assessors enable community values to filter into legal decision-making in criminal cases. In addition, there seems to be a good fit between the German court culture of consensus and cooperation, and the lay assessors and professional judges' culture of consensus and cooperation during deliberations.

Marie Comiskey's chapter, "The Jury in Canada: Testing the Comprehensibility of Styles of Jury Instructions and the Effectiveness of Aids" (Chapter 9), focuses on jurors in Canada and how to improve their understanding of jury instructions. Canada has had traditional juries "almost since the beginning of the development of the separate English colonies that eventually became the nation of Canada" (Vidmar, 2000, p. 217). Comiskey undertook an experiment with mock jurors in which they observed an abridged criminal trial based on an actual case. She arranged for lawyers to present the case in a courtroom presided over by a judge, after which the juries deliberated for up to 45 minutes. Comiskey tried to replicate the courtroom experience as closely as possible.

Comiskey wanted to see which version of jury instructions – the traditional legal language of *CRIMJI: Canadian Criminal Jury Instructions* ("*CRIMJI*"), the integrated step instructions of the Canadian *Watt's Manual of Criminal Jury Instructions* ("*WATT*"), or the concise plain language instructions of *California Criminal Jury Instructions* ("*CALCRIM*") – led to greater mock juror comprehension. She also tested some aids, including a written copy of the instructions and a decision tree (that reduces the instructions to a visual chart with a list of questions), to see whether either aid helped mock jurors understand the instructions read aloud by the judge. Comiskey hypothesized that the aids would provide mock jurors with more than one way of acquiring the legal knowledge conveyed by the instructions. Comiskey looked to the jury instruction literature from several countries, including the United States, Australia, and New Zealand, in designing her experiment, and she used jury instructions from California to see if they would be a more effective model than the Canadian versions.

Comiskey found that the mock jurors who received the *WATT* integrated step style instructions achieved the highest overall comprehension scores of the three instructions. She also discovered that the mock jurors who had been given both aids (written instruction and decision tree) had the highest comprehension levels, but that the decision tree alone had little effect.

Although Comiskey examined jury instructions in Canada, the challenge is one that magistrates in England and Wales and lay assessors in Germany also face, which is how to convey legal concepts to lay participants most effectively. In England and

Wales, the magistrates can seek explanations from the legal adviser, and in Germany, the lay assessors can raise their questions with the professional judges on their mixed tribunal. In Canada, as in the United States, judges explain the law to jurors through jury instructions. The jurors listen to the judge read the instructions aloud in open court. They are not typically given the opportunity to ask any questions immediately after the reading. Instead, they go into the jury room where they can ask their fellow jurors. If no one is able to answer the question, the foreperson can send a note with the question to the judge. Typically, the judge calls everyone back to the courtroom and may answer the question or may simply reread the part of the instruction that led to the jury's question. Jurors do not typically find the latter very helpful. The problem of how to convey the law to a lay participant remains the same in England, Germany, and Canada, but the lay participant has different ways of seeking an answer in each of these countries.

Although jury instructions can leave jurors frustrated, the experience of being a juror, like the experience of being a magistrate or a lay assessor, is usually one that the lay participant finds meaningful. In these countries, lay participation, whether as a magistrate, a lay assessor, or a juror, provides a way of introducing community values into legal decision-making. It is also a way of having those who are trained in the law and those who are untrained in the law work together. Each of these forms of lay participation – magistrates in England and Wales, lay assessors in Germany, and jurors in Canada – has a long history, and over time the professional judges and lay participants have come to appreciate each other's contributions to the process. Although lay participation has endured in these countries, there is always room for reform, as each of these chapters also makes clear.

CHALLENGES TO LAY PARTICIPATION IN LAW

Chapters in Parts I and II illustrate some of the factors that have led legal reformers to introduce lay participation and that are key elements in the successful maintenance of existing systems. Whether the systems are new or old, there is continuing debate over the desirability and the scope of lay participation. There is also pressure from legal elites, who want to maintain or expand their roles in legal decision-making.

Support for lay participation – among the public at large, among political actors, and among legal elites such as judges and lawyers – is central to maintaining a broad and vibrant system of lay participation. Roberts and Hough (2009, 2011) reviewed opinion surveys conducted in a broad range of countries with jury systems. They confirmed the broad and deep public support for and confidence in the jury trial. However, exceptions to this picture of strong public support emerged in two instances: in *terrorism cases* and in the aftermath of *unpopular verdicts* (Roberts & Hough, 2009). Half the British respondents in one poll agreed that denying the right to trial by jury to people who were charged with terrorist offenses was a "price worth paying," indicating that they were willing to relinquish jury trial rights in such cases (Roberts & Hough, 2009, p. 22).

Unpopular verdicts also affect support. In the early days of the new jury system in Spain, public support dropped following the high-profile *Otegi* case, described by Jimeno-Bulnes in her chapter in this volume (Chapter 6). After the jury's roundly criticized acquittal of Otegi, the Spanish public reported lower willingness to be tried by a jury, illustrating the power of a single unpopular verdict on support for a fragile jury system. In Uruguay, reaction to what appeared to be an unjustified acquittal of a prominent businessman led to public denunciations of trial by jury and subsequent abolishment of its more than 50-year-old jury system (Bado, 2014).

Political and legal elites, policy-makers, and members of the public marshal a range of claims as they argue for reducing the scope of lay participation in law, or for replacing lay jurors or lay judges with legally trained judges. These claims include doubts about lay participants' fact-finding competence, concerns about lay participants' ability to understand and apply the law, and worries about the fairness of lay decision-making. Assertions of bias go both ways; lay participants are said to be either too lenient or too harsh in their treatment of criminal defendants. Policy-makers also point to the expense and inefficiency in the use of lay participation. Finally, critics have expressed concern about the use of general verdicts instead of reasoned verdicts because the general verdict does not provide a written explanation of the basis for the decision. The chapters in Part III show how these claims have been deployed to limit the scope of lay participation in law.

Anna Offit's chapter, "Dismissing the Jury: Mixed Courts and Lay Participation in Norway" (Chapter 10), on Norway, documents a marked trend away from exclusive reliance on laypeople as decision-makers in favor of mixed courts with professional and lay decision-makers. Norway's all-layperson jury system was launched in 1887, but over the course of the following century, concerns about the exclusive reliance on laypeople to make decisions in Norwegian criminal cases rose. By 1981, politicians succeeded in replacing the all-layperson jury trial with a mixed court of lay and professional decision-makers. By 2017, politicians agreed that a mixed court would replace the all-layperson juries that had previously participated in appellate trials.

Offit's interviews with lawyers and judges revealed some of their concerns about the use of an all-layperson jury, and the reasons why these legal elites viewed mixed courts as a superior alternative. Norwegian judges expressed worry about the competence of an all-layperson jury in understanding the law and the facts. In their instructions to the jury, judges also summarized and commented upon the evidence in the case. Yet practices across judges varied tremendously; some judges avoided commenting on the evidence, whereas others took a more expansive approach, creating inequality. Attorneys and judges asserted that professional judges would be better able to explain the fine points of the evidence and the law if they worked together with laypeople on a mixed court, as opposed to instructing them as an independent jury.

Lawyers and judges also drew attention to what they viewed as the problematic absence of written explanations underlying jury verdicts. Without a requirement to provide written reasons for a verdict, mistaken understanding of facts and law might not emerge until the sentencing stage. Other judges asserted that the writing of reasons was a tool that helped a fact-finder to decide what the verdict should be.

Finally, Offit's chapter illustrates the power of unpopular verdicts to undermine support for lay participation. In a high-profile rape case in Norway, an all-layperson appellate jury acquitted the defendants after a mixed court had previously convicted them. This controversial decision by the lay jury, which many saw as based on prejudice against rape victims, created demands that laypeople be excluded from deciding rape cases entirely.

Claire M. Germain's comparative assessment, "Trials by Peers: The Ebb and Flow of the Criminal Jury in France and Belgium" (Chapter 11), sounds similar themes. An offspring of the French Revolution, the French jury was an iconic representation of democratic self-governance. Enthusiasm for the lay jury declined, though, as juries showed over time what some felt was unwarranted generosity toward sympathetic criminal defendants. Jurors' confusion about the evidence was also seen as a source of unjustified jury acquittals. In 1941, the Vichy government made a dramatic change, replacing the all-layperson jury with a mixed court of professional and lay judges. The French "jury" (which is still called a jury) remains a mixed court today.

Germain describes contemporary political debates over the French jury, and the reforms that resulted. Trial by jury became something of a political football, engaging then-president Nicolas Sarkozy in a war against the professional judges whom he (in a twist) saw as overly lenient. Sarkozy expanded the reach of lay participation in a variety of ways. Although the expansion was popular with the public, judges and lawyers were generally opposed, accurately viewing the legal constriction of their roles as evidence of mistrust. When the French government changed in 2012, it abandoned the expansion on the grounds of excessive cost and undue burdens. Of course, the judges' distrust of citizens interfering with the judicial roles was also a crucial factor, underscoring the importance of support from legal elites to the flourishing of a lay participation system.

In the end, a host of reforms, stimulated by concerns about jury fact-finding, jury bias, and a lack of reasoned verdicts, expanded the role of the professional judges in France. To make the trial more understandable to laypeople, the professional judge now summarizes the facts, the indictment, and the elements of each side's case. The French jury now must generate a reasoned verdict, reflecting the political and legal context following *Taxquet* v. *Belgium* (2010). An experimental program has removed many rape cases from the *Cour d'assises*, insulating them from the presumed biases of lay fact-finders in cases of sexual assault.

Until 2016, the Belgian jury was composed only of laypeople. Germain explains that in that year, the Belgian jury became a mixed court of three professional judges and three lay citizens. What is more, the types of cases to be heard by the mixed court were severely restricted; most cases were reclassified to be eligible to be tried by a court with professional judges only, leaving only a small number to be heard by lay and professional judges in the mixed court. Although the reforms were not popular with the public, legal elites, including the justice minister and the judges' union, strongly supported the changes, pointing to the high cost of jury trials, the complexity of evidence, and the problems with juries rendering reasoned verdicts. Once again, elite support, or in this case elite opposition, can have a powerful effect on the scope of lay participation.

In contrast to the long-existing systems of lay participation in the European countries of Belgium, France, and Norway, the chapters on Russia and Georgia describe introductions of trial by jury. As these chapters make clear, new jury systems face considerable obstacles, especially if elite support is weak or nonexistent. The concerns expressed about lay participation in new jury systems, however, resemble those in long-standing lay participation systems such as Belgium, France, and Norway.

Russia introduced (or reintroduced) jury trials in 1994, during a period of significant political change following the dissolution of the Union of Soviet Socialist Republics (USSR). In their chapter, "The Russian Jury Trial: An Ongoing Legal and Political Experiment" (Chapter 12), Nikolai Kovalev and Sergei Nasonov note that the Russian people have long distrusted professional judges. Thus, the introduction of trial by jury held out the promise of greater legitimacy for the criminal courts. However, as the Russian government worked to craft a new jury system appropriate for the country, it kept careful control over the trial procedures to ensure the judge's strong supervisory role. Kovalev and Nasonov report that judges and prosecutors resisted reforms to give more independence to the jury. Instead, trial judges could (and did) halt jury trials with insufficient evidence for conviction and return cases to the prosecutor for further investigation, even when juries had already begun to hear the case. Jury acquittals could also be overturned by appellate courts, and the case tried again with a new jury. These procedural elements effectively undermine the jury's power and independence. Again this shows the crucial importance of elite support for lay participation.

Russia also removed juries from political trials, ostensibly because of anti-government bias and jury intimidation, according to Kovalev and Nasonov. The jury is a fundamentally political institution, allowing communities to incorporate their ideas about justice and fairness into legal decisions, even though community sentiments may be at odds with the law on the books. It is striking that a number of countries have eliminated trial by jury in terrorism and other politically charged trials. In Spain, the government removed political cases from the jury following the *Otegi* case. Another example is Northern Ireland's Diplock courts, which heard serious criminal cases without juries during intense nationalist conflict in that country (Jackson & Doran, 1995). One might argue that political cases are exactly the ones where a strong community voice in the form of a jury would be most important. Yet, to the extent that such cases include crimes linked to terrorism, these cases are also ones in which the public is most willing to abandon the right to a jury trial (Roberts & Hough, 2011).

The new jury system in Georgia also exemplifies the challenges facing lay participation systems. These difficulties pose stronger challenges because Georgia's contemporary jury system is still in its infancy. Nikolai Kovalev and Giorgi Meladze's chapter, "Trial by Jury in Georgia: A Catalyst for Evolving Independent Courts" (Chapter 13), describes how the Georgian jury system has been hampered by minimal government support, skepticism among legal elites, and an uninformed public. The newly independent country included trial by jury as a constitutional guarantee in the early 2000s. Even though advisors from the United States and other common-law countries provided support for the introduction of trial by jury, it was slow to take hold. The first jury trial did not occur until 2011, and as of 2019, just 40 jury trials have taken place.

Analyzing the slow and deliberate pace in Georgia's adoption of jury trials provides clues about the factors that limit lay participation. As in Russia, where judges have wide latitude to limit the impact of jury decisions, the constitutional provision for jury trials in Georgia only describes it as an acceptable alternative to trial by professional judges, allowing circumvention of the jury trial right. Kovalev and Meladze describe how critics of jury trials voiced concerns about jury competence and fairness during debates over the introduction and reform of trial by jury in Georgia.

The Georgian jury trial in the case of Lasha Makharadze also adds to our examples of the oversized impact of an unpopular verdict on public and elite support for lay participation. In that case, the jury could not agree on a verdict, leading the prime minister of Georgia to label the trial's outcome a failure and the Ministry of Justice to introduce a bill limiting jury trials. Critics championed the desirability of reasoned verdicts, even though in the end they were not successful in dislodging the current practice of the jury's general verdict.

Although the five countries analyzed in chapters in Part III vary widely, one can observe common issues. Legal elites in all these countries have attempted to hold onto their scope of authority vis-à-vis lay participants, with varying degrees of success. As justification, they point to concerns about cost, efficiency, competence, fairness, and verdict transparency. On all these dimensions, critics claim, professionally trained judges have decided advantages over lay decision-makers.

GLOBAL PERSPECTIVES ON LAY PARTICIPATION

Most of the chapters in this book, regardless of whether they are describing advances in lay participation, enduring systems of lay participation, or the challenges in lay participation, provide nuanced and fine-grained explorations of lay participation. In their in-depth approach, rich with details and contextual information, the authors describe the evolution of the specific forms of lay participation in their countries, the ways in which the systems have been put into effect, and their current challenges.

Several of the chapters shift the lens to capture the perspectives of their close geographic neighbors or even some of their more distant geographic neighbors, but with a longer history of the same form of lay participation. Almeida and colleagues (Chapter 2) illustrate how the recent introduction of juries in several Argentine provinces has attracted the attention of their South American neighbors. In another chapter, Kovalev and Meladze (Chapter 13) elaborate on the Russian historic influence on the development of the jury in Georgia. While writing about the juries in another part of the world, Comiskey (Chapter 9) assesses the effectiveness of Canadian and US jury instructions on a sample of Canadian residents.

In Part IV of the book, the lens widens further, as the chapters purposely take a global perspective. Such an approach opens doors to the exploration of how ideas about lay participation spread across the world, how existing knowledge about specific legal procedures could be combined to develop new models of lay participation, and how widespread lay participation tends to be around the world. In a world of globalization and movement away from pure models of inquisitorial and adversarial procedures, a global perspective could help spread the ideas and prepare the ground for successful legal transplants, including the jury, mixed tribunals, magistrates, and lay courts.

Nancy S. Marder's chapter, "What Hollywood, USA, Teaches the World (Incorrectly and Correctly) about Juries" (Chapter 14), studies the accuracy with which the US film industry presents the American jury and how local film industries in other countries have adjusted the image to fit their local conditions. The movie that Marder has selected to analyze – *12 Angry Men* – depicts how a group of strangers learns to work together as a jury by examining the evidence, challenging each other's biases, and ultimately reaching a verdict in spite of their personality differences. As Marder argues, this movie is an easily accessible way for worldwide audiences to get an in-depth look at the operation of an American jury.

The movie focuses on a single holdout juror, skillfully played by Henry Fonda, who ultimately changes the minds of eleven other jurors. While the movie's emphasis on the holdout juror and his struggle against the will of the majority is used as an effective cinematic technique that creates tension as part of the storytelling, it also poignantly projects the difficulty and complexity of reaching a fair judgment. Even 50 years after the release of the movie, participants in a law review symposium – lawyers and experts on legal issues – debated whether the jury made the right decision in the case (Marder, 2007).

As Marder aptly points out, although such cinematic technique is an excellent tool in storytelling, the movie is somewhat misleading in its focus on a holdout juror because the cases with holdout jurors, some of which eventually become cases with hung juries, are quite rare in American courtrooms. In fact, according to the National Center for State Courts' four-year study of hung juries (Hannaford, Hans, & Munsterman, 1999), the rate of hung juries is just about 2.5% in federal courts and about 6.2% in state courts. Marder points out that, although the jury unanimity rule is required in serious cases in US federal and state courts, new jury systems frequently forgo the unanimity requirement.

The appeal of the movie extends beyond the movie itself because it shows how a group of everyday citizens can work as a team to make legal decisions (Marder, Chapter 14). Marder has identified at least eight countries across the world, some of which do not have lay participation at all (e.g., India, the Netherlands) or use a completely different form of lay participation (e.g., China, Germany), in which foreign remakes of the movie have been made. These foreign remakes, which follow the original movie plot line closely, have been adjusted to local contexts, including prejudices toward Jews (Russia) and people from rural provinces (China). Acted by local actors and in a range of different languages, the remakes of the American original confirm the global appeal of movies as a medium to share how a group of ordinary people can engage in decision-making.

John D. Jackson's chapter, "The Case for a Hybrid Jury in Europe" (Chapter 15), raises the issue of cross-fertilization across European legal systems and proposes a model of a hybrid jury that can suit the needs of both common-law and civil-law countries. In the process, Jackson contrasts the two forms of lay participation: the traditional jury consisting exclusively of lay citizens who reach a general verdict, and mixed tribunals consisting of citizens and professional judges who jointly provide a reasoned verdict.

While the jury seems to be more closely associated with common-law systems, which tend to use adversarial procedure, mixed tribunals are more likely to be associated with civil-law systems, which tend to use inquisitorial procedure. Jackson argues that, unlike inquisitorial systems that rely on the hierarchical structures of authority and see the purpose of administration of justice as managing society, adversarial systems that rely on the decentralization of power in the courtrooms and focus on conflict resolution between two citizens may be more suitable grounds for the juries. Critical procedural elements of inquisitorial procedure that do not mesh well with the jury and the public oral trial include the reliance on the case dossier and the need to expose the decision-maker to evidence that could be prejudicial.

Jackson and Kovalev's two surveys of lay participation in the Council of Europe countries (2006; 2016), conducted a decade apart, demonstrate a decrease in the number of countries that use traditional juries and, within countries that retain juries, some evidence toward narrowing of their jurisdiction. A traditional jury is a legal transplant from a common-law system into a civil-law system and, as such, it may be challenged in its new environment (see, e.g., Langer, 2004). Hence, Jackson attributes the jury's decline in civil-law countries to the potential mismatch between the characteristics of the legal procedure used in civil-law countries and the characteristics of the legal procedure that might be more suitable for juries. To survive, juries need not only a legal procedure that allows them to thrive but also a legal culture that supports lay participation, as the Russian example illustrates (e.g., Kovalev & Nasonov, Chapter 12).

Jackson's central argument is that a hybrid jury, required to provide a reasoned decision, could appeal to the countries that rely either on adversarial procedure or on inquisitorial procedure. In common-law countries, verdicts that incorporate reasons for the decision would outline the rationale to the public, help generate legitimacy for the jury's verdict, and allow appellate courts to review jury decisions. At the same time, in civil-law countries with inquisitorial procedures, reasoned decisions would also make a traditional jury fit better into the mold of an inquisitorial procedure in which the emphasis is on truth-finding, rather than on both resolution of a conflict between the two parties and fact-finding. The proposed model of a hybrid jury would fit well with the European Court of Human Rights Grand Chamber's decision in *Taxquet* v. *Belgium* (2010), which suggested that the defendant and the public should both be able to understand the verdict.

Sanja Kutnjak Ivković and Valerie P. Hans's chapter, "A Worldwide Perspective on Lay Participation" (Chapter 16), explores the nature and prevalence of lay participation in criminal courtrooms across the world. Based on the data set collected through surveys and internet and library research, Kutnjak Ivković and Hans present the first worldwide map of lay participation. The authors report that two-thirds of the countries in the world rely on lay participation in their criminal courtrooms. Lay participation is found in all corners of the world, from the Americas, Europe, and Africa, to Asia, Australia, and Oceania. This strong worldwide prevalence of lay participation in quite diverse legal systems likely reflects a political recognition of its legitimizing effects. It is a testament to its adaptability and, ultimately, to its endurance.

Kutnjak Ivković and Hans show that lay participation in a country appears closely related to its dominant legal traditions. Common-law, civil-law, and socialist-law traditions are more likely to be fertile grounds for lay participation than is the Islamic-law tradition. However, a particular form of lay participation is not restricted to only one legal tradition; as chapters in this book demonstrate, juries can be found not only in common-law countries such as Canada, the United Kingdom, and the United States, but also in civil-law countries including Argentina, Russia, and Spain. On the other hand, mixed tribunals are typically reserved for countries with the civil-law tradition such as Germany and Norway. Because the socialist-law tradition is closely associated with the civil-law tradition, it comes as no surprise that mixed tribunals have been used in many former communist countries and countries in transition.

Chapter 16 features geographic coverage of many traditionally overlooked parts of the world, particularly the Global South. Whereas prior research on lay participation is particularly limited in Africa, Kutnjak Ivković and Hans's chapter demonstrates that the continent has a plenitude of lay participation in various forms. The chapter also brings into the spotlight lay magistrates and lay courts, two rarely studied forms of lay participation. The survey findings demonstrate the importance of lay participation in decision-making, and provide a valuable stepping stone for future explorations of the relation between democracy and lay participation.

LOOKING TO THE FUTURE

The breathtaking coverage of the world in the following chapters shows that lay participation is a pervasive feature in the criminal justice systems of democratic countries around the globe. Despite the availability of professional judges in most countries worldwide, in the first global survey of lay participation, Kutnjak Ivković and Hans (Chapter 16) reveal nearly two-thirds of *all* nations currently involve lay citizens as decision-makers in their justice systems. The other chapters in this book offer in-depth looks at the variety of approaches taken by these legal systems in the forms of lay participation they include. Some use a classic common-law jury, others choose mixed courts of lay citizens and professional judges, and still others employ lay judges and magistrates. But these categories do not capture the rich diversity of approaches these chapters show in the institutions and uses of lay participation they examine.

Lay participation offers the promise of incorporating societal perspectives into legal outcomes and greater legitimacy for the legal system and for verdicts. These attractions may explain why the countries in Asia, Europe, and South America discussed in this volume have made recent and substantial advances toward lay citizen decision-making. At the same time, we see that elsewhere around the globe some countries have been pulling back from their commitment to popular participation in law, cabining lay involvement or changing its form.

The reader may be surprised that none of the chapters focuses on the US jury, a much studied institution of lay participation (from the country that the four editors call home). This is entirely intentional. Our purpose here has been to try, to the extent possible, to avoid the all-too-frequent ethnocentric bias that arises when lay participation is discussed. Our only quasi-US chapter attempts to turn outward. Marder (Chapter 14) examines the impact (and often misleading picture) supplied by Hollywood movies on the American jury. As the other chapters show, the American jury is only one piece of the global lay participation landscape.

The in-depth looks at lay institutions in countries around the world in this volume supply the groundwork for a full and nuanced understanding of lay participation. Like any other evaluation of the past and present, however, it cannot provide confident predictions about the shape of the future. The close examinations of past and present practices around the globe raise new questions that should stimulate future investigations, a particularly appropriate stance in our world of constantly evolving uses of lay participation. These questions fall into three primary categories.

First are questions about the development of lay participation. We find that a search for enhanced transparency and legitimacy of the legal system, sometimes coupled with an interest in bringing the outcomes of the legal system more in line with the values and perspectives of the community, can motivate calls for lay participation, but are there other conditions that are needed? What accounts for the embrace of lay participation by some countries and its rejection by others? What explains the form that lay participation takes? Are there some cultural contexts that encourage use of lay decision-makers and others that do not? Why are juries more prevalent in common-law countries and mixed tribunals more prevalent in civil-law countries? How is the type of legal procedure related to the introduction of a particular form of lay participation?

Second are questions about the operations of lay participation systems. Many countries collect information about the activities of their legal systems, but the information collected is typically neither comprehensive nor finely tuned enough to tightly monitor the performance of lay institutions operating within those larger systems. Thus, it is difficult to answer the question: What difference does having lay participation make in the decisions that legal institutions make? This is particularly important for new and changing systems.

Third, there are many unanswered questions about the impact of lay participation. In addition to monitoring effects on perceived legitimacy and trust in the legal system, researchers have the opportunity to use the new institutions, as well as changing institutions and procedures, as natural experiments. These interventions can enable us to understand how the introduction of lay participation, or the form of lay participation, affects decisions, has spillover effects on the legal system, and influences the lay participants beyond their service in court. Thus, does the introduction of lay participation always bring other changes to a legal system? What changes does it bring? How does enhancement of lay participation, or its restriction, affect the civic engagement of laypersons or their ability to speak for the community?

As we have followed developments around the world, we have been impressed by the tireless energy and boundless passion of those committed to working on improving their justice systems, whether it is by introducing or by substantially reforming the process by which lay citizens are given a voice in legal decision-making. We look forward to much collaborative research in the future with colleagues in our global village to build on the wealth of knowledge about lay participation systems described in this volume. While we are no doubt unreasonably optimistic, we aspire to a comprehensive understanding of lay participation that will enable us to set out the contours of best practices for incorporating lay fact-finders in the legal system.

REFERENCES

Abel, R. L., & Lewis, P. S. C. (Eds.). (1995). *Lawyers in society: An overview*. Oakland: University of California Press.

Bado, W. (2014). El crimen de "La Ternera" [The crime of "La Ternera"]. www.derechocomercial.edu.uy/WBcrimen_de.htm

Constable, M. (1994). *The law of the other: The mixed jury and changing conceptions of citizenship, law, and knowledge*. Chicago: University of Chicago Press.

Green, T. A. (1985). *Verdict according to conscience: Perspectives on the English criminal trial jury 1200–1800*. Chicago: University of Chicago Press.

Hannaford, P. L., Hans, V. P., & Munsterman, G. T. (1999). How much justice hangs in the balance? A new look at hung jury rates. *Judicature*, 83(2), 59–67.

Jackson, J., & Doran, S. (1995). *Judge without jury*. Oxford: Clarendon Press.

Jackson, J. D., & Kovalev, N. P. (2006). Lay adjudication and human rights in Europe. *Columbia Journal of European Law*, 13, 83–123.

(2016). Lay adjudication in Europe: The rise and fall of the traditional jury. *Oñati Socio-Legal Series*, 6, 368–395. http://ssrn.com/abstract=2782413

Kutnjak Ivković, S. (1999). *Lay participation in criminal trials: The case of Croatia*. Lanham, MD: Austin & Winfield.

Langer, M. (2004). From legal transplants to legal translations: The globalization of plea bargaining and the Americanization thesis in criminal procedure. *Harvard International Law Journal*, 45, 1–64.

Marder, N. S. (Ed.). (2007). Symposium: The 50th anniversary of 12 *Angry Men*. *Chicago-Kent Law Review*, 82, 551–899.

Roberts, J. V., & Hough, M. (2009, February). *Public opinion and the jury: An international literature review*. London: Ministry of Justice Research Series 1/09.

(2011). Public attitudes to the criminal jury: A review of recent findings. *Howard Journal of Criminal Justice*, 50, 247–261. https://doi.org/10.1111/j.1468-2311.2011.00664.x

Vidmar, N. (2000). The Canadian criminal jury: Searching for a middle ground. In N. Vidmar (Ed.), *World jury systems* (pp. 211–248). Oxford: Oxford University Press.

PART I

Advances in Lay Participation

2

The Rise of the Jury in Argentina

Evolution in Real Time

Vanina G. Almeida, Denise C. Bakrokar, Mariana Bilinski, Natali D. Chizik, Andrés Harfuch, Lilián Andrea Ortiz, Maria Sidonie Porterie, Aldana Romano, and Shari Seidman Diamond

The jury in Argentina is a new institution with a long history. It was prominently included in three separate sections of the Constitution of 1853, an extraordinary feature for the primary legal document of a civil-law country. And although the Constitution was amended multiple times, the current version adopted in 1994 retains those three sections from the original document specifying that juries are the appropriate decision-makers in criminal trials.

Despite the clarity of this constitutional mandate, the jury is still a debt that remains to be paid at the national level. In recent years, however, several provinces have introduced jury trials, and that number has been growing. The province of Córdoba began the contemporary experiment, implementing a mixed jury in which lay citizens and professional judges deliberate together to reach a majority verdict. The provinces of Neuquén, Buenos Aires, Mendoza, Chaco, and Río Negro have implemented the classic form of the jury system in which jurors deliberate and decide separately from the professional judge; and similar jury bills have been passed in San Juan, Entre Ríos, and Chubut. Other provinces are currently considering jury bills in their legislatures as well. After the long period of inaction, recent change has come and appears to be gathering speed. Argentina thus presents a unique opportunity to watch legal evolution in real time.

In this chapter, we trace the introduction of the modern jury in Argentina, considering the reasons for its implementation after an unfulfilled promise of more than 150 years, the relation of the jury to changes in the legal system as a whole, the different forms jury systems are taking as the provinces forge their own paths, the special features of the Argentine jury systems, and an analysis of what we have learned about the operation of the new jury trials from the perspective of those participating in the new tribunals: the judges, the attorneys, and the jurors. We then take a brief look at the growing interest that the juries in Argentina have been generating in other parts of Latin America.

CONSTITUTIONAL BACKGROUND

Argentina's National Constitution of 1853 specified that the National Congress shall promote the implementation of trial by jury. Although the 1853 Constitution has been amended several times, today's document, as in 1853, provides for the jury in three separate sections. Part One describes the rights and guarantees that the national government must give citizens, and includes in section 24 the obligation of Congress to establish trial by jury (Constitución de la Nación Argentina, 1994). Part Two, which describes the powers and functions of the various branches of government, includes two sections that provide for jury trials. Section 75 specifies that Congress shall enact the laws that are needed to provide for jury trials, and section 118 stipulates that jury trials will be required in all ordinary criminal cases once the system is enacted.

As this coverage shows, the promise of the jury trial has been repeatedly recognized in the nation's fundamental law. Yet even today, the National Congress, although charged with providing for trial by jury, still has yet to fulfill this constitutional promise. Although bills for the implementation of all-citizen jury trials have been introduced at least every other year since 2004 and every year since 2010 (Porterie & Romano, 2016), national legislation has thus far failed to provide for jury trials. The provinces, in contrast, have taken action in recent years, beginning to fill the gap.

WHY NOW?

The groundwork for the recent renewed interest in trial by jury in Argentina was laid by dissatisfaction with the legal system run exclusively by professionals operating in a civil-law structure marked by a lack of transparency and long delays. With the legitimacy of the legal system under attack (Porterie & Romano, 2016), scholars and reformers, including members of the judiciary, saw the jury as one potential response to citizen dissatisfaction. Together they mobilized governmental support for a change in the legal system that, through a more democratic approach, offered a potential way to reconnect with citizens. A similar impetus for lay participation in the province of Córdoba had contributed to the introduction of a mixed tribunal system in 2004 (Chapter 3, this volume).

The background dissatisfaction among citizens of Argentina was reflected in opinion surveys that reveal the extent to which the justice system has suffered in recent years from problems of legitimacy. For example, an average of two-thirds of those surveyed in multiple national opinion polls evaluated the performance of the judicial branch as bad or very bad, while an average of only one in four rated it as good or very good (Latinobarómetro, 2006, 2007, 2008, and 2015; Porterie & Romano, 2018). Respondents in these surveys reported that their trust in the judicial branch was not only lower than their trust in the church, the most trusted institution, but also lower than their trust in the government, the state, and even the armed forces.

Chayer, Spector, and Zacchino (2010) constructed an index of perceived level of trust in justice that includes measures of impartiality, efficiency, and honesty. In the year 2010, the perception index in Argentina was 29.9 on a scale where 0 indicates the minimum of trust and 100 the maximum. This low opinion was also reflected in public opinion surveys of attitudes toward the criminal justice system. For example, a 2010 survey in 26 countries in the Americas found that country-level percentages of measured confidence in the effectiveness of the criminal justice system ranged from 31 to 56. Among the Argentine respondents, just 37% expressed confidence; respondents in only seven other countries indicated less confidence than respondents in Argentina (Herrmann, MacDonald, Tauscher, & Layton, 2011).

Despite these low ratings for the performance and trustworthiness of the judicial branch and the criminal justice system, the majority of respondents surveyed in national polls in Argentina show strong support for democracy, with an average of two-thirds (68%) indicating that democracy is preferable to any other kind of government (Latinobarómetro, 1995–2015, excluding 1999 and 2012 when no surveys were conducted; Porterie & Romano, 2018). This support is even higher (81%) for agreement with the statement "democracy can have problems but it's the best government system" (Latinobarómetro 2015, Q. 13A). The contrast between perceptions of what democracy can offer and evaluations of what the existing justice system has provided may explain why the modern era has supplied a fertile ground for advocates of the jury to reassert the promise of the jury system as part of a set of reforms that can instill greater trust consistent with the democratic values the citizens of Argentina support.

The characteristics of the pre-jury justice system show features of the legal system that contributed to this lack of trust in the justice system (e.g., lack of transparency, lengthy time to verdict). The need to change these characteristics in order to implement jury trials reveals the jury as a Trojan horse: the jury carries with it a set of other procedural elements that necessarily change the justice system as a whole.

ARGENTINA'S CRIMINAL PROCESS: THE CIVIL-LAW CULTURE

As a former colony of Spain, Argentina inherited the inquisitorial legal system of a civil-law country. Throughout most of the twentieth century, its legal system maintained the basic procedural rules of the inquisitorial system consisting of a nonpublic investigation and trial relying solely on written evidence. It was only in 1992, in an attempt to soften the strongest features of the inquisitorial system, that Argentina enacted national legislation requiring oral trials in criminal matters. This federal criminal process, similar to procedures used on today's European continent, consists of three stages. The first stage is primarily inquisitorial, a secret and written investigation (*inquiry*) conducted by the judge. The judge can delegate the investigation to the prosecutor, but is able to reassume control at his or her own discretion (sections 26 and 196 of the Código Procesal Penal de la Nación Argentina, 1991). The compiled information of this inquiry constitutes the evidence, which is incorporated in a file (*dossier*) (Thaman, 1999), and these written minutes are used to support the verdict and the sentence, as well as to inform any appeals (Maier, 2004).

The intermediate stage, which is also written, is handled by a single professional judge. The judge informs the parties that they can give written reasons why the case should be continued or dropped, and then decides whether there is sufficient evidence to take the case to trial.

If the case is referred to trial, a new court conducts the trial. This trial consists of an oral public hearing before a panel of three professional judges. The parties present witnesses and other evidence that was in the dossier, including reports of the testimony from witnesses who had been interviewed earlier. The judges then deliver a verdict, but the verdict is provisional and may be appealed by either party.

The trial itself resembles a traditional inquisitorial trial rather than an adversary proceeding. The judges at the trial have the primary responsibility to search for truth and, just as in a traditional inquisitorial trial, they actively control the production of evidence. They question the witnesses and the defendants, and they search for information in the files of the case. The parties occupy a decidedly secondary role, so the adversary nature of the process is only superficial. The prosecutors do not assume a leading role in the inquiry, limited by the constrained authority that the judges give to them. Similarly, although in principle the defense attorneys are permitted to present alternative sources of evidence, in general their activity is limited to denying the charges. Cross-examination does not occur (Hendler, 2008).

Throughout all three stages of the process, in general, judicial functions are delegated to lower-level court employees, not all of whom are lawyers, and who, among other tasks, produce and write the explanation for the verdict and the sentence that is later signed and delivered by the judges. The overall procedural structure thus reflects a vertical judicial organization with bureaucratic-judicial career judges who decide cases based on written testimony, written evidence, and official documentation (Damaška, 1986). The oral trial of the last phase adds little to the process because, as we describe in the next paragraph, the written dossier remains the key focus in the appeal.

Following the trial, there is an appeal stage usually known as the *second instance*, in which the appellate court reviews the full dossier, which includes documents from the pretrial investigation, as well as the evaluation of the evidence by the pretrial and trial judges, and the justification given for their decisions (Maier, 2004). The parties typically give more importance to this stage than the previous one, and usually what is written is more important than what was said during the trial. In this scenario, the parties have little incentive to prepare for an oral trial and instead focus their efforts on later appeals (Almeida, Bakrokar, & Bilinski, 2016). The result is that the oral and public trial occupies a decidedly secondary role in these federal trials (Código Procesal Penal de la Nación Argentina, 1991; Hendler, 2008).

When oral proceedings at the trial stage were introduced in 1992, those advocating the new procedures anticipated major changes in the role played by the parties and in the transparency of the trial, consideration of opposing evidence and arguments, and impartiality of the decision-making. However, in response to strong resistance from legal actors who remained rooted in the inquisitorial culture, the changes promised by an oral trial were only superficially implemented. Written content remained the foundation for decision-making in federal trials (Binder, 2012).

In 2015, Argentina's National Congress (*Congreso de la Nación*) passed a law providing for a full shift to the adversary system. The then President Mauricio Macri, however, suspended by decree the implementation of that system, and therefore the procedural criminal system at the federal level remains a mixed system.

In contrast, recent history has taken a different course at the provincial level, as some provinces adopted many features of the adversarial system. For example, the provinces of Buenos Aires and Santa Fe adopted oral trial systems. Other provinces, such as Neuquén, Chubut, and the City of Buenos Aires, made more significant changes, such as implementing hearings in all stages of the process (investigation, trial, and appeal).

These changes have not been adopted without resistance from both judges and attorneys, and in some places the new practices were strangled by the old inquisitorial traditions (Binder, 2015). Formality and written procedures were inconsistent with full implementation of the new adversarial style. Although parties began to be more active, many judges resisted giving up their traditional control. It is in this context that trial by jury burst in and disrupted the old practices in the Argentine justice system.

TRIAL BY JURY AS TROJAN HORSE

A good way to characterize the introduction of trial by jury into the inquisitorial civil-law fortress is as the Trojan horse that brings with it the end of the inquisitorial system (Harfuch, 2015). The jury not only involves the presence of 12 laypersons who are called to decide a case. It is more. The jury brings with it a trial model, the central feature of which is the public and adversarial trial. In accordance, it is hard to imagine a pure inquisitorial system coexisting comfortably with the jury trial (Hans, 2014; Kovalev, 2010).

The jury trial is a democratic institution. Citizen participation by decision-makers who have no prior connection with the legal system promotes impartiality. The structure of the adversary criminal jury trial requires the prosecution as an organ of the state to shoulder the burden of producing evidence, and empowers the defense to present opposing evidence and arguments. Jury trials in an adversary system give to the parties the responsibility to produce their own evidence and the opportunity to provide contrary evidence (Binder, 2012).

The presence of the jury in the courtroom requires that all evidence be produced at a hearing. This requirement puts an end to the centrality of the written file and places the trial at the center of the process. A jury trial also requires new techniques to present the facts through the use of direct and cross-examination coupled with opening and closing statements.

In addition, the presence of the jury requires that the language used and the presentation as a whole be accessible to nonlawyer members of the public. To communicate with the lay jurors, attorneys and the judge, as well as litigants, must (at least try to) speak in plain language, bolstering the transparency of the legal proceedings.

EVOLUTION OF THE JURY IN THE PROVINCES

Faced with resistance and unwillingness to change at the federal level, it is not surprising that the provinces were the sites of the modern jury movement in Argentina. The first of the provinces to add laypersons to its justice system was Córdoba. Its initial step in 1998 was modeled on the German *Schöffen*, with a tribunal composed of three professional judges and two laypersons, a structure that maintained professional control. But in 2004, Córdoba broadened the participation and control of laypersons by adopting a mixed court system composed of three professional judges and eight lay judges (Chapter 3, this volume).

Although the mixed tribunal system engendered initial distrust and there are still some questions about its operation, including concerns about potential undue influence from the professional judges in the jury room, the movement toward lay participation in Córdoba has been viewed favorably (Chapter 3, this volume; Hendler, 2001–2002). The positive impressions judges received of the jurors on these mixed tribunals allayed some fears about lay competence, laying the groundwork for acceptance when reformers introduced the classic (all-lay) jury systems in other provinces.

After a quiet period, the province of Neuquén in 2011 adopted a new criminal procedure code (Ley de Juicio por Jurados de Neuquén, 2011) that introduced classic jury trials, employing 12 laypersons who deliver a general verdict without issuing an opinion providing reasons for their decision. The first jury trial was held in Neuquén in 2014, and more than 45 jury trials had taken place there by July 2018.

The activity in Neuquén stimulated more widespread interest in enacting the classic trial by jury, and in 2013 the province of Buenos Aires, Argentina's largest province, with more than 15 million inhabitants, passed its own jury law (Código Procesal Penal de la Provincia de Buenos Aires [Act 14.543], 2013), also adopting the classic jury of 12 laypersons. Buenos Aires held its first jury trial in 2015, and the number of jury trials in the province increased in each of the following years. By July 2018, 225 jury trials had taken place in the province.

The next provinces that moved to implement trial by jury were Río Negro (Código Procesal Penal de la Provincia de Río Negro, 2014) and Chaco (Ley de Juicio por Jurados de Chaco, 2015). Chaco originally planned to have its first jury trials in 2016, but postponed implementation; the first jury trial was held in November 2019. In the province of Río Negro, the first jury trial took place in March 2020, after the province finished with the first stage of implementing the accusatory system. Mendoza joined the move to jury trials later, passing its jury law in October 2018 (Ley de Juicio por Jurados de Mendoza, 2018), but as of March 2020 had already held 15 jury trials. San Juan too passed a jury law at the end of 2018 (Código Procesal Penal de la Provincia de San Juan, 2018). Entre Ríos (Ley de Juicio por Jurados de Entre Ríos, 2019) and Chubut (Ley de Juicio por Jurados de Chubut, 2019) followed in 2019.

As of this writing, 9 of Argentina's 23 provinces (Córdoba, Buenos Aires, Neuquén, Chaco, Río Negro, San Juan, Mendoza, Entre Ríos, and Chubut) have laws that explicitly include lay participation, and 5 of the 8 with classic all-lay jury laws have already conducted jury trials. Other provinces have jury laws under consideration in their legislatures.

How has this rapid evolution occurred? The convergence of fertile ground and a legal foundation are only part of the story. The speed of this contemporary evolution can only be understood in the context of an unprecedented grassroots force of reformers with energetic leadership from the Instituto de Estudios Comparados en Ciencias Penales y Sociales (INECIP) and the Asociación Argentina de Juicio por Jurados (AAJJ). With this collaboration, provinces have been introducing lay participation in their criminal justice systems, filling the constitutional space that the National Congress has left unoccupied.

It is important to recognize how dramatic this change has been and how much effort has been invested to make the abstract idea a reality. In addition to arranging and promoting international educational conferences and meetings between legal professionals and jury scholars, and publishing books consisting of theoretical and practical information on jury systems (Binder & Harfuch, 2016; Diamond, 2016; Hans & Gastil, 2014; Harfuch, 2014, 2019b), INECIP and the AAJJ have conducted more than 100 mock jury trials throughout the country to show how a jury system functions (e.g., Asociación Argentina de Juicio por Jurados, 2018).

To effectively implement jury trials, the legal systems have faced not only the need for facilities that can accommodate public jury trials and the development of jury lists of individuals to be called as jurors, but also the need to train attorneys, both prosecutors and defense attorneys, in new skills for handling litigation involving oral trials and requiring communication with laypersons. The changes required have been challenging. The energy and persistence of those involved in the implementation, accompanied by the willingness of trial participants and provincial judicial organizations to engage in systematic research that is tracing and assessing the responses to the new systems (e.g., Porterie & Romano, 2018), may be unprecedented.

DIFFERENCES IN LAY-PARTICIPATION SYSTEMS AMONG PROVINCES

Each province engaging in jury reform has approached the jury question with new eyes, resulting in a diverse array of procedures. While most provinces that enacted jury laws have opted for the traditional common-law model, they vary in their choices on a number of dimensions: whether the jury trial is mandatory or optional, types of cases eligible for jury trial, and procedures required to reach a verdict. Table 2.1 provides a summary of similarities and differences, which we discuss in greater detail in the remainder of this section.

The systems are still too new for robust comparisons, but the variations across provinces have set up the opportunity to evaluate the impact of these choices,

TABLE 2.1 *Features of the new Argentine juries*

Province	Year of bill	Mandatory or optional	Jury-eligible	Decision rule	When required vote not reached
Neuquén	2011	Mandatory	> 15 yr penalty requested	8 of 12 to convict	Acquit
Buenos Aires	2013	Optional	Life impris. possible	Unanimous to convict	Acquit unless 9 to 11 for conviction; one retrial
	2013	Optional	> 15 yr penalty requested	10 of 12 to convict	Acquit unless 9 for conviction; one retrial
Río Negro*	2014 (2019)	Mandatory	> 12 yr penalty possible	Unanimity (delayed acceptance ≥ 10 of 12)	Acquit
San Juan	2018	Mandatory	Life impris. possible	10 of 12 to convict	Acquit unless 7 to 9 for conviction; one retrial
	2018	Mandatory	≥ 20 yr penalty possible	8 of 12 to convict	Acquit unless 7 for conviction; one retrial
Chaco	2019	Mandatory	Life impris. possible, homicide, & some sexual offenses	Unanimous to convict or acquit	Hung; if hung on retrial, acquit

TABLE 2.1 *(continued)*

Province	Year of bill	Mandatory or optional	Jury-eligible	Decision rule	When required vote not reached
Mendoza	2019	Mandatory	Aggravated homicide	Unanimous to convict or acquit	Hung; if hung on retrial, acquit
Entre Ríos	2019	Mandatory	≥ 20 yr penalty possible	Unanimous to convict or acquit	Hung; if hung on retrial, acquit
Chubut	2019	Mandatory	≥ 14 yr penalty possible	10 of 12 to convict	Hung; if hung on retrial, acquit

* In November 2019, Río Negro's legislature voted to remove the 7-person jury from Río Negro's law and to require all juries to have 12 members, matching the 12-member jury size mandated in all of the other jury provinces.

treating the provinces, as US Supreme Court Justice Brandeis once described the US states, as "laboratories of democracy" (*New State Ice Co.* v. *Liebmann*, 1923). We begin with a look at the differences in the jury procedures and decision rules in the provinces that have already had jury trials and those that are on the cusp of implementing a jury system.

Mandatory or Optional?

The provinces of Neuquén and six others specify that trial by jury is mandatory (consistent with section 118 of the National Constitution of Argentina), while the province of Buenos Aires allows the defendant to waive this right and choose a bench trial in lieu of a jury trial. The differences in these provisions reflect political choices rooted in concerns about the costs of a mandatory system, but they also reflect differences of opinion about the normative role of the jury.

Those who favor an obligatory trial by jury consider it a guarantee for the accused, but also a right and duty of the people to participate in the administration of justice (section 118 of the National Constitution), especially in the most serious crimes. To the extent that jury trials can build confidence in the legal system, the attraction of the mandatory jury trial is that more such trials will take place and more citizens will be involved (Harfuch, 2013). In contrast, those who oppose a mandatory jury see the jury trial as a defendant's right (Cafferata Nores, 2012). Thus, in their eyes only the defendant should be able to decide whether to be tried by a jury or by a professional judge.

Neuquén instituted a mandatory jury system, which brought objections from some defense attorneys who claimed that the mandatory jury violated the principles established in the Magna Carta. They viewed jury trials as a right of the defendant and not of the State (Cafferata Nores, 2012). They also argued that the mandatory jury violates the rights of defendants by generating an imbalance in power between the parties (Ministerio Público de la Defensa, 2015).

The reviewing court in Neuquén rejected these arguments, explaining that although section 24, which provides for the establishment of trial by jury, is included in Part One of the Constitution, which sets out the principles, rights, and guarantees to citizens, not every section in Part One refers to guarantees to defendants. In addition, the way in which provinces comply with the constitutional mandate is reserved to every province (Carvajal D. A. y otros s/homicidio doblemente calificado, 2015). In 2019, another case from Neuquén brought the final word from the Supreme Court of Argentina, which determined that provinces are free to choose a mandatory jury trial system (Canales, Mariano Eduardo y otros, 2019). The Supreme Court recognized and endorsed the pattern that is emerging in the new jury systems of Argentina: the provinces are designing their own jury systems and are making different choices at some points.

What Crimes Are Eligible for Jury Trial?

Although section 118 of the Constitution specifies that jury trials will be required in all ordinary criminal cases once the system is enacted, the new jury systems have to this point focused exclusively on serious crimes. In the province of Buenos Aires, a trial is jury-eligible for any offense if the crime the defendant is charged with could result in a prison sentence of more than 15 years (Act 14.543, section 22bis). In Neuquén, San Juan, and Río Negro, a trial is jury-eligible based on the length of the prison sentence requested by the prosecution. In Neuquén, jury trials are limited to cases involving crimes against the person or his/her sexual integrity or any other offense resulting in his/her death or serious injuries if the prosecutor requests a penalty of more than 15 years in prison (Ley de Juicio por Jurados de Neuquén [Act 2784], section 35). In San Juan, the law mandates a jury trial if a penalty of life imprisonment is possible, or if the maximum possible penalty is 20 years or more. In Entre Ríos, a jury trial is mandated if the possible penalty is 20 years or more; in Chubut, the jury mandate applies if the possible penalty is 14 years or more. Finally, in Río Negro, as of 2019, defendants are tried by a jury if the sentence requested is more than 12 years in prison.

In other provinces, the offense directly determines whether there will be a jury trial. In Chaco, jury trials are limited to crimes that are eligible for a penalty of life in prison, but mandatory for all crimes of homicide, including those cases in which the homicide is committed to perpetrate a robbery, and cases involving some types of sexual abuse or against the sexual integrity of a minor (Ley de Juicio por Jurados de

Chaco [Act 7661], section 2). In Mendoza, all aggravated homicides are tried before a jury (Ley de Juicio por Jurados de Mendoza [Act 9106], section 2). All of these mandatory systems create an incentive for the prosecutor who wants to avoid a jury trial to request fewer years in prison or charge an offense that carries a lesser penalty.

How Many Votes Are Required for a Verdict?

Two aspects of the verdict requirement worried legislators as they considered the design of their new jury systems. First, there was concern that a system requiring unanimity would result in failure to convict guilty defendants. Second, if unanimity was required and the jury failed to reach agreement, what should the outcome be?

Neuquén dealt with these concerns by requiring a majority of 8 out of 12 to deliver a guilty verdict. Failure to achieve the required majority results not in a hung jury, but in an acquittal (Act 2784, section 207). The province of Buenos Aires took a different approach, requiring unanimity for conviction in cases with a penalty of life imprisonment and a majority of 10 out of 12 for other felony convictions. Chubut requires 10 out of 12 for conviction in all jury cases. San Juan has chosen a third variation, requiring a majority of 10 out of 12 for felonies in which life imprisonment is possible, and 8 out of 12 when the maximum possible penalty is 20 years or more.

Río Negro is taking yet a fourth approach. Its law adopts a variant on the English approach (United Kingdom Juries Act, 1974). The jury is instructed to reach a unanimous decision to convict or acquit. However, if jurors fail to reach a verdict after a reasonable time of deliberation, they are to be informed that a majority verdict (10 of 12) is acceptable. Finally, the laws adopted in Chaco (Act 7661, section 86), Mendoza (Act 9106, section 33), and Entre Ríos (Ley de Juicio por Jurados de Entre Ríos [Act 10.746]) have established the classical model: 12 jurors with unanimity required for both guilty and not-guilty verdicts. These various choices regarding decision rule have implications for the potential occurrence of a hung jury.

What Happens When Jurors Are Unable to Reach a Verdict?

The solutions adopted by each province are very different. In Neuquén, a hung jury cannot occur because failure to achieve the required majority of eight for conviction results in an acquittal (Act 2784, section 207). However, in the province of Buenos Aires, which requires at least 10 out of 12 to favor a conviction or unanimity if life imprisonment is possible, a jury that does not reach the required number for conviction will be asked to return to the jury room to deliberate again up to three times (Act 14.543, section 371 quater). If the final vote is 8 or fewer for conviction, the defendant will be acquitted, but if 9 favor conviction (or between 9 and 11 vote for conviction in cases in which life imprisonment is possible), the jury will be declared hung. If the prosecutor chooses to try the case again, there will be a new trial in front of a new jury, but if the second jury hangs, the judge will acquit the defendant (Harfuch, 2014). Similarly, San Juan's law will produce a hung jury if a majority of at least 7 jurors favors conviction but the number is less than the majority required for a conviction and if after three further votes the jury fails to achieve the required majority (i.e., 8 out of 12 in cases in which the maximum possible penalty is 20 years or more; 10 out of 12 in cases in which life imprisonment is possible). If a new trial similarly fails to achieve the required majority, the defendant will be acquitted.

In Chaco, Mendoza, and Entre Ríos, where unanimity is required for either an acquittal or a conviction, hung juries can occur if agreement is not reached. In Chaco, the law specifies that the court, in an effort to overcome disagreement on the jury (Act 7661, section 87), can employ techniques pioneered in Arizona, USA, by reopening the trial to take further evidence, giving additional instructions, or directing the attorneys to make additional closing arguments (Dann & Logan, 1996). If the deadlock persists as the jury still cannot reach a unanimous verdict, there can be a new trial at the prosecutor's request, but with the same restriction as in the province of Buenos Aires: if the second jury hangs, the judge will acquit the defendant. The provinces of Mendoza (Act 9106, section 34), Entre Ríos (Act 10.746), and Chubut (Ley de Juicio por Jurados de Chubut [Act XV No. 30, Decree No. 78]) have adopted the same solution.

Finally, the law of the province of Río Negro does not permit hung juries. If the jury fails to reach unanimity or an agreement from 10 of 12 to convict after reasonable deliberation, the jury shall render a not-guilty verdict.

In the United States, where unanimous verdicts were typically required in criminal cases until 2020 when the US Supreme Court mandated them in all criminal cases (*Ramos* v. *Louisiana*, 2020), hung juries have been rare, occurring in a modest 5.5 to 6.2% of cases (Hannaford-Agor, Hans, Mott, & Munsterman, 2002). Among its benefits, the requirement of unanimity brings a more robust debate among jurors (Diamond, Rose, & Murphy, 2006), while conferring a heightened legitimacy on jury decisions. Although it is early in the life of the jury in Argentina in the provinces where the decision rule permits a hung jury, few hung juries have occurred in those provinces.

Between 2015 and 2017, hung juries in Argentina were impossible in Neuquén because of its decision rule, but could happen in the province of Buenos Aires in the absence of unanimity (or if nine voted for conviction on a charge involving less than life imprisonment). Only three hung juries occurred, constituting 3/173 = 1.7% of the verdicts in the province of Buenos Aires. The province of Mendoza, which requires a unanimous verdict, had 15 jury trials before the coronavirus suspended court activity in March 2020. Although the number is too small to compute a meaningful hung jury rate, all but one resulted in a unanimous verdict. The one exception involved the controversial case of a longtime victim of domestic violence on trial for killing her husband with a knife. She claimed self-defense. After six hours of deliberation, the jury reported that it was divided. The prosecutor swiftly responded to the jury's deadlock by announcing that he would not put the defendant on trial a second time, and the judge acquitted and released her (Asociación Argentina de Juicio por Jurados, 2019).

DISTINCTIVE FEATURES OF THE COMPOSITION OF THE ARGENTINE JURY

Jury trials in Argentina have adopted some distinctive features, one shared by all provinces that have introduced jury trials, and one crafted to meet the specific sociocultural context of the province.

Gender Equality

All of the provincial jury laws, as well as the mixed court in Córdoba, require that the jury be composed of equal numbers of men and women. Unlike common-law countries, which do not specify the particular gender composition of a jury, the Argentine provinces have attempted to eliminate any potential gender discrimination in jury selection by requiring that each jury has equal numbers of men and women. This also ensures that each jury, at least with respect to gender, will be representative of society and will not disproportionately include jurors of either gender. One question that future research in Argentina may answer is whether the explicit equal membership of men and women on each jury is reflected in foreperson choice on the jury and more equal participation of men and women during jury deliberations (Diamond & Hans, 2019).

The Indigenous Jury

The interest in representative juries in Argentina is further shown in an innovative provision for an indigenous jury, designed to ensure representation for the Aboriginal minority population. In Chaco, which has a substantial indigenous community, the law provides that when both the accused and the victim of a crime belong to the native tribes, Qom, Wichí or Mocoví, half the jury must be members of the same indigenous community (Chizik, 2018; Harfuch, Bilinski, & Ortiz, 2017). Although the province of Neuquén does not explicitly provide for an indigenous jury, it does require that at least half the jury belongs to the same cultural environment of the accused. In the Middle Ages, resident foreigners in England were entitled to a jury of half natives and half aliens, but that mixed jury system was abolished in 1870 (Constable, 1994). Unique in the modern world, the Argentine indigenous jury is an experiment to watch and to evaluate as an instrument of impartiality and fairness. At this point, the only Argentinian trial involving an indigenous jury has occurred in the province of Neuquén ("Sociedad: El pueblo," 2015).

EVALUATING IMPLEMENTATION OF THE NEW JURY SYSTEMS: THE PROVINCES OF BUENOS AIRES AND NEUQUÉN

A remarkable feature of the new Argentine jury systems is that those implementing them have recognized the need to monitor their implementation and to take stock along the way of how they are being received by both the legal professionals and the jurors. In the first three years of its operation, the jury system in the province of Buenos Aires conducted 173 jury trials, with the number increasing each year. Sidonie Porterie and Aldana Romano of INECIP were able to gather court statistics and conduct surveys and interviews with the professionals who participated in those trials (Porterie & Romano, 2018).

Similarly, Valerie Hans of Cornell University, Maria Sidonie Porterie, Aldana Romano, and Andrés Harfuch of INECIP, Shari Diamond of Northwestern University and the American Bar Foundation, John Gastil of Pennsylvania State University, and Paula Hannaford-Agor of the National Center for State Courts joined the Court Administration of Neuquén in ongoing research, studying the reactions of both professionals and jurors who are participating in the jury trials in that province. The empirical findings have corrected many of the mistaken predictions about the decisions juries would reach and how citizens would behave as they encountered the legal system face-to-face.

Prior to the implementation of the law, many predicted that juries would consistently convict, regardless of the evidence shown at the trial, because the public was seen as overly punitive (Porterie & Romano, 2018). Professionals in particular believed the Argentinian society was not prepared to participate in judicial decisions (Elhart, 2017). To the surprise of many, the first four jury trials conducted in the province of Buenos Aires ended in acquittals. Later trials resulted in convictions, but even so, these early acquittals were significant, contradicting the expectation that juries would inevitably convict.

How to interpret the initial string of acquittals was the subject of some controversy. Some prosecutors began to raise questions about the ability of jurors to make decisions. Others suggested that the difficulty was not with the jurors, but with the strength of the evidence prosecutors were presenting at trial (Porterie & Romano, 2018). Although a professional judge might be willing to fill in gaps left by a prosecutor, the jurors required those gaps to be filled by the evidence presented to them. The tacit alliance between judges and prosecutors had been interrupted by the demands of the public jury trial. If sufficient evidence was not presented, publicly demonstrating proof beyond a reasonable doubt, it was appropriate for the jurors to acquit. Thus, according to some observers, what the jurors were saying with their early acquittals was: "*This evidence is not enough to convict. Bring a better and stronger one*" (Observatorio Permanente de Juicios por Jurados de la Universidad Nacional del Sur, 2016).

Some prosecutors sought relief in a series of unsuccessful appeals challenging the constitutionality of the jury law, but they failed on appeal when the appellate courts responded by endorsing and providing further support for the jury system (López, Mauro Gabriel s/ recurso de Queja interpuesto por Agente Fiscal, 2016). Other prosecutors coped with the challenge posed by the jury by increasing their preparation in jury cases. The new system, as many recognized, requires both greater preparation for trial and a new set of professional skills. Although the jury conviction rate in 2015 was 53%, that percentage rose in the following years: 69% in 2016 and 65% in 2017.

In their study of the first three years of juries in the province of Buenos Aires, Porterie and Romano (2018) surveyed 25 judges, 57 prosecutors, and 25 defense attorneys who had participated in jury trials; 75% of these legal professionals evaluated the jury system as positive or very positive, 16% were neutral, and only 9% gave a negative rating. This result revealed a remarkable level of approval for a dramatic change in the legal system from the professionals who implemented it. Similar enthusiasm was expressed by the professionals in a study of 17 jury trials conducted in Neuquén where Valerie Hans and her colleagues found that all 17 judges and 74% of the lawyers were positive or very positive about the jury system (Hans, Porterie, & Romano, 2018). Post-trial surveys of jurors in both Neuquén and Buenos Aires showed similar enthusiasm. In Neuquén, 90% of the jurors said their experience resulted in positive or very positive evaluations of the jury system (Hans et al., 2018). In Buenos Aires, surveys conducted in 2015 by the Ministry of Justice of the province of Buenos Aires showed that 95.5% of the surveyed jurors found the experience of serving on a jury to be a positive experience and 90.5% of them reported that the experience helped to improve their image of the criminal justice system (Porterie & Romano, 2016).

The legal professionals studied by Porterie and Romano (2018) in Buenos Aires provided important insights about the key elements and operation of the new jury system. The research also identified crucial issues to be addressed to optimize the system. When the judges were asked if they would have reached a different verdict than the one reached by the jury in any of the trials in which they participated, 76% answered negatively (Porterie & Romano, 2018). This level of agreement is strikingly similar to the results from studies of judge/jury agreement in the United States: 78% in the classic study by Kalven and Zeisel (1966), and 75% in the more recent study by Eisenberg and his colleagues (Diamond, Porterie, & Romano, 2018; Eisenberg, Hannaford-Agor, Hans, Waters, Munsterman, Schwab, & Wells, 2005; Kalven & Zeisel, 1966).

In cases of disagreement with the jury, the judges in Buenos Aires, like those in the United States, generally viewed the jury's verdict as reasonable and not arbitrary. When asked which three of six attributes (arbitrariness, efficiency, costliness, hard-working, impartiality, and legitimacy) they associated with the jury, the three groups of legal professionals were all more likely to select legitimacy than any other feature, with impartiality second, and with arbitrariness least likely to be selected (Porterie & Romano, 2018). Confidence in the new jury system was further reflected in the surveys of legal professionals. When the legal professionals were asked, "If you or a family member were accused of a homicide, which system would you prefer?" a strong majority (67%) of the respondents said that they would prefer a jury trial to a bench trial (Porterie & Romano, 2018). Studies in the United States that have asked laypersons about their preferences for a jury trial versus a bench trial have shown similar preferences for the jury (MacCoun & Tyler, 1988; Rose, Ellison, & Diamond, 2010). The distinctiveness of the Buenos Aires survey is that it found the same jury preference pattern among legal professionals.

The implementation of the jury trial was challenging for all of the legal professionals involved and for the judicial system and government of Buenos Aires. Adjustments included making building changes, adapting the hearing rooms and the deliberation room, and instituting training in litigation skills necessary for trials under the new rules. When asked to evaluate the success of the implementation, 41% of the legal professionals rated it as successful or very successful, 43% were neutral, and only 10% saw it as deficient (Porterie & Romano, 2018). These legal professionals recognized that the new features of the jury are imposing new challenges on the judges and attorneys who are responsible for conducting these trials. Asked to rate each of nine trial features (theory of the case, preliminary hearing, *voir dire*, opening statement, direct examination, cross-examination, closing statement, instructions, and the penalty hearing), respondents rated *voir dire* and closing arguments as most challenging, but more than half of them rated six of the nine features as challenging or very challenging (Porterie & Romano, 2018). The new jury system was imposing new demands on legal professionals trained under a very different model of legal decision-making. It thus is not surprising that 92% of them expressed the view that it is necessary or very necessary for universities to adapt their curricula so that future lawyers have litigation tools (Porterie & Romano, 2018).

The initial response of both jurors and professionals to the new jury system in Buenos Aires has been strikingly positive. In addition to the survey responses described in the preceding paragraphs, Porterie and Romano (2018) conducted interviews with legal professionals to get their observations about their initial jury experiences. Several themes emerged. The first was surprise. As one defense attorney reported: "Although I thought that they were going to be more prejudiced, or that the penalties were going to be more severe, or that they were going to be less fair, it seems to me that citizens, when you give them the responsibility to decide, are very responsible. What I see is [the jury] has a lot of common sense" (Porterie & Romano, 2018, p. 55). A second theme was the observation that the jurors took their responsibility seriously. As one prosecutor said, "The juries have become very deeply involved; they have made the judgments fresh. It is not that they take the task lightly, without consequences [...] they really made a very important commitment to their task" (Porterie & Romano, 2018, pp. 52–53). A third theme echoed the impartiality ratings from the survey, with interviewees suggesting that laypersons are in a position to be more objective than professionals. As one judge reported: "When a person is put on trial and we make our best effort to be impartial, the fact that we have worked on 200, 300, 400 cases unconsciously prevents us from having the same vision that a citizen coming from outside the system has [. . .] such a person comes, sits, and decides that case and does not judge any other case in their life; they take it differently" (Porterie & Romano, 2018, p. 51). And in the words of a defense attorney, "The jurors are not contaminated by the judicial file or the people; they only decide a particular case and have no coercion, threat, pressure, nothing. Therefore, they are really independent" (Porterie & Romano, 2018, p. 58). A final theme reflects an appreciation for the advantages associated with the new procedures that have produced a realignment of professional roles. As one judge observed, "For me, for the judiciary, it seems to me that it is even calmer and you begin to understand what the function is of each one [. . .] so that each one truly fulfills their function" (Porterie & Romano, 2018, p. 71). Or in the words of a prosecutor, "I tell you that we really have a trial when we judge by juries" (Porterie & Romano, 2018, p. 77).

The jury systems in Buenos Aires and Neuquén are still new, and challenges remain. Yet the results from the preliminary empirical research described here provide reasons for optimism as other provinces prepare to implement jury trial systems and jury trials become more common throughout Argentina.

ELSEWHERE IN LATIN AMERICA

Neighbors in other parts of Latin America share the same history as Argentina from the two Western judicial cultures: the common-law adversary system brought by the English, which includes the public oral jury trial, and the civil-law inquisitorial system, brought by the Spaniards, French, and Portuguese, with its written and secret procedures. The jury in Argentina has been bringing these two different traditions together (Harfuch, 2018).

The modern jury initiatives in Argentina have not gone unnoticed. For example, in the first ruling on trial by jury in its 39 years of existence, the Inter-American Court of Human Rights (IACHR) cited with approval features from all of the existing provincial jury laws of Argentina, endorsing various features of the common-law jury: the general verdict, *voir dire*, judicial instructions on the law, and the acceptability of not requiring the jury to provide explicit reasons for its verdict (VRP, VPC, and others v. Nicaragua, 2018; see also Harfuch, 2019a). At this point, the evidence that Argentina's jury system is currently functioning very well in several provinces and is rapidly expanding to other provinces has triggered interest from neighboring countries such as Chile, Uruguay, and Paraguay. For example, the IV Congreso Internacional de Juicio por Jurados (Fourth International Congress on Trial by Jury) held in Mendoza, Argentina, in March 2019 included a panel of representatives from Bolivia, Chile, Paraguay, Perú, and Uruguay, all discussing the prospects for jury systems in their countries. Future developments await.

NEW CHALLENGES

It took over 150 years to introduce the first classic jury trial in Argentina. Resistance was powerful and still exists, but the jury has taken root and is expanding. Citizen-jurors have demonstrated commitment and competence. The jurors who managed to arrive amid flooding to serve in the first trial in Neuquén and the juror in San Isidro, Buenos Aires, who offered to fix a courtroom's leaky ceiling when the trial ended (Coelho, 2016) represent examples of the citizens' appetite for inclusion in the democratic process. As described earlier in this chapter, post-trial juror surveys show that these positive reactions to participation in the justice system are not idiosyncratic.

Courts too have demonstrated an increasing appreciation for lay participation and the lay autonomy that the jury brings. The most recent manifestation of this judicial recognition in Argentina occurred in Córdoba when the Supreme Court of the province ruled that the lay members of the mixed court should deliberate on their own, before being joined by the professional judges, rather than deliberating together from the start as had been the procedure earlier (Protocolo de Actuación, 2017). That change partially addresses, although it does not eliminate, one of the charges leveled at the mixed tribunal: excessive influence by the professional judges (Hendler, 2008). It also signals the growth in respect for the lay members of the mixed court. If this view is more widely embraced, the Córdoba mixed jury may yet move further in the direction of Argentina's more recently created provincial jury systems.

Trial court judges as well as jurors have expressed their enthusiasm, sometimes to their surprise, at the effective performance of the jurors (Porterie & Romano, 2018). It is too soon to assess that payoff for the legal system as a whole, but the positive reactions from jurors and legal professionals in the early post-trial surveys conducted in the provinces of Buenos Aires and Neuquén bode well for the contribution the new jury systems can make to the legitimacy of the criminal justice system in Argentina. Reflecting the enthusiasm for the new juries, the governor of Mendoza announced in May 2020 that he planned to expand jury trials in Mendoza to serious offenses beyond aggravated homicide and even to some civil cases involving public corruption (Las reformas clave que Suárez impulsara en la Justicia, 2020). And Argentinian President Alberto Fernández announced in March 2020 that he supports a federal jury bill that will be sent to the Congress for its approval (Asociación Argentina de Juicio por Jurados, 2020).

Challenges do remain for this new vehicle – this Trojan horse – that has introduced dramatic change in the legal systems of Argentina. Abandoning a written system and adopting oral trials has created the need to train lawyers to communicate effectively with laypersons in order to achieve the effectiveness and legitimacy that the public jury trial can offer. Procedures, rules of evidence, and clear jury instructions are needed to determine what jurors will be told and how that information will be conveyed. The choices that Argentina makes will be instructive far beyond its borders.

Authors' Note: All of the authors of this chapter presented papers at a series of panels at the Law and Society Association Meetings in 2016 (New Orleans), 2017 (Mexico City), 2018 (Toronto), and 2019 (Washington, DC) which accompanied the growing activity of juries in Argentina. The meetings and International Research Collaborative (IRC) funding from the National Science Foundation (grant number SES-1556070) facilitated the collaboration reflected in this chapter.

REFERENCES

Almeida, V., Bakrokar, D., & Bilinski, M. (2016, June). From civil law to common law in Argentina: The jury's great potential to put an end to the Inquisition's culture [Paper presentation]. Law and Society Association meeting, New Orleans, USA.

Asociación Argentina de Juicio por Jurados [Argentina Association of Trial by Jury]. (2018). Mendoza: Multitudinaria conferencia y simulacro de juicio por jurados [Mendoza: Multitudinous conference and mock jury trial]. www.juicioporjurados.org/2018/08/mendoza-multitudinaria-conferencia-y.html

(2019). Mendoza: Absolvieron a la mujer que mató a su marido en Godoy Cruz [Mendoza: The woman accused of murdering her husband was acquitted in Godoy Cruz]. www.juicioporjurados.org/2019/05/mendoza-absolvieron-la-mujer-que-mato.html#more

(2020). Argentina's President Alberto Fernández announced that the federal jury bill will be sent to the Congress for its approval. www.juicioporjurados.org/2020/03/argentinas-president-alberto-fernandez.html

Binder, A. M. (2012). *La implementación de la nueva justicia penal adversarial* [The implementation of the new adversarial criminal justice]. Buenos Aires: Ad Hoc.

(2015). *Contra la inquisición: Notas y ensayos breves sobre la justicia penal* [Against the inquisition: Notes and short essays about criminal justice]. Buenos Aires: Ad Hoc.

Binder, A. M., & Harfuch, A. (2016). *El juicio por jurados en la jurisprudencia nacional e internacional: Sentencias comentadas y opiniones académicas del common law, del civil law y de la Corte Europea de Derechos Humanos* [Trial by jury in the national and international jurisprudence: Commented rulings and scholarly opinions from the common law, the civil law, and the European Court of Human Rights]. Buenos Aires: Ad Hoc.

Bruzzone, G. (2000). *El juicio por jurado en el proceso penal* [Trial by jury in a criminal proceeding]. Buenos Aires: Ad Hoc.

Cafferata Nores, J. (2012). *Manual de derecho procesal penal* [Handbook of criminal procedural law]. Córdoba, Argentina: Advocatus.

Canales, Mariano Eduardo y otros, Corte Suprema de Justicia, 461/2016/RH1 (2019).

Carvajal, D. A. y otros s/homicidio doblemente calificado, Tribunal Penal de Impugnación Penal de Neuquén (2015). http://181.168.124.69:81/cgi-bin/koha/opac-detail.pl?biblionumber=135

Chayer, J., Spector, H., & Zacchino, P. (2010). Index of trust in justice. www.scribd.com/document/50547049/indice-2010-di-tella

Chizik, N. (2018, June). The aboriginal jury in Argentina and the possibility of a "grafting-transplant" [Paper presentation]. Law and Society Association meeting, Toronto, Canada.

Código Procesal Penal de la Nación Argentina [Code of Criminal Procedure of the Argentine Nation] (1991). http://servicios.infoleg.gob.ar/infolegInternet/anexos/0-4999/383/texact.htm

Código Procesal Penal de la Provincia de Buenos Aires [Code of Criminal Procedure of the Province of Buenos Aires (Arg.)], Act 14.543 (2013).

Código Procesal Penal de la Provincia de Río Negro [Code of Criminal Procedure of the Province of Río Negro (Arg.)], Act 5020 (2014); (amended 2019).

Código Procesal Penal de la Provincia de San Juan [Code of Criminal Procedure of the Province of San Juan (Arg.)], Act 1851 (2018).

Coelho, J. M. (2016). First verdict "not guilty" of San Isidro: Interview with Judge María Coelho. www.juicioporjurados.org/2016/03/no-culpable-en-san-isidro-entrevista-la.html

Constable, M. (1994). *The law of the other: The mixed jury and changing conceptions of citizenship, law and knowledge*. Chicago: University of Chicago Press.

Constitución de la Nación Argentina [National Constitution of Argentina] (1994). http://servicios.infoleg.gob.ar/infolegInternet/anexos/0-4999/804/norma.htm

Damaška, M. R. (1986). *The faces of justice and state authority: A comparative approach to the legal process*. New Haven, CT: Yale University Press.

Dann, B. M., & Logan, G. (1996). Jury reform: The Arizona experience. *Judicature*, 79, 280–286.

Diamond, S. S. (2016). *Las múltiples dimensiones del juicio por jurados: Estudios sobre el comportamiento del jurado: Jurado penal y jurado civil* [The many dimensions of trial by jury: Studies of jury behavior. Criminal and civil jury trials]. Buenos Aires: Ad-Hoc Publishers.

Diamond, S. S., & Hans, V. P. (2019, May). Gender on the Argentine jury [Paper presentation]. Law and Society Association meeting, Washington, DC, USA.

Diamond, S. S., Porterie, S., & Romano, A. (2018, June). The power of the jury: Discovering the jury trial in the province of Buenos Aires [Paper presentation]. Law and Society Association meeting, Toronto, Canada.

Diamond, S. S., Rose, M. R., & Murphy, B. (2006). Revisiting the unanimity requirement: The behavior of the non-unanimous civil jury. *Northwestern University Law Review*, 100, 201–230.

Eisenberg, T, Hannaford-Agor, P. L., Hans, V. P., Waters, N. L., Munsterman, G. T., Schwab, S. J., & Wells, M. T. (2005). Judge-jury agreement in criminal cases: A partial replication of Kalven and Zeisel's *The American jury*. *Journal of Empirical Legal Studies*, 2, 171–207.

Elhart, R. (2017, June). Juicio por jurados: El otro paradigma [Trial by jury: The other paradigm]. *Pensamiento Penal LJ*, pp. 1–2. www.pensamientopenal.com.ar/system/files/2017/06/doctrina45389.pdf

Hannaford-Agor, P. L., Hans, V. P., Mott, N. L., & Munsterman, G .T. (2002). Are hung juries a problem? www.ncsconline.org/WC/Publications/Res_Juries_HungJuriesPub.pdf

Hans, V. P. (2014). ¿Cuál es la diferencia que hace un jurado? [What difference does a jury make?] In Hans & Gastil, 2014 (pp. 21–45).

Hans, V. P., & Gastil, J. (Eds.). (2014). *El juicio por jurados: Investigaciones sobre la deliberacíon, el veredicto y la democracia* [Trial by jury: Studies on deliberation, verdict, and democracy]. Buenos Aires: Ad Hoc.

Hans, V. P., Porterie, S., & Romano, A. (2018, June). A new jury system at work [Paper presentation]. Law and Society Association meeting, Toronto, Canada.

Harfuch, A. (2013). *El juicio por jurados en la provincia de Buenos Aires: Ley provincial 14.543 anotada y comentada. El modelo de jurado clásico* [Trial by jury in the province of Buenos Aires: Notes on the provincial law 14.543. The classic jury model]. Buenos Aires: Ad Hoc.

(2014). *El jurado clásico: Manual modelo de instrucciones al jurado. Ley modelo de juicio por jurados* [The classic jury: Handbook guide for jury instructions. Trial by jury model law]. Buenos Aires: Ad Hoc.

(2015). La firmeza (finalidad) del veredicto del jurado [The finality of the jury's verdict]. In G. Letner & L. Piñeyro (Eds.), *II congreso internacional de juicio por jurados* [Second international conference of trial by jury] (pp. 85–112). Buenos Aires: Jusbaires.

(2018, June). The status of trial by jury in Latin America [Paper presentation]. Law and Society Association meeting, Toronto, Canada.

(2019a, May). The Inter-American Court of Human Rights ruling and the expansion of the jury in Argentina and Latin America [Paper presentation]. Law and Society Association meeting, Washington, DC, USA.

(2019b). *El veredicto del jurado* [The verdict of the jury]. Buenos Aires: Ad Hoc.

Harfuch, A., Bilinski, M., & Ortiz, A. (2017). El jurado indigena en Argentina [The indigenous jury in Argentina]. In G. Letner & L. Piñeyro (Eds.), *Juicio por jurados en el procedimiento penal* [Trial by jury in a criminal procedure] (pp. 25–32). Buenos Aires: Jusbaires.

Hendler, E. S. (2001–2002). Lay participation in the judicial process: The situation in Argentina. *Saint Louis–Warsaw Transatlantic Law Journal*, *2001–2002*, 81–88.

(2008). Lay participation in Argentina: Old history, recent experience. *Southwestern Journal of International Law*, *15*, 1–29.

Herrmann, S., MacDonald, D., Tauscher, R., & Layton, M. L. (2011). Perspectivas desde el barómetro de las américas: 2011. Confianza en el sistema de justicia penal de las Américas, N°62 [Prospects from America's barometer: 2011. Confidence in America's criminal justice system, No. 62]. www.vanderbilt.edu/lapop/insights/I0862es2.pdf

Kalven, H., Jr., & Zeisel, H. (1966). *The American jury*. Boston: Little, Brown and Company.

Kovalev, N. (2010). *Criminal justice reform in Russia, Ukraine and the Former Republics of the Soviet Union: Trial by jury and mixed courts*. Lewiston, NY: Edwin Mellen Press.

Las reformas clave que Suárez impulsara en la Justicia [The key justice reforms that Suárez will push]. (2020). *El Sol*. www.elsol.com.ar/las-reformas-clave-que-suarez-impulsara-en-la-justicia

Latinobarómetro [Latinobarometer]. (1995–2015, excluding 2012 and 1999). www.latinobarometro.org/lat.jsp

Ley de Juicio por Jurados de Chaco [Jury Trial Law of Chaco (Arg.)], Act 7661 (2015).

Ley de Juicio por Jurados de Chubut [Jury Trial Law of Chubut (Arg.)], Act XV No. 30, Decree No. 78 (2019).

Ley de Juicio por Jurados de Entre Ríos [Jury Trial Law of Entre Ríos (Arg.)], Act 10.746 (2019).

Ley de Juicio por Jurados de Mendoza [Jury Trial Law of Mendoza (Arg.)], Act 9106 (2018).

Ley de Juicio por Jurados de Neuquén [Jury Trial Law of Neuquén (Arg.)], Act 2784 (2011).

Lopez, Mauro Gabriel s/recurso de Queja interpuesto por Agente Fiscal, Tribunal de Casación Penal de la Provincia de Buenos Aires. (2016). www.defensapublica.org.ar/JURISDICCIONAL/Jurisprudencia/tribunal_de_casacion/Fallos_por_temas/Juicio_x_Jurados/Recurso_Fiscal_Juicio_x_Jurados.pdf

MacCoun, R. J., & Tyler, T. (1988). The basis of citizens' perceptions of the criminal jury: Procedural fairness, accuracy, and efficiency. *Law and Human Behavior, 12*, 333–352.

Maier, J. B. J. (2004). *Derecho procesal penal tomo II, encuadernados* [Procedural criminal law, Vol. 2, bound]. San Juan: University of Puerto Rico Press.

Ministerio Público de la Defensa [Public Ministry of Defense (Arg.)]. (2015, June 9). Diez: "El juicio por jurados es una garantía del imputado" [Diez: "Trial by jury is a right for the defendant"]. www.mpdneuquen.gob.ar/index.php/2-sin-clasificar/302-diez-el-juicio-por-jurados-es-una-garantia-del-imputado

New State Ice Co. v. Liebmann, 285 U.S. 262 (1923).

Observatorio Permanente de Juicios por Jurados de la Universidad Nacional del Sur [Permanent Observatory of Jury Trials of Universidad Nacional del Sur]. (2016). *Juicio por jurados. Informe.* [*Trial by jury. Report.*] Editorial de la Universidad Nacional del Sur. Ediuns.

Porterie, S., & Romano, A. (2016). Juries and democratic legitimacy: The jury trial in the public debate in Argentina. www.academia.edu/32284058/

(2018). *El poder del jurado: Descubriendo el juicio por jurados en la Provincia de Buenos Aires* [The power of the jury: Discovering trial by jury in the province of Buenos Aires]. Buenos Aires: INECIP.

Protocolo de Actuación en Juicios con Jurados Populares: Acuerdo 260, Serie "A," Tribunal Superior de Justicia de la Provincia de Córdoba [Protocol with guidelines on trial by jury: Agreement 260, "A" Series, Superior Court of Justice of the Province of Córdoba (Arg.)] (2017, May 8).

Ramos v. Louisiana, 140 S. Ct. 1390 (2020).

Rose, M. R., Ellison, C., & Diamond, S. S. (2010). Judges and juries in the public's mind. *Judicature*, 93, 194–200.

Sociedad: El pueblo, más sabio que los abogados [Society: The people, wiser than the attorneys]. (2015, November 5). *Página/12*. www.pagina12.com.ar/diario/sociedad/3-285450-2015-11-05.html

Thaman, S. C. (1999). Europe's new jury systems: The cases of Spain and Russia. *Law and Contemporary Problems*, 62, 233–259.

United Kingdom Juries Act (1974). www.legislation.gov.uk/ukpga/1974/23/contents

VRP, VPC, and others v. Nicaragua, Inter-American Court of Human Rights (ser. C) No. 350 (2018, March 8).

3

Twelve Years of Mixed Tribunals in Argentina

María Inés Bergoglio

Although implementation has been recent, trial by jury has deep historical roots in Argentina. Understood as a guarantee against the abuse of state power, trial by jury can be found in drafts proposed during the first Constitutional Assembly, held in 1813, as well as in the Constitutions of 1819 and 1826 (Cavallero & Hendler, 1988). The 1853 National Constitution prescribed trial by jury in three articles. After the 1994 Reform of the Constitution, the placement of the provisions changed, but the content remained the same. The long-standing presence of trial by jury in these documents is a clear indicator of Argentina's profound democratic aspirations, as well as its ample tolerance of the gap between written law and social practices.

It was not until 2004 that Córdoba became the first province to pass a law (Ley No. 9182) that would add lay participation to criminal decisions. The tribunal, composed of eight lay jurors and three professional judges, deliberates and decides jointly by majority vote. This mixed court deals with cases of aggravated homicide, various crimes that resemble "felony-murder" cases, and cases that involve public officials.

The law was passed in the context of a national debate concerning what measures were required to fight against the fear of crime. This debate was inspired by public demands for harsher penalties and judicial reform to improve urban safety. Supporters saw citizen participation in criminal justice decisions as a tool to adjust punishment levels to social demands and to correct the approach generally held by judges, which was considered to be too benign.

The desirability of greater punitiveness was the subject of some difference of opinion, however. One popular movement considered it desirable and included it in their demands (Kessler, 2009). Some sectors of the legal profession opposed jury trials for this reason. For example, the prestigious criminal lawyer Zaffaroni (who later served on the Supreme Court of Argentina) declared that the idea of employing jury trials was dangerous for it may become "a quick lynching tool for the poor" (Zaffaroni, 2012).

The arguments offered in the provincial legislature when the initiative was presented emphasized another issue. During the parliamentary debate, it became clear that a major aim of the law was to restore the judiciary's prestige. In the words of legislator Cid, who presented the bill:

> [T]he Argentine people demanded justice for they felt they had none; the Argentine people demanded security for they felt none; the Argentine people demanded to believe in their institutions for they no longer believed. So, we legislators in Córdoba must provide answers to the people's demands and create those institutions which will allow us to restore the social contract that has been lost, in order to generate a bridge between the people and their leaders; to generate that belief that got lost in time. We must reconstruct the social contract. That is why trial by jury is necessary because it is an instrument that leads toward the aforementioned goal (Ferrer & Grundy, 2005, p. 101).

Other social actors also expressed the goal of rebuilding confidence in the judiciary through lay participation in judicial decision-making. The president of the Judges Association, Victor Velez, declared in a press interview at the time of the parliamentary debate: "(lay participation in criminal courts) is an open door, allowing the entrance of a natural sense of equity and fairness, and the exit of better opinions on how the justice administration works" ("Piden debate sobre jurados populares," 2004).

The main resistance to the initiative was led by members of the legal profession who feared that lay participation in criminal trials could lead to a tougher penal system. They raised constitutional objections to the procedure, but the Provincial High Court rejected the objections and has repeatedly supported the innovation in response to later challenges (Bergoglio, 2011).

The formative stages of the law revealed the variety of actors interested in matters of judicial politics (Bergoglio, 2008) and the different social goals they were trying to achieve. Now, after more than a decade of lay participation in criminal trials, one can analyze whether the institution of mixed tribunals has fulfilled the expectations held by those who promoted this innovation and those who resisted it. This review of the Córdoba experience with mixed tribunals summarizes the main findings of a research program initiated in 2008. It focuses on three issues:

(1) the differences between jury and judge decisions and the actual levels of lay participation obtained when judges and juries sit and deliberate together,
(2) the tensions between the approaches of professional judges and the social demand for penal harshness associated with fear of crime, and
(3) the contribution of lay participation in the courts toward legitimizing the judiciary, a key issue in a society where trust in justice has been chronically low.

Data sources are varied and include a set of 445 verdicts reached between 2005 and 2017, supplemented by interviews with lawyers and judges as well as citizens who served as jurors. A total of 51 interviews were conducted in different stages of this project, with 10 judges, 4 prosecutors, 4 judicial clerks, 15 lawyers, and 18 jurors. In addition, there were four focus groups of jurors, with a total of 26 participants. Data from two public opinion surveys conducted in Córdoba in 1993 and 2011 were also used to assess the effects of lay participation on the legitimacy of the judiciary.

LAY PARTICIPATION IN CÓRDOBA MIXED TRIBUNALS

Jury scholars have described the benefits and challenges of lay citizens' participation as legal decision-makers (Hans, 2008; Voigt, 2008). Jury service provides laypersons with the experience of sitting in the seat of government, deliberating with fellow citizens, and rendering decisions that have meaningful consequences. This type of public participation may also boost their sense of civic responsibility (Gastil, Deess, Weiser, & Simmons, 2010).

In Córdoba, lay participation in criminal trials follows the civil-law tradition, in which jurors sit together in mixed courts with professionally trained judges. This model is used in several European countries, including Germany, Italy, France, and Poland. A mixed court is also employed in Japan's new system of lay participation (Goldbach & Hans, 2014).

The mixed court is composed of three professional judges and eight lay citizens (four men and four women), whose names are obtained from a list randomly chosen each year from the voter rolls. Voting is compulsory in Argentina; the voting rolls include all citizens aged 18 or more and are complete. The professionals and lay citizens deliberate and jointly decide questions of fact by majority vote. The presiding judge, who can only vote in the case of a tie, is charged with explaining the reasoning behind the lay citizen votes if it differs from the judges' decision. Sentencing decisions are made by the three professional judges alone.

The 445 trials that occurred before mixed tribunals between 2005 and 2017 involved 721 defendants and 500 victims. Table 3.1 shows the distribution of the offenses the defendants were charged with.

The principal offenses dealt with in the trials were homicides, effective or attempted (80%). Trials for crimes of corruption, in which government officials were charged, were rare (8.6%) and most involved low-ranking public officials (Rusca, 2014).

TABLE 3.1 *Offenses in cases tried by Córdoba mixed tribunals, 2005–2017*

Offenses	N	%
Homicides	528	73.2
Attempted murders	49	6.8
Sexual abuse followed by death	9	1.2
Offenses against the state	62	8.6
Property offenses	33	4.6
Other offenses	40	5.5
Total number of defendants	721	100.0%

The conviction rate for the 721 defendants was 82.5%, but lower (70%) for corruption cases. Of the 595 defendants who were convicted, 147 were sentenced to life terms in prison.

Judge and Jury Decisions in Córdoba

Empirical research on differences between jury and judge decisions started in the United States when Kalven and Zeisel collected data on over 3,500 criminal trials. They surveyed professional judges who reported on jury trials the judge had presided over and found that judges and juries usually agreed on the proper outcome of a case (78%). When they disagreed, the juries were more likely to acquit than the judges (Kalven & Zeisel, 1966).

This method has been intensely debated (Eisenberg, Hannaford-Agor, Hans, Waters, Munsterman, Schwab, & Wells, 2005; Farrell & Givelber, 2010; Hans & Vidmar, 1991). Although the approach ensures that the judge and jury are responding to the same case, the judges are expressing post hoc opinions. Those opinions may differ from the verdict the judge would have reached if deciding the case. Lack of consequences may have distorted their judgments. Moreover, they could have simply forgotten the important characteristics of the cases or even adapted their opinion to the jury to validate the jury's verdict.

The present work avoids the methodological limitation of the Kalven–Zeisel approach by taking advantage of the features of the mixed Córdoba court. Córdoba provides a useful opportunity to analyze differences between judge and jury decisions based on the written registry of the decisions made by each of the judges and jurors who took part in the deliberations. According to legal provisions, the participation of laypersons is restricted to deciding two issues: whether the crime charged was committed and whether the defendant was the person who committed the crime. In this way, lay participants are called to assess facts together with the judges, while legal issues (such as the duration of the sentence) are left to judges alone.

The information pertaining to the votes in each decision is restricted, of course, to the final decision of each member of the tribunal and reflects neither the richness of the debates nor the dynamics of the participation. It is nonetheless very useful to analyze the differences in the perspectives of judges and jurors in the same cases. The research analyzed the outcomes in 445 trials involving verdicts for 721 defendants (see Table 3.2).

Because the judges and jurors all sit together during the deliberations, judges have the chance to manage the discussion and influence the lay votes. Reviewing research on mixed courts in different countries, Hans (2008) notes that unanimity rates over 90% are frequent in these systems. This raises questions about the actual levels of participation of citizens in the deliberations. In South Korea, a study of the first three years of advisory jury trials found that judges and juries agreed on the verdict in most

TABLE 3.2 *Final votes on Córdoba mixed tribunals*

Final vote distribution	N	%
Unanimity	587	81.4
Majority composed of:	134	18.6
All professional judges and at least 4 jurors*	104	14.4
1 professional judge and at least 5 jurors	25	3.5
6 or more jurors	5	0.7
Total defendants	721	100.0%

Source: Author's study of 445 registered trials in the 2005–2017 period (on file with author).

* In 13 of these cases the presiding judge voted due to a tie.

cases (91.4%; 89.1% for the cases in which the defendant had not confessed) (Kim, Park, Park, & Eom, 2013). Orias Arredondo (2013), who studied mixed courts in Bolivia, reported a unanimity rate of 89%.

The level of concurrence between judges' and citizens' opinions is a little lower in Córdoba: in 81% of the cases the verdict was unanimous, a figure close to the agreement percentage obtained by Kalven and Zeisel, where the jury had deliberated alone (see Table 3.2). In most of the cases resolved by majority vote, the number of dissenters was limited to one or two persons (54%). So, if we take the unanimous decisions and the decisions reached by majorities composed of two professional judges and a half or more of the jurors, the convergence level of the opinions of the laypersons and professionals reaches more than 90%.

A clue to the paths followed to build consensus came from an interview with one of the judicial clerks, who reported that unanimity is facilitated by the strength of the evidence. "The evidence is usually so strong that the defendant is already in jail. The judicial practice ensures that cases that arrive at the jury are not hard to prove," declared the judicial clerk.

The organization of the deliberation that follows the presentation of the evidence at trial varies in different courts; this may influence the role played by laypersons during the deliberation. A judge interviewed for this project, who clearly favors lay participation, reported that the professional judges leave the jurors to talk alone as long as they need, while the judges deliberate in another room. They join the lay jurors to discuss together and vote only when the lay citizens call them back. This practice was endorsed by the Provincial High Court in 2017.

The dynamic may be different in other courts, where there is joint discussion throughout the entire deliberation. A judge who had publicly argued against the introduction of mixed tribunals when the legislature was considering this initiative indicated that, in his experience, one of the judges explains his position first, asserting judicial authority with technical reasons. This practice leaves little space for laypersons to argue for a different position.

The data from the laypersons who have served on the mixed tribunals present a more complex picture. The Provincial Supreme Court commissioned a study of the opinions of the citizens who had acted as jurors. The survey included 1,040 respondents. A large majority of them (83%) declared that they had been able to present their own views on the case during the deliberation (Tarditti & Ferrer, 2016).

Amietta (2011) has described the practices by which professional judges attempt to govern jurors and keep their behavior as decision-makers under control in the Córdoba mixed tribunals. His analysis derives from Foucault's notions of power, discipline, and governmentality. Summarizing his findings, he reports:

> The narratives of the participants showed how, besides teaching them the norms of judging, judges also observe, control and, if necessary, correct jurors' conduct. I described this relationship as a pedagogical one, reproducing and reinforcing power relations largely demarked by knowledge: the possessors of a legitimate body of knowledge become legitimate educators and evaluators in the face of those who lack it. My work also showed how these practices are accompanied and supported by demonstrations of courtesy and respect to jurors and, relevantly, by bestowing on them small signs of the privileged status they hold "as judges" (Amietta, 2011, p. 25).

In the interviews, most jurors reported that they felt respected during deliberations. Lay jurors said that they were able to take part in the tribunal's deliberation, and while professional judges oriented them in cases of doubt, the judges did not attempt to influence their decisions. However, 2 of the 44 jurors interviewed affirmed that the judges pressed them to change their point of view. Both professionals and laypersons interviewed for this project admitted that jurors had access to the prosecution file of the case, a practice forbidden by Ley No. 9182, which has been pointed out by Amietta (2011) as a regular practice used by judges to influence jurors' opinions.

In sum, the disagreement rates in cases tried by Córdoba's mixed tribunals suggest that lay participation levels are slightly higher than in other jurisdictions using this type of court. However, available evidence suggests that the actual level of autonomy reached by citizens in their decisions is debatable and may vary depending on the procedure used by a particular tribunal.

JURY AND JUDGE DECISIONS OUTSIDE ARGENTINA

When discussing trial by jury, those who favor lay participation maintain that it performs a control function. Lay participation has historically been viewed as a mechanism that narrows judicial authority. Therefore, it can contribute to verdicts that are consistent with the moral standards present in the community and promote procedurally fair trials (Machura, 2003). Kutnjak Ivković (2015) observes that by being present in the tribunal, lay judges compel the professional judges to make the reasoning of the decision explicit and transparent. Their presence performs the latent function of strengthening judicial independence.

Traditionally, jurors were expected to be more likely to acquit than judges, and that pattern was found by Kalven and Zeisel in the United States. More recent research has replicated that result (Eisenberg et al., 2005), but a few studies have produced evidence of some exceptions to that pattern. Levine (1983) compared conviction rates in jury and bench trials in the 1970s, reporting higher conviction rates in jury trials. He attributed the difference to a conservative reaction connected to fear of crime, although the strategic choice of a jury or a bench (judge) trial makes this comparison and others like it potentially a comparison of nonequivalent cases.

Using government records of over 75,000 federal criminal trials decided between 1945 and 2002, Leipold (2005) described the evolution of conviction rates in jury and bench trials. Between 1945 and 1964, judges invariably convicted at higher rates than juries. In the second phase (1964–1988), the conviction rates were quite similar. Although jury conviction rates remained stable between 1989 and 2002, judge conviction rates began to drop. Beginning in 1992, bench trials resulted in substantially more acquittals than jury trials as conviction rates in bench trials dropped. Leipold acknowledged that in this last period, some of the gap in conviction rates may be explained by identifiable features of those cases that defendants directed toward judges rather than juries and to the effect of sentencing guidelines on the judges' willingness to acquit in order to avoid a severe mandatory sentence. No study has shown this effect in the state courts that handle the majority of criminal trials in the United States.

Recent criminological research has connected the long-term trend toward greater levels of incarceration in the United States to the increased use of plea bargaining and the decline of jury trials, which has meant that more judicial decisions are made by professionals. These arguments have been developed by Dzur (2012), who associates the growth of the contemporary penal state with the increasing bureaucratization of the criminal justice system. He concludes by proposing to revitalize the jury trial in order to produce a better judicial system.

The evidence from other countries is varied. In Russia, where the new Constitution established juries following the Anglo-Saxon model in 1993, Machura (2003) concluded that juries are more likely to acquit than judges. He reported that generally, Russian courts acquit in 0.4% of the cases, while Russian juries acquitted in 12% of the cases in 2002. Comparing over 80,000 verdicts in cases decided with and without juries in Spain between 1891 and 1932, Toharia (1987) concluded that the final outcomes with both procedures were quite similar. The acquittal rate reached 45% when there were laypersons among the decision-makers and 42% when the decision was made by the judge alone.

The evidence on agreement rates within mixed tribunals is growing. Han, Párraga, and Morales (2006) analyzed the experience in the region of Zulia, Venezuela, between 2001 and 2004, and found that the introduction of lay participation had not changed conviction rates. In Bolivia, Orias Arredondo (2013) reported different patterns of response from judges versus juries. While ordinary citizens often react more severely in cases of homicide, they are more inclined to acquittal in crimes connected with drug use or trafficking.

As noted in the previous section, a study of the first three years since the introduction of the advisory jury system in South Korea found that judges and juries agreed on the verdict in most cases. When they disagreed, juries had a greater tendency to acquit than did judges (7.4% where the jury acquitted when the judge would have convicted and 1.2% where the judge would have convicted when the jury acquitted, respectively; excluding confession cases, the disagreement rates were 9.4% and 1.5%) (Kim et al., 2013).

TRENDS IN ATTITUDES TOWARD PUNISHMENT

In Córdoba, the political and social context in which Ley No. 9182 was passed may be described as marked by "penal populism": a growing call for harsher penal policies (Dzur, 2012, describing the concept introduced by John Pratt in 2007). These policies were seen as the only tool available to compensate for feelings of insecurity and the fear of crime in a society in which the sensationalization of crime has been a staple of the media. Penal populism seems also to be connected to people's feelings of insecurity as a result of social fragmentation and the erosion of social bonds characteristic of modern neoliberal politics. In these conditions, criminal justice reform was viewed as a tool to lessen the worries of groups frustrated by the state's inability to address the insecurities of modern life.

Given the widespread feelings of insecurity about crime, its inclusion on the public agenda is not surprising. In 1995, only 2% of Argentines placed insecurity at the top of their list of problems. However, in 2011, according to the Latinobarómetro (2011), 34% of respondents selected it as the most important problem. Even if insecurity levels do not precisely track trends in criminal activity levels, crime rates almost doubled between 1993 and 2014 in Córdoba (from 2,413 to 4,257 offenses per 100,000 inhabitants) and more than doubled nationally over the same period (from 1,650 to 3,750 offenses per 100,000 inhabitants) (Dirección Nacional de Política Criminológica, 2017).

In this context, it is interesting to see how attitudes toward criminal punishment changed over the 18-year period between 1993 and 2011 (Table 3.3). In both years, most of the respondents favored a harsh criminal policy. Dissatisfaction with the level of criminal punishment in our society has been widespread and persistent, with almost half of the respondents agreeing that a tough response is a solution to the problem of crime, a proportion that has not changed substantially in recent years. Similarly, attitudes that emphasize offenders' accountability for their actions are widely held.

Nonetheless, these preferences for a harsh criminal policy do not translate into extreme attitudes. The majority of respondents oppose the death penalty. Similarly, they reject "vigilante" justice, which involves the taking of law enforcement into private hands, instead showing support for judicial power.

Table 3.3 also indicates some evolution in these attitudes toward punishment in recent years. Although the image of offenders as fully responsible for their actions has grown significantly, adherence to hard policies that combat crime has basically remained stable. Dissatisfaction with the level of criminal punishment has experienced a small, but statistically significant, reduction.

ATTITUDES TOWARD PUNISHMENT IN JURY TRIAL DECISIONS

We may now ask whether these preferences for a tough penal policy reveal themselves in the verdicts of Córdoba's mixed tribunals. How do citizens behave when the judgment ceases to be a conversation subject and becomes a decision for which

TABLE 3.3 *Attitudes toward punishment, Córdoba, 1993–2011*

Attitude		Year		Chi-square*
		1993	2011	
If the state were tougher on crime, the crime problem would end.	Agree	51.1%	53.3%	9.78,
	Undecided	24.8%	16.6%	$p < .008$
	Disagree	24.1%	30.1%	
Total		100.0%	100.0%	
Offenders should be treated more like patients than as criminals.	Agree	21.4%	20.8%	20.32,
	Undecided	31.5%	18.8%	$p < .001$
	Disagree	47.1%	60.4%	
Total		100.0%	100.0%	
Do you think offenders receive enough punishment here?	Yes	10.0%	15.4%	5.42,
	No	90.0%	84.6%	$p < .02$
Total		100.0%	100.0%	
Concerning the death penalty, you:	Strongly agree	15.8%	13.4%	9.64,
	Agree	16.6%	14.4%	$p < .02$
	Disagree	27.1%	21.2%	
	Strongly disagree	40.5%	51.0%	
Total		100.0%	100.0%	
No circumstances may justify the taking of law enforcement into one's own hands.	Agree	38.4%	46.7%	18.49,
	Undecided	32.3%	19.4%	$p < .001$
	Disagree	29.3%	33.9%	
Total		100.0%	100.0%	

Source: General population surveys, Córdoba, 1993 (N = 400) and 2011 (N = 434).

* The Chi-square test assesses whether paired observations on two variables, expressed in a contingency table, are independent of each other (Freedman, Pisani, & Purves, 2007).

responsibility is shared? To answer this question, I have analyzed the differences between the judgments of judges and lay jurors responding to the same cases, using 445 decisions reached by mixed tribunals in the province of Córdoba between 2005 and 2017.

As indicated earlier, 82.5% of the verdicts were unanimous, indicating a high rate of concurrence between the jury and judge on the final verdict. As described earlier, Córdoba's mixed tribunals consist of three professional judges and eight lay citizens who deliberate and jointly decide by majority vote. The presiding judge can only vote in the case of a tie. This means that for each case, we have three possibilities amongst the jurors and three amongst the judges: agreement on acquittal, agreement on conviction, or divided decision.

To assess the differences between judges and jurors, it is necessary to analyze the composition and orientation of votes in the 134 cases between 2005 and 2017 that were decided by a majority.

In 33 out of the 134 nonunanimous decisions, one professional judge was among the majority and the other was aligned with the minority. This division suggests that these were borderline cases, where the evidence did not strongly favor either the prosecution or the defense.

In the remaining 101 cases, however, the professionals and laypersons were divided: all voting judges voted for the same verdict, opposing a group composed entirely of jurors. In 96 of these instances, the laypersons made up the minority; in only five cases was a juror majority able to impose its decision on the legal professionals. In 62 of these 101 cases (61%) in which juror decisions differed from those of the judges, the jurors' preferred verdict was more lenient than that adopted by the judges, either because the jurors would have acquitted or because they would have favored conviction on a less serious charge.

To sum up, there is no evidence that lay participation in criminal matters has resulted in a greater conviction rate. Jurors generally tend to agree with judges, and many of the decisions are made by unanimous vote. However, when lay citizens favor a different verdict, it is generally more favorable to the defendant than the one favored by the professional judges. Considering these results, the fears of greater punitiveness due to lay participation in judicial decisions can be rejected.

The attitudinal evidence thus suggests that attitudes toward punishment have become stricter in recent years. The changes are relatively modest and have been accompanied by a rejection of extreme positions, and progressive consolidation of attitudes supporting the rule of law. However, the detailed analysis of the positions of judges and ordinary citizens expressed in the verdicts delivered by mixed tribunals confirms that during their 13-year period of lay participation in judicial decisions, jurors have not produced harsher verdicts. Even if the introduction of lay participation took place in a context marked by demands for tougher punishment, and feelings of insecurity are widespread, the data do not indicate a trend toward increased eagerness to convict defendants. Decisions made by judges and jurors generally coincide; when divergence between professional judges and lay participants occurs, the jurors are generally less likely to side with the prosecution.

The comparison between the public opinion data and the verdicts analysis highlights the gap between expressing a point of view on a political issue and making a meaningful decision about it. This distance has also been noted by other researchers. For example, after reviewing research on this issue in several countries, Roberts and Hough (2009) argued that when people are given new information about crime and justice in experimental settings their attitudes are less punitive than expected. Also, analyzing attitudes toward punishment in Spain from a wide variety of empirical sources, Varona Gómez (2009) observed the contrast between responses to general opinion questions and those obtained in response to a hypothetical case presented by the researcher.

LAY PARTICIPATION AND TRUST IN JUSTICE

Scholars have argued that lay participation contributes to the legitimation of judicial power. For example, Tocqueville (1840, p. 316) observed the positive impact of interactions between judges and citizens on the prestige of the judiciary: "The jury, then, which seems to restrict the rights of the judiciary, does, in reality, consolidate its power; and in no country are the judges so powerful as where the people partake their privileges." More recently, Machura (2003) and Marder (2005) have pointed out that citizen participation in judicial decisions has positive effects on trust in justice. Working with data from more than 80 countries, Voigt (2008) reports positive correlations between confidence in the legal system and lay participation.

This position has also received support from theorists of deliberative democracy, who emphasize that the deliberation on public issues can benefit the legitimacy of political institutions. Researchers working on this conceptual framework have observed that jury deliberations arguably approach the ideal speech situation, offering a space for unconstrained deliberation, in which no force except that of a better argument is exercised (Gastil, 2018; Gastil et al., 2010; Iontcheva, 2003). Newly emerging systems offer an interesting opportunity to observe whether the public legitimacy of a legal system is affected when citizens participate as decision-makers, an issue difficult to study within stable existing systems (Hans, 2008). From a Latin American perspective, this question is particularly relevant, since confidence in justice has been chronically low in the region.

To advance this discussion, I review changes in confidence in justice in Córdoba, Argentina, where mixed tribunals were introduced in 2005. Data from two public opinion surveys, conducted in 1993 and 2011, are used to explore the changes. Survey data (Latinobarómetro, 1995–2011) are also employed to understand these changes within the Argentina context.

Legitimacy and Trust in Justice: Theoretical Remarks

Max Weber's theory of legitimacy (Weber, 1978) is the starting point for most contemporary work on legitimacy. From his perspective, legitimacy arises when people feel an inner need to follow the rules or decisions of an existing power. Therefore, every domination will look for more stability by trying to raise the *belief* in the legitimacy of that domination. Following this approach, legitimacy should be analyzed within an existing social relationship, since it implies both the claim from the power or institution to be considered rightful and the belief in the correctness of such a claim made by those who are subject to this domination.

Rosanvallon (2009) pointed out that in contemporary societies, where elections have become less central, new ways to approach the idea of general interest and novel forms of legitimacy have arisen. He calls these legitimacy of impartiality, legitimacy of reflexivity, and legitimacy of proximity; all three types are defined by the qualities of the bond between rulers and subjects. Hence, these new forms are never definitively acquired. They always remain open to challenge and dependent on social perceptions of institutional behavior; authorities face the need for continual relegitimation.

The relational perspective is the main Weberian legacy present today in this field of research. As noted by Lembcke (2008), it has been adopted by those who choose a top-down approach and who concentrate on describing the efforts of the institutions to gain acceptance for their claims of legitimacy. In contrast, a bottom-up perspective is taken by those who focus on citizens' subjective convictions. In this case, attention is directed to the motives of assent to the demands of power. The present project adopts this perspective, which calls on us to assess the extent of approval regarding a specific system of domination and its dynamic processes of transformation.

Empirical analysis of judicial legitimacy is generally grounded in the concept of diffuse support, developed by Easton (1965, p. 273), who refers to "a reservoir of favorable attitudes or goodwill that helps members to accept or tolerate outputs to which they are opposed or the effects of which they see as damaging to their wants." Specific support is related to consent in response to particular decisions. But authorities would be fragile if there were only such agreements since decision-making involves favoring some and disfavoring others. Authorities survive thanks to a cushion of general support, not linked to particular outcomes, which allows them to exercise discretion.

Diffuse support occurs when people have confidence in institutions to make, in the long run, desirable public policy. Applied to the study of judicial legitimacy, this notion has been conceptualized as institutional loyalty, which helps citizens tolerate outputs that they are opposed to, without necessarily undermining their basic commitment to supporting the institution (Gibson, Caldeira, & Spence, 2005; Gibson, Lodge, & Woodson, 2014). This notion is also employed here.

Trust in Justice: Methodological Issues

In Latin America, empirical research on institutional legitimacy generally uses survey data from Gallup or Latinobarómetro. Both sources are appropriate for comparative analysis in the region since they include common questions about trust in different institutions. For example, they both ask respondents: "Please tell me how much confidence you have in each of the following groups, institutions or persons mentioned on this list: a lot, some, a little or no confidence? The Congress, the Judiciary, political parties, etc." Survey data are especially useful to develop a cross-national, regional perspective, as well as to describe trends in legitimacy levels over time. The Latinobarómetro project, inaugurated in 1995, provides annual surveys in 18 countries, analyzing mass support for democracy and confidence levels in different institutions.

Power and Cyr (2010) have observed that the reliability of an institution is reflected not only by what individuals say but also by what they do or are willing to do in connection with it. In their view, an adequate operationalization of legitimacy should encompass both attitudes (such as trust in institutions) and behavior (e.g., measures of compliance). Their remark is particularly relevant in a country such as Argentina, where low trust in the judiciary is accompanied by a high rate of litigation (Smulovitz, 2008).

This project, oriented toward analyzing changes in judicial legitimacy throughout a longer period, has used only attitudinal indicators to maintain data comparability. Two different measures of trust in justice were included in the research. The first one focuses on judges as persons, and may be easier for laypersons to answer ("Do you believe that a judge inspires confidence and the sensation of being protected?" Alternative answers: a lot, some, little, or no). The second is the traditional question about trust in institutions, employed in cross-national research.

Data were obtained from two public opinion surveys conducted in the city of Córdoba in 1993 and 2011. The first survey (400 respondents) measured the trust in judges as persons, as well as opinions about the independence, impartiality, honesty, and efficiency of judges. The second survey (434 respondents) included the same questions and added a measure of trust in the judiciary as an institution. In the second survey, it was possible to measure the correlation between confidence in judges as persons and in the judiciary as an institution. The correlation was .44 ($p < .001$), suggesting that the two questions tap into similar sources.

Trust in Justice in Argentina

The public opinion data for Argentina indicate that the legitimacy of the most basic political institutions, including the judiciary, is quite low, though not below average when compared with other Latin American countries. Latinobarómetro (2011) data report that only one out of three citizens (33%) showed much or some confidence in the courts in 2011. Average confidence levels in Latin America were 29.1% for the same year. Power and Cyr (2010), who have mapped legitimacy levels in Latin America, have pointed out the connection between the confidence in justice and democracy strength. In this region, countries where democracy has been more stable, such as Uruguay (49.5%), exceed the regional mean. It is interesting to observe that Brazil – where lay participation in judicial decisions was introduced as early as 1822 (Amietta, 2010) – had confidence levels that were also higher: 39%.

Legitimacy levels are higher in societies with more advanced levels of human development, a feature also documented by Power and Cyr (2010). This is not surprising since the prestige of political institutions increases as those institutions produce positive economic results for citizens over long periods.

Analyzing changes in institutional legitimacy levels in Argentina between 1984 and 2006, Turner and Carballo (2010) have shown considerable variation in the confidence in the judiciary since the end of the military dictatorship. The level has fluctuated between 19% and 58% over that period.

This review clarifies why, from a relational approach, confidence in the judiciary is a complex variable, which is influenced by diverse factors. Therefore, the following analysis must be considered as an exploratory study of its relationship with lay participation in judicial decision-making.

Trust in Justice in Córdoba

The survey data reveal changes in confidence in the judiciary and relative stability in attitudes toward lay participation between 1993 and 2011. They also document some of the variables involved in these modifications. During this 18-year period, confidence in judges improved slightly (Table 3.4). Even though the increase in positive answers has been small, negative responses have clearly diminished. The proportion of those who felt little or very little confidence was 53% in 1993, but this figure dropped to 40% by 2011.

The surveys included two questions on public support for lay participation. The first one explored the public reaction to the jury system in general terms. The second question asked members of the public to imagine that they had been charged with a criminal offense and to state whether they would prefer to be tried by a lay jury or a professional judge.

A clear preference emerged in the responses to these questions: much of the sample supported lay participation and preferred to be tried by a jury. That preference did not change over time. Research has shown that a more positive image of juries compared to judges is general in common-law countries such as England and Wales, New Zealand, and the United States, while civil-law countries reveal a mixed pattern of findings regarding preferences for a jury (Roberts & Hough, 2009).

By 2011, the implementation of mixed tribunals had not brought about significant changes in general attitudes toward the jury system. There was a slight increase in positive opinions in 2011, which resulted from respondents moving from neutral to

TABLE 3.4 *Changes in attitudes toward lay participation, Córdoba, 1993–2011*

Attitude		Year 1993	Year 2011	Chi-square
Confidence in judges				
Do you believe that a judge inspires confidence and the sensation of being protected?	**A lot**	3.6%	3.7%	21.66,
	Some	14.5%	16.6%	$p < .001$
	Fair	28.7%	39.4%	
	Little	38.1%	23.7%	
	Very little	15.2%	16.6%	
Total		100.0%	100.0%	
Attitudes toward trial by jury				
Concerning trial by jury, you are	**In favor**	58.9%	62.3%	1.43,
	Neither for nor against	25.3%	21.9%	Not significant
	Against	15.8%	15.8%	
Total		100.0%	100.0%	
If you found yourself on trial, you would prefer to be tried by	**A judge alone**	33.8%	38.0%	1.51,
	A jury	66.2%	62.0%	Not significant
Total		100.0%	100.0%	

Source: General population surveys, Córdoba, 1993 (N = 400) and 2011 (N= 434).

positive, but the increase was not significant. These increases in support for lay participation increased primarily among those with low levels of education.

We also examined views on the independence of the judiciary from political power, impartiality, and equality in the treatment of affairs of common people. Other aspects studied included the honesty of the judges – understood as the absence of corruption – and efficiency in their job, in general, and regarding an adequate level of criminal punishment. In reviewing changes in public opinion on these issues, it is important to consider that personal experience with the justice administration became more frequent during this period. The proportion of people who had contact with the courts was 33% in 1993 and reached 45% in 2011, probably due to an increase in civil litigation during that interval.

As Table 3.5 shows, the views of citizens on the independence of courts from political power became less negative over this time period, which may in part be due to changes initiated in 2000 in the process of appointing judges. Perceptions of the honesty of judges increased. The assessment of judicial efficiency also improved. These statistically significant changes may be connected to enhanced transparency of judicial activities obtained thanks to lay participation in courts.

TABLE 3.5 *Perceptions of the judiciary, Córdoba, 1993–2011*

		Year		
		1993	2011	Chi-square
Independence of the courts	**Very high**	5.8%	6.2%	18.19, $p < .001$
	Rather high	13.7%	19.9%	
	Rather low	32.0%	40.7%	
	Low	48.5%	33.3%	
Total		100.0%	100.0%	
Impartiality in criminal proceedings	**Agree**	31.9%	30.5%	0.18, Not significant
	Disagree	68.1%	69.5%	
Total		100.0%	100.0%	
Impartiality in civil proceedings	**Agree**	20.8%	26.0%	2.95, Not significant
	Disagree	79.2%	74.0%	
Total		100.0%	100.0%	
Equal treatment to all in criminal proceedings	**Yes**	7.1%	8.3%	0.46, Not significant
	No	92.9%	91.7%	
Total		100.0%	100.0%	
There is enough punishment for crime	**Yes**	10.0%	15.4%	5.42, $p < .02$
	No	90.0%	84.6%	
Total		100.0%	100.0%	
Cases of corruption among judges are:	**Frequent**	23.5%	20.9%	12.17, $p < .007$
	Occasional	42.5%	33.9%	
	Rare	28.9%	41.4%	
	Never	5.1%	3.8%	
Total		100.0%	100.0%	
Judicial efficiency	**Very high/high**	16.0%	27.7%	26.39, $p < .001$
	Fair	62.5%	55.2%	
	Low/ Very low	21.5%	17.1%	
Total		100.0%	100.0%	

Source: General population surveys, Córdoba, 1993 (N = 400) and 2011 (N =434).

In addition, Table 3.5 reports that the proportion of citizens who believe that the level of criminal punishment is adequate increased over time. As our earlier analysis showed, this satisfaction cannot derive from higher conviction rates. Instead, this result suggests that lay participation improved the legitimacy of criminal sentences, moderating external criticism of verdicts (Park, 2010).

Table 3.5 indicates that the negative assessment of the ability of judges to perform their tasks without social or economic considerations remained stable. In 2011, two-thirds of those interviewed still doubted the impartiality of judges in criminal and civil cases, no change from the proportion in 1993. The negative opinions about fair treatment in criminal courts were even higher: more than 90% believed that judges are sensitive to social and economic pressures, both in 1993 and 2011. These data suggest that special efforts are needed to accomplish the ideals of equality before the law in the contact between citizens and the administration of justice.

Small positive changes in the opinions about the independence and honesty of the judges, the efficiency of courts, and the levels of criminal punishment offer some explanation for the slight improvement of the confidence in the judiciary in Córdoba during the 1993–2011 period. As Table 3.6 illustrates, all these dimensions are significantly correlated with trust in justice.

TABLE 3.6 *Correlations between confidence in judges and other perceptions of the judiciary*

	A judge inspires confidence:	
Other perceptions of the judiciary:	1993	2011
Independence from political power	.18**	.13*
Impartiality in criminal proceedings	.25**	.24**
Impartiality in civil proceedings	.26**	.30**
Equal treatment to all in criminal proceedings	.23**	.19**
Efficiency of the courts	.37**	.36**
Frequency of cases of corruption among judges	−.30**	−.32**
There is enough punishment for crime	.16**	.15**

Note. Ns for 1993 were between 309 and 394; Ns for 2011 were between 394 and 434.
* $p < .05$
** $p < .01$

Data included in Table 3.6 provide evidence that the views on the impartiality of judges and their ability to offer equal treatment to citizens – dimensions negatively assessed in both surveys – are also correlated with confidence in the judiciary. This is useful in explaining the modest increase in trust in the judiciary observed in 2011 and offers clues to design policies oriented toward improving the relationship between judges and citizens.

The relationship between lay participation in judicial decision-making and confidence in the judiciary is complex. Comparative research has pointed out that the call for popular participation in the administration of justice is more likely in contexts characterized by dissatisfaction with judicial performance and lack of confidence in justice. In the long run, however, we can expect lay participation to have a positive effect on trust in justice.

There are at least three microprocesses by which this occurs. First, as pointed out by Park (2010) in his analysis of Korea's experience with juries, the very existence of a system for jury trials might reduce external criticism of penal decisions. This result is more likely when jury trials receive widespread media coverage.

Secondly, as Tocqueville (1840) observed, differences in knowledge and technical skills become evident during the interaction between judges and citizens, which consolidates the prestige of judges. Mixed tribunals, where judges and laypersons share the deliberation process, offer ample opportunities for this type of interaction.

In addition, those who participate in a jury trial are likely to communicate information about their experience throughout their social networks. If they are satisfied with their experience and share that reaction, the legitimacy of the whole judicial system will be bolstered.

Recall that in Córdoba, mixed tribunals were created in a context characterized by low legitimacy of the judicial system. The connection between a lack of confidence in the judiciary and support for lay participation was also present in 2004, during the parliamentary debate of Ley No. 9182.

Public opinion data collected in 2011, after seven years of mixed tribunals, showed an increase in confidence in the judiciary; the increase was small but statistically significant. To interpret these changes, it is necessary to determine if the microprocesses explaining the link between lay participation and the legitimation of the judiciary are also present.

In Córdoba, media coverage of cases tried by the new mixed tribunals has been intense. The primary local newspaper, *La Voz del Interior*, published 162 articles about jury trials in 2007. In other small towns, jurors interviewed for this project complained about the intensity of media coverage (Bergoglio, 2011). As a result, one can expect, as Park (2010) hypothesized, a reduction in the external criticism of criminal decisions. Accordingly, 2011 survey data showed greater satisfaction with criminal punishment, as the results in Table 3.5 showed.

Qualitative studies on the experience of mixed tribunals have reported that the interactions between judges and jurors in Córdoba are frequently framed as a teaching relationship, where judges are always available to assist citizens with their knowledge and to answer questions (Amietta, 2011). These practices are suitable for rebuilding the prestige of judges.

In addition, those who have served as jurors report satisfaction with the experience, and their opinion about the administration of justice has improved, as the surveys conducted in 2006 and 2011 show.

Given these favorable conditions, why is the impact of lay participation in the confidence in justice still rather modest? It is necessary to take into consideration that the experience in Córdoba with mixed tribunals is quite limited: in a seven-year period before the 2011 survey, only 215 cases had been tried with citizens included among the decision-makers. Even if those who serve share their positive experience with others, relatively few people had that experience to share. International comparisons about the number of summons delivered per year are useful here. Park (2010) estimates that 2 million summons are mailed each year in the United States, amounting to 1 per 154 persons. In Córdoba 4,822 summons were delivered in 2009; that is 1 per 686 inhabitants.

This analysis suggests that the participation of citizens in judicial decision-making could build confidence in judges in the long term, as has been suggested by previous sociolegal research (Iontcheva, 2003; Machura, 2003; Marder, 2005). Therefore, we could expect that the consolidation of the experience of mixed tribunals in Córdoba will contribute decisively to the legitimation of the judiciary.

CONCLUSION

Drawing on a variety of sources, we have assessed whether the Córdoba mixed tribunals have fulfilled the expectations held by those who promoted this innovation. Evidence on the level of lay participation in the mixed tribunals provides mixed results on the effective autonomy of the lay citizens during deliberations. Unanimity rates are somewhat lower than in other mixed tribunal systems, but may suggest that Córdoba jurors are more willing to dissent and not simply follow the decisions of professional judges.

It is worth noting that this participation has not led to higher conviction rates, even though the introduction of mixed tribunals took place in a context marked by demands for tougher sentencing and stricter attitudes toward punishment. The comparative analysis of the positions of judges and ordinary citizens, as expressed in the verdicts reached by mixed tribunals, confirms that lay participation in judicial decisions has not produced higher conviction rates. While decisions made by judges and lay jurors often agree, when they diverge, the jurors generally favor acquittal or conviction on a less serious offense.

Finally, public opinion data suggest that citizen participation in judicial decision-making has improved confidence in the judiciary; the changes are small but statistically significant. This could increase trust in judges in the long term. Consequently, we expect in the future that the experience with mixed tribunals in Córdoba will contribute to the legitimation of the judiciary.

Our findings also help to confirm that deliberative spaces promote responsible citizen participation. As new initiatives to introduce trial by jury multiply in different parts of the country, these results are interesting. They show that citizens pressed to consider information about criminal offenses, and placed in a dialogic space, share the moral responsibility for judging criminal responsibility and do not adopt extreme attitudes. In this way, lay participation in judicial decision-making contributes to the collective construction of a democratic society.

REFERENCES

Amietta, S. A. (2010). Tendencias en juicios por jurados en Latinoamérica [Latin American trends in trials by jury]. In M. I. Bergoglio (Ed.), *Subiendo al estrado: La experiencia cordobesa de juicios por jurados* [Getting on the stand: Cordoba's experience with jury trials] (pp. 37–51). Córdoba, Argentina: Advocatus.

(2011). Governance in Córdoba's mixed tribunal: A study on microphysics of power. *Oñati Socio-Legal Series*, *1*(1), 1–33. http://opo.iisj.net/index.php/osls/article/view/43

Bergoglio, M. I. (2008). New paths toward judicial legitimacy: The experience of mixed tribunals in Córdoba. *Southwestern Journal of International Law*, *14*(2), 319–339.

(2011). Metropolitan and town juries: The influence of social context on lay participation. *Chicago-Kent Law Review*, *86*, 831–853.

Cavallero, R., & Hendler, E. (1988). *Justicia y participación: El juicio por jurados en materia penal* [Justice and participation: Jury trials in criminal matters]. Buenos Aires: Universidad.

Dirección Nacional de Política Criminológica [National Directorate of Criminal Intelligence (Arg.)]. (2017). https://datos.gob.ar/dataset/seguridad-estadisticas-criminales-republica-argentina-por-provincias

Dzur, A. W. (2012). *Punishment, participatory democracy and the jury*. New York: Oxford University Press.

Easton, D. (1965). *A systems analysis of political life*. New York: John Wiley & Son.

Eisenberg, T., Hannaford-Agor, P. L., Hans, V. P., Waters, N. L., Munsterman, G. T., Schwab, S. J., & Wells, M. T. (2005). Judge-jury agreement in criminal cases: A partial replication of Kalven and Zeisel's *The American jury*. *Journal of Empirical Legal Studies*, *2*, 171–207. https://doi.org/10.1111/j.1740–1461.2005.00035.x

Farrell, A., & Givelber, D. (2010). Liberation reconsidered: Understanding why judges and juries disagree about guilt. *Journal of Criminal Law*, *100*, 1549–1586. http://iris.lib.neu.edu/slaw_fac_pubs/27

Ferrer, C., & Grundy, C. (2005). *El nuevo juicio penal con jurados en la provincia de Córdoba* [The new criminal jury trial in the province of Córdoba]. Córdoba, Argentina: Ed. Mediterránea.

Freedman, D., Pisani, R., & Purves, R. (2007). *Statistics*. New York: W. W. Norton.

Gastil, J. (2018). The lessons and limitations of experiments in democratic deliberation. *Annual Review of Law and Social Science*, *14*, 271–291. https://doi.org/10.1146/annurev-lawsocsci

Gastil, J., Deess, E. P., Weiser, P. J., & Simmons, C. (2010). *The jury and democracy: How jury deliberation promotes civic engagement and political participation*. New York: Oxford University Press.

Gibson, J. L., Caldeira, G. A., & Spence, L. K. (2005). Why do people accept public policies they oppose? Testing legitimacy theory with a survey-based experiment. *Political Research Quarterly*, *58*(2), 187–201. https://doi.org/10.1177/106591290505800201

Gibson, J. L., Lodge, M., & Woodson, B. (2014). Losing, but accepting: Legitimacy, positivity theory, and the symbols of judicial authority. *Law & Society Review*, *48*, 837–866. https://doi.org/10.1111/lasr.12104

Goldbach, T., & Hans, V. (2014). *Juries, lay judges, and trials*. In G. Bruinsma & D. Weisburd (Eds.), *Encyclopedia of criminology and criminal justice* (pp. 2716–2727). New York: Springer.

Han, P., Párraga, J., & Morales, J. (2006). La participación ciudadana en la justicia penal venezolana [Citizen participation in Venezuelan criminal justice]. *CENIPEC*, *2*(25), 247–269.

Hans, V. P. (2008). Jury systems around the world. *Annual Review of Law and Social Science*, *4*, 275–297. https://doi.org/10.1146/annurev.lawsocsci.4.110707.172319

Hans, V. P., & Vidmar, N. (1991). *The American jury* at twenty-five years. *Law & Social Inquiry*, 16, 324–351.
Iontcheva, J. (2003). Jury sentencing as democratic practice. *Virginia Law Review*, 89, 311–383.
Kalven, H., & Zeisel, H. (1966). *The American jury*. Boston: Little, Brown and Company.
Kessler, G. (2009). *El sentimiento de inseguridad: Sociología del temor al delito* [The feeling of insecurity: Sociology of the fear of crime]. Buenos Aires: Siglo XXI.
Kim, S., Park, J., Park, K., & Eom, J.-S. (2013). Judge–jury agreement in criminal cases: The first three years of the Korean jury system. *Journal of Empirical Legal Studies*, 10, 35–53.
Kutnjak Ivković, S. (2015). Ears of the deaf: The theory and reality of lay judges in mixed tribunals. *Chicago-Kent Law Review*, 90, 1031–1067.
Latinobarómetro [Latinobarometer]. (1995–2011). www.latinobarometro.org/latOnline.jsp
Ley No. 9182, Legislación Provincial de Córdoba [Law No. 9182, Legislature of the Province of Córdoba (Arg.)] (2004).
Leipold, A. D. (2005). Why are federal judges so acquittal prone? *Washington University Law Quarterly*, 83, 151–227.
Lembcke, O. W. (2008). The dynamics of legitimacy: A critical reconstruction of Max Weber's concept. *Recht der Werkelijkheid*, 3, 33–47.
Levine, J. P. (1983). Jury toughness: The impact of conservatism on criminal court verdicts. *Crime & Delinquency*, 29, 71–87. https://doi.org/10.1177/001112878302900103
Machura, S. (2003). Fairness, justice, and legitimacy: Experiences of people's judges in South Russia. *Law & Policy*, 25, 123–150.
Marder, N. (2005). *The jury process*. New York: Foundation Press.
Orias Arredondo, R. (2013). Jueces ciudadanos: Democratizando la justicia en Bolivia [Citizen judges: Democratizing justice in Bolivia]. *Revista Sistemas Judiciales*, 9(17), 26–38.
Park, R. Y. (2010). The globalizing jury trial: Lessons and insights from Korea. *American Journal of Comparative Law*, 58, 525–582. https://doi.org/10.5131/ajcl.2009.0049
Piden debate sobre jurados populares [They are calling for a debate on popular juries]. (2004, August 7). *La Voz del Interior*. http://buscador.lavoz.com.ar
Power, T. J., & Cyr, J. M. (2010). Mapping political legitimacy in Latin America. *International Social Science Journal*, 60, 253–272.
Roberts, J. V., & Hough, M. (2009). *Public opinion and the jury: An international literature review*. London: Ministry of Justice. http://eprints.bbk.ac.uk/3795/
Rosanvallon, P. (2009). *La legitimidad democrática: Imparcialidad, reflexividad, proximidad* [Democratic legitimacy: Impartiality, reflexivity, proximity]. Buenos Aires: Manantial.
Rusca, B. (2014). La implementación del juicio por jurado en delitos de corrupción: Un análisis de la experiencia cordobesa [The implementation of the jury trial in corruption crimes: An analysis of the Córdoba experience]. *Revista de La Facultad. Facultad de Derecho y Ciencias Sociales de La Universidad Nacional de Córdoba (UNC)*, 5, 107–124.
Smulovitz, C. (2008). La política por otros medios: Judicialización y movilización legal en Argentina [Politics by other means: Judicialization and legal mobilization in Argentina]. *Desarrollo Económico*, 48, 287–305.
Tarditti, A., & Ferrer, C. (2016). El juicio con jurados populares: A diez años de su aplicación en la provincia de Córdoba [The trial with popular juries: Ten years after its application in the province of Córdoba]. In *Investigaciones aplicadas en el ámbito del Poder Judicial de Córdoba III* [Applied research in the area of the Córdoba Judicial Power III] (pp. 49–84). Córdoba: Centro Judicial Ricardo Nuñez. http://campusvirtual.justiciacordoba.gob.ar/moodle/repository/investigacion/publica/tomo11/11_02.pdf

Tocqueville, A. de. (1840). *Democracy in America*. Translated by Henry Reeve. Pennsylvania State University, Electronic Classics Series. http://seas3.elte.hu/coursematerial/LojkoMiklos/Alexis-de-Tocqueville-Democracy-in-America.pdf

Toharia, J. J. (1987). *Pleitos tengas ... Introducción a la cultura legal española* [Disputes you have ... Introduction to Spanish legal culture]. Madrid: Centro de Investigaciones Sociológicas.

Turner, F. C., & Carballo, M. (2010). Cycles of legitimacy and delegitimation across regimes in Argentina, 1900–2008. *International Social Science Journal*, 60, 273–283.

Varona Gómez, D. (2009). ¿Somos los españoles punitivos? Actitudes punitivas y reforma penal en España [Are we Spaniards punitive? Punitive attitudes and penal reform in Spain]. *InDret*, 1/2009, 2–31.

Voigt, S. (2008). The (economic) effects of lay participation in courts: A cross-country analysis. *CESifo Working Paper Series No. 2365*. http://papers.ssrn.com/sol3/papers.cfm?abstract_id=1226682

Weber, M. (1978). *Economy and society: An outline of interpretative sociology*. Edited by G. Roth & C. Wittich. Los Angeles: University of California Press. https://archive.org/details/MaxWeberEconomyAndSociety

Zaffaroni, R. (2012, November 12). El juicio por jurados no funciona [Trial by jury doesn't work]. *Página/12*. www.pagina12.com.ar/diario/elpais/subnotas/76068–24551-2006–11-12.html

4

Lay Participation in the Criminal Trial in Japan

A Decade of Activity and Its Sociopolitical Consequences

Dimitri Vanoverbeke and Hiroshi Fukurai

Japan has adopted varied forms of lay participation in its justice system over the course of its history. These lay systems have included: (1) an American-style all-citizen, 12-member criminal jury (from 1928 to 1943); (2) a grand jury called the Prosecution Review Commission (PRC, or *Kensatsu Shinsakai*), in which a panel of 11 citizens is asked to make an indictment decision (from 1948 to the present); (3) a 12-member American-style jury in both criminal and civil cases on the island of Okinawa (from 1963 to 1972); (4) a 9-member grand jury to make an indictment decision in Okinawa (from 1963 to 1972); and (5) a mixed *Saiban'in* tribunal in criminal cases (from 2009 to the present). The *Saiban'in* system is unique in that it is Japan's first mixed tribunal system in which a collegial panel of professional and lay judges is asked to render a verdict on conviction and penalty. All other lay adjudication systems adopted in Japan, including the current PRC system, have excluded participation by professional judges in the deliberative process.

The *Saiban'in* trial was introduced after the Law on the Participation of Lay Judges in the Criminal Procedure (Saiban'in no sanka suru keiji saiban ni kan suru hōritsu [Jury Law]), Law no. 63, came into effect on May 21, 2009, following a preparatory period of five years. The legislative intent was to contribute to the promotion of the public's understanding of the judicial system and thereby raise their confidence in it (Jury Law, Art. 1; see Anderson & Saint (2005) for its English translation). In the 1980s, newspapers extensively covered several wrongful convictions in death penalty cases, which fueled a public challenge to the way that justice was rendered in Japan. The most widely circulated newspaper in Japan – the *Yomiuri Shimbun* – devoted more than 35 editorials to the issue of wrongful convictions in the 1980s, with such evocative titles as "The Bitter Taste of a Wrongful Conviction" ("Shasetsu: Enzai ni nigai aji," 1980), "Wrongful Convictions Caused by Brute Investigations" ("Shasetsu: Enzai o unda gōin na sōsa," 1984), and "Investigations Dependent on Confessions Is What Should Be Questioned" ("Shasetsu: Towareru jihaku izon no sōsa," 1988). Failures in criminal procedure were being exposed in the 1980s because, inter alia, new evidence made it undeniable that convicted defendants such as Sakae Menda, Shigeyoshi Taniguchi, Masao Akahori, and Yukio Saitō could not have committed the murders that had led to their convictions, and to the death penalty, decades earlier. The media began to pay greater attention to the unwillingness of judges to recognize fallacies and weaknesses in the prosecutors' reports. This analysis also revealed that judges were inclined to accept uncritically the written conclusions of the prosecutor (Hirano, 1985, 1989; Isa, 2006). Ryūichi Hirano, a prominent Japanese legal scholar, wrote that the criminal justice system was terminally ill and could only be saved by introducing lay judges in criminal trials (Hirano, 1985, 1989).

The Jury Law stipulates that a panel of six randomly selected citizens and three professional judges deliberate jointly on the facts and, if the defendant is convicted, on the sanction. The *Saiban'in* jury is used at the district court for those crimes punishable by death, imprisonment for an indefinite period, or imprisonment with hard labor. The selection of the lay judges is made by the three professional judges in the presence of the prosecutor and defense counsel. This selection process is not open to the public (Art. 33, 1). The prosecutor and defense counsel may each remove up to four candidates without providing any reasons (Art. 36, 1). Once this procedure is complete, six lay judges and two or three additional lay judges are selected by lottery (Art. 37, 1). The expectation is that the *Saiban'in* jurors shall perform their duties truthfully and fairly (Art. 39, 2), and that they will have to express their opinion (Art. 66, 2) in the deliberations. It is the duty of the presiding judge to inform the lay judges about the relevant law and about procedural aspects related to the trial (Art. 66, 3). The penalty related to disclosing the content of the deliberations (i.e., the secrecy provision) is set at a fine of up to ¥500,000 (US$5,000) and/or imprisonment for up to six months (Art. 108). Several scholars have criticized the secrecy provision as an impediment to realizing the primary purpose of this new procedure, because former lay judges are prohibited from sharing their experiences (Levin & Tice, 2009).

The introduction of the *Saiban'in* system was largely hailed as a positive development by the media, legal professionals, progressive scholars of the legal system and procedures, and such civil rights organizations as the Japan Federation of House Wives (*Shufuren*) and the National Federation of the Prosecution Review Commission (*Zenkoku Kensatsu Shinsakai Rengōkai*), among many others. However, the limitations on the independence of the lay judges drew expressions of dismay and disappointment from others, such as Research Group on Jury Trial (RGJT) president Chihiro Isa. He argued that the benefits of trial by jury would not be realized in the *Saiban'in* system because the lay judges would not be able to serve as independent actors in a procedure that remained under full control of the professional judges (Isa, 2006).

Isa served as a juror in a criminal jury trial on the island of Okinawa when the island was under US military rule. In 1963, the US military government introduced the jury trial in both civil and criminal matters; the amendment to the Penal Code of Okinawa established trial by jury on March 8, 1963 (Vanoverbeke, 2015). In 1964, *United States of America* v. *Megumi Yoshihisa* led to the fourth criminal jury trial. Isa was chosen as a juror, along with two other Okinawan residents and nine American citizens who resided on the island (Fukurai, 2007; Vanoverbeke, 2015). Four Okinawan youths were accused of murdering a drunken American soldier and were subsequently acquitted on the murder charge. Isa described his jury experience in a book called *Reversal: A Jury Trial in Okinawa Under US Rule* (*Gyakuten: Amerika Shihaika Okinawa no Baishin Saiban*), in which he embraced the democratic value of citizen participation in the adjudication of serious and violent criminal charges brought by the prosecution against the members of their own community. After his book received the prestigious *Ohya Sōichirō* nonfiction book award in 1977, Isa formed the first organized civic movement to introduce the jury trial in Japan. In April 1982, he joined with several progressive and well-respected lawyers and civil rights activists to launch Japan's first pro-jury civil organization, the Research Group on Jury Trial (RGJT). Prominent members of RGJT included English legal scholar Hideo Niwayama, news reporter and columnist Katsuhiko Iimuro, law professor Mitsuru Shinokura, and criminal defense lawyers Jitsuzō Shigeta, Tetsuji Kurata, Isamu Sekihara, and Shōjirō Gotō. Gotō won the prestigious Human Rights Award from the Tokyo Bar Association in 1991 after working on many famous wrongful conviction cases (Fukurai, 2007).

Members of the RGJT agreed that most wrongful convictions resulted from the uncritical decisions of professional judges who routinely accepted defendants' forced confessions as the queen of evidence in rendering their convictions, thereby leading to a 99.9% conviction rate of all defendants indicted. Japanese judges are career bureaucrats who rarely render judgments that contradict the general interests and policies of the government, corporate oligarchy, or powerful political organizations and their personnel (Foote, 1996; Fukurai, 2007). Isa and other RGJT members believed that lay judges could raise doubts in the evaluation of the authenticity or voluntary character of confessions (Isa, 2006). Voluminous research has long substantiated that many confessions have been extracted and concocted under extreme physical abuse and psychological duress (Foote, 1991; Hamada, 2001; Johnson, 2002).

The Justice System Reform Committee (JSRC) first suggested the introduction of the lay judge system to the government in June 2001, after two years of intense activity, which included 63 public meetings (Vanoverbeke, 2015; Yanase, 2016). The JSRC argued that it was necessary to inject a strong sense of sovereignty into ordinary residents by empowering them to adjudicate the crimes that occurred in their own community (as reflected in "Prime minister's policy speech," 2001). This idea of sovereignty also appeared repeatedly in the preparatory stage of the lay judge system, referred to as the idea of subjective engagement (*shutaisei*), meaning that the citizens do not merely defer to authority. The importance of this concept in academic research and policy making originated after World War II, when it was argued that the expression of one's individual opinion was necessary to induce a social transition from the paternalism of a state-centered society to a citizen-centered community based on individual rights and freedom (Kawashima, 1963, 1967; Koschmann, 1996).

Isa's disappointment with the *Saiban'in* system is thus understandable in light of his view that the participation of professional judges in the deliberation leads to their undue influence upon citizen judges, thus reducing citizens' independent deliberative engagement (Vanoverbeke, 2015). Isa argued that the participation of professional judges in the deliberations would fail to emancipate the citizens from state power. The fear was that the lay judges would not dare to differ from the professional judges' opinions and would therefore merely rubber-stamp the legal professionals' view (Ishimatsu, Tsuchiya, & Isa, 2007). Critical voices stressed that the lay judge system would not be a real departure from the past, but merely an opportunity for the public to learn how excellent the criminal procedure is and how wrong the critics are (Odanaka, 2001).

THE LAY JUDGE SYSTEM AFTER A DECADE

This section examines the performance of *Saiban'in* trials during the first decade of its operation. As of May 2019, over 90,000 citizens had served as lay participants in *Saiban'in* trials (n = 92,056) and rendered decisions on over 12,000 defendants (n = 12,179) (Supreme Court of Japan, 2019). The sociodemographic breakdown of citizen participants indicated that a majority were males (55.2%) and a majority of all lay judges were between 40 and 69 years old (61.4%). Full-time employees made up over half of all lay judges (56.3%). The second largest group were part-time employees (15.4%). Homemakers made up nearly one-tenth of *Saiban'in* participants (9.3%), while self-employed or freelancers (6.9%) and those without jobs (7.1%) also acted as jurors in the *Saiban'in* trials to an important degree. The remaining lay judges were students (0.8%), others (2.2%), and those with unknown backgrounds (2.0%) (Supreme Court of Japan, 2019).

The average trial in 2018 took 10.8 days, up from a length of 3.7 days in the first year of the lay system (Table 4.1). Deliberations in 2009 took, on average, 6.6 hours, but in 2018 took, on average, 12.9 hours (Table 4.2).

These results drew mixed commentaries in the newspapers assessing this first decade of the *Saiban'in* (e.g., "Saiban'in 10 nen, tegotae to kadai," 2019). On the one hand, a genuine impact on the trial was reported, with, for example, much more comprehensible language being used in the courts and greater opportunity for the accused to prepare his or her defense, due to more frequent approval of bail ("Shasetsu: Saiban'in seido 10 nen, shihō to shimin," 2019). On the other hand, concern with the increasing burden on the *Saiban'in*, resulting in a decline of public support for the system, was noted in such editorials as "The Number of People Refusing [to serve as a *Saiban'in*] Is a Real Problem" ("Saiban'in seido 10

TABLE 4.1 Saiban'in *public trial duration in days (2009–2018)*

Year	All trials	Trials in which the defendant confessed	Trials in which the defendant denied guilt
2009	3.7	3.5	4.7
2010	4.9	4.0	6.6
2011	6.2	4.5	8.5
2012	7.4	5.0	10.1
2013	8.1	5.8	10.5
2014	8.2	5.9	10.8
2015	9.4	6.2	13.0
2016	9.5	6.7	12.6
2017	10.6	7.2	13.5
2018	10.8	7.3	14.0

Note. Adapted from Supreme Court of Japan, 2019.

TABLE 4.2 *Duration of Saiban'in deliberations in hours (2009–2018)*

Year	All trials	Confession trials	Denial trials
2009	6.6	6.2	7.9
2010	8.4	7.3	10.3
2011	9.4	7.8	11.6
2012	10.3	7.9	13.1
2013	10.5	8.3	12.9
2014	11.2	8.8	13.9
2015	11.9	9.0	15.2
2016	12.1	9.3	15.2
2017	12.6	9.6	15.2
2018	12.9	9.7	15.9

Note. Adapted from Supreme Court of Japan, 2019.

nen, jitairitsu no zōka," 2019; see also "Shasetsu: Saiban'in seido 10 nen, shihō to shimin," 2019).

The Supreme Court has been very rigorous in monitoring the *Saiban'in* system by means of frequent opinion surveys of lay judges and the public. In one of the recurrent questions in the annual opinion survey, approximately 50% of former lay judges expressed their initial disinclination to serve in the trial. In 2018, 14.8% of former lay judges reported they ***absolutely*** had not wanted to act as a *Saiban'in*, and a further 29.3% said they had preferred not to become a *Saiban'in*. Yet, after the trial, the overwhelming majority of the respondents said that their *Saiban'in* experience was good (32.9% in 2018) to very good (63.8% in 2018) (Supreme Court of Japan, General Secretariat, 2019, figure 1).

The conviction rate in *Saiban'in* trials remained extremely high throughout the first decade of operation; however, a slight decrease can be seen in recent years (Table 4.3).

TABLE 4.3 *Saiban'in trial conviction rates (2009–2018)*

Year	Total defendants	Convicted	Found not guilty	Other[A]	Conviction rate (%)[B]
2009	149	142	0	7	100.00
2010	1530	1504	2	24	99.87
2011	1568	1514	10	46	99.35
2012	1526	1488	9	29	99.40
2013	1415	1374	12	29	99.07
2014	1220	1195	7	18	99.42
2015	1206	1171	8	17	99.33
2016	1104	1090	12	2	98.92
2017	993	931	20	27	97.90
2018	1039	1007	19	13	98.15

Note. Calculated from the various reports published by the Supreme Court of Japan and Ministry of Justice (Japan), 2018.

[A] These cases were either dropped or were transferred to different jurisdictions.

[B] The computation was based on the number of convictions divided by the sum of both convicted and acquitted cases.

During the first seven years of *Saiban'in* operation, the conviction rate was 99.43%. In 2017, the conviction rate dropped slightly, but not significantly, to 97.90%, with 20 acquittals and 931 convictions, yielding an acquittal rate of 2.1%. The conviction rate was 98.15% in 2018. In the entire decade, *Saiban'in* found only a total of 99 defendants not guilty among more than 11,000 defendants (n = 11,750). Thus, while the acquittal rate increased slightly in the last few years, the acquittal rate in the *Saiban'in* trials has remained at 2% or less throughout the decade.

The distribution of sentences appeared to change with the *Saiban'in*, with prison sentences becoming longer, but probation and suspended sentences occurring more frequently. The *Saiban'in* rendered longer sentences in many criminal categories than those rendered by professional judges in similar cases before the *Saiban'in* system was introduced. This mainly occurred when charges included rape, sexual molestation, and assault with injury (Hirayama, 2012). The 13-to-15-year prison term was the most frequent sentence by the *Saiban'in* in murder trials (previously 11-to-13 years in bench trials); and the 5-to-7-year imprisonment was the *Saiban'in's* most frequent sentence for rape resulting in death or injury, as well as bodily injury resulting in death (previously 3-to-5 years in bench trials for both crimes) ("Saiban'in seido dōnyū," 2019; Supreme Court of Japan, 2019). From 2010 to 2013, the number of cases in which the *Saiban'in* rendered sentences beyond prosecutors' recommendations gradually increased (e.g., 5 cases in 2010; 10 in 2011; 19 in 2012; and 14 in 2013). In response to these occasional longer and more severe sentences, the Judicial Research and Training Institute investigated the sentencing pattern. In 2013, Tokyo High Court commuted three death penalty decisions, which had exceeded the prosecutor's original recommendation, to life sentences (Supreme Court of Japan, 2019). Accordingly, the high court's reversal of *Saiban'in* decisions also increased from none in 2009 to 7.8% in 2011, 14.2% in 2015, and 11.9% in 2018 ("Saiban'in hanketsu no haki-ritsu," 2019).

In contrast, the *Saiban'in* rendered suspended sentences for arson (40%) and murder (8%) more frequently than the professional judges had before the introduction of the *Saiban'in* system (24% and 5%, respectively). The *Saiban'in* also rendered a probationary decision overall (55%) more often than had the professional judges (35%) ("Saiban'in seido dōnyū," 2019).

One possible explanation for the difference in sentencing patterns may be a difference in the cases adjudicated previously by professional judges versus *Saiban'in* trials. While the largest number of *Saiban'in* trials were held in 2011 (n = 1,568), their number has steadily declined, with a rather significant reduction in recent years. For example, in 2014, a total of 1,220 defendants were tried, with a significant drop of 350 defendants from 2011 (22.3% reduction). In 2017, an even smaller number of defendants were tried (n = 993), which is 575 defendants fewer (or a 36.6% reduction) than in 2011. Possible explanations for this include the continuous declining crime rate in Japan (Ministry of Justice (Japan), 2018) and the increase of contestation of the facts by the suspects, which results in fewer indictment decisions by the prosecutors, as they are widely known to want to be confident that their cases will lead to a conviction.

Another notable change has been in the rate of confessions by the accused and the corresponding rate of denials by those charged with crimes in *Saiban'in* trials. In the first year of the *Saiban'in* trials, almost 20% denied guilt and 80% confessed. The percentage of denials increased to 46% by 2012, and in 2017 and 2018 more than half of the accused (53.5% and 51.7%) denied guilt (Table 4.4).

The rise in denials by the accused reflects a growth in the involvement of defense attorneys and their advice not to confess or to sign the investigator's reports swiftly, according to attorney Akira Sugeno ("Saiban'in saiban, fueru hinin," 2018). Moreover, interrogations of suspects charged with crimes likely to be tried by the *Saiban'in* have been partially recorded on a voluntary basis by investigators since the start of the *Saiban'in* system in May 2009. This initiative was announced by Hiroto Yoshimura, the director-general of the National Police Agency, after the start of the system, in order to make it easier to demonstrate the voluntary character of the confessions (Shasetsu: Enzai o unda, 2009). It has indeed become more difficult to

TABLE 4.4 *Confessions and denials in Saiban'in trials (2009–2018)*

Year	*Saiban'in* trials (aggregate)	Confession	Denial	Percentage of denials
2009	142	114	28	19.7
2010	1,506	970	536	35.6
2011	1,525	885	640	41.9
2012	1,500	806	694	46.2
2013	1,387	725	662	47.7
2014	1,202	644	558	46.4
2015	1,182	623	559	47.2
2016	1,104	568	536	48.5
2017	966	449	517	53.5
2018	1,027	496	531	51.7

Note. Adapted from Supreme Court of Japan, 2019.

pressure the suspects to confess, also due to the increasing refusal of the judges to allow custody, which can amount to 23 days without being charged. It has been reported that the number of requests for detention that were refused was 10 times greater in 2018 than it was in 2000 ("Yōgisha no jinken," 2018; see also Supreme Court, General Secretariat, 2019). This increase occurred because of the increased media attention to the *Saiban'in* trials. The public had become more aware of the possibility of wrongful convictions, leading to more attention to the preservation of the human rights of the suspect ("Yōgisha no jinken," 2018). These changes may help to explain why the suspects increasingly resist the prosecutors' pressure to confess.

As seen in Table 4.5, there has been a decline in the number of potential *Saiban'in* responding to their summons. In 2010, more than 120,000 *Saiban'in* candidates were identified from the source list (n = 126,455). After initial screenings of these candidates, jury summons were sent to qualified jurors (n = 94,210). Some summons failed to reach juror candidates, while many candidates requested the cancellation of their summons for *Saiban'in* duty (n = 34,146). Of those who received the summons, the large majority appeared at the courthouse for further juror selection processes (n = 48,422 or an in-court appearance rate of 83.9%). However, the court appearance rate of lay participants has been steadily declining in recent years, falling from 40.3% in 2009 to 22.6% in 2017 and 22.7% in 2018. As we observed earlier, the length of the average *Saiban'in* trial has increased, and that could be one factor in helping to explain the declines in in-court appearance rates. As a result, despite the large juror candidate pool, the absolute number of those who reported to the courthouse declined significantly from 48,422 in 2010 to 32,598 in 2015, and even further to 27,152 in 2017. The courts are granting the cancellation of the summons for *Saiban'in* duty rather easily, and

TABLE 4.5 *Saiban'in selection processes from 2009 to March 2018*

Year	Total candidates	Summons sent	Cancellation accepted	In-court appearance[A]	In-court appearance rate[B]	Total appearance rate[C]
2009	13,423	9,638	3,185	5,415	83.9	40.3
2010	126,465	94,220	34,147	48,422	80.6	38.3
2011	131,880	94,109	37,756	44,150	78.4	33.5
2012	135,535	97,047	42,443	41,543	76.0	30.6
2013	135,207	95,541	43,451	38,527	74.0	28.5
2014	123,059	86,304	40,351	32,833	71.5	26.7
2015	132,831	92,076	43,806	32,598	67.5	24.5
2016	127,811	88,326	41,563	30,313	64.8	23.7
2017	120,187	84,176	41,707	27,152	63.9	22.6
2018	127,490	87,787	44,907	28,961	67.5	22.7
TOTAL	1,173,888	829,224	373,316	329,914	75.2	30.4

Note. Adapted from Supreme Court of Japan, 2019.
[A] These cases were either dropped or were transferred to different jurisdictions.
[B] The computation was based on the number of candidates summoned to appear in court divided by the number of in-court appearances.
[C] The computation was based on the total number of candidates divided by the number of in-court appearances.

the more that people are aware of the possibility of refraining from acting as a *Saiban'in*, the more they may give a reason that is likely to be accepted by the court.

SUMMARIES OF JUROR EXPERIENCES

The lay judges have indicated overwhelming satisfaction with their experience in a criminal trial, using the word for accomplishment and reporting that their personal views of the justice system have changed. In Mrs. Eguchi's words, "I notice that I had totally changed [... and] my whole family changed" (Taguchi, 2013, p. 29). Mrs. Eguchi was a former *Saiban'in*, 1 of 14 former lay judges whose experiences have been compiled by Masayoshi Taguchi, himself a former lay judge who is very active in organizing networks of former *Saiban'in*. Noteworthy in the reports is that many former *Saiban'in* use words such as duty and responsibility to explain their positive feelings about having participated in the *Saiban'in* trials. One lay judge, for example, reported on the survey by the Supreme Court in 2013, "I am older and am very happy to have been of some use, once in my life, as a Japanese citizen" (Supreme Court of Japan, 2013, p. 151). Another said, "I was glad to have been a lay judge out of a feeling of duty as a Japanese citizen and to contribute to society" (Supreme Court of Japan, 2013, p. 151). According to yet another juror, "It was a good opportunity to broaden my horizons and it was my duty as a Japanese citizen" (Supreme Court of Japan, 2013, p. 151).

Jury scholar Masahiro Fujita has studied the impact of lay judge experience on public consciousness, concluding that the *Saiban'in* system has contributed to promoting public interest and trust in the criminal justice system (Fujita, 2018). In sum, the satisfaction of having served as a lay judge expressed by more than 95% of the former lay judges is relevant not only to the way that the judiciary is respected and trusted, but also to the lay judges themselves as members of society because, in the words of Rieko Kage, "it is rewarding, empowering, and educational" (Kage, 2017, p. 6).

Although lay judges often express appreciation for the recognition they received from the national authorities, they also frequently mention feelings of frustration and stress that can coexist with positive feelings. Former *Saiban'in* have called for more and better assistance in mental health care for former lay judges who suffer from acute stress disorder. When talking about their feelings after the trial, former *Saiban'in* often use expressions such as "heavy" (Taguchi, 2013, p. 84), a "mental burden" (Taguchi, 2013, p. 98), and "heavy pressure" (Taguchi, 2013, p. 111). Stress is an important concern for lay judges due to, inter alia, pictures of the victim shown in court, the emotions of the parties in the trial, and the secrecy obligation with which lay participants must comply. Stress as an issue for lay judges became widely known when a former *Saiban'in* in the prefecture of Fukushima was diagnosed with acute stress disorder and sued the government for damages ("Saiban'in keikensha kataru," 2018). The Supreme Court ruled that the stress suffered was within reasonable limits and rejected her claim.

SOCIOPOLITICAL IMPACTS OF THE LAY JUDGE SYSTEM

This section explores three of the significant sociopolitical impacts that have emerged from the introduction of the *Saiban'in* system. A first example relates to the political consciousness of the citizens who served in a *Saiban'in* trial in Okinawa, noting that the lay judge system could contribute to political action on issues unrelated to the particular criminal procedure, through empowering former lay judges (Kage, 2017). The second example relates to policy-making. Former lay judges have created five collaborative organizations of their own (Ii, 2019) and have begun to engage in lobbying activities to engineer specific policy reforms, such as a possible moratorium on the death penalty. A third example involves the implementation of recordings and videotaping of interrogations as a result of the *Saiban'in* system.

Saiban'in *Trials in Okinawa: Empowerment of a Grassroots Movement*

Since 2009, a total of 153 decisions have been rendered in the *Saiban'in* trials at the Naha District Court in Okinawa. Three of them involved four American military personnel charged with serious crimes committed against Okinawan residents. The first *Saiban'in* trial, which occurred in 2010, involved the prosecution of a 19-year-old soldier who allegedly attacked and injured a local taxi driver. A second trial, in 2012, involved a US soldier who was accused of sexual assault (Fukurai, 2012). The third trial in 2013 involved two young soldiers accused of gang-raping a local woman (Tritten & Sumida, 2013). In each of these three trials, a panel of six local residents and three professional judges convicted the defendants and sent them to Japanese prison (Fukurai, 2014).

These trials mark a significant departure from past practices. As stated earlier, Okinawa once operated an American-style, 12-member jury trial in the 1960s and early 1970s for both criminal and civil cases (Dobrovolskaia, 2004; Fukurai, 2011; Vanoverbeke, 2015). The jury trials involving local residents led to the empowerment of former jurors such as Chihiro Isa, who became an important activist for judicial reforms in the 1980s and beyond (Vanoverbeke, 2015). The last criminal jury trial took place in 1971 and involved the drug offense of a 16-year-old American youth, a son of military personnel; the last civil jury trial occurred in 1972, immediately prior to Okinawa's reversion to Japan. For nearly 40 years (1971–2009), Okinawan residents were excluded from participation in the adjudication of crimes committed by military personnel or their dependents residing in Okinawa (Fukurai, 2012). During that period, the majority of alleged crimes committed by soldiers and their families were prosecuted and tried in the US military courts. Even in cases in which the Japanese government exercised primary jurisdiction, US service personnel and dependents were tried exclusively by Japanese professional judges, adding to dissatisfaction with the way Okinawa was ruled by both the US and Japanese governments (Tanji, 2007). This situation dramatically changed in 2010 when the first *Saiban'in* panel in Okinawa tried a young American soldier accused of assaulting a local taxi driver (Fukurai, 2011). This case became the first criminal trial in which Okinawans participated in the adjudication of crimes committed against local residents by a foreign soldier stationed on the island.

The adjudication of serious and violent crimes committed by US military personnel and their dependents continues to draw widespread and significant attention from the residents of Okinawa, who have long viewed themselves as victimized by their foreign occupiers (Tanji, 2007). This situation dates back to the end of the Battle of Okinawa in 1945, when the US government began constructing military bases and facilities in Okinawa. Today, nearly three-quarters of all the US military bases in Japan are found on the island of Okinawa (Fukurai, 2014). This judicial participation also raised the political consciousness of, and provided a strong sense of empowerment to, Okinawans on the island. Okinawan attorney Toshio Ikemiyagi, who led Okinawa's largest administrative lawsuit against the noise pollution at the Kadena US Air Force base, stated that now is the time to introduce the American-style, all-citizen jury system in both criminal and civil cases (Fukurai, 2020). He also witnessed Okinawans' participation in jury trials in the 1960s and early 1970s. Lay participation has energized the Okinawans by inserting them into the role of powerfully presiding over a trial through the system of lay participation in the justice system.

Saiban'in *Trials and Policies on the Death Penalty*

Another sociopolitical impact is the significant role played by former lay judges in policy-making activities. Japan continues to retain the death penalty, and despite decades of international pressure calling for its abolition (Reiterer & Vanoverbeke, 2011, 2014), there seems to be little chance of an official moratorium or abolition of the death penalty in the near future (Bacon, Reiterer, & Vanoverbeke, 2017). The minister of justice insisted in 2013 that any debate over capital punishment should be based on Japan's domestic situation, including public sentiment and maintaining public order, rather than movements beyond Japan's borders (Ito, 2013). The Japan Federation of Bar Associations issued a statement in 2016 advocating abolition of the death penalty by 2020. Serious debate on the death penalty had been revived immediately after the first death penalty sentence was rendered by the *Saiban'in* on November 16, 2010, at the Yokohama District Court. The then presiding judge Yoshifumi Asayama made an unprecedented statement urging the defendant to file an appeal. In the post-trial press conference, a *Saiban'in* also advised the defendant to appeal ("First death penalty handed down," 2010). Four *Saiban'in* and two alternates who attended the press conference disclosed how difficult it was to decide on the death penalty, urging that there be broader public discussions on whether or not to retain capital punishment in Japan ("First death penalty handed down," 2010).

Today, there is little public discussion regarding the abolition of the death penalty. Even so, the introduction of the lay judge system has certainly triggered serious debate on lay judges' participation in death penalty cases. As was pointed out in a commentary in the *Japan Times*:

> [the secrecy requirement of] the [*Saiban'in*] system needs to be revised. At present, even the simple matter of whether a death sentence was unanimous or based on a majority opinion cannot be divulged. [. . .] the current system [also] prohibits lay judges [. . .] to share with other citizens what they thought and how they may have agonized over their decision. ("Too close to the death penalty," 2010)

A former lay judge in a trial that resulted in a death penalty sentence explains, "[W]e all are troubled. We had doubts about the sentence of death penalty [. . .]. Only the fact of having been part of rendering a death sentence was a heavy burden. Probably because of this I often woke up at night. Not only influencing a life but the burden is heavy of the ultimate decision to take a life" (Taguchi, 2013, p. 164). Some lay judges reported that the experiences in court made them conscious of how they should behave in and contribute to society. A former *Saiban'in* elaborates,

> Until now, I was just considering myself as one of the crowd. I began to realize that I was in trial because I am a citizen and felt that I had to become a responsible citizen. I also realized that until the trial, I was very passive and obedient in doing what the government told me. I did not feel anything about this responsibility, as I lived in a very narrowly confined world. I realized that from now on, I should be more actively involved [in societal affairs] as a citizen (Taguchi, 2013, p. 98).

In February 2014, 20 former *Saiban'in* presented a petition to the minister of justice, asking for a moratorium on the death penalty and calling for wider public discussions ("Saiban'in keikensha 20 nin," 2014). One of the founders of the Former Lay Judge Network, Masayoshi Taguchi, stressed, "If jurors remain silent about their experience, this would be a loss for society. [...] The duty of the former lay judge is to talk about the present situation and future of the judiciary" (Taguchi, 2013, p. 2). A similar reaction from lay judges has been observed in France (Jellab & Giglio-Jacquemot, 2012), where some former lay judges report that they feel they have a duty to contribute to the reforms of the criminal procedure based on their experience. Currently, five organizations of former *Saiban'in* participants continue to organize symposia and discuss policies related to the criminal justice system, including the abolition of the death penalty in Japan (Ii, 2019).

Saiban'in *and the Admission of the Videotaping of Interrogations*

A third example of a sociopolitical impact of the *Saiban'in* system is the advocacy for the recording and taping of prosecutorial interrogations of suspects. There has long been criticism of the prosecutors' reliance on confessions for conviction, as well as their zeal in obtaining them (Foote, 1991; Johnson, 2002). A number of former lay judges have called for the possible recording of the interrogations in order to assess the authenticity of the confession ("Saiban'in keikenshara 'kashika' iken," 2015). In parallel with the recent cases revealing miscarriages of justice, including a wrongful conviction, the call by former *Saiban'in* for a complete videotaping of interrogations has been increasing over the years. The belief is that videotapes represent the only source that can enable lay judges to arrive at a well-informed and fair conclusion ("Saiban'in keikenshara 'kashika' iken," 2015). This claim by former lay judges was built on the call for recorded interrogations in a 2010 case not tried by *Saiban'in*. In this case, it became known that a prosecutor had tampered with evidence in order to increase the likelihood of convicting a senior civil servant who had been politically targeted by the government (Johnson, 2012).

The pressure for criminal procedure reforms, including the recording of interrogation and its admission in court, emerged in 2009 as a key item on the political agenda of the Democratic Party of Japan (DPJ) when it took over power from the more conservative Liberal Democratic Party (LDP). The window of opportunity was open for further judicial reforms. Media and public attention to the issue of coerced confessions was accompanied by the statements of former lay judges who agonized over the assessment of the voluntary character of confessions. These discussions led to the videotaping of interrogations being placed higher on the political agenda (Murakami, 2018). In June of 2011, newly appointed DPJ Justice Minister Satsuki Eda established the Special Subcommittee on the Criminal Justice System in a New Era (Miyazawa & Hirayama, 2017).

In December 2012, however, the conservative LDP returned to power, and the momentum for far-reaching criminal justice reforms waned, although the activities of the special subcommittee continued. An intermediate report was submitted, suggesting that interrogations be taped in their entirety for those cases tried by lay judges (about 3% of all criminal cases), with exceptions permitted in cases in which recording would make it impossible to obtain a meaningful confession (Miyazawa & Hirayama, 2017). The Bill was passed in May 2016 and became effective in May 2019. Confining mandatory recording to this small group of cases demonstrates the waning window of opportunity for more drastic measures in relation to the danger of forced confessions. Masayuki Suo, a member of the Special Subcommittee, who was frustrated by the shifting mood in the committee, wrote about his frustration, recording his seemingly vain fight for reform of a criminal procedure that would reduce the likelihood of wrongful convictions (Suo, 2015).

It was clear that the *Saiban'in* system played a significant role in accelerating wider discussions on judicial reforms. Yet, as was the case in the Bill on Videotaping of Interrogations, the window of opportunity for change can close rapidly if the political context becomes unreceptive. As Miyazawa and Hirayama argue, "The requirement of videotaped interrogations was conceptualized and initiated by a reformist minister, but the policy-making process was controlled by former and current members of the criminal justice establishment who were supported by academics working closely with them" (Miyazawa & Hirayama, 2017, p. 164).

CONCLUSION

The *Saiban'in* trial celebrated the tenth anniversary of its operation in 2019. This tribunal is Japan's newest lay participation system, as Japan once operated an American-style, all-citizen 12-member jury trial before the end of World War II. The American jury experiment continued in Okinawa in the 1960s and 1970s in both civil and criminal cases. The acquittal rate of the prewar jury trial was 17%, while the large majority of the postwar criminal charges were rejected by the criminal juries in Okinawa prior to its reversion to Japan in 1972 (Fukurai, 2020). The near 99% conviction rate of *Saiban'in* trials suggests that the introduction of the *Saiban'in* system has not led to significant changes in the conviction rates originally expected by jury scholars in Japan and beyond.

Nevertheless, the sociopolitical influences on society, including the impacts on former lay judge participants, should not be overlooked. The *Saiban'in* trial allowed Okinawan residents, for the first time, to adjudicate the crimes committed by US military personnel who had long terrorized and victimized them, dating back to 1945, when the first US military base was built. Drawing on court experiences, former lay judges have also begun to speak out and participate in public meetings with citizens, prosecutors, and professional judges regarding a possible moratorium on the death penalty, as well as the requirement that interrogations be videotaped. They have also begun to give lectures on their jury experiences and to create their own networks and organizations in order to share the importance of civic engagement with wider audiences.

Prominent legal scholar Daniel Foote once stated that the number of lay judge participants remains too small to allow a conclusion about its immediate and significant impact on the democratic arrangement of Japanese society (Foote, 2014). Our analysis leads us to the hope that the lay judge system can contribute to improved functioning of democratic and participatory society, both within and outside the courtroom. The importance of citizen participation was first pointed out by French jurist Alexis de Tocqueville, who stated, "A nation may be considered in the light of a jury which is empowered to represent society at large, and to apply the great and general law of Justice" (Tocqueville, 2003/1838, p. 240). While more time may be needed to confirm the definitive impact of the *Saiban'in* in Japan, there are encouraging signs that it has already contributed to an enhanced civic engagement and the raising of political consciousness, just as it has in other countries that have embraced lay participation in their justice systems (Gastil, Deess, Weiser, & Simmons, 2010).

Acknowledgments: The authors wish to thank Valerie P. Hans, Shari Seidman Diamond, Makoto Ibusuki, and David T. Johnson, who read the earlier manuscript and provided their extremely helpful comments and suggestions. We also wish to thank Mark Levin and other participants in the Conference on Japanese Law at Harvard University, Law School, on October 28 and 29, 2018.

REFERENCES

Anderson, K., & Saint, E. (2005). Japan's quasi-jury (*Saiban-in*) law: An annotated translation of the act concerning participation of lay assessors in criminal trials. *Asian-Pacific Law & Policy Journal*, 6, 233–283.

Bacon, P., Reiterer, M., & Vanoverbeke, D. (2017). Recent developments on the death penalty in Japan: Public opinion and the lay judge system. In W. Benedek, M. C. Kettemann, R. Klaushofer, K. Lukas, & M. Nowak (Eds.), *European Yearbook on Human Rights* (pp. 103–118). Vienna: NWV.

Dobrovolskaia, A. (2004). An all-laymen jury system instead of the lay assessor (*Saiban'in*) system for Japan? Anglo-American-style jury trials in Okinawa under the US occupation. *Vanderbilt Journal of Transnational Law*, 37, 966–973.

First death penalty handed down by lay judges. (2010, November 17). *Japan Times*. www.japantimes.co.jp/news/2010/11/17/national/first-death-penalty-handed-down-by-lay-judges/#.XbBE7i2B3_Q

Foote, D. H. (1991) Confessions and the right to silence in Japan. *Georgia Journal of International & Comparative Law*, 21, 415–488.

(1996). Judicial creation of norms in Japanese labor law: Activism in the service of stability. *UCLA Law Review*, 43, 635–709.

(2014). Citizen participation: Appraising the *Saiban'in* system. *Michigan State International Law Review*, 22, 755–775.

Fujita, M. (2018). *Japanese society and lay participation in criminal justice: Social attitudes, trust, and mass media*. Singapore: Springer.

Fukurai, H. (2007). The rebirth of Japan's petit quasi-jury and grand jury systems: Cross national analysis of legal consciousness and lay participatory experience in Japan and the US. *Cornell International Law Journal*, 40, 315–354.

(2011). Japan's quasi-jury and grand jury systems as deliberative agents of social change: De-colonial strategies and deliberative participatory democracy. *Chicago-Kent Law Review*, 86, 789–829.

(2012). Lay prosecution of US military crimes in Japan by prosecutorial review commissions and the *Saiban'in* trial. In H. N. Scheiber & T. Ginsburg (Eds.), *Japanese legal system: An era of transition* (pp. 131–160). Berkeley, CA: Robbins Collection Publisher.

(2014). Okinawa's citizen judge panels vs. US military hegemony: Wikileaks' secret US cable document on the lay adjudication of American soldier criminal cases in Japan's *Saiban'in* trials. *International Journal of Okinawan Studies*, 4, 13–30.

(2020). *Unprecedented trials in Asia and beyond: Okinawa's global jury in criminal and civil cases under the US military occupation and search for the right to self-determination*. London: Palgrave Macmillan.

Gastil, J., Deess, E. P., Weiser, P. J., & Simmons, C. (2010). *The jury and democracy: How jury deliberation promotes civic engagement and political participation*. New York: Oxford University Press.

Hamada, S. (2001). *Jihaku no shinrigaku* [Psychology of confession]. Tokyo: Iwanami shinsho.

Hirano, R. (1985). Gendai keiji soshōhō no shindan [Diagnosis of the current code of criminal procedure]. In Y. Hiraba, R. Hirano, T. Takada, T. Fukuda, H. Ōtsuka, T. Kagawa, K. Naitō, & K. Matsuo (Eds.), *Dandō Shigemitsu hakase koki shukuga ronbunshū* [Collection of essays to celebrate Dr. Shigemitsu Dandō's seventieth birthday] (Vol. 4, pp. 423–462). Tokyo: Yukikaku.

(1989). Diagnosis of the current code of criminal procedure. *Law Japan*, 22, 129–142.

Hirayama, M. (2012). Lay judge decisions in sex crime cases: The most controversial area of *Saiban-in* trials. *Yonsei Law Journal*, 3, 128–160.

Ii, T. (2019). *Anata mo asu wa saiban'in!?* [You will also become a Saiban'in tomorrow!?] Tokyo: Nihon hyōronsha.

Isa, C. (2006). *Saiban'in seido wa keijisaiban o kaeru ka: Baishin seido o motomeru riyū* [Will the Saiban'in system change the criminal trial? Why the jury system is necessary]. Tokyo: Gendai jinbunsha.

Ishimatsu, T., Tsuchiya, K., & Isa, C. (2007). *Enzai o umu saiban'in seido: Baishin saiban no fukkatsu ni mukete* [The Saiban'in system that manufactures wrongful convictions: The effort to resurrect the jury system]. Tokyo: Gendai jinbunsha.

Ito, M. (2013, February 21). Three murderers sent to the gallows. *Japan Times*. www.japantimes.co.jp/news/2013/02/21/national/crime-legal/japan-executes-three-inmates/#.Xajh_fZFw2w

Jellab, A., & Giglio-Jacquemot, A. (2012). Des profanes en justice, les jurés d'assises: Entre légitimité et contestation du pouvoir des juges [Public jury trials and the challenges of the court of law: Between nonprofessional legitimacy and questioning judges' power]. *L'Année sociologique*, 62, 143–193.

Johnson, D. T. (2002). *The Japanese way of justice: Prosecuting crime in Japan*. New York: Oxford University Press.

(2012). Japan's prosecution system. *Crime and Justice*, 41, 35–74.

Kage, R. (2017). *Who judges? Designing jury systems in Japan, East Asia, and Europe*. Cambridge: Cambridge University Press.

Kawashima, T. (1963). Dispute resolution in contemporary Japan. In A. T. Von Mehren (Ed.), *Law in Japan: The legal order in a changing society* (pp. 41–72). Cambridge, MA: Harvard University Press.

(1967). *Nihonjin no hōishiki* [The law consciousness of the Japanese]. Tokyo: Iwanami shinsho.

Koschmann, J. V. (1996). *Revolution and subjectivity in postwar Japan*. Chicago: University of Chicago Press.

Levin, M., & Tice, V. (2009). Japan's new citizen judges: How secrecy imperils judicial reform. *Asia-Pacific Journal*, 19(7): 6–9.

Ministry of Justice (Japan). (2018). *Heisei 30 nenban, hanzai hakusho: Susumu kōreika to hanzai* [White paper on crime]. http://hakusyo1.moj.go.jp/jp/65/nfm/mokuji.html

Miyazawa, S., & Hirayama, M. (2017). Introduction of videotaping of interrogations and the lessons of the Imaichi case: A case of conventional criminal justice policy-making in Japan. *Washington International Law Journal Association*, 27, 149–176.

Murakami, S. (2018, June 18). Japan's criminal justice reforms aim to enhance transparency of interrogations: Are they working? *Japan Times*. www.japantimes.co.jp/news/2018/06/18/reference/japans-criminal-justice-reforms-aim-enhance-transparency-interrogations-working/

Odanaka, T. (2001) Konpan no shihō seido kaikaku no "gyakukaikaku" teki honshitsu [The "counter-reformative" essence of today's judicial reforms]. *Hō to minshushugi*, 360, 36–38.

Prime minister's policy speech. (2001, May 8). *Japan Times*. www.japantimes.co.jp/news/2001/05/08/national/prime-ministers-policy-speech/#.XbBFPi2B3_Q

Reiterer, M., & Vanoverbeke, D. (2011). Japan and the death penalty from a European perspective: At a crossroads to a changing discourse on human rights? In W. Benedek, F. Benoit-Rohmer, W. Karl, & M. Nowak (Eds.), *European Yearbook on Human Rights* (pp. 267–281). Vienna: NWV.

(2014). ASEAN's regional approach to human rights: The limits of the European model? In W. Benedek, F. Benoit-Rohmer, W. Karl, M. Kettemann, & M. Nowak (Eds.), *European Yearbook on Human Rights* (pp. 185–196). Vienna: NWV.

Saiban'in hanketsu no haki-ritsu no suii [Transitions of reversal rates of *Saiban'in* verdicts]. (2019, May 20). *Jiji.com*. www.jiji.com/jc/graphics?p=ve_soc_saiban20190520j-05-w390

Saiban'in 10 nen, tegotae to kadai [A decade of the *Saiban'in* system: Impact and concerns]. (2019, June 13). *Yomiuri Shimbun*. Retrieved from Yomidas Rekishikan Yomiuri Database Service.

Saiban'in keikensha kataru, "shuhigimu sutoresu" hōsōsansha to ikenkōkan = Shiga [The former *Saiban'in*'s voice: Stress because of the secrecy obligation exchanging opinions with the three legal professions, Shiga Prefecture]. (2018, February 28). *Yomiuri Shimbun*. Retrieved from Yomidas Rekishikan Yomiuri Database Service.

Saiban'in keikensha 20 nin "shikei shikkō teishi o" hōsō ni yōbō [Twenty former lay judges submit a demand for a moratorium on the execution of the death penalty]. (2014, February 18). *Asahi Shimbun*. Retrieved from Kikuzo II Visual.

Saiban'in keikenshara "kashika" iken kōkan [The former *Saiban'in* talk "Recordings of interogations" exchanging views]. (2015, July 17). *Yomiuri Shimbun*. Retrieved from Yomidas Rekishikan Yomiuri Database Service.

Saiban'in no sanka suru keiji saiban ni kan suru hōritsu [Law on the participation of lay judges in the criminal procedure]. (2009), Law no. 63.

Saiban'in saiban, fueru hinin sakunen hatsu no 50% koe, shinri chōkika, futanzō [*Saiban'in* trials: Increasing denials, last year for the first time over 50%, drawn-out trials, increasing burden]. (2018, May 22). *Yomiuri Shimbun*. Retrieved from Yomidas Rekishikan Yomiuri Database Service.

Saiban'in seido dōnyū 10-nen deno omona henka [Major changes of *Saiban'in* system for the last 10 years]. (2019, May 15). *Jiji.com*. www.jiji.com/jc/graphics?p=ve_soc_saiban20190515j-07-w390

Saiban'in seido 10 nen, jitairitsu no zōka ga kigakari da [A decade of the *Saiban'in* system: The number of people refusing (to serve as a Saiban-in) is a real problem]. (2019, May 19). *Yomiuri Shimbun*. Retrieved from Yomidas Rekishikan Yomiuri Database Service.

Shasetsu: Enzai no nigai aji o kamishimeyo [Editorial: The bitter taste of a wrongful conviction]. (1980, November 7). *Yomiuri Shimbun*. Retrieved from Yomidas Rekishikan Yomiuri Database Service.

Shasetsu: Enzai o unda gōin na sōsa [Editorial: Wrongful convictions caused by brute investigations]. (1984, July 12). *Yomiuri Shimbun*. Retrieved from Yomidas Rekishikan Yomiuri Database Service.

Shasetsu: Saiban'in seido 10 nen, shihō to shimin, kitae ate mae e [Editorial: A decade of the *Saiban'in* system: The judiciary and the citizens are strengthening each other but should proceed]. (2019, May 20). *Asahi Shimbun*. Retrieved from Kikuzo II Visual.

Shasetsu: Towareru jihaku izon no sōsa [Editorial: Investigations dependent on confessions is what should be questioned]. (1988, February 10). *Yomiuri Shimbun*. Retrieved from Yomidas Rekishikan Yomiuri Database Service.

Suo, M. (2015). *Soredemo boku wa kaigi de tatakau: Dokyumento keiji shihō kaikaku* [Even then I will fight in the meeting: Document on the reform of the criminal law]. Tokyo: Iwanami shoten.

Supreme Court of Japan (Eds.). (2013). Saiban'in tō keikensha ni taisuru ankēto chōsa kekka hōkokusho, Heisei 24 nendo [Report on the results of the survey of the former lay judges (the 24th year of the Heisei era = 2012)]. www.saibanin.courts.go.jp/vcms_lf/h24_keikensya.pdf

(Eds.). (2017). Saiban'in saiban no jisshi jōkyo – keikensha no koe mo o shirase shimasu [The situation of the implementation of the *Saiban'in* trials: Informing about the former lay judges' voices too]. www.saibanin.courts.go.jp/vcms_lf/h28_jissi_matome.pdf

(Eds.). (2018). Saiban'in saiban no jisshi jōkyo ni tsuite (seido shikkō~Heisei 30 nen 3 gatsu matsu • sokuhō) [Report on the results of the implementation of the *Saiban'in* trials (from the start of the implementation until March 2018)]. www.saibanin.courts.go.jp/vcms_lf/h30_3_saibaninsokuhou.pdf

(Eds.). (2019). Saiban'in saiban no jisshi jōkyo ni tsuite (seido shikkō~Reiwa gannen 5 gatsumatsu • sokuhō) [Report on the results of the implementation of the *Saiban'in* trials (from the start of the implementation until the end of May 2019)]. www.saibanin.courts.go.jp/vcms_lf/r1_5_saibaninsokuhou.pdf

Supreme Court of Japan, General Secretariat. (2019). Saiban'in seido 10 nen no sōkatsu hōkokusho [Summary report of one decade of the *Saiban'in* system]. www.saibanin.courts.go.jp/vc-files/saibanin/file/r1_diagram.pdf

Taguchi, M. (2013). *Saiban'in no atama no naka: 14 nin no hajimete monogatari* [Inside the heads of the jurors: The unique story of 14 people]. Tokyo: Gendai jibunsha.

Tanji, M. (2007). *Myth, protest and struggle in Okinawa*. London: Routledge.

Tocqueville, A. de (2003). *Democracy in America*. Translated by Henry Reeve. Clark, NJ: Lawbook Exchange. (Originally published, New York: Adlard and Saunders, 1838.)

Too close to the death penalty. (2010, November 20). *Japan Times*. www.japantimes.co.jp/opinion/2010/11/20/editorials/too-close-to-the-death-penalty/#.XbBDUC2B3_Q

Tritten, T. J., & Sumida, C. (2013, March 31). Sailors sentenced for gang-rape in case that sparked curfew. *Stars and Stripes*. www.stripes.com

Vanoverbeke, D. (2015). *Juries in the Japanese legal system: The continuing struggle for citizen participation and democracy*. New York: Routledge.

Wilson, M., Fukurai, H., & Maruta, T. (2015). *Japan and civil jury trials: The convergence of forces*. Cheltenham: Edward Elgar.

Yanase, N. (2016). Deliberative democracy and the Japanese *Saiban'in* (lay judge) trial system. *Asian Journal of Law and Society*, 3, 327–349.

Yōgisha no jinken, tsuyomaru hairyo, kōryū kyakka ritsu 2000 nen no 10 baichō [The human rights of the accused: Increasing attention, the rejection of the request for detention 10 times higher than in 2000]. (2018, August 26). *Yomiuri Shimbun*. Retrieved from Yomidas Rekishikan Yomiuri Database Service.

5

The Korean Jury System

The First Decade

Jaihyun Park

On February 12, 2008, South Korean citizens witnessed a historic criminal trial held at the Daegu District Courthouse (Pang, 2008). The trial was momentous, not because of the litigants or the details of the alleged criminal charges, but because it gave a group of lay citizens the unprecedented opportunity to participate in legal decision-making. Nine ordinary people were selected as the jurors to decide a robbery and assault case. After listening to all the arguments and observing the evidence, including witness testimony from both sides, the jurors were excused from the courtroom to deliberate. After over two hours of deliberation, the jury found the defendant guilty, but suggested a suspended sentence, presumably having taken into account that the defendant had attempted to take the victim to a hospital as she was bleeding (Pang, 2008). The judge accepted the jury's verdict and imposed a suspended sentence.

This represents the first ever jury trial (officially known as "citizen participation trial") in South Korea after the country introduced this new form of trial into its justice system at the beginning of 2008 (Kukmineui hyeongsajaepan chamyeoeh gwanhan beobryul, 2007). Contrary to the serious concerns and skepticism that some legal professionals had expressed (Hwang, 2010), this panel of Korean citizens was able to perform the unfamiliar task of fact-finding in the trial and deliberate to reach a verdict. The new jury system, however, gave the jury's verdict no binding effect; it was only advisory to the professional judge, who had the sole authority to make the final legal decision (S. Kim, Park, Park, & Eom, 2013).

The Korean jury system has a unique set of jury trial practices, largely taking the form of the classic common-law all-citizen jury (Hans & Vidmar, 1986; Kalven & Zeisel, 1966), but incorporating a few features of mixed tribunals (Hans, Fukurai, Kutnjak Ivković, & Park, 2017). When jury trials were first instituted in 2008, the South Korean government initially favored an all-citizen jury as the appropriate form of lay participation in legal decision-making, as recommended by the Judicial Reform Committee (Kukmineui hyeongsajaepan chamyeoeh gwanhan beobryul, 2007). In large part, the Korean jury system is similar to its American counterpart (Vidmar, 2000): A group of citizens is selected from the community to serve as the trier of fact, and the jurors deliberate independently, outside the presence of the judge, to render a verdict. However, the Korean jury also incorporates some features of mixed tribunals (S. Kim et al., 2013; J. Park, 2010). For instance, if the jurors do not reach a unanimous decision, they must consult with the presiding judge before deciding by a simple majority vote. Korean jurors also make a recommendation for sentencing once the defendant is found guilty. In addition, the Korean system has a few idiosyncrasies: the defendant has the right to request a jury trial (Kukmineui hyeongsajaepan chamyeoeh gwanhan beobryul, 2007, Art. 3), but the judge can reject the request under some circumstances (Art. 6); a jury consists of five, seven, or nine jurors, depending on the severity of the crime (Art. 13).

The most important characteristic of Korean jury trials, however, is the advisory nature of the jury's verdict. The jury's verdict is not legally binding, but only advisory to the judge (Hans et al., 2017; J. Park, 2010). The advisory nature of the jury verdict has received considerable attention from researchers and practitioners (Hwang, 2010; D.-S. Kim, 2018; S. Kim et al., 2013; Kwak, 2018; Song, 2018). Reluctance to institute a legally binding jury verdict reflects concerns about an anticipated charge of unconstitutionality (Hans et al., 2017), which will be discussed in the next section, but at the same time, it has become a significant impediment to the ability of Korean jurors to exercise their right to decide criminal cases.

Thus far, the Korean jury system has been implemented without any interruption since the first jury trial in 2008. More than 2,000 jury trials have been held in the past decade (Song, 2018). Many, if not most, researchers and legal professionals view the jury system as a successful feature of the Korean justice system (I.-G. Lee, 2017). This chapter, following a brief historical account of how the new form of trials was introduced, describes the jury trials conducted in South Korea in the first 10 years of the system, and addresses the key issues that have significant implications for the future of the jury system in the country.

JURY TRIALS IN SOUTH KOREA (2008–2017)

A Brief History

Ordinary citizens had never participated in legal decision-making in Korea until the recent introduction of jury trials (Ahn & Han, 2005; J. S. Lee, 2016; J. Park, 2010). No governmental document or public record has been found to indicate any form of lay participation in law in the modern history of Korea since its liberation from the colonial rule of Japan in 1945 and the ensuing Korean War (1950–1953) (J. S. Lee, 2016). For many years following the war, the oppressive regimes in South Korea had little, if any, interest in including lay citizens in legal decision-making. Instead, they often exerted controlling influence on trials and judicial practices for the purpose of maintaining their ruling power. This action prompted collective but unsuccessful resistance from judges in 1971 and occasionally thereafter (Ahn & Han, 2005). Under such social and political circumstances, it was not conceivable for ordinary citizens to participate in trials. Legal decision-making power belonged exclusively to a small number of legal elites (Ahn & Han, 2005; J. Park, 2010).

In 1987, South Korean citizens made significant strides toward the democratization of the country. A long fight against the oppressive military government led to the amendment of the Constitution of South Korea, instituting direct presidential elections by the citizens instead of by the members of the electoral college who could be more easily manipulated by the authorities (J. Park, 2010). In addition, as a result of democratization, judicial processes became mostly independent from the ruling power (Ahn & Han, 2005), although subsequent regimes continued to attempt occasionally to influence the judiciary. Despite the fact that the 1987 democratization made significant changes in the political arena, Korean citizens still could not participate in legal decision-making. The demand for further democratization, however, led to a remarkable move. In the 1990s, some legal professionals, scholars, and civic groups began to discuss the need for a judicial reform to enhance the democratic legitimacy of and public confidence in the trial processes (Ahn & Han, 2005; J. S. Lee, 2016). One of their proposals was to include citizen participation in legal decision-making (Ahn & Han, 2005).

As a result of these efforts, the Judicial Reform Committee was formed in 2003 and included lay participation in law as part of its official agenda the following year (Ahn & Han, 2005). The committee initially debated whether an all-citizen jury or a mixed tribunal would be more suitable in the Korean social and political context. After long and intense discussions, the committee decided to adopt an all-citizen jury system as the main form of lay participation (Ahn & Han, 2005). This was believed to be more conducive to enhancing democratic legitimacy and political transparency than a mixed tribunal (Ahn & Han, 2005; J. S. Lee, 2016; J. Park, 2010). The committee suggested that jury trials should be conducted for five years from 2008 through 2012, whereupon a comprehensive evaluation would be performed to determine the final form of the system (J. S. Lee, 2016). The reform bill, the Act for Civil Participation in Criminal Trials (2007), was finally approved by the National Assembly of Korea on April 30, 2007, to be effective as of January 2008 (J. Park, 2010).

Although the reform bill was eventually approved, the Judicial Reform Committee faced serious challenges along the way. Some legal professionals and scholars, for instance, expressed their doubts and concerns about the ability of ordinary citizens to decide criminal cases according to the law without being influenced by extralegal factors such as emotion or prejudice (Hwang, 2010). The Act addressed this issue of jury competence by providing, as noted in the previous paragraph, for an empirical evaluation of the system after five years. A more critical issue was the constitutionality of the system. The present South Korean Constitution states that "all citizens have the right to a trial by a judge as stipulated by the Constitution and the law" (Daehanminkuk Hunbeob, 1987, Art. 27). The opponents of jury trials argued for a literal interpretation of "a judge" in the Article, which would have made trial by jury unconstitutional (Ahn & Han, 2005). This was one of the major reasons that the Judicial Reform Committee made jury verdicts only advisory, as will be discussed later in this chapter.

Under the Act, the initial plan was to conduct jury trials for the first five years while monitoring the result of each trial in order to ensure the validity and accuracy of lay citizens' legal judgments (Kukmineui hyeongsajaepan chamyeoeh gwanhan beobryul, 2007; S. Kim et al., 2013). An official evaluation of the jury trials held during the period was to follow. Accordingly, at the beginning of 2013, the Committee for Citizen Participation in Law of the Supreme Court of Korea undertook an extensive review of the more than 800 jury trials that had been conducted to that point. Using descriptive data from the trials (e.g., case, outcome) and survey data from various groups of citizens (e.g., former jurors, defendants, the general public), the committee reviewed a variety of issues, including the number of jurors, jury competence, decision rules, and appeal rates. Based on the results of the review, the committee recommended that the practice of jury trials be continued, while suggesting several procedural modifications (Kukmin sabeob chamyeo weewonhoi, 2013). The major recommendations included (a) abolishing the five-person jury, (b) changing the decision rule (the proportion of jurors needed to reach a verdict) from a simple majority to a supermajority (three-quarters), and (c) stipulating that the jury verdict must be respected unless the procedure or the result of the jury verdict is in violation of the Constitution, laws, acts, and regulations, or there is a reason to believe that either the procedure or outcome is invalid. None of these recommendations was adopted in the revised law (Kukmineui hyeongsajaepan chamyeoeh gwanhan beobryul, 2017); therefore, the basic framework of the Korean trial has remained intact.

Number of Cases

In the first 10 years of South Korea's jury system, 2,267 jury trials were conducted across the entire 18 district courthouses in South Korea (Beobwon haengjeongcheo, 2018). The number of jury trials per year has increased over time since 2008, although there has been some fluctuation during the period (see Table 5.1). The total number of jury trials represents about 40% of the 5,701 cases in which the defendant made an initial request for a trial by jury. That proportion has ranged from 29.8% to 51.2%, depending on the year.

In the other 60% of cases in which the defendant initially requested a jury trial but none was held, either the defendant withdrew the request or the judge determined that the case should not be tried by a jury. Defendants who had initially requested jury trials withdrew their requests in about 40% of cases (n=2,277) (with a range of 36.0% to 44.8%). The reasons for withdrawing the initial request in each case are not known; defendants are not obligated to reveal them. Surveys of the defendants, however, indicate that the reasons

TABLE 5.1 *The number of jury trials in South Korea in the first 10 years*

Year	Requested by defendant	Tried by jury	Excluded by judge	Withdrawn by defendant	Sum of three columns
2008	233	64 (29.8%)	61 (28.4%)	90 (41.9%)	215
2009	336	95 (30.8%)	75 (24.4%)	138 (44.8%)	308
2010	438	162 (39.1%)	75 (18.1%)	177 (42.8%)	414
2011	489	253 (51.2%)	63 (12.8%)	178 (36.0%)	494
2012	756	274 (40.5%)	124 (18.3%)	278 (41.1%)	676
2013	764	345 (43.3%)	118 (14.8%)	334 (41.9%)	797
2014	608	271 (44.4%)	107 (17.5%)	233 (38.1%)	611
2015	505	203 (38.6%)	106 (20.2%)	217 (41.3%)	526
2016	860	305 (38.9%)	151 (19.3%)	328 (41.8%)	784
2017	712	295 (37.2%)	195 (24.6%)	304 (38.3%)	794
Total	5,701	2,267 (40.3%)	1,075 (19.1%)	2,277 (40.5%)	5,619

Note. The sum of cases for the three columns (i.e., "tried by jury," "excluded by judge," and "withdrawn by defendant") in a year differs from the number of cases in the second column (i.e., "requested by defendant") for the year because some of the cases in which defendants requested trial by jury were actually tried in the following year. In 2008, for instance, the difference of 18 cases (between 233 and 215 cases) could not be tried in the same year for some reason (e.g., the requests of trial by jury were accepted by the court at the end of the year). These 18 cases were tried in the next year and included in the number of cases that were "tried by jury" in 2009. Likewise, every year, a varying number of cases was tried a year after the request was accepted by the court. As indicated in the last row, the difference of 82 cases (between 5,701 and 5,619 cases) represents those that were pending at the end of 2017 to be tried in 2018. The percentages in the parentheses were computed from the number of cases in the last column ("sum of three columns").

include: (a) suggestions by defense lawyers, (b) the limited (advisory) effect of a jury verdict, (c) concerns that the jury sentence would be more severe than if a judge decided the case, and (d) the perceived unpredictability of juries' verdicts in comparison with judges' verdicts (Song, 2018; Tak & Choi, 2011).

In the remaining 20% (n=1,075) of the cases in which the defendant initially requested a jury, the judge denied the request for a jury trial. Under the current law, judges can exclude cases from jury trial for various reasons, including: (a) when there are concerns about a possible threat against jurors, juror candidates, reserve jurors (equivalent to alternate jurors in the United States), or their families; (b) when a victim in a sexual assault case prefers to have a judge rather than a jury trial and vetoes the defendant's preference; (c) when one or more of a defendant's accomplices object; and (d) when the judge believes that it is not appropriate to have the case tried by a jury (e.g., if there are too many witnesses, the key issues are too complex, or one or more witnesses are victims of sexual assaults in a sexual assault case) (Kukmineui hyeongsajaepan chamyeoeh gwanhan beobryul, 2017). The information about the judge's actual reasons for denying a jury trial in each case is not available.

Types of Crimes

Initially, jury trials were limited to serious criminal cases such as murder, robbery, assault, and rape (Kukmineui hyeongsajaepan chamyeoeh gwanhan beobryul, 2007). However, the scope of relevant crimes was broadened in 2012 to include all severe criminal cases that must be tried by a judicial panel of three judges in district courts (Song, 2018). This change is reflected in the growth in the number of jury trials. According to Song (2018), from 2008 through 2011, the number of applicable criminal cases each year ranged from 4,287 to 6,040. From 2012 through 2017, however, the number substantially increased, ranging from 19,521 to 21,397. Of the total number of applicable criminal cases each year, the proportion of crimes that were *not* murder, robbery, assault, or rape was low between 2008 and 2011, ranging from 4.67% to 18.52%, whereas the comparable proportion went up noticeably from 2012 through 2017, ranging from 57.82% to 65.12%. In 2015, jury trials were further extended to include certain less serious criminal cases over which a single judge usually presides (Kwak, 2018).

According to the National Court Administration of Korea (2018), the most common types of crimes dealt with in jury trials during the past 10 years have been murder (20.7%), robbery (14.8%), sexual crimes (14.5%), violent crimes (6.4%), and assault (4.3%). Other criminal charges resulting in jury trials have included arson (4.5%), theft (1.0%), fraud (0.8%), and criminal traffic offenses (1.8%). About 20% of the crimes were placed in an unspecific category of violations of the Act on Aggravated Punishment of Particular Crimes (Teukjeongbeomjoi Gajoongcheobeol deungeh gwanhan beobryul, 2010).

The proportion of cases not tried by juries despite the defendant's initial request, whether due to the defendant's withdrawal of the request or the judge's exclusion of the case, has varied by type of crime (Song, 2018). For instance, among the murder cases, 26.5% were withdrawn by the defendants and 12.8% were excluded by the judges; for robbery, 39.5% were withdrawn and 17.4% were excluded; for sexual crimes, 44.9% were withdrawn and 30.0% were excluded; for assault, 32.6% were withdrawn and 11.4% were excluded. Murder cases had the lowest levels of withdrawal and exclusion combined. The sexual crimes, in contrast, had a highest rate of exclusion (30%), mostly because the victims, for privacy reasons, preferred not to have jury trials.

Duration of Jury Trial

Unlike bench trials in Korea, which often last for months (S. Kim et al., 2013), jury trials are completed in a short period of time; the vast majority of jury trials during the first 10 years (2,045 of 2,267, or 90.2%) took only one day (Kwak, 2018). Often, the trial day lasted until very late (e.g., midnight). Most jurors involved in the trial preferred this extended day to the alternative of adjourning and coming back the next day (Kwak, 2018). In the remaining 9.8% of the cases, the trial lasted two days or more.

Jury trial length has, however, increased over time. In the first five years, fewer than 5% of the cases took more than one day, while in the next five years, about 13% did (Kwak, 2018). The reason for this trend is not clear. It may be that Korean citizens' reluctance to serve for longer periods of time has eased somewhat over the years as they have become more accustomed to this new form of trial. In addition, as attorneys have become more familiar with jury trials, they may engage in further efforts to produce evidence that they believe will be persuasive to jurors.

Defendant's Dispute on Guilt

The defendant pleaded not guilty in 1,521 of 2,267 cases that have been tried before juries (67.1%) (Song, 2018). This proportion is substantially higher than that in comparable criminal cases that were decided by judges in district courthouses (Kwak, 2018). When defendants plead guilty, some trials are held primarily for the purpose of sentencing if certain conditions are met. This is further discussed in the sections that follow.

Number of Jurors

Juries can consist of five, seven, or nine members, depending on the severity of the crime (Kukmineui hyeongsajaepan chamyeoeh gwanhan beobryul, 2017, Art. 13). According to this law, a nine-person jury should be used if conviction can lead to a death penalty or life imprisonment (e.g., murder or manslaughter cases). For other serious crimes (e.g., robbery, assault, or rape), the court generally uses a seven-person jury. A five-person jury *can* be used, but only when there is no room for dispute because the defendant admits his or her guilt for the charged crime or, if there are multiple offenses, for *all* the charged crimes; the jury then determines only the sentence. Song (2018) noted that the court showed a tendency to use five-person juries sparingly.

Two-thirds of the 2,267 jury trials used seven-person juries. Nine-person juries were employed in 608 cases (26.8%), seven-person juries in 1,548 cases (68.3%), and five-person juries in 111 cases (4.9%) (Kwak, 2018). It should be noted that the Committee for Citizen Participation in Law (Kukmin sabeob chamyeo weewonhoi, 2013) recommended elimination of the five-person jury because some legal professionals had argued that the five-person jury is not cost effective due to its primary role merely in sentencing. The 2017 revision of the law, however, did not incorporate the recommendation.

Decision Rule

Jurors may render a verdict if they agree unanimously (Kukmineui hyeongsajaepan chamyeoeh gwanhan beobryul, 2017, Art. 46). Before reaching a verdict, jurors may consult the presiding judge to ask his or her opinion about their prospective verdict if a majority of them wish to do so, but they may render a unanimous verdict without such consultation if no majority wishes to seek professional advice. If the jurors cannot reach a unanimous decision, they must consult the judge before deciding by a simple majority vote.

Among the 1,868 cases in which juries reached a verdict on a single charge or the same verdict on multiple charges against the same defendant, juries reached unanimous verdicts in 1,543 cases (82.6%) (Kwak, 2018). It should be noted, however, that this figure may include the cases in which jurors were initially split in their judgments but made a unanimous decision after consulting the judge. Unfortunately, no information is available on how often this consultation occurred; the actual impact of such consultation appears to be limited, however, since a survey of actual jurors indicated that only one-third of actual jurors who said they had listened to the judge's opinion reported that they changed their decisions (Tak & Choi, 2011). In the remaining 325 cases (17.4%), jurors reached nonunanimous verdicts. Specific statistics about the final vote distributions are not available. Given the report of S. Kim and colleagues (2013) that the proportion of unanimous verdicts for the 323 cases during the first three years of the jury system (2008–2010) was 82.0%, it appears that the proportion has not shifted over the course of the first decade.

Conviction/Acquittal Rates

Juries convicted the defendant in 2,037 of the 2,267 cases of jury trials (89.9%) during the period, although 746 of the convictions arose from guilty pleas (32.9%) rather than jury verdicts (1,291 or 57.0%). Although the 10.9% acquittal rate in jury trials is more than twice the 4.2% rate in bench trials for comparable crimes in district courts during the same period, this comparison is misleading for two reasons (Song, 2018). First, while only a third of the defendants in jury trials plead guilty, the vast majority of defendants in South Korean bench trials plead guilty (S. Kim et al., 2013). Second, the counting rule used in the government statistics leads to a higher rate of convictions in bench trials because if the defendant is found guilty in a bench trial on any of the multiple charges it is counted as a conviction, whereas the outcome on each charge in a jury trial is counted separately (S. Kim et al., 2013). Thus, a defendant who is tried on two charges and found guilty on one charge would yield a 100% conviction rate in a bench trial but only a 50% conviction rate in a jury trial.

When compared cross-nationally, the conviction rate in Korean jury trials is higher than that in the United States, as reported by the Chicago Jury Project (67% for Kalven & Zeisel, 1966) and the NCSC hung jury study (68% for Eisenberg, Hannaford-Agor, Hans, Waters, Munsterman, Schwab, & Wells, 2005). However, the vast majority of cases in the United States end with a guilty plea rather than a trial (S. Kim et al., 2013). Guilty plea cases are not included in the base number of jury trials in the United States. If one were to remove from the number of Korean jury trials the 746 cases in which defendants pleaded guilty, the conviction rate in Korea would drop from 89.9% to 84.9%. Either way, contrary to the claims of critics (e.g., Hwang, 2010), the conviction rate of Korean jury trials is not especially low compared with that of jury trials in the United States. Moreover, without the data on the conviction rate in bench trials not involving guilty pleas and using the same measures as those applied to jury verdicts, any comparisons between conviction rates in bench and jury trials in South Korea must be interpreted with caution.

Judge–Jury Verdict Agreement

Among the 2,267 cases tried by juries, judges and juries reached the same verdict in 2,112 cases, an agreement rate of 93.1% (Beobwon haengjeongcheo, 2018). It should be noted that a jury renders a verdict first, which is only advisory, and that the judge is expected to use his or her own discretion to decide the case without necessarily adopting the jury's verdict. Judges and juries agreed on conviction in 2,026 cases (89.3%) and agreed on acquittal in 86 cases (3.8%). Among the 155 cases in which judge and jury disagreed about the defendant's guilt (6.8%), juries acquitted when judges convicted in 144 cases (92.9%); juries convicted when judges acquitted in 11 cases (7.1%). Thus, when they disagreed, juries were much more likely than judges to acquit the defendant. According to S. Kim et al. (2013), the judge–jury agreement rate in jury trials in Korea during the first three years was 91.4% when all 323 jury trial cases were included, and 89.1% when the cases in which the defendant confessed were excluded. It appears, therefore, that the agreement rate has been quite consistent over the entire period.

Judge–Jury Agreement on Sentencing Judgment

One of the unique features of the Korean jury system is that jurors can recommend a sentence if the defendant is convicted (Hong, 2018). Before jurors offer their opinions, the presiding judge must instruct the jurors on sentencing regulations, such as the range of sentencing for the convicted crime and the factors that need to be considered in sentencing. Hong (2018) reported that, counting a difference in sentence of no more than one year of imprisonment as "agreement," judges and juries "agreed" on the sentence in 89.6% of conviction cases (1,713 out of 1,911 cases). When judges and juries disagreed (198 out of 1,911 cases, or 10.4%), in a majority of those cases (60%), judges passed harsher sentences than what juries recommended, while juries' recommendations were harsher in the remaining cases (39.4%). Thus, the judge–jury agreement rate has been nearly as high in sentencing as it has been in judgments of guilt, with a similar greater leniency from juries on both decisions.

RESOLVED AND UNRESOLVED ISSUES

Jury Competence

One of the major questions critics have raised about the viability of the Korean jury system is whether ordinary citizens are capable of deciding criminal cases in accordance with the facts and the law, given that most jurors have little, if any, legal education and training (e.g., Hwang, 2010; J. Park, 2010). While this concern is plausible, it can be effectively addressed through empirical evidence, as many researchers have done (Chesterman, Chan, & Hampton, 2001; Eisenberg et al., 2005; Goodman-Delahunty, Brewer, Clough, Horan, Ogloff, Tait, & Pratley, 2008; Heuer & Penrod, 1994; Kalven & Zeisel, 1966; S. Kim et al., 2013).

As in previous studies, one way to evaluate jury competence empirically is to examine the judge–jury verdict agreement rate on verdicts (Eisenberg et al., 2005; Goodman-Delahunty et al., 2008; Heuer & Penrod, 1994; Kalven & Zeisel, 1966; S. Kim et al., 2013). According to the data reported by the National Court Administration of Korea (2018), the percentage of cases during the first 10 years of the Korean jury system (2008–2017) in which the judge and the jury rendered the same verdict was 93.1% (2,112 of 2,267 cases). This high rate of agreement between judges and juries has been consistently documented; S. Kim et al. (2013) reported an agreement rate of 91.4% during the first three years. In the relatively few instances in which judges and juries disagreed, juries had a far greater tendency to acquit the defendant; juries acquitted when judges convicted in 92.9% of those cases. S. Kim et al. (2013) also reported a similar pattern during the first three years.

While the high rate of judge–jury agreement on legal decisions in South Korea is striking, two additional points should be considered. First, the agreement rate, like other statistics reported in this chapter, comes from *all* the jury trials held during the first 10 years. In previous studies conducted in other countries, scholars computed agreement rates using sampled cases (Eisenberg et al., 2005; Goodman-Delahunty et al., 2008; Heuer & Penrod, 1994; Kalven & Zeisel, 1966). In each of these studies, questions can be raised about the representativeness of these samples. In contrast, the figures reported in this chapter for South Korea represent population statistics. Thus, the Korean judge–jury agreement statistics are free from any possible sampling error or bias. Second, Korean jury verdicts are only advisory to the judge. Judges are supposed to use their own discretion to decide and need not adopt the jury's verdict. Considering these two characteristics, the judge–jury agreement rate in South Korea appears to be very high even when it is compared with similar data from countries with longer histories of jury trials.

In addition, other empirical data also provide evidence suggesting that Korean jurors feel that they have the competence to make valid legal decisions. Song (2018) reported results of surveys from former jurors and reserve jurors. Among 18,081 jurors and reserve jurors who attended their respective trials, 28.1% stated they "fully understood the case materials"; 60.6% stated they "mostly understood"; 10.6% stated they "understood half the materials"; and only 0.7% stated they "did not understand at all." When asked how difficult it was to reach a final decision as a juror, 18.5% of the former jurors selected "not at all difficult"; 32.1% "slightly difficult"; 35.5% "somewhat difficult"; and 13.6% "very difficult."

Although such responses represent jurors' subjective impressions, it is still significant that over 89% believed that they understood case materials well. These responses appear to have some credibility because it is unlikely that the judge–jury agreement rate on verdicts would have been as high as it was had the jurors not understood the case materials relatively well (Kwak, 2018). In addition, more than half the jurors reported that they did not find it difficult to reach their decisions on the defendant's guilt; only 13.6% of them said they had substantial difficulty in deciding. Furthermore, S. Kim and colleagues (2013) reported that, based on the analysis of the jury trial data for the first three years, when two independent legal professionals rated overall evidentiary complexity of each case on a five-point scale from Level 1 (low) to Level 5 (high), the judge–jury agreement rates were consistent across all five levels of evidentiary complexity. They did not find any indication that complexity leads to greater judge–jury disagreement.

Do the empirical data from jury trials alleviate the concerns about the competence of Korean jurors to make good legal decisions? Some researchers think so (e.g., I.-G. Lee, 2017; H.-H. Park, Kim, & Kim, 2017). In addition, the National Court Administration of the Supreme Court of Korea, which has held regular conferences to discuss and evaluate various aspects of jury trials, has in recent years rarely focused on lay citizens' competence in legal decision-making. It appears that empirical evidence has helped resolve the initial skepticism about jury competence.

Advisory Effect of Jury Verdicts

A distinctive aspect of the Korean jury system, already noted, is that the jury's decision has only an advisory effect. The professional judges consider the jury's verdict but independently make a binding decision; they have no obligation to adopt the jury's verdict. The current law clearly states that "the verdict and the opinion [of the jury] do not bind the Court" (Kukmineui hyeongsajaepan chamyeoeh gwanhan beobryul, 2017, Art. 46). The advisory nature of jury verdicts has been one of the primary issues that legal practitioners and academic researchers have debated since the beginning of the new system.

Why did the Korean government impose such a crucial restriction on the effect of jury verdicts? One reason may be that the mixed support for the jury system when it was first instituted in 2008 made the introduction of the jury a tentative experiment. Many legal professionals, as discussed in the brief history section, initially expressed concerns about jury competence (Hwang, 2010). Such concerns and skepticism prevented the Korean government from granting full decision-making power to lay citizens. Instead, the government took a more cautious approach. The initial plan was to conduct jury trials for five years, at which point the government would undertake an extensive review of the new system, the results of which would determine the system's viability (Kukmineui hyeongsajaepan chamyeoeh gwanhan beobryul, 2007).

Perhaps more importantly, there were serious concerns that allowing lay citizens to make legally binding decisions would be unconstitutional. The current Korean Constitution states that "all citizens have the right to a trial by a judge" (Daehanminkuk Hunbeob, 1987, Art. 27). From the time that the judicial reform bill (which included the jury system) was enacted in 2007 until today, the interpretation of "a judge" has aroused great controversy among researchers, practitioners, and legislators. Critics of jury trials have tended to stick to a literal interpretation of the word, which is limited to professional judges, while proponents have argued for a broader interpretation that includes lay citizens (Ahn & Han, 2005; D.-S. Kim, 2018; S. Kim et al., 2013). It appears that the notion of advisory juries was a practical solution to defuse the anticipated charge of unconstitutionality from the opponents of the jury system, which could have crippled the plan to introduce jury trials before it began.

As jury trials have become a more settled part of the Korean justice system following the first 10 years of largely successful implementation, the advisory effect of jury verdicts has emerged again as a key issue (Hong, 2018; D.-S. Kim, 2018; Song, 2018). The results of more than 2,000 jury trials have substantially assured most researchers, practitioners, and lawmakers that Korean citizens are competent to make legal decisions according to the law. Some researchers have recently argued that if the judge–jury agreement rate is reliably over 90%, the jury's verdict should be granted binding effect (Hong, 2018; I.-G. Lee, 2017; H.-H. Park et al., 2017). They also argue that, since the primary purpose of introducing jury trials is to enhance the democratic legitimacy and procedural transparency of the judicial system, that purpose could be fulfilled more effectively by giving juries actual decision-making power.

The Korean government, however, has maintained a conservative stance on this issue (Kukmineui hyeongsajaepan chamyeoeh gwanhan beobryul, 2017). The Committee for Citizen Participation in Law addressed the topic of "effects of jury verdicts" when it undertook an extensive review of jury trials in early 2013. Considering opinions from both sides of the debate and statistics from jury trials, the committee concluded that more decisional power should be granted to juries than their advisory verdicts had previously been understood to possess. While the committee found it premature or even risky to grant *full* binding effect to the jury because the problem of unconstitutionality was not yet completely resolved, the committee recommended that the jury's verdict be granted "*de facto* binding effect" (D.-S. Kim, 2018). According to the committee, "*de facto* binding effect" means that the judge must "respect" the jury's verdict when judging whether to convict the defendant; the judge should be able to reach a different verdict only in certain circumstances (i.e., when the jury's verdict is against the Constitution, Laws, Acts, or Regulations; when it is against logical or empirical rules; or when there is a reason to believe that the contents of the verdict or the procedure that produced it are illegitimate) (Kwak, 2018).

Many researchers have found this concept of "*de facto* binding effect" to be abstract and unclear (e.g., D.-S. Kim, 2018). They have also pointed out that, because the Committee for Citizen Participation in Law's notion of "*de facto* binding effect" allows so many exceptions, it is not practically different from "advisory effect." After considerable discussion, the government bill to revise the law, which was proposed in 2017, eliminated the concept of "*de facto* binding effect." The 2017 revision, which is currently the law, thus retains the merely advisory nature of the jury's verdict (Kukmineui hyeongsajaepan chamyeoeh gwanhan beobryul, 2017).

Another rationale behind the Korean government's conservative approach to addressing the effect of jury verdicts is the lack of consensus among Korean citizens on granting more decisional power to laypersons. Of the 1,300 citizens randomly selected from the general public whom Tak and Choi (2011) asked about the effect of jury verdicts, 60.5% agreed that "the jury's opinion should be advisory" while 35.1% agreed that "the jury's opinion should be binding." According to this study, of the 147 respondents who were former jurors or juror candidates, 80.3% agreed that "the jury's opinion should be advisory" while 17.0% agreed that "the jury's opinion should be binding." By contrast, a majority of the 360 defendants in jury trials who were surveyed (54.2%) agreed that "the jury's opinion should be binding," while 35.6% agreed that "the jury's opinion should be advisory" (Tak & Choi, 2011). In addition, among 93 incumbent judges who presided over jury trials between 2015 and 2018 and who responded to a recent survey (Kwak, 2018), 52% believed that it is desirable to have the jury's verdict advisory (as it currently is); 24% responded that it would be desirable for the jury's verdict to have *de facto* binding effect; 23% thought that it would be desirable for the jury's verdict to have limited binding authority; and only 1% thought that it would be desirable to give the jury's verdict full binding effect. Thus, with the exception of defendants, the majority of judges and Korean citizens appear to believe, at least at present, that it is appropriate for the jury's verdict to remain only advisory.

Decision Rule

The decision rule by which jurors reach a verdict has also been the subject of considerable discussion. Under the current law (Kukmineui hyeongsajaepan chamyeoeh gwanhan beobryul, 2017), Korean jurors must unanimously agree on what the verdict should be in order to reach a verdict without consulting the presiding judge. If unanimity is not obtained, they must consult the presiding judge. After listening to the judge's "opinions," jurors can reach a verdict by a majority vote. The simple majority rule, however, has been criticized by many researchers and practitioners. For instance, Hong (2018) pointed out that the current decision rule is merely a rule of convenience that allows jurors to reach a quick decision without attempting to incorporate the opinions of the minority. He also argued that the simple majority rule makes it difficult for jurors to take into consideration the principle of "proof beyond a reasonable doubt" when deciding a criminal case and prevents jurors from actively engaging in full deliberation to find the facts.

As some researchers and policy-makers have recently suggested that juries should have greater decision making power (Hong, 2018; I.-G. Lee, 2017; H.-H. Park et al., 2017), the decision rule has become even more important. Many have expressed concerns that the simple majority rule is insufficient to realize the purposes of jury trials (e.g., achieving democratic legitimacy in legal decisions, reflecting the voice of the community in trials; Hong, 2018; S. Kim et al., 2013; I.-G. Lee, 2017; J. Park, 2010; H.-H. Park et al., 2017). To address these concerns, the Committee for Citizen Participation in Law (Kukmin sabeob chamyeo weewonhoi, 2013) suggested that the simple majority rule be replaced by a supermajority rule (three-quarters); if jurors do not reach a verdict under the supermajority rule, the judge should decide the case by himself or herself. Although the supermajority rule may appear to be a reasonable modification, some researchers have questioned its practicability (e.g., Hong, 2018). They have argued that a more stringent rule will make it more likely that juries cannot reach a verdict at all and thus may end up losing the opportunity to participate in making legal decisions, even in an advisory manner.

Indeed, survey data indicate that only a third of jurors changed their judgments after listening to the judge's opinion (Tak & Choi, 2011). Nearly half (47.3%) responded that the judge's opinion had little or no influence on their decision-making, while 39.5% indicated that the judge's opinion had some influence. Given that the judge's opinion appears to have only limited influence in persuading jurors to reach a unanimous verdict when they have not been able to do so on their own, adopting the supermajority rule might increase the risk of hung juries, which may eventually reduce the opportunities of lay citizens to participate in legal decision-making. In addition, the prospect of a hung jury would raise concerns about wasting social resources. In fact, the revised law has maintained the simple majority rule (Kukmineui hyeongsajaepan chamyeoeh gwanhan beobryul, 2017).

Appeal to Higher Courts: Is It Necessary to Impose a Limitation?

Korean jury trials have generated a high rate of appeals to higher courts: 81.0% during the first 10 years (Beobwon haengjeongcheo, 2018). This figure is noticeably higher than the appeal rate from bench trials held in district courts for comparable criminal cases (61.5%) (S. Kim et al., 2013). It seems that the higher proportion of appeals in jury trials has been driven primarily by the prosecution: The prosecution has filed appeals in only 28.1% of bench trials, but in 48.4% of jury trials (Beobwon haengjeongcheo, 2018). Defendants were understandably more likely to file appeals in general in view of the higher frequency of convictions than acquittals, but they filed at only a slightly higher rate in jury trials (59.2%) than in bench trials (51.2%). These numbers include the cases in which both the prosecution and the defendant filed an appeal. The higher rate of appeals by prosecutors in jury trials than in bench trials is particularly remarkable when considering the conviction rate in these cases (89.1%); in many cases, apparently, even when the jury votes to convict, the prosecution still appeals the sentence or the particular conviction offense when the jury convicted of a lesser charge than the prosecutor requested. This tendency leads to a suspicion that Korean prosecutors may have little confidence in legal decisions in which ordinary citizens participate.

Interestingly, however, the decisions by the "high court," the appellate court in South Korea, appear to reflect a different assessment of the validity and accuracy of legal decisions in which lay citizens participated (Song, 2018). It should be noted that, unlike appellate proceedings in other countries (e.g., the United States), the high court can retry the appealed case. In the 1,747 cases that the high court retried involving appeals from jury verdicts, the high court affirmed the verdict in 1,234 (70.6%) and overturned the decision in 497 (28.4%); the remaining 16 cases were withdrawn (0.9%). In contrast, in bench trials in comparable cases, the high court overruled the decision 40.5% of the time, a substantially higher reversal rate than for jury trials (Song, 2018). It is not clear how many of the appeals were on the sentence only, as the relevant statistics are not available. However, Song (2018) reported that the sentence was changed for 423 of 1,747 appealed jury cases (24.2%) while the comparable proportion in bench trials was 32.0%; in addition, the sentence was reduced for 298 of 1,747 jury cases (17.1%) while the corresponding proportion in bench trials was 24.9%.

The fate of cases appealed to the Supreme Court of Korea has indicated a similar pattern (Song, 2018). Appealing to the Supreme Court, as in many other countries, represents the final step in the linear sequence of the appellate procedure. Of the 703 cases appealed that were initially tried by jury in district courts, the Supreme Court dismissed the appeal in 645 (91.7%) and overruled the verdict in only 8 (1.1%). The rest of the cases (7.2%) were withdrawn. Of the comparable criminal cases initially tried by the bench in district courts, the Supreme Court overruled 3.7%. Overall, then, an appeal was more likely to be filed when the case was tried by a jury than when tried by the bench at district courts, but the higher courts were less likely to overturn the initial decision when a jury participated in making it.

As described in the preceding paragraphs, the higher rate of appeal in jury trials may be attributable to the prosecution. Despite the fact that jury verdicts are only advisory, the prosecution appears to place little, if any, trust in the judgments when lay citizens participated in making them. The higher courts in Korea, however, have been less inclined to overrule the initial decisions from jury trials than bench trials.

Thus, many law professionals have argued that the high rate of appeal by the prosecution has wasted public resources and that measures should be taken to limit the prosecution's proclivity to appeal verdicts from jury trials (Song, 2018).

Two Supreme Court cases appear to provide potential support for such a limitation. In one appealed case, the Supreme Court of Korea overturned the ruling by the high court and affirmed the decision from a lower court in a robbery and assault jury trial (Daebeobwon Pangyeol, 2009D014065). A jury of nine citizens had participated in deciding this case and reached a unanimous verdict that the defendant was not guilty. The presiding judge adopted the verdict, ruling in favor of the defendant. The prosecution appealed the ruling to the high court, where the case was tried by the bench. The high court reversed the decision based on further questioning of the victim, but without examining any new evidence. The Supreme Court then overturned the decision of the high court and reinstated the verdict of acquittal. The Supreme Court ruled that the high court cannot reverse the decision from a lower court unless a clear and convincing situation emerges through a new investigation of evidence, when (1) a criminal case is tried by a jury; (2) the jury returns a unanimous verdict that the defendant is not guilty; and (3) the judge adopts the verdict and rules accordingly. It is also notable that the Supreme Court of Korea emphasized, in the same statement, that the jury decision needs to be "respected" when these conditions are met unless clear and convincing new evidence is found that sufficiently opposes the decision by the jury. It is very rare for the Supreme Court to make such a comment about the decision of a district court (S. Kim et al., 2013). Moreover, this decision was not a fluke. A year later, the Supreme Court used the same standard to overturn the reversal of a jury verdict in another case (Daebeobwon Pangyeol, 2010D04450).

The upshot of these decisions is to make certain decisions in which lay jurors participated effectively unappealable, which should discourage the prosecution from filing appeals in those sorts of cases and thus reduce the total number of appeals from jury trials. The three conditions that the Supreme Court set forth have guided proposals for prohibiting appeals (S. Kim et al., 2013). In addition, by recognizing the important role of the jury, the statement set a new principle for the practice of criminal law. The Committee for Citizen Participation in Law (Kukmin sabeob chamyeo weewonhoi, 2013) adopted the conditions in making its recommendations. The legislators' bill to revise the law (on jury trials), which was proposed in early 2017, also employed the three conditions to restrict appeals by the prosecution. However, the 2017 revision did not incorporate the restriction (Kukmineui hyeongsajaepan chamyeoeh gwanhan beobryul, 2017).

CONCLUSION

The introduction of jury trials to South Korea was part of an effort by a former government to carry out a judicial reform program that was initiated in 2004 when the Judicial Reform Committee officially included a jury system as part of its agenda. Proponents anticipated that jury trials could enhance the legitimacy, transparency, and public confidence in trial processes by allowing lay citizens to participate in legal decision-making (S. Kim et al., 2013; J. Park, 2010).

During the first 10 years of the new system, over 2,000 jury trials took place and a substantial amount of trial data have been collected, allowing researchers, practitioners, and lawmakers to make informed evaluations of the operation of Korean jury trials. The data provide evidence that Korean citizens are competent to make valid legal decisions according to the law (Kwak, 2018; Song, 2018).

While initial concerns about jury competence have gradually waned over the years, new issues have emerged. At the heart of those issues lies the effect of the jury's verdict. Many researchers have consistently argued that the mere advisory effect of jury verdicts is not sufficient, and that the jury's verdict should be binding in order to achieve the ultimate goal of lay participation in legal decision-making (Hong, 2018; I.-G. Lee, 2017; H.-H. Park et al., 2017). So far, however, the Korean government has resisted making this change. Although the Committee for Citizen Participation in Law (Kukmin sabeob chamyeo weewonhoi, 2013) proposed that greater decision-making power should be granted to juries by giving jury verdicts "*de facto* binding effect," the government version of the bill to revise the law eliminated the recommendation and did not make any change concerning the effect of the jury's verdict in the 2017 revision (Kukmineui hyeongsajaepan chamyeoeh gwanhan beobryul, 2017). Presumably, as the issue of constitutionality regarding lay participation in law has yet to be resolved, the Korean government will remain unwilling to make what it perceives as a risky move. The debate is still underway and the conflict concerning the effect of jury verdicts is still unresolved. It is by no means clear what the ultimate outcome will be. It seems clear, however, that employing lay citizens as legal decision-makers has had a positive influence on the legal system in South Korea (I.-G. Lee, 2017) and is anticipated to make meaningful contributions to further democratization of its society in the years to come.

REFERENCES

Ahn, K., & Han, I. (2005). *Baeshimjewa shimineui sabeobchamyeo* 배심제와 시민의 사법참여 [Jury system and civil participation in law]. Seoul: Jip-mun dang.

Beobwon haengjeongcheo 법원 행정처 [National Court Administration (S. Kor.)]. (2018). *Kukminchamyeojaepan gyeolgwa bunseok* 국민참여재판 결과 분석 [An analysis of results of citizen participation trials].

Chesterman, M., Chan, J., & Hampton, S. (2001). *Managing prejudicial publicity: An empirical study of criminal jury trials in New South Wales*. Sydney: Law and Justice Foundation of New South Wales.

Daebeobwon Pangyeol 대법원 판결 [Supreme Court of Korea Decision] 2009Do14065, decided March 25, 2010.

Daebeobwon Pangyeol 대법원 판결 [Supreme Court of Korea Decision] 2010Do4450, decided May 3, 2011.

Daehanminkuk Hunbeob 대한민국 헌법 [Constitution of the Republic of Korea] (1987).

Eisenberg, T., Hannaford-Agor, P. L., Hans, V. P., Waters, N. L., Munsterman, G. T., Schwab, S. J., & Wells, M. T. (2005). Judge–jury agreement in criminal cases: A partial replication of Kalven and Zeisel's *The American Jury*. *Journal of Empirical Legal Studies*, 2(1), 171–206.

Goodman-Delahunty, J., Brewer, N., Clough, J., Horan, J., Ogloff, J. R. P., Tait, D., & Pratley, J. (2008). *Practices, policies and procedures that influence juror satisfaction in Australia*. Canberra: Australian Institute of Criminology.

Han, I. (2010). Sabeob minjoohwa gwajeonggwa kukminjaepaneui taedong: yeoksajeok euimi 사법 민주화 과정과 국민재판의 태동: 역사적 의미 [The process of judicial democratization and the birth of trial by citizens: The historical meanings]. In I. Han & S. Han (Eds.), *Kukmineui sabeobchamyeo* 국민의 사법참여 [Citizen participation in law] (pp. 37–45). Seoul: Kyungin.

Hans, V. P., Fukurai, H., Kutnjak Ivković, S., & Park, J. (2017). Global juries: A plan for research. In M. B. Kovera (Ed.), *The psychology of juries*. Washington, DC: American Psychological Association.

Hans, V. P., & Vidmar, N. (1986). *Judging the jury*. Cambridge, MA: Perseus.

Heuer, L., & Penrod, S. (1994). Trial complexity: A field investigation of its meaning and its effects. *Law and Human Behavior*, *18*, 29–51.

Hong, S. (2018). Kukminchamyeojaepanehseo baeshimwon pangyeoleui bangshikgwa hyoryeokeui baramjikhan gaeseon bangan 국민참여재판에서 배심원 판결의 방식과 효력의 바람직한 개선 방안 [A study on the way of decision making of the jury and the effect of the verdict of participatory trial]. *Wonkwang Beobhak* 원광 법학, 34, 155–177.

Hwang, B.-D. (2010). Baeshimjaepan shihangeui munjejeomgwa daechaek 배심재판 시행의 문제점과 대책 [Problems and solutions for implementing the jury trials]. *Hanyang Beobhak* 한양 법학, 21(2), 33.

Kalven, H., & Zeisel, H. (1966). *The American jury*. Boston, MA: Little, Brown and Company.

Kim, D.-S. (2018). Kukminchamyeojaepan baeshimwon pyeonggyuleui hyoryeokeh daehan gochal 국민참여재판 배심원 평결의 효력에 대한 고찰 [A study on the effect of jury verdict in the citizen participation trial]. *Beobhaknonchong* 법학논총, 40, 41–60.

Kim, S., Park, J., Park, K., & Eom, J.-S. (2013). Judge–jury agreement in criminal cases: The first three years of the Korean jury system. *Journal of Empirical Legal Studies*, 10, 35–53.

Kukmin sabeob chamyeo weewonhoi 국민사법참여위원회 [Committee for Citizen Participation in Law]. (2013). *Kukmin chamyeojaepaneui choijong hyeongtae gyeoljeongeul weehan cheongmunhoi gyeolgwa bogo* 국민 참여재판의 최종 형태 결정을 위한 청문회 결과 보고 [Outcome report of hearings for determining the final form of civil participation trial]. Seoul: Supreme Court of Korea.

Kukmineui hyeongsajaepan chamyeoeh gwanhan beobryul 국민의 형사재판 참여에 관한 법률 [Act for Civil Participation in Criminal Trials (S. Kor.)] (2007), Korean Government Code 8495.

Kukmineui hyeongsajaepan chamyeoeh gwanhan beobryul 국민의 형사재판 참여에 관한 법률 [Act for Civil Participation in Criminal Trials (S. Kor.)] (2017), Korean Government Code 14839, Amendment of Other Laws.

Kwak, D. (2018). *Kukminchamyeojaepan hwalseonghwareul weehan jaepanshilmoo jeokjeonghwa bangan* 국민참여재판 활성화를 위한 재판실무 적정화 방안 [A plan to optimize trial practice for the purpose of vitalizing citizen participation trial] [Paper presentation]. 2018 Conference on Citizen Participation Trials, Supreme Court of Korea.

Lee, I.-G. (2017). Kukminchamyeojaepaneui gaejeongbeobryulaneh gwanhan ilgo 국민참여재판의 개정법률안에 관한 일고 [A brief thought on the revised act of Korean jury trial system]. *Beobhakyeongoo* 법학연구, 17, 245–278 [published by the Korean Law Association].

Lee, J. S. (2016). Transplanting jury trials in South Korean legal soils: Comparative analysis with jury trials in the United States. *Asian Journal of Criminology*, 11, 111–133.

Pang, J.-H. (2008, February 13). Chut kukminchamyeojaepan yeolrin daegujibeob gaboni 첫 국민참여재판 열린 대구지법 가보니 [Visiting Daegu District Courthouse in which the first citizen participation trial was held]. www.mk.co.kr/news/print/2008/78148

Park, J. (2010). *Baeshimjewa beobshimrihak* 배심제와 법심리학 [The jury system and legal psychology]. Seoul: Ore.

Park, H.-H., Kim, M.-D., & Kim, J.-H. (2017). Kukminchamyeojaepaneh gwanhan noneui: Kukminchamyeojaepan panryereul joongshimeuro 국민참여재판에 관한 논의: 국민참여재판 판례를 중심으로 [A study on the civil participation in criminal jury trial: focused on precedent analysis]. *Wonkwang Beobhak* 원광 법학, 33, 57–80.

Song, O. (2018). *Kukminchamyeojaepaneui hyunhwanggwa gwaje* 국민참여재판의 현황과 과제 [The status and the future tasks of citizen participation trials] [Paper presentation]. 2018 Conference on Citizen Participation Trials, Supreme Court of Korea.

Tak, H., & Choi, S. (2011). *Kukmineui hyungsajaepanchamyeo pyungga yeongooreul joongshimeurohan hyungsajeongchaekgwa sabeobjedo yeongoo* 국민의 형사재판참여 평가연구를 중심으로한 형사정책과 사법제도 연구 [Studies on the criminal justice policies and judicial systems with a focus on evaluation research on civil participation in criminal trials]. Seoul: Korean Institute of Criminology.

Teukjeongbeomjoi Gajoongcheobeol deungeh gwanhan beobryul 특정범죄 가중처벌 등에 관한 법률 [Act on Aggravated Punishment of Particular Crimes (S. Kor.)] (2010), Korean Government Code 10210.

Vidmar, N. (2000). *World jury systems*. New York: Oxford University Press.

6

The Twenty-Fifth Anniversary of the Spanish Jury

Mar Jimeno-Bulnes

Article 125 of the 1978 Spanish Constitution contemplates the right of the public to participate as jurors in jury trials. It provides as follows: "Citizens may engage in popular action and participate in the administration of justice through the institution of the jury, in the manner and with respect to those criminal trials as may be determined by law." It is undoubtedly the most representative way for citizens to participate in judicial administration (Burgos Ladrón de Guevara, 1997). However, it is not the same as the right to trial by jury as guaranteed in common-law countries (Esparza Leibar, 1995) and included in the procedural guarantees provided by the Sixth Amendment to the US Constitution (Marder, 2005). Interestingly, Article 125, which provides for trial by jury, also gives crime victims and any member of the public the right to bring private and popular prosecutions that supplement a public prosecution (Pérez Gil, 2003).

After several drafts propounded by different political groups, organizations, and legal scholars, the new law entered into force under the government of Felipe González. Organic Law 5/1995, on the Jury, noted as *indatada* because no date was included in its title (Pérez-Cruz Martín, 1995), became known as the Jury Law (1995). The new law was the subject of much discussion and attention (Jimeno-Bulnes, 2004). Surprisingly, and by the express choice of the minister of justice at the time, Juan Alberto Belloch, Spain opted for the "purist" model of a classic jury trial system, modelled on the Anglo-Saxon jury, which was considered the best solution in keeping with Spanish tradition (Martín Ostos, 1990; Thaman, 1998), rather than the mixed court system (*escabinado*) in the continental style. Even so, the modern Spanish jury differs in several ways from the original Anglo-Saxon jury, especially with respect to rules about the verdict. The Spanish verdict, which is *sui generis*, is far removed from common-law procedures in general, and American jury procedures in particular, as I will explain.

The Spanish Jury Law passed its twentieth anniversary in 2015 quietly, in comparison with its tenth anniversary, when it was at least applauded in academic circles (Cano Barrero, 2007; Lorca Navarrete, 2005; Martín Pallín, 2006). Now it is time to prepare for the celebration of its twenty-fifth anniversary in 2020. This chapter provides some assessment of whether or not the experiment of the jury has been successful in Spain. In my view, the Spanish jury functions well in general thanks to the efforts of law professionals and the public in fulfilling their respective tasks. In fact, despite the criticism levelled at the beginning, Spanish citizens have gained confidence in the jury over the years. Nevertheless, media coverage has caused some disruption in high-profile jury trials, potentially endangering the impartiality of the jurors (Jimeno-Bulnes, 2014). For this reason, I shall pay specific attention to this last topic.

JURY TRIAL IN SPAIN: LEGAL BACKGROUND

The Spanish Jury Law (*Ley Orgánica 5/1995, de 22 de mayo, del Tribunal del Jurado*) has been in force since November 24, 1995. In addition to its initial amendments in Organic Laws 8/1995 of November 16 and 10/1995 of November 23 (Ley Orgánica 5/1995 [Jury Law], 1995), the Spanish Jury Law has only undergone one additional reform: Organic Law 1/2017 of December 13, which "guarantee[s] the participation of people with disabilities without exclusions" in jury service. Since its approval, people living with disabilities can request appropriate means of support and the necessary adjustments to be able to serve as jurors under equal conditions.

This section will describe some of the most significant features of the Spanish jury from both institutional and procedural perspectives. It outlines some of the ways in which the Spanish criminal justice system had to adapt to the introduction of the jury in Spain. As mentioned, Spain chose to follow the common-law model based on the adversarial system with the traditional jury trial (Hans, 2002), rather than the mixed court model, in which professional judges and lay assessors work together to "decid[e] both the guilt of the defendant and the appropriate sentence" (Kutnjak Ivković, 2015, p. 1031; see also Kutnjak Ivković, 2003). Although a full adversarial system does not exist in Spain, an authentic jury trial has developed with distinctive characteristics that recall the earlier legal history of Spain (Gleadow, 2000). This development reinforces the idea that the line between an accusatorial and an inquisitorial system is blurring and that Anglo-American and European criminal procedural systems are converging due to mutual influence (Jimeno-Bulnes, 2013).

Jury and Jury Proceedings in Spain

The jury in Spain consists of nine citizens who serve on a court presided over by a trial judge, a magistrate from a superior jurisdictional body (*Audiencia Provincial*). As a general rule, these courts function only within the ambit of that jurisdictional body, with the exception of "privileged persons" standing trial before a regional court or the national Supreme Court. All of these courts share the same criminal procedural tasks: the jurors have to reach a verdict in light of which the trial judge will pronounce judgment and, when necessary, impose a sentence (Jury Law, 1995).

Nevertheless, Spain regulates the participation of citizens as jurors in a very particular way in terms of a "duty/right"; in addition, there is a complicated system of causes for their qualification or disqualification, including requirements, incapacities, ineligibilities, disqualifications, and excuses (Jury Law, 1995).

According to a rights perspective, the Jury Law's implementing regulations offer remuneration for daily jury service; according to a duty perspective, the same provisions contemplate financial penalties for failure to participate in jury service. The most controversial question with regard to this duty to serve as a juror is the absence of any regulation of "conscientious objection." In Spain, as in other countries, such a right is only observed in relation to military obligations (Constitución Española [Spanish Constitution], 1978, Art. 30(2)). The question is whether a citizen can decline to serve as a juror because he or she feels unable to serve. There are opinions in favor (Bermúdez Requena, 1998; Martínez Torrón, 1996) and against (Belloch Julbe, 2000) any such regulation. The Constitutional Court appears to permit conscientious objection and with it, the admission of an appeal for protection (*recurso de amparo*) on the grounds of a violation of a fundamental right. Conscientious objection is specifically provided by Article 54(2) of the Spanish Constitution as a fundamental right. Given the absence of any pronouncement on the merits from the Constitutional Court, it is not clear whether a provision for conscientious objection actually exists; in judicial practice, however, conscientious objection operates as a "hidden" excuse for not serving as a juror (Ferrer Ortiz, 2003, p. 10; Jimeno-Bulnes, 2011).

In addition to conscientious objection, there is also a marked tendency by those who work in certain professions or live in certain geographical areas to resist jury service more than do others. The typical ground for avoiding jury service, in addition to conscientious objection, is economic hardship as a result of time spent away from work in the case of a lengthy trial and in spite of the legally required juror pay (Toharia, 1985, 1994). However, early in the jury's existence in Spain, there was another more compelling reason that citizens did not want to serve as jurors, and that was their apprehension or even their fear of serving (Fidalgo Gallardo, 1998). In spite of various proposals, such as permitting a change of venue, protecting the identity of the jurors (Sanjurjo Rebollo, 1998), and addressing the needs of special regions in which there has been terrorism (Jimeno Bulnes, 2001), none of these proposals appears to be a panacea.

The jury proceeding is considered a "special criminal proceeding" (Gómez Colomer, 1996; for a contrary view, see Gimeno Sendra, 2015) in which the jury acts as the lawful and exclusive judge under Article 24(2) of the Spanish Constitution, which provides that "all persons have the right of access to the ordinary judge predetermined by law" (Spanish Constitution, 1978). The Constitutional Court in Judgment num. 47/1983 of May 31 (STC, May 31, 1983) reinforced the view that this is a fundamental right established in the Spanish Constitution that can never be forsaken (De Vega Ruiz, 1989). Thus, according to constitutional law and interpretation, the criminal jury is to judge specific legally defined offenses (Jury Law, 1995), which include unlawful killing, intimidation, failure of the duty to assist, trespassing a dwelling, and forest fires. The jury also hears offenses against public administration, such as disloyalty in the custody of documents, corruption, influence peddling, embezzlement, fraud and illegal taxation, negotiations in which civil servants cannot engage, and disloyalty in the custody of prisoners.

In general, the Spanish jury trial follows established criminal procedures and the general rules contained in the 1882 Spanish Criminal Procedure Act (Ley de Enjuiciamiento Criminal [LECrim], 1882), which essentially maintains the inquisitorial system. However, perhaps the most interesting feature of the jury trial in Spain is the use of the adversarial system (but see Grande, 2016, who argues that the jury trial has strengthened nonadversarial features of the Spanish justice system). Every piece of evidence must now be presented in the oral proceedings or the "plenary" session of the trial. The jurors, unlike the trial judge, have no access to the file and/or "investigative dossier" prepared during the pretrial investigation (Thaman, 2008, p. 32). The Preamble of the Spanish Jury Law makes it clear that the adversarial system is to govern the jury procedure: "the present Act conceives the trial by jury as a way to eradicate the aforesaid procedural malformations, by means of the examination of all evidence before the said jury" (Jury Law, 1995, Part 3.1).

The Spanish Jury Law, rather than regulating only the trial procedure during the "plenary" or "oral" proceedings (*juicio oral*) also includes pretrial procedures led by the investigating judge (*Juez de Instrucción*) during the investigative phase and the so-called interim phase. This essential step in the Spanish criminal process leads to the opening of the trial or the dismissal (*sobreseimiento*) of the case. The investigating judge evaluates the merits of the criminal investigation before the trial commences. The Jury Law provides for a preliminary hearing, which includes an oral session with all parties to the case (Jury Law, 1995, Arts. 30 et seq.). The Jury Law also provides procedural guarantees such as an oral proceeding or "verbal hearing" and a "contradiction" (*principio de contradicción* and/or *audiencia bilateral*). The contradiction principle implies the compulsory presence and participation of all involved parties in the criminal procedure, such as the prosecution (public prosecution and, if it is the case, private and popular prosecution) and the defense.

However, the most distinctive characteristics of the jury proceedings in Spain occur during the jury trial itself. The trial begins with the jury selection process or "constitution of the jury" and ends with the announcement by the trial judge of the "object of the verdict" to the jury with the provision of instructions or summing up (Jury Law, 1995, Arts. 38, 52–54). The court clerk plays an essential role. He or she is the person the jury might turn to with questions about the law (Jimeno-Bulnes & Hans, 2016). In fact, the clerk, as a public-sector employee trained in the law, has a duty to provide general assistance in all judicial proceedings, including jury proceedings. The clerk is the only person authorized to enter the jury room for the purposes of assisting the jury in recording its verdict according to Article 61(2) of the

Jury Law. Textually, "at the request of the spokesman [who is a member of the jury], the trial judge may authorize the court clerk or an assistant officer to draw up or record the minutes. Likewise, the designated minute-taker appointed to substitute for the spokesman may also request the aforesaid."

The Spanish Jury Law is peculiar in that it contemplates a verdict of a special kind that is quite different from the verdict required in common-law countries (Jimeno-Bulnes, 2007). In brief, the Spanish jury verdict has two distinctive features. One feature is that the verdict requires only a majority vote; it does not need to be unanimous. According to this rule, five votes are required to prove a fact that is "favorable" to the criminal defendant, but seven votes are needed to prove a fact that is "unfavorable" to the criminal defendant. The other feature is that the jury must provide reasons for the verdict (Jimeno-Bulnes, 2007). This is unheard of in the traditional jury system. Article 61(1)(d) of the Jury Law sets forth the requirements that the minutes of the votes must include. One of the requirements is "a succinct explanation of the reasons why the jurors have declared or refused to declare those points of fact as proven" (Jury Law, 1995). The meaning of the phrase "a succinct explanation of the reasons" has been widely debated. Legal academics have argued in favor of juries giving reasons (Lorca Navarrete, 2003) and in opposition (Esparza Leibar, 2000). The requirement of providing reasons for a verdict has come to be known as "a reasoned verdict."

The reasoned verdict has practical consequences for the Spanish jury. A verdict that does not include reasons or that includes reasons that the trial judge finds to be inadequate can be returned to the jury. An appeal to the jury's final verdict must be lodged on specific legal grounds, which is not usual in Spain for ordinary appeals; for this reason, it is considered to be an extraordinary proceeding (Villagómez Cebrián, 1998). After an initial appeal, the only other extraordinary appeal to the verdict must take place before the Supreme Court in Madrid (LeCrim, Art. 847). This extraordinary appeal, called cassation (*casación*), can occur when a High Court Justice delivers a judgment that the jury has made an "error in the evaluation of the evidence," but it is unclear what constitutes such an error (Montero Aroca, 1998). To reduce the likelihood of error, the court clerk is permitted to participate in the drafting of the verdict and to assist the jurors in providing their reasons so that they can achieve clarity of expression. Although the law limits the court clerk to assisting the jurors with strictly "drawing up" or "recording" the minutes, it is sometimes difficult to draw the line between the court clerk's assistance with merely writing and his or her assistance with providing reasoning (Jimeno-Bulnes & Hans, 2016). Jimeno-Bulnes and Hans (2016) found that court clerks took different approaches to their duties, with some adopting a narrow interpretation of acceptable assistance and others providing a broader range of assistance to the jury.

There has been a lot of debate about what constitutes adequate reasons for a jury verdict (Lorca Navarrete, 2012; Pedraz Penalva, 1992). After all, Article 120(3) of the Spanish Constitution provides that "judgments shall always contain the grounds therefore, and they shall be delivered in a public hearing." If the Spanish legislature had intended jurors to give reasons, it could have opted for the mixed court model. Requiring juries to give reasons for their verdicts has proven to be a stumbling block for many juries. In the early years of the Spanish jury system, close to half of the jury verdicts lacked adequate reasoning (Serra Domínguez, 2001). Although Spanish juries continue to be challenged by the requirement to give reasons for their verdict, the reasoned verdict enjoys support among some academics (Blom-Cooper, 2019; Coen & Doak, 2017) and in the European Court of Human Rights (*Taxquet* v. *Belgium*, 2010; Daly, 2010; Thaman, 2011).

Adapting the Spanish Judicial System to the Jury

The introduction of trial by jury in Spain required some changes in the way that lawyers, judges, and other participants in the trial perform their roles. Judges, prosecutors, and defense counsel have yet to adapt fully to the presence of jurors and to this new form of jury trial (Ramos Méndez, 1997). A group of experts circulated a list of linguistic suggestions to help judges and lawyers communicate more effectively with jurors and the public at large (Casanovas Romeu, 1997, 1999). Yet judges and lawyers continue to use formal language in the courtrooms, and jurors do not always understand it. The judge's need to communicate effectively with jurors becomes most acute when the judge is "summing up" (instructions, or *instrucciones*) the case for the jury. The Spanish judge is not the only one to face this challenge. Judges in common-law countries, such as the United States, face this problem when they deliver jury instructions. In the United States, for example, "jury instructions are written in a language intended for lawyers rather than laypersons and [...] jurors have difficulty understanding the instructions" (Marder, 2006, p. 451); in the words of the same author, "[jury instructions] rely on legal terms of art, complex sentence structure, and an overarching organization that is difficult to discern" (Marder, 2006, p. 451). Pattern instructions exacerbate the problem because "the language is typically drawn from case law or statutes and written in general terms" (Marder, 2006, p. 451). Spanish judges in their summing up, like American judges in their jury instructions, face similar challenges. They both have to communicate important information to jurors in language that they can understand.

The Preamble of the Spanish Jury Law makes clear "one of the keys to the success or failure of trial by jury is contained in the instructions" (Jury Law, 1995, Part 5.2) delivered by the trial judge to the jury. The instructions are critical because they make up "for any deficiencies that may arise from technical ignorance of the law" (Jury Law, 1995, Part 5.2).

At the same time, the judge's summing up is to help the jury reach a verdict that is consistent with the facts as presented at trial and the law as instructed by the judge. However, the traditional jury, as found in many common-law countries, and now adopted for certain offenses in Spain, leaves it to the jurors to decide how the law that the judge has given them should be applied to the facts as they have found them. Jurors try to reach a verdict that makes sense to them. Some social scientists have observed that juries follow a "story model" in that they try to put together the evidence in the case so that it creates a coherent narrative (Hastie, Penrod, & Pennington, 1986). One justification for having jurors give reasons for their verdict is so that it is clear to the parties and the public that their verdict is based on acceptable reasons, but jurors cannot always articulate the reasons for their verdict or agree with one another on the same reasons (Jimeno-Bulnes, 2007).

The trial judge gives instructions in "a didactic manner directed at ensuring that the verdict will be in keeping with the requirements of the law," and for this reason, "the communicative skills of the trial judge assume a very important role" (Valero Romero, 2018, p. 48). Early case law in Spain recognized this important function of the trial judge's instructions. For example, the Supreme Court in Judgment num. 364/1998 of March 11 (STS, March 11, 1998) explained that "the fundamental purpose of the instructions to the jury is so that they can be effectively understood by ordinary people, in other words, by laypersons with no knowledge of the law."

With respect to the timing of the instructions, one recommendation is to give all or some of the instructions at the beginning of the trial (*juicio oral*) so that jurors have a framework in which to understand the trial (Smith, 1991). When the judge provides instructions early in the proceedings, the instructions can serve as a "guide or frame of reference" for jurors to interpret the evidence as it is presented during the trial (De Paul Velasco, 1993a, p. 86). For example, if jurors are instructed about the presumption of innocence and the standard of "beyond a reasonable doubt" before the evidence is presented in court, then they will be able to keep those concepts in mind as they view the evidence. Moreover, if jurors have a deeper understanding of the trial, it will help them to defer any decision until the deliberations, rather than drawing hasty conclusions.

Early instructions are also important because they help keep the jury focused on its task throughout the trial. Without early instructions, there is a danger that extralegal elements might have greater influence on jurors (De Paul Velasco, 1993b). For example, it is important for jurors not to be swayed by the parties' background characteristics such as their race, gender, or religion. The instructions remind jurors to focus on the evidence, not on these other characteristics, just like American judges instruct jurors to focus on the evidence and not on other considerations (Marder, 2015). It is difficult to reconcile any consideration of extralegal factors with the guarantee of the impartiality of the jury and the right of the defendant (and victim) to a fair trial, as provided in Article 24(2) of the Spanish Constitution, Article 6(1) of the European Convention of Human Rights, and other international treaties also recognized in the Spanish Constitution under Article 10(2).

Many observers of the Spanish jury assume that legally trained professional judges in Spain are immune to bias from extralegal factors. However, a line of research based on US and Canadian judges shows that professionally trained judges are also susceptible to such influences (Hans, 2012). Therefore, the assumption that Spanish judges are immune to factors that influence lay jurors may not be warranted.

Another extralegal factor of a different type is the publicity that can surround cases prior to the trial by jury, which must indeed have certain limits (Marder, 2009). According to empirical research, pretrial publicity can influence jurors. Today, the power of media is complex; there are myriad forms of media, including radio, newspapers, television, the internet, and social media. With the omnipresence of media, jurors may be influenced not only during the pretrial phase, but also during the trial itself (Vidmar, 1999), in spite of any specific instructions to ignore what they have already read or seen and to avoid any media coverage of the trial while they are serving as jurors.

STATE OF THE JURY: SOME STATISTICS AND EXAMPLES

This section will provide a snapshot view of how the Jury Law is working in Spain by offering statistics and examples from the 25 years that the Jury Law has existed. In terms of statistics, the reports published by public institutions in Spain reveal interesting differences in how the jury is working in different regions and provinces in Spain. Several examples are based on firsthand experiences in the courts of the province of Burgos. In Spain, there are cameras in the courthouses, unlike in federal courts in the United States, where the debate still "arouses strong passions on both sides" (Marder, 2012, p. 1491). As a result, high-profile jury trials in Spain receive extensive coverage in the media; this fact can be more harmful in jury trials than in trials before judges.

Assessing the Spanish Jury according to Its Statistics

The General Council of the Judiciary Branch (*Consejo General del Poder Judicial*, or CGPJ) posts annual reports and statistics on its website. Statistics by the CGPJ reveal significant differences between the number and type of criminal cases decided in each Spanish province. The CGPJ published reports in 1998, 1999, and on the occasion of the twentieth anniversary of the Jury Law in 2015. The General Attorney's Government Office (*Fiscalía General del Estado*, or FGE) also serves as a source of information about the Jury Law in Spain. Jury trial statistics from the early years of the Spanish jury and from its twentieth anniversary offer an interesting comparison in terms of the challenges faced by new and established jury systems.

The Spanish Jury in the Early Years

In the first 14 months following the introduction of the Jury Law, from November 23, 1995, until March 31, 1997, there was a total of 76 jury proceedings in Spain (CGPJ

Report, 1998). Provinces varied in their adoption of jury trial procedures: 31 provincial courts had jury trials; there were no jury trials in the other 20 provincial courts during this period. Some provinces had a greater number of jury trials in the early years of the Jury Law than in more recent years. For example, Barcelona and Madrid had the highest number of jury trials (nine each) in this early period.

The length of jury proceedings during this early period of the Jury Law also varied considerably, from the receipt of the file in the provincial court, through pretrial proceedings, and ending at the judgment. Jury proceedings ranged from three months, for a criminal case in Ciudad Real (Castile–La Mancha) for bribery to over two years for a jury trial in Valencia for a crime of failure to render assistance. Typically, however, jury proceedings took between 6 to 13 months, with the average proceeding lasting 9 months.

Similarly, there was a difference in the types of offenses that were heard by a jury in this early period of the Jury Law. Juries heard unlawful killing cases most often (42 cases), followed at some distance by trespassing a dwelling (19 cases), intimidation (15 cases), crimes against public administration (8 cases), failure in the duty to assist (7 cases), and, finally, forest fires (2 cases). The small number of cases for certain offenses, such as those against the public administration, is significant. The number of cases for failure in the duty to assist was also low, as was the even lower number of cases for forest fires. The low number of both of these types of cases might be attributable to the difficulty of identifying the guilty party.

The most surprising statistic was for offenses involving intimidation. In spite of how often this crime is perpetrated, the number of cases judged in the jury courts remained very low. The reason might be because the same facts involved in the crime of intimidation can also be the basis for misdemeanors or minor offenses. Misdemeanors or minor offenses are heard by the investigating judge, rather than by the jury. The General Council of the Judiciary Branch has described this situation as "escaping the jury trial" (CGPJ Report, 1998, p. 74). The outcomes change from one province to another depending on how the offense is categorized for each specific case.

Admittedly, the numbers provided by this report offer only a snapshot. However, if those cases that ended with a "conformity sentence" or "handing down" (plea bargaining) and therefore never proceeded to trial by jury are excluded, then the revised numbers based on types of crime would be as follows: 32 jury trials for unlawful killing, 8 jury trials for trespassing a dwelling, 4 jury trials for intimidation, 2 jury trials for failure in the duty to assist, and 1 jury trial for forest fires. Interestingly, plea bargaining is used most often in crimes against the public administration (7 cases).

The early CGPJ report also suggested that juries might be more inclined to render not-guilty verdicts. Of the 54 verdicts delivered during the period of the first report, 30% of the juries' verdicts were not-guilty verdicts, whereas 20% of the verdicts by professional judges and tribunals were not-guilty verdicts. Although the selection of cases for jury proceedings might also be responsible for these differences, the figures hint at the greater "benevolence" of the jury and support the traditional view that juries are more lenient than judges, which is a characteristic for which juries have been both praised and criticized (Devine, Olafson, Jarvis, Bott, Clayton, & Wolfe, 2004; Hans, 2012). This is one of the standard arguments used both for and against the institution of the jury. Some writers have attributed the leniency of the jury to the presence of female jurors (Fletcher, 1996). However, studies in the United States found that gender did not affect verdict outcomes, except in two specific types of cases (death penalty and rape cases) (Marder, 1987). A landmark study in the United States found that criminal juries were more lenient than judges in certain grey areas of the law, but in three-quarters of the cases in that study, judges and juries reached the same verdict (Kalven & Zeisel, 1966).

The second CGPJ report (1999) examined the jury trials that occurred between April 1, 1997, and March 31, 1998. Compared with the 76 jury cases in the first report, the 195 cases in the second report represents a very substantial increase in a single year. One explanation for the small number of jury cases observed in the first report could be that the investigation for a jury trial took longer than for a judge trial; thus, some of the cases that arose during the first report were still being investigated in the first year and were not heard by a jury until the second year of the Jury Law. During the period covered by the second report, 44 provincial courts heard jury cases, up from 31 provincial courts in the first 14 months of adoption of the Jury Law. Thus, between the first report and the second, the number of jury trials had increased and the provinces in which there were jury trials had also expanded.

However, even by the time of the second CGPJ report, there was still disagreement among provincial courts about which types of cases should be heard by a jury. As in the first reporting period, some cases were still "escaping the jury trial." These cases include either the reclassification of the offense as a misdemeanor to be heard by an investigating judge or a plea bargain giving rise to a conformity sentence, as I will next describe.

In terms of guilty or not-guilty verdicts, 30% of not-guilty verdicts in the first 14 months decreased to 19% (excluding plea bargains) in the second time period (CGPJ Report, 1999). The lower percentage of not-guilty verdicts delivered by juries in the second time period is the same as the percentage of acquittals (20%) handed down by professional judges and courts in that same time period. The report also noted some improvements. As explained earlier, the Spanish Jury Law has a requirement that the jury must provide reasons for its verdict, which was problematic and led to appeals and the setting aside of jury verdicts. In the period covered by the second report, the General Council of the Judiciary Branch found that juries' reasons for their verdicts improved. Approximately half of the jury verdicts contained an acceptable reason, as deduced from the verdict minutes.

The reports of the first few years of trial by jury in Spain showed a new institution gradually gaining acceptance across the provinces. Trials became more common and most provinces held jury trials. Fully 322 jury cases were successfully resolved by the end of 1998, though large differences remained among the various provinces. However, several problems emerged or persisted during this time period, including lack of adequately reasoned verdicts, cases that were not sent to the jury, reclassification of crimes so that judges would decide those cases, and plea bargaining.

The Spanish Jury at 20 Years

The General Council of the Judiciary Branch report in 2015 was drafted in commemoration of the twentieth anniversary of the Spanish Jury Law, covering the period from the implementation of the Jury Law in 1995 until its twentieth anniversary in 2015. It offers a useful picture of longer-term development and the current status of trial by jury in Spain. During this period, there was a general decline in the number of jury trials across Spain. For example, the number of jury trials in 2015 was just 50% of the jury trials in the early years. This is attributable to two developments. One development was the increasing restrictions on when juries could hear cases, as articulated by Supreme Court case law. The other development was the growing use of plea agreements between criminal defendants and the prosecution.

A total of 10,407 new cases were identified for jury trial proceedings in Spain between 1996 and 2014 (CGPJ Report, 2015). An additional 392 cases were reinstated, adding to the total. Again, there are differences in numbers according to the different Spanish regions. The highest number of new cases for jury trials was in Andalusia (1,919 cases) and Catalonia (1,821 cases), followed by Madrid (1,251 cases). The high numbers in Andalusia and Catalonia are not surprising because these regions are the most populous in Spain. The lowest number of jury cases was in La Rioja (61 cases), which is the least populated region in Spain.

During the same period, 1996–2014, the courts resolved a total of 10,440 cases. Yet just 5,848 cases were forwarded from the offices of the investigating judge to the provincial courts, where jury trials are held. Only those cases that go to the provincial courts can proceed to the trial phase (*juicio oral*), assuming the offense is one that is entitled to a jury trial. The case can be dismissed for the same reasons contained in the general rules (LECrim, Arts. 637 and 642), such as the lack of evidence that a crime has been committed or the existence of facts that do not constitute a crime. Regional courts such as High Courts of Justice may also hold jury trials.

Contrary to studies elsewhere that have found that juries are more lenient than judges, the statistics in Spain from 1995 to 2015 show that juries reached guilty verdicts in 89.2% of the cases they heard. A total of 6,171 judgments in jury proceedings by provincial courts and High Courts of Justice were delivered between 1996 and 2014, of which 5,503 were convictions and only 664 were acquittals. The percentage of convictions (89%) in jury trials was higher than the percentage of convictions in other criminal proceedings determined by judges, such as the ordinary proceeding provided for more serious offenses with punishment up to nine years of imprisonment (84%) and abbreviated proceedings provided for offenses punished under or equal to nine years of imprisonment or other penalties (80%).

The twentieth anniversary report provides figures that show that plea bargaining continues to play a role in resolving criminal cases, which could pose a threat to the jury in Spain. In fact, according to Article 50 of the Jury Law, a plea bargain should only be reached after the completion of the jury trial. However, in some cases, a plea bargain was in fact reached before the jury trial and even before the commencement of jury selection. For example, in a case of unlawful killing before the Provincial Court of Lugo, in which the criminal defendant suffered a temporary mental illness, the prosecution and the defense disagreed only over the type of custodial sentence to be imposed, and their disagreement was settled in a hearing before a judge, rather than a jury. This approach has now become the general practice (Jimeno-Bulnes, 2011).

HIGH-PROFILE JURY TRIALS AND THE ROLE OF THE MEDIA

Several high-profile cases over the past 25 years of jury trials in Spain illustrate the challenges posed by the reasoned verdict and the effect of extensive media coverage. Without a doubt, the *Otegi* case was the most controversial case in Spain's past 25 years of jury trials and attracted an inordinate amount of media attention (Thaman, 1998). The *Otegi* case illustrates the challenges of both the reasoned verdict and the role of the media in covering jury trials in Spain. Other high-profile cases received enormous public attention and media coverage; such cases included well-known victims who were local or regional politicians and the unlawful killing of women and minors.

The Otegi *Case and the Role of the Reasoned Verdict*

The most surprising verdict in the past 25 years of jury trials in Spain was the verdict in the well-known *Otegi* case. Several foreign and national writers have written commentaries on the case (Hendler, 2006; Igartúa Salaverria, 1998; Thaman, 1998). Mikel Otegi Unanue, the defendant in the *Otegi* case, was a sympathizer of "Jarrai," the youth wing of the *Coordinadora Abertzale Socialista*, a nationalist group sympathizing with the terrorist organization *Euskadi Ta Askatasuna* (Basque Country and Freedom, henceforth ETA). Otegi considered himself to be constantly harassed by the Basque police. One day, after drinking at a bar with friends, he returned home in the afternoon and opened the door to two policemen, who were afterward found shot in his house with his shotgun. Public and private prosecutors charged Mikel Otegi with two counts of murder and two counts of attacks on public officials. The defense alleged the complete excuse of temporary insanity due to drunkenness and extreme emotional disturbance caused by Basque police harassment. The jury's verdict declared that Mikel Otegi was not guilty of the murder of the two Basque policemen and the acquittal was announced by the trial judge of the Provincial Court of Guipúzcoa on March 10, 1997 (SAP Guipúzcoa, March 10, 1997). Many described the acquittal as "scandalous" (Hernández, 2000). There was stern criticism as well as a heated debate in the media about the viability of the Spanish jury system. Defense counsel also took the opportunity to make public its point of view (Forest, 1997).

However, the High Court of Justice of the Basque Country overruled the acquittal on appeal on June 26, 1997 (STSJ País Vasco, June 26, 1997), based on "the existence of errors in the verdict" according to Article 846 bis (a) of the Criminal Procedure Act. In brief, the High Court held that the jury verdict was not supported by adequate reasons. Moreover, the nullity of the verdict was confirmed by the Supreme Court in a final appeal or cassation through Judgment num. 364/1998 of March 11 (STS, March 11, 1998). The Supreme Court's reversal of the jury's verdict in the *Otegi* case should have led to another trial before a different jury, but it never took place because the defendant fled. Spanish criminal procedural law requires the presence of the criminal defendant at the trial, except in certain limited instances. In the wake of the *Otegi* case, there were several proposed amendments to the Jury Law, including a change from the classic jury to a mixed court system. However, this draft law, proposed by the conservative Popular Party on March 11, 1997 (Proposición no de Ley presentada por el Grupo Parlamentario Popular en el Congreso, de reforma de la Ley Orgánica del Tribunal del Jurado), was unsuccessful (Fairén Guillén, 1997).

Jury Trials and Media

Other high-profile cases illustrate the effect of extensive media coverage. The media coverage is due more to extralegal factors than to the legal dispute, such as the severity of the offense (usually unlawful killing) and the circumstances and identity of the perpetrators or victims. In some cases, perpetrators or victims are well-known politicians in local or regional governments; in other cases, the victims are women and minors, whose greater defenselessness attracts public attention in a special way. In all of these cases, there is extensive media attention in a variety of types of media (national and local newspapers, radio, television, and internet).

The *Wanninkhof* case (SAP Málaga, September 25, 2001) was another high-profile case involving a reversal of a jury's decision on the ground of an inadequately reasoned verdict. The High Court of Justice of Andalusia in Granada delivered its judgment on February 1, 2002. It reversed a guilty verdict because of the absence of individualized evidence in the reasoning of the jury. The case involved the murder of a 19-year-old, Rocío Wanninkhof. The Supreme Court affirmed the reversal of this judgment on March 12, 2003 (STS, March 12, 2003). It was headline news in *El País*. The newspaper reported that "the Supreme [Court] orders a new jury to judge the 'Wanninkhof case': four magistrates against one considered that the verdict contained deficient reasoning" (De la Cuadra, 2003). However, the *Wanninkhof* case became well-known as the first example of a wrongful conviction in a jury trial. The real murderer, Tony Alexander King, was later found guilty after a DNA test implicated him, and the defendant was released after having served 17 months in prison. The case left the jury "up against the ropes" yet again, with some scholars arguing for its demise (Igartúa Salaverria, 2004).

The *Gürtel* case (Jimeno Bulnes, 2014), which involved politicians in public institutions, town halls, and regional governments, also attracted media attention in Spain and caused a public furor. Several politicians were accused of various offenses related to their duty in public administration. One of the greatest high-profile criminal proceedings involved Francisco Camps Ortiz, former president of the Valencian Autonomous Community. The trial was colloquially dubbed the "trial of suits" because of the excessive number of suits that Francisco Camps was alleged to have been given as gifts in return for political favors. The case had also a second colloquial name: *Gürtel*, the German word for "belt," after the surname of the presumed leader of the extortion, Francisco Correa (*correa* means "belt" in Spanish). The investigation of the case and the jury trial were broadcast daily on television, so that Camps and the other three defendants became familiar faces. Their acquittals were announced in Judgment num. 2/2012 of January 30 by the High Court of Justice of the Valencian Community (STSJ Comunidad Valenciana, January 30, 2012). The not-guilty verdict was very controversial, but the Supreme Court affirmed the verdict following a final appeal, in Judgment num. 323/2013 of April 23 (STS, April 23, 2013).

There have been further controversial and high-profile cases in the past decade, such as the *Asunta* case (SAP A Coruña, November 11, 2015) and the *Carrasco* case (SAP León, March 10, 2016). The first one related to the murder of a 12-year-old girl of Chinese origin, and the second one involved the murder of a well-known politician in Castile and León where, for the first time, the trial judge amended the verdict by acquitting one of the accused. These cases received a lot of media attention, as will other cases in the future. In all of these cases there is a risk that the media coverage will influence the public in general and the jurors in particular (Groscup, 2019). It is a fact that jury trials attract special attention by the media; there are not many jury trials in Spain and a great number of them involve the most serious crimes, such as unlawful killing. Such "media overexposure" produces almost a "parallel trial" taking place outside of the courtroom and developing at the same time as the court case (Campaner Muñoz, 2019, p. 183). Of course, no information on jurors' personal data is given out, but much information on victims, perpetrators, and the circumstances of the crime are publicized throughout Spain. Commentators have debated whether this excessive publicity of the criminal proceedings in general before and during the trial is compatible with the right to a fair trial (Jimeno-Bulnes, 1993).

CONCLUSION

The development of jury trials in Spain over the past 25 years has been peaceful, but there has been a significant decrease in the number of jury trials. There are several reasons for the decline in the number of jury trials, including restrictions on types of cases that juries can decide, and plea-bargaining agreements between prosecution and defense even before the selection of the jury (Jimeno-Bulnes, 2011). Moreover, the trial judges' increasing power can jeopardize the impartiality of the jury through the instructions and the rules of evidence applied to jury trials under Article 46 of the Jury Law (Domingo Monforte, Sala Paños, Gimeno, & Pellicar, 2018).

As countervailing forces to these challenges to the jury trial in Spain, I would point to the jury's social and legal acceptance. The jury institution has overcome many of the initial problems, such as inadequately reasoned verdicts. Finally, the jury system enforces the accusatorial and adversarial characteristics of Spanish criminal procedure in contrast to any other Spanish criminal proceedings carried out according to the inquisitorial model. Now every charge must be proven during the trial without any reference to the investigative dossier, which is not shown to the jurors.

However, this chapter has identified some weaknesses of the jury system in Spain as revealed by 25 years of experience. One weakness is the tremendous media coverage of some jury trials, which interferes with the normal development of the criminal process and runs the risk of unfairness to the parties. Also, the different applications and interpretations of the Jury Law in the provincial courts in Spain has led to imbalances in the prosecution of offenses under the jurisdiction of the Jury Court.

In spite of these problems and multiple efforts to amend the Jury Law, it has remained basically unchanged since 1995. The sole exception is the guarantee of the participation of people with disabilities (Garcimartín Montero, 2018). Currently, the jury is not on the list for further reforms of criminal procedure in Spain. For these reasons, I believe that the jury will continue to endure in Spain. Moreover, jury trials have spread to a number of countries, especially in Latin America (Porterie & Romano, 2018; Ríos Patio & Espinoza Bonifaz, 2018). Although this expansion might be due to the influence of the North American jury system, it might also be due to the influence of the Spanish jury system, as there is little doubt that we speak the same language.

Acknowledgments: My special gratitude to Professors Valerie Hans and Nancy Marder for their support as well as to Antony Ross Price for his English review of the manuscript.

REFERENCES

Belloch Julbe, J. A. (2000). La ley del jurado [The jury law]. *Revista Vasca de Derecho Procesal y Arbitraje*, *12*, 323–333.

Bermúdez Requena, J. M. (1998). La objeción de conciencia y el jurado [Conscientious objection and the jury]. *Actualidad Penal*, *27*, 489–498.

Blom-Cooper, L. (2019). *Unreasoned verdict: The jury's out*. Oxford: Bloomsbury.
Burgos Ladrón de Guevara, J. (1997). La institución del jurado en España: Delimitación constitucional y legal [The institution of the jury in Spain: Constitutional and legal limits]. *Justicia*, 3–4, 1127–1140.
Campaner Muñoz, J. (2019). *Publicidad y secreto del proceso penal en la sociedad de la información* [Publicity and secrecy of criminal proceedings in the information society]. Madrid: Dykinson.
Cano Barrero, J. (2007). *La ley del jurado: Jurisprudencia comentada. Diez años de la aplicción de la ley del jurado* [The Jury Law: Annotated jurisprudence. Ten years of the application of the Jury Law]. Cizur Menor, Spain: Aranzadi.
Casanovas Romeu, P. (1997). Pragmática de las decisiones judiciales: Diferencias de razonamiento y lenguaje ante el jurado [Pragmatics of judicial decisions: Differences in reasoning and language before the jury]. In J. Bayo Delgado (Ed.), *Lenguaje judicial* [Legal language] (pp. 109–142). Madrid: Consejo General del Poder Judicial.
(1999). Intervención de las partes en el proceso de selección y designación de los jurados: Atención a los criterios de decisión de los candidatos; estrategias de comunicación [Involvement of the parties in the process of selection and appointment of jurors: Attention to the criteria for deciding on candidates; communication strategies]. In Ministerio de Justicia (Ed.), *Estudios jurídicos: Cuerpo de secretarios judiciales V-1999* [Legal studies: The group of court clerks V-1999] (pp. 383–400). Madrid: Centro de Estudios de la Administración de Justicia.
Coen, M., & Doak, J. (2017). Embedding explained jury verdicts in the English criminal trial. *Legal Studies*, 37, 786–806.
Consejo General del Poder Judicial [General Council of the Judiciary Branch (Spain)] reports. (1998, 1999, & 2015). www.poderjudicial.es/cgpj/es/Temas/Estadistica-Judicial/Estadistica-por-temas/Actividad-de-los-organos-judiciales
Constitución Española, aprobada por las Cortes el 31 de octubre de 1978 [Spanish Constitution, approved by the Courts on October 31, 1978]. www.congreso.es/constitucion/ficheros/c78/cons_ingl.pdf
Daly, T. (2010). An endangered species? The future of the Irish criminal jury system in light of *Taxquet v. Belgium*. *Irish Criminal Law Journal*, 20, 34–43.
De la Cuadra, B. (2003, March 15). El Tribunal Supremo ordena que un nuevo jurado sentencie sobre la muerte de Rocío Wanninkhof [Supreme Court orders new jury to rule on Rocio Wanninkhof's death]. *El País*. https://elpais.com/diario/2003/03/15/espana/1047682808_850215.html
De Paul Velasco, P. (1993a). De la composición y del veredicto del jurado: Comentarios psicológicos al Anteproyecto de Ley del Jurado [Of the composition and verdict of the jury: Psychological comments on the Jury Law's draft bill]. *Jueces para la democracia*, 20, 84–86.
(1993b). Factores extralegales que influyen en la toma de decisiones de los miembros del jurado [Extra-legal factors influencing jury members' decision-making]. *Cuadernos de Política Criminal*, 50, 657–666.
De Vega Ruiz, J. A. (1989). El jurado y el juez ordinario y predeterminado por la ley [The jury and the ordinary judge, predetermined by law]. *La Ley*, 3, 899–908.
Devine, D. J., Olafson, K. M., Jarvis, L. L., Bott, J. P., Clayton, L. D., & Wolfe, J. (2004). Explaining jury verdicts: Is leniency bias for real? *Journal of Applied Social Psychology*, 34, 2069–2098.
Domingo Monforte, J., Sala Paños, D., Gil Gimeno, C., & Calvo Pellicer, S. (2018). Triada y triage de cuestiones problemáticas en el juicio con tribunal de jurado [Triad and triage of problematic issues in the jury trial]. *Diario La Ley*, 9142. http://diariolaley.laley.es

Esparza Leibar, I. (1995). El jurado en los Estados Unidos de Norteamérica: Problemática general. El procedimiento de selección [The jury in the United States of America: General issues. The selection process]. *Revista de Derecho Procesal*, *1*, 295–311.

(2000). Algunas cuestiones sobre el veredicto en la ley del jurado [Some questions about the verdict in jury law]. *Revista Tribunales de Justicia*, *4*, 451–460.

Fairén Guillén, V. (1997). Sobre la "proposición no de ley" para la reforma de la Ley orgánica del Tribunal del Jurado, de 11 de marzo de 1997 [On the "non-legislative proposal" (bill draft) for the reform of the Organic Law on the Jury Court, of March 11, 1997]. *Revista de Derecho Procesal*, *3*, 695–744.

Ferrer Ortiz, J. (2003). La objeción de conciencia al jurado [Conscientious objection to the jury]. *Revista General de Derecho Canónico y Derecho Eclesiástico del Estado*, *2*. www.iustel.com

Fidalgo Gallardo, C. (1998). La intimidación de los jurados [The intimidation of jurors]. *Justicia*, *1–2*, 171–276.

Fiscalía General del Estado [General Attorney's Government Office (Spain)] reports. (2019). www.fiscal.es/documentación

Fletcher, G. (1996). *Las víctimas ante el jurado* [The victims before the jury]. (Spanish edition). Valencia: Tirant lo Blanch. (Original work, *With Justice for Some: Victims' Rights in Criminal Trials*, published 1995).

Forest, E. (1997). *¿Proceso al jurado?: conversaciones con Miguel Castells* [Jury trial: conversations with Miguel Castells]. Hondarribia, Spain: Hiru D. L.

Garcimartín Montero, R. (2018). *La inclusion de las personas con discapacidad en el Tribunal del Jurado: Un análisis a la luz de la reforma de la LO 1/2017, de 13 de diciembre* [The inclusion of people with disabilities in the Jury Court: An analysis in the light of the reform of LO 1/2017 of December 13]. San Sebastián: Instituto Vasco de Derecho Procesal.

Gimeno Sendra, V. (2015). *Manual de derecho procesal penal* [Handbook of criminal procedure law]. Madrid: Castillo de Luna Ediciones Jurídicas.

Gleadow, C. (2000). *History of trial by jury in the Spanish legal system*. Lewinston, NY: Edwin Mellen Press.

Gómez Colomer, J. L. (1996). *El proceso penal especial ante el tribunal del jurado* [The special criminal procedure before the jury court]. Madrid, Spain: Civitas.

Grande, E. (2016). Rumba justice and the Spanish jury trial. In J. E. Ross & S. C. Thaman (Eds.), *Comparative criminal procedure* (pp. 365–395). Cheltenham, UK: Edward Elgar Publishing.

Groscup, J. L. (2019). The impact of legally relevant media exposure on criminal juror decision-making. In C. J. Najdowski & M. C. Stevenson (Eds.), *Criminal juries in the 21st century* (pp. 133–154). New York: Oxford University Press.

Hans, V. P. (2002). US jury reform: The active jury and the adversarial ideal. *Saint Louis University Public Law Review*, *21*, 85–97.

(2012). What difference does a jury make? *Yonsei Law Journal*, *3*, 37–54.

Hastie, R., Penrod, S. D., & Pennington, N. (1986). *La institución del jurado en los Estados Unidos: Sus intimidades* [The institution of the jury in the United States: Its intimacies]. (Spanish edition.) Madrid: Civitas. (Original work, *Inside the Jury*, published 1983.)

Hendler, E. S. (2006). *El juicio por jurados: Significados, genealogías, incógnitas* [The trial by jury: Significance, genealogies, unknowns]. Buenos Aires: Editores del Puerto.

Hernández, J. A. (2000, February 4). El escándalo del caso Otegi [The scandal of the Otegi case]. *El País*. https://elpais.com/diario/2000/02/04/sociedad/949618802_850215.html

Igartúa Salaverria, J. (1998). El jurado y la motivación de su veredicto (A propósito de la STS sobre el "caso Otegi") [The jury and the reasons for its verdict (About STS on the "Otegi case")]. *Revista vasca de Administración Pública*, 51, 215–235.

(2004). El caso Wanninkhof ¿un tiro de gracia al jurado? [The Wanninkhof case: A coup de grace to the jury?] *Jueces para la democracia*, 50, 63–74.

Jimeno-Bulnes, M. (1993). El principio de publicidad en el sumario [The principle of publicity in pretrial instruction]. *Justicia*, 3–4, 645–717.

(2001). La institución del jurado en el Reino Unido y el régimen especial de Irlanda del Norte [The institution of the jury in the United Kingdom and the special regime in Northern Ireland]. *Revista de Derecho Procesal*, 1–3, 343–404.

(2004). Lay participation in Spain: The jury system. *International Criminal Justice Review*, 14, 164–185.

(2007). A different story line for *12 Angry Men*: Verdicts reached by majority rule – The Spanish perspective. *Chicago-Kent Law Review*, 82, 759–775.

(2011). Jury selection and jury trial in Spain: Between theory and practice. *Chicago-Kent Law Review*, 86, 585–611.

(2013). American criminal procedure in a European context. *Cardozo Journal of International and Comparative Law*, 21, 409–459.

(2014). Un ejemplo emblemático de juicio por Jurado en España: "El caso *Gürtel*" [An emblematic example of trial by jury in Spain: "The *Gürtel* case"]. *Revista Vasca de Derecho Procesal y Arbitraje*, 26, 1–26.

Jimeno-Bulnes, M., & Hans, V. P. (2016). Legal interpreter for the jury: Role of the clerk of the court in Spain. *Oñati Socio-Legal Series*, 6, 197–615.

Kalven, H., Jr., & Zeisel, H. (1966). *The American jury*. Boston: Little, Brown & Co.

Kutnjak Ivković, S. (2003). An inside view: Professional judges' and lay judges' support for mixed tribunals. *Law & Policy*, 25, 93–122.

(2015). Ears of the deaf: The theory and reality of lay judges in mixed tribunals. *Chicago-Kent Law Review*, 90, 1031–1067.

Ley de Enjuiciamiento Criminal, Real Decreto de 14 de septiembre de 1882 [Criminal Procedure Act (Spain), Royal Decree, of September 14, 1882]. English version updated October 6, 2015. www.mjusticia.gob.es/cs/Satellite/Portal/es/servicios-ciudadano/documentacion-publicaciones/publicaciones/traducciones-derecho-espanol

Ley Orgánica 5/1995, de 22 de mayo, del Tribunal del Jurado [Organic Law 5/1995, of May 22, on the Jury (Spain)]. www.mjusticia.gob.es/cs/Satellite/Portal/es/servicios-ciudadano/documentacion-publicaciones/publicaciones/traducciones-derecho-espanol

Lorca Navarrete, A. M. (2003). La deliberación del Jurado en la declaración del hecho probado y proclamación de la culpabilidad e inculpabilidad del acusado en la doctrina y en la reciente jurisprudencia [The deliberation of the jury in declaring the proven facts and proclaiming the guilt or innocence of the accused in doctrine and recent jurisprudence]. *La Ley*, 2, 1413–1420.

(2005). Décimo aniversario de la ley del jurado (1995–2005) [Tenth anniversary of the Jury Act (1995–2005)]. *Revista Vasca de Derecho Procesal y Arbitraje*, 17, 1–130.

(2012). *El veredicto del jurado* [The jury's verdict]. San Sebastián: Instituto Vasco de Derecho Procesal.

Marder, N. S. (1987). Gender dynamics and jury deliberations. *Yale Law Journal*, 96, 593–612.

(2005). *The jury process*. New York: Foundation Press.

(2006). Bringing jury instructions into the twenty-first century. *Notre Dame Law Review*, 81, 449–512.

(2009). From "practical obscurity" to web disclosure: A new understanding of public information. *Syracuse Law Review*, 59, 441–457.
(2012). The conundrum of cameras in the courtroom. *Arizona State Law Journal*, 44, 1489–1574.
(2015). Juror bias, voir dire, and the judge–jury relationship. *Chicago-Kent Law Review*, 90, 927–956.
Martín Ostos, J. (1990). *Jurado y escabinado (participación popular en la administración de justicia)* [Jury and mixed court (popular participation in the administration of justice)]. Madrid: Dykinson & Instituto Vasco de Derecho Procesal.
Martín Pallín, J. A. (2006). *La ley del jurado en su X aniversario* [The law of the jury on its tenth anniversary]. Cizur Menor, Spain: Aranzadi.
Martínez Torrón, J. (1996). Ley del jurado y objeción de conciencia [The law of the jury and conscientious objection]. *Revista Española de Derecho Constitucional*, 48, 119–143.
Montero Aroca, J. (1998). Ambito del recurso de casación en el proceso especial ante el tribunal del jurado (con ocasión de la STS, Sala 2ª, de 24 de febrero de 1998) [Scope of the appeal in the special proceedings before the jury (on the occasion of the STS, 2nd Chamber, February 24, 1998)]. *Revista de Tribunales de Justicia*, 8–9, 831–841.
Pedraz Penalva, E. (1992). Motivación y control de las resoluciones jurisdiccionales [Grounds for and review of judicial decisions]. *Revista de Ciencias Jurídicas (El Salvador)*, 1, 31–125.
Pérez Gil, J. (2003). Private interests seeking punishment: Prosecution brought by private individuals and groups in Spain. *Law & Policy*, 25, 151–171.
Pérez-Cruz Martín, A. J. (1995). Anotaciones a la competencia y composición del tribunal del jurado: Especial consideración de los arts.1 y 5 de la LO 5/1995 del Tribunal del Jurado *indatada* [Annotations to the competence and composition of the jury court: Special consideration of articles 1 and 5 of the LO 5/1995 of the "non-dated" Jury Court]. *Justicia*, 3–4, 63–97.
Porterie, S., & Romano, A. (2018). *El poder del Jurado: Descubriendo el juicio por jurados en la Provincia de Buenos Aires* [The power of the jury: Discovering the jury trial in the Province of Buenos Aires]. Buenos Aires: INECIP.
Proposición no de Ley presentada por el Grupo Parlamentario Popular en el Congreso, de reforma de la Ley Orgánica del Tribunal del Jurado, Boletín Oficial de las Cortes Generales (BOCG) de 24 de marzo de 1997, Congreso de los Diputados, VI Legislatura, Serie D, Núm. 118, p. 8 [Draft law num. 162/000110 (Spain). BOCG March 24, 1997. Congress. VI legislative period. Series D, num. 118, 8]. www.congreso.es/portal/page/portal/Congreso/Congreso/Iniciativas
Ramos Méndez, F. (1997). La implantación del jurado en el sistema del enjuiciamiento criminal español [The implementation of the jury in the Spanish criminal trial system]. In J. L. Gómez Colomer & J. L. González Cussac (Eds.), *La reforma de la justicia penal. Estudios en homenaje al Prof. Klaus Tiedemann* [Criminal justice reform. Studies in homage to Prof. Klaus Tiedemann] (pp. 337–348). Castellón, Spain: Universitat Jaume I.
Ríos Patio, G., & Espinoza Bonifaz, A. R. (2018). La conveniencia de establecer el sistema de jurado en la justicia penal de los países periféricos hispano americanos [The convenience of establishing the jury system in the criminal justice of the peripheral Hispanic American countries]. *Revista Vasca de Derecho Procesal y Arbitraje*, 30, 273–286.
Sanjurjo Rebollo, B. (1998). Jurados anónimos: Caso de Estados Unidos c. Bowles (Minnesota 1995) [Anonymous jurors: *United States* v. *Bowles* (Minnesota 1995)]. *Revista de Derecho Procesal*, 1, 147–162.

Sentencia de la Audiencia Provincial (SAP) de A Coruña de 11 de noviembre de 2015, JUR 2015/289211 [Provincial Court of A Coruña (Spain), Judgment JUR 205/289211 of November 11, 2015]. https://insignis.aranzadidigital-es

Sentencia de la Audiencia Provincial (SAP) de Guipúzcoa de 10 de marzo de 1997, JUR 1999/211124 [Provincial Court of Guipúzcoa (Spain), Judgment JUR 1999/211124 of March 10, 1997]. https://insignis.aranzadidigital-es

Sentencia de la Audiencia Provincial (SAP) de León de 10 de marzo de 2016, JUR 2016/50968 [Provincial Court of León (Spain), Judgment JUR 2016/50968 of March 10, 2016]. https://insignis.aranzadidigital-es

Sentencia de la Audiencia Provincial (SAP) de Málaga de 25 de septiembre de 2001, ARP 2002/290 [Provincial Court of Málaga (Spain), Judgment ARP 2002/290 of September 25, 2001]. https://insignis.aranzadidigital-es

Sentencia del Tribunal Constitucional (STC) 47/1983, de 31 de mayo [Constitutional Court (Spain), Judgment num. 47/1983 of May 31, 1983]. http://hj.tribunalconstitucional.es/HJ/es/Resolucion/Show/175

Sentencia del Tribunal Superior de Justicia (STSJ) de Andalucía en Granada de 1 de febrero de 2002, ARP 2002/50 [High Court of Justice of Andalusia in Granada (Spain), Judgment ARP 2002/50 of February 1, 2002]. https://insignis.aranzadidigital-es

Sentencia del Tribunal Superior de Justicia (STSJ) del País Vasco de 26 de junio de 1997, ARP 1998/3079 [High Court of Justice of the Basque Country, Judgment ARP 1998/3079 of June 26, 1997]. https://insignis.aranzadidigital-es

Sentencia del Tribunal Superior de Justicia (STSJ) de Comunidad Valenciana de 30 de enero de 2012, ARP 2012/81 [High Court of Justice of the Valencian Community, Judgment ARP 2012/81 of January 30, 2012]. https://insignis.aranzadidigital-es

Sentencia del Tribunal Supremo (STS) 364/1998, de 11 de marzo [Supreme Court (Spain), Judgment num. 364/1998 of March 11, 1998]. www.poderjudicial.es/search/index.jsp

Sentencia del Tribunal Supremo (STS) 279/2003, de 12 de marzo [Supreme Court (Spain), Judgment num. 279/2003 of March 12, 2003]. www.poderjudicial.es/search/index.jsp

Sentencia del Tribunal Supremo (STS) 373/2013, de 23 de abril [Supreme Court (Spain), Judgment num. 373/2013 of April 23, 2013]. www.poderjudicial.es/search/index.jsp

Serra Domínguez, M. (2001). El jurado: Éxito o fracaso [The jury: Success or failure]. In J. Picó i Junoy & X. Abel Lluch (Eds.), *Problemas actuales de la justicia penal* [Current criminal justice issues] (pp. 59–66). Barcelona: Bosch.

Smith, V. L. (1991). Impact of pretrial instruction on jurors' information processing and decision making. *Journal of Applied Psychology*, 76, 220–228.

Taxquet v. Belgium, Judgment num. 926/05 (November 16, 2010). http://hudoc.echr.coe.int/eng?i=001–101739

Thaman, S. C. (1998). Spain returns to trial by jury. *Hastings International and Comparative Law Review*, 21, 241–537.

(2008). *Comparative criminal procedure: A casebook approach*. 2nd ed. Durham, NC: Carolina Academic Press.

(2011). Should criminal juries give reasons for their verdicts? The Spanish experience and the implications of the European Court of Human Rights Decision in *Taxquet* v. *Belgium*. *Chicago-Kent Law Review*, 86, 613–668.

Toharia, J. J. (1985). Los españoles ante el juicio con jurado [Spaniards at the jury trial]. *Documentación Jurídica*, 45–46, 285–297.

(1994). *Actitudes de los españoles ante la Administración de Justicia: Opiniones y aptitudes* [Attitudes of Spaniards toward the administration of justice: Opinions and aptitudes]. Madrid: Centro de Investigaciones Sociológicas.

Valero Romero, M. A. (2018). *La argumentación lingüística en los juicios con Jurado* [Linguistic argumentation in jury trials]. Valencia: Tirant lo Blanch.
Vidmar, N. (1999). Foreword. *Law and Contemporary Problems*, 62, 1–5.
Villagómez Cebrián, M. (1998). *La "apelación" de la sentencia en el juicio con jurado: Estudio del recurso establecido por la L.O. 5/1995 del Tribunal del Jurado* [The "appeal" of the sentence in the jury trial: Study of the appeal established by the Jury Court Law 5/1995]. Bologna, Italy: Real Colegio de España.

PART II

Enduring Systems of Lay Participation

7

"... And My Right"

The Magistrates' Courts in England and Wales

Stefan Machura

Visitors to a court in England and Wales will typically find a panel of lay judges sitting under the royal coat of arms with its inscription *Dieu et mon droit* (God and my right). The legal system of England and Wales is unique in its extensive use of laypersons as decision-makers. In addition to using citizens as jurors and members of administrative and employment tribunals, the legal system calls on citizens to serve as lay magistrates in the magistrates' courts and the Crown Court. Magistrates' courts hear by far most of the criminal cases against adults and minors (there is also the family court, not discussed in this chapter). Magistrates are arbiters of fact and law, and they also sentence offenders, thus exercising the powers of both judge and jury. My discussion here focuses on England and Wales, which make up most of the population of Great Britain. Scotland and Northern Ireland have their own distinctive justice systems.

According to the "union" of magistrates, the Magistrates Association (2016), the role of the magistrates is to provide local justice: "Although the office has evolved significantly, the core principle that justice is participatory *with the community* it serves, rather than something which is simply *done to the community*, is as immutable as it is enduring" (p. 1, emphasis in the original).

Others agree that the goals are to serve the idea of "local justice" and bring in "broader 'experience in life'" than professional judges have (Ames, Szyndler, Burston, Phillips, Keith, Gaunt, Davies, & Mottram, 2011, pp. 17–18). The views and experiences of the people of the court circuit are intended to influence the work of the courts. The contrast is with professional judges who may not be from the area and who have been shaped by legal training and a long legal career. Yet, magistrates have become part of a "centralized bureaucracy" (Donoghue, 2014, p. 944).

The bold involvement of laypersons in a state apparatus is not unproblematic. For example, a basic tension underlying the work of the magistrates arises between the idea of "local justice" and the application of legally established sentencing guidelines, interpreted to the lay judges by their professional court clerk, the legal adviser. Sentencing guidelines are an attempt to structure the magistrates' decision-making so that criminal law is evenly applied. Yet the guidelines limit the discretion of magistrates to tailor the punishment to case facts and the defendant's circumstances (Ward, 2017). The speedy disposal of cases is one of the key objectives of magistrates' courts (Ward, 2017). The government has put in place measures intended to facilitate swift disposal of cases, such as video links and the closure of outlier courts. Forms of diversion remove cases from magistrates. Many cases go into "pre-court diversion," where the police or the prosecution organize programs to deal with minor offending, avoiding a court trial and yielding a less punitive outcome (Robin-D'Cruz & Whitehead, 2019). In addition, there have been cuts to legal aid, the prosecution service, and the police. Together, these developments in the last decade threaten to undermine the ideal of "justice."

The magistrates of England and Wales are a unique legal decision-making group, even compared with lay decision-makers in other parts of the world. They differ from juries (such as criminal juries in the United States), and they differ from lay assessors in mixed courts (such as the *Schöffengericht* in the German lower criminal court). Table 7.1 shows key features of the three types of courts. Whereas a jury is selected for one case and it is up to chance if jurors have prior experience in their role, the magistrates spend many days and years in court, and in most sessions they hear several cases. The German *Schöffengericht* falls between those two, although the lay assessors typically gain some experience. Jurors in the United States are initially selected randomly, but in a subsequent step, the parties can challenge individual jurors, which happens frequently, as defense and prosecution aim for a sympathetic jury. At the magistrates' court and the *Schöffengericht*, challenges are very rare. Lay judges can be suggested by others for their role. In Germany, they are frequently suggested by political parties or other organizations, but they may also volunteer in response to a public call. Lay magistrates in England and Wales have to apply, and they are often asked to apply by sitting magistrates, but they too may come forward in response to a public call. The prestige of the office also differs fundamentally: being a US juror is seen as a citizen's duty, and the random selection process means that those selected for jury service have no reason to view it as a special honor. German lay assessors (*Schöffen*) may feel a sense of duty, but also of honor as the selection process involves many steps and checks. Being a magistrate is a highly esteemed position in English and Welsh society, for reasons explained later in this chapter.

The magistrates essentially *are* the court because they *are* the decision-makers. They have a high feeling of belonging to their bench, whereas *Schöffen* only occasionally work in the lower criminal court which otherwise is run by professional judges, and US jurors are only called up for a very limited period of service. It is thus difficult for *Schöffen* and impossible for jurors to develop the same feeling of belonging to the court.

Table 7.1 also shows the decision-making powers given to the three types of lay decision makers. The court-approved powers are most limited for the US criminal jury, which primarily decides on the guilt of the accused, although it plays an important role in death penalty sentencing and decides on both guilt and sentence in a small number of states. Magistrates make all decisions at the Magistrates' Courts, including for example pretrial remand in custody, procedural directions, guilt, and the sentence. German lay assessors have the same rights as a professional judge in running the hearing; they decide together on procedure, guilt, and sentence, but they have no involvement in the pretrial phase.

The size of US juries varies, with most juries in felony criminal cases consisting of 12 jurors, but in a few jurisdictions the number is smaller. Magistrates typically sit in groups of three, occasionally in groups of two. One of them chairs the trial. There also is a "single judge procedure" with only one magistrate. The German mixed court has a presiding professional judge and two lay assessors.

As the comparison in Table 7.1 shows, the magistrates are the lay decision-makers with the most power: they are involved in pretrial decisions and they have comprehensive powers in the main hearing. The US jury typically hears only the evidence

TABLE 7.1 *Comparison of US criminal jury, magistrates in England and Wales, and lay assessors at German mixed courts* (Schöffen)

	US criminal jury	Magistrates	*Schöffen*
Times of service per year, years of service	jury typically selected for one case	13 days and more, typically with several cases, serve for at least 5 years	about 8–10 days, mostly with several cases, serve for at least 5 years
Selection	randomized procedure, then challenges	self-recruitment; responses to public calls	suggested by organizations, or self-application
Prestige of office	citizen duty	a special honor	duty and honor
Decision powers	generally decide on guilt only; death penalty*	comprehensive, including pretrial decisions	comprehensive, but excluding pretrial decisions
Composition	12 lay jurors*	3 (2) lay magistrates, 1 of them chairperson**	1 presiding professional judge, 2 lay judges
Case investigated by	prosecution and defense	prosecution and defense primarily**	professional judge
Deliberation	jury in deliberation room	magistrates on the bench or in deliberation room (may ask legal adviser to join)	professional and lay judges in deliberation room
Feeling of belonging to court	none	strong identification	minimal

Source: Adapted from Machura, 2001, p. 51.
* There is some variation among states.
** Different for the single judge procedure.

the judge permits and the prosecutor and defense attorney present in arguing their cases. Should a conflict arise between the two parties on a procedural point, a presiding professional judge decides it independently from the jurors. In contrast, the magistrates themselves make those decisions. The case is presented to the magistrates usually by prosecution and defense. In German courts, the presiding professional judge, rather than the parties, investigates the case during the hearing, but any decisions are made together with the lay assessors. Jurors deliberate with each other, separated in their own room. In clear-cut cases, magistrates often decide quickly on the bench, but otherwise they retire into a deliberation room, and they can call their legal adviser to join them. The German mixed court is defined by the joint deliberation, led by the presiding professional judge (Chapter 8, this volume). To summarize, these are three very different forms of lay participation, and the magistrates in England and Wales wield the most power in the cases they handle.

Recent research on how trials are conducted at magistrates' courts suggests that in their current form, the magistrates' courts need reform. Procedural justice requires that defendants be fairly treated by the judges (e.g., Haller & Machura, 1995; Tyler, 2006), that the defendants' views are heard, and that decision-makers are unbiased and respect the rights of defendants. A well-organized, competently conducted trial is also key (Green, Sprott, Madon, & Jung, 2010; Thomas, Ely, & Estep, 2018). It will be shown that several circumstances militate against meeting some of those requirements in magistrates' courts in England and Wales.

With a colleague, the author visited a youth court in a large city for a day in 2015. Then in 2016, the author observed six trial days at the youth court, in three different locations belonging to two different benches in semirural areas. In one court (two observation days), the youth court magistrates also heard adult cases during sessions. Together with postgraduate students, and aided by an observation form, the author watched trials at magistrates' courts on eight days between 2017 and 2019. One court, observed on seven days, was in a semirural location; the other was in a city area. We were able to see several panels of magistrates in different courtrooms, and on three days the work of a district judge magistrates' court. Over the years, the author also had many conversations with magistrates, social workers, lawyers, prosecutors, and other professionals. Some of these occurred in the courtroom during breaks between cases; others took place in court offices or at conferences.

This chapter focuses on the main settings in which lay magistrates work: as a panel of lay judges and sometimes as a single judge. It describes how panels of lay magistrates function, and how they are supported by a legal adviser. Next, the procedures in trials of adults in magistrates' courts are analyzed, followed by an assessment of the impact on the proceedings of court architecture and the use of video links. Issues of social representation are also considered. Professional judges partially replace lay panels at the magistrates' courts, allowing a comparison. Appeals of decisions by magistrates' courts are heard by a panel of a professional judge and lay magistrates at the Crown Court. A closer look at reductions in the number of magistrates, in the number of cases they decide, and in the courts themselves, follows. The youth court is special and is covered in the penultimate section, setting the scene for concluding remarks.

MAGISTRATES' COURTS

The number of professional judges in England and Wales is low relative to other countries. There are roughly 3,000 professional judges "with a primary appointment in judicial roles in courts" (and a further 1,703 judges in administrative and employment tribunals; Ministry of Justice, 2018b, pp. 2–3), whereas Germany, for example, has about 20,300 (Bundesamt für Justiz, 2016). Per capita, there is one professional judge per 12,500 inhabitants in England and Wales (based on a population estimate for 2017 by the Office of National Statistics, 2018), but one per 4,100 in Germany (based on a population estimate for 2018 by Statistisches Bundesamt, 2019). The participation of a large number of lay judges in the administration of justice, as magistrates and to a lesser extent as members of administrative tribunals, makes this low number of professional judges in England and Wales possible.

Magistrates' courts are a time-honored institution, commonly traced back to the Justices of the Peace Act of 1361. The magistrates, sometimes referred to as "Justices of the Peace," numbered 15,003 in April 2018 (Ministry of Justice, 2018b, p. 11). Their main jurisdiction is criminal law. Magistrates sign police search warrants, conduct trials, and make bail and sentencing decisions. They hear by far most of all criminal cases at the magistrates' court, but also participate in appeals at Crown Courts, where they sit in panels with professional judges. Magistrates dealt with the cases of 1.4 million defendants in the 12 months ending September 2017, convicting 1.2 million of them (Ministry of Justice, 2018a).

Criminal cases in England and Wales are divided into three offense categories that determine how they will be handled. In all three categories, magistrates have a function.

1. The most severe crimes ("indictable only cases"), such as murder, robbery, and rape, move to the Crown Court following a finding by the magistrates that the prosecution has a prima facie case. If a case goes to trial in the Crown Court, a professional judge presides over a jury trial, although most defendants plead guilty rather than go to trial.
2. "Triable either way offenses," which include theft, burglary, arson, and some assaults, can be dealt with by the magistrates' courts or the Crown Court. The magistrates will consider whether their sentencing powers – detailed in the next section – are sufficient for the case. If not, they pass it on. Scholars assert that magistrates tend to follow the prosecution's recommendation (Cammiss & Cunningham, 2015; Cownie, Bradney, & Burton, 2013). The recommendation tends to be the product of negotiation between prosecutor and defense lawyer,

taking into account court practice (Herbert, 2004). Defendants pleading not guilty can choose to move the case to Crown Court. Most do not (Darbyshire, 2017), as they risk harsher sentences. In the end, about one-quarter of the triable-either-way offenses are tried at the magistrates' courts (Darbyshire, 2017).

3. The least severe of the three categories of crimes ("summary only") is the exclusive preserve of the magistrates' courts. The longest custodial sentence magistrates can impose is 6 months in prison for one offense and 12 months for more than one offense. If after convicting a defendant the magistrates deem their sentencing powers inadequate because the defendant deserves a longer sentence, they can refer the case to the Crown Court for sentencing. Fines were previously limited to 5,000 pounds, but limits now vary by offense, as statutorily determined (Darbyshire, 2017).

While being a magistrate is an honor, it also entails a significant commitment. A magistrate must sit at least 13 days or 26 half-days per year (Courts and Tribunals Judiciary, n.d.-b), a minimum that most magistrates seem to exceed (Darbyshire, 2017). Magistrates are unpaid, but they can claim travel, subsistence, or financial loss allowances (Courts Act 2003, Provision 15). No legal qualification is required (although occasionally magistrates have a legal background). They initially serve for five years and many continue beyond that period.

Magistrates receive training according to national standards, consisting of basic and more advanced seminars, as well as court observations. The initial training consists of three and a half days (Transform Justice, 2016, p. 10). New magistrates have an experienced colleague as a mentor. Those who after at least three years go on to become presiding magistrates attend a two-day course (Transform Justice, 2016, p. 10). Magistrates are reappraised every three years. Training budgets have been reduced in recent years, limiting the training that magistrates receive (Darbyshire, 2017).

Legally trained professionals hold key roles at the magistrates' courts. This is important because their work patterns influence the proceedings.

- Magistrates are supported by a clerk who is usually legally qualified and acts as a legal adviser. He or she administers the hearing schedule, moving things along, and introduces a case at the hearing. Legal advisers provide procedural advice as well as explanations of the law, applicable sentencing guidelines, and court practice. When defendants are not represented by a lawyer, legal advisers guide them through the court procedure.
- Prosecutors at the magistrates' courts are mostly employed by the Crown Prosecution Service (CPS). They are either lawyers or trained paralegals.
- The defendant is usually represented by a lawyer (solicitor), thanks to legal aid. Alternatively, the free duty solicitor can "provide brief advice" on the day of the trial (Ward, 2017, p. 40). Law firms have to be successful in competitive tendering for access to the legal aid market. To get legal aid, defendants must

pass a "public interest" test and a means test. The public interest test takes into account consequences for the defendant or third persons (e.g., defendants may lose their livelihood or a child's parent may receive custody; Gov.UK, 2019). Increasingly, defendants are excluded from the program to avoid public expense, yet still lack the financial means to pay for a lawyer privately (Ward, 2017). This adds to the other difficulties that most defendants face, often including mental health and substance abuse problems, or learning difficulties.

- Probation officers also have specialist training, as do the representatives of multiagency Youth Offending Teams (YOTs) in youth trials. YOT staff have sometimes studied law. They are usually seasoned social workers.

Despite this heavy involvement of professional and legal elements, the lay magistrates are the defining feature, if only because advocates must address and make all arguments understandable to them. However, the legal adviser certainly is a strong figure as well. All of the regular professional participants of the court tend to form a team, bound together by mutual dependence and interest in smooth-running proceedings (Darbyshire, 2011).

PANELS OF LAY JUDGES AND SINGLE JUSTICE PROCEDURES

The magistrates' court usually sits with three lay judges to avoid a draw. It is however considered sufficient for two magistrates to hear the case if, for example, a third magistrate is unavailable on the day. The idea is that "three minds are better than one" (Raine, 1989, p. 79). The magistrates have been likened to a "mini jury" (Ames et al., 2011, p. 19). Similarly, other countries prefer panels of judges over single judges in many cases, for example at the German *Schöffengericht* (Machura, 2016a).

Each trial in magistrates' courts before a lay panel is presided over by a senior chairperson. "Wingers," that is, the junior lay judges who sit at the side of the presiding judge, are often seen whispering additional ideas (e.g., for questions, or occasionally to correct the chairperson). The personality of the chairperson determines whether wingers are encouraged and supported in bringing ideas to the attention of the panel or discouraged from actively participating (Burney, 1979). This is akin to findings on presiding professional judges in mixed courts (Machura, 2016b). Even the influence of the legal adviser depends on the figure of the chairperson. A strong chairperson leaves limited space for the adviser (own observation; Burney, 1979).

Empirical research has established that magistrates' courts have developed local punishment policies (Tarling, 2006), policies on forwarding cases to Crown Courts (Herbert, 2004), and policies on granting bail (Cownie et al., 2013). In some cases, the judges do not even retire into a backroom, but go through a quick whispered deliberation on their bench. A culture of consensus, to come to joint decisions and to avoid disputes, is also typical for German mixed courts (Machura, 2016b).

Recently, a "single justice procedure" has been introduced. Hundreds of thousands of cases are decided each year *in camera* by individual magistrates aided by a legal adviser and on the basis of written evidence as well as in the absence of the defendant and prosecutor. This procedure is applicable only when an adult has pleaded guilty to a summary-only nonprisonable offense (e.g., a traffic offense). Critics argue that this cost-cutting move sacrifices the advantages of decision-making by a group of magistrates (Donoghue, 2014).

LEGAL ADVISERS

Legal advisers have a key role vis-à-vis lay magistrates. They not only administer cases in the courtroom, but also provide advice on the law and court practice. Thus, advisers occupy some of the roles played by judges in a US jury trial, with the important difference that legal advisers may in addition join the magistrates in the deliberation room. There are about 2,000 of these "career assistants" at magistrates' courts and in line with an international drive toward greater efficiency, their role is expanding (Holvast, 2016, pp. 18, 22, 25). In the eyes of government and higher courts, the proper administration of the law is safeguarded only by appropriate collaboration between the lay judges and their legal advisers (Lauermann, 1987). The magistrates normally depend on their adviser when it comes to questions of law (Darbyshire, 1999). Yet, genuine legal issues are often inextricably mixed with other aspects of a case. To avoid any impression that magistrates are not being independent judges (Burney, 1979), legal advisers join them in the deliberation room only on invitation. In addition, legal advisers are required to inform the parties of any advice given outside the courtroom. In many of the trials observed by the author and his students, legal advisers did not supply parties with any information about the advice they gave when they joined the magistrates.

England and Wales have reduced their spending on legal aid drastically. The cuts have burdened legal advisers with additional work. If a defendant is unrepresented, the legal adviser has to "assist" (Ames et al., 2011, p. 22), but avoid becoming the defendant's "representative" (Holvast, 2016, p. 18).

Judicial authorities have created criminal procedure and rules of evidence for use by professional judges (Darbyshire, 2017). Legal advisers struggle with an avalanche of new criminal offenses, resulting from competition among political parties, media, and lobbyist groups. The unsystematic law is "a nightmare to apply for judges, magistrates' legal advisers and lawyers" (Darbyshire, 2017, p. 261).

Trials are often unpredictable: all advance planning is subverted when defendants fail to appear in court, videos cannot be shown due to technical glitches, or prosecution and police lose files. On a daily basis, court advisers must juggle essential court management tasks, firefight sudden problems, and advise the magistrates. In extreme cases, some advisers are confused or subdued by events in the courtroom, while others take the reins firmly and dominate the courtroom, much like an authoritarian presiding judge (own observation, similar to Malsch, 2009). For example, in one case the author observed, a seasoned legal adviser clearly took charge of almost all steps but the decision, bringing in the full authority and complete knowledge of the procedures developed over a long work life.

TRIALS AGAINST ADULT DEFENDANTS

A preliminary hearing at the magistrates' court determines whether the defendant will be released on bail, whether the defendant is legally represented, and whether the defendant is ready to plead guilty. The court also notes if any witnesses have to be scheduled. These hearings are very short and the legal adviser is central here. According to McConville, Hodgson, Bridges, and Pavlovic (2013), the lack of case detail at the bail application phase results in magistrates erring on the side of caution.

At criminal court, the principles of adversary procedure apply, although, in practice, the defendant's side does not necessarily fight through to the end of the trial for an acquittal. The magistrates receive the case file only as the trial begins, so they cannot prepare in advance. The magistrates are presented with arguments by prosecution and defense, sometimes with the addition of the statement from a probation officer. Prosecution witnesses are not usually required to appear in person and their evidence is summarized in the prosecutor's opening statement. Most of the time, those case "facts" are not disputed. On the rare occasions when the defense offers an opposing witness, that witness testifies in person. In our observations, lay magistrates for the most part simply listen to the presentations. In a typical trial, they ask few questions because the defendant usually accepts the facts or swiftly pleads guilty. For example, defense lawyers declare that the client admits being at fault (or admits to some of the accusations) and introduces arguments in mitigation, at minimum that the client feels remorse.

When the defendant is legally represented, a hearing (preliminary or other) becomes a conversation between lawyers, marginalizing the defendant (own observation; Raine, 1989). Reductions in the availability of legal aid have led to fewer defendants being represented by a lawyer. At magistrates' courts, the quality of lawyers varies. Many have little personal contact with their client (Ward, 2017). In some cases, for example if the defendant failed to pay fines, the legal adviser acts as "collecting officer of the court." The adviser no longer appears as an impartial adviser but interrogates the defendant and may leave the defendant with an impression that the proceedings are unfair (Darbyshire, 1999, pp. 385–386).

Despite crowded court schedules, magistrates often take time to look deeply into a case. In sentencing, the magistrates commonly consider a set of diverse goals that may include retribution, education, and rehabilitation of the offender, or deterring the offender or other people from committing crimes. The magistrates' penal philosophy emphasizes the "needs" of defendants, but cannot be reduced to one maxim (Ward, 2017). Case characteristics and those of the lay judges become decisive in the outcome. For example, defendants with severe substance addiction repeatedly appearing in court received custody sentences quickly in cases observed. In contrast, a young law student got away lightly for driving under the influence of cannabis in response to an appeal not to impede his future career in the legal profession. In other cases, the magistrates drew on their own knowledge about or experience with the local roads as drivers: "We all know the approach to the petrol station from the motorway," a chairman replied to a defendant claiming poor visibility at night time.

The communication style of hearings at magistrates' courts is generally business-like and routine. Within the confines of an adversarial trial, and when pragmatically accepting the consequences of underfunding, it even appears as fair. On closer inspection, there may be questions.

Trials, McConville et al. (2013) suggest, proceed under an implicit assumption of guilt, as mainly cases in which guilt seems somewhat clear are brought to a full trial in front of the magistrates. The outcome thus becomes almost predictable. This is a wider problem that is not confined to magistrates' courts, or to England and Wales.

Welsh (2017) emphasized that the current legal aid regime leads lawyers to decide case strategy with incomplete knowledge, either because the fees do not cover extended research, or because the client's application for legal aid is still pending when court action begins. The latter situation can result in the lawyer advising the client to plead not guilty just to have the case continued. McConville and his collaborators studied the work of lawyers and their law firms in the 1990s. Some defendants who thought they had a good case to go to trial, or at least a wish to have their day in court, were persuaded by lawyers to plead guilty. "Many lawyers do not check whether there is a factual basis for a plea of guilty" (McConville et al., 2013, p. 189).

There also is a "get it over with" attitude among defendants, leading the fearful and disillusioned to forgo their procedural rights (Darbyshire, 2011, p. 156). Prosecutors and lawyers can easily strike a deal, as the former need only to get some kind of conviction (McConville et al., 2013). McConville and his colleagues found that insisting on an examination of the evidence did not result in a harsher sentence, but lawyers tended to believe their clients were guilty (see also Newman, 2012) and that magistrates are inclined to favor the prosecution, so lawyers avoided trials if possible (McConville et al., 2013). According to McConville and his colleagues (2013), the principal aim of the lawyers was a lenient sentence, which they could achieve in magistrates' courts where there is a particular emphasis on speedy trials.

According to observations by McConville and collaborators (2013) in magistrates' courts in the 1990s, defendants who insisted on a full hearing often profited from that demand if the prosecution was unprepared and evidence was not at hand. The circumstances allowed defense lawyers to influence the court through their oral performance (McConville et al., 2013). Such findings coincide with the author's own observations two decades later. In addition, experienced defense lawyers use arguments that will persuade the magistrates. These arguments in trials observed by the author included an early guilty plea, reputational damage suffered in the community, and the fact that a defendant was in line for a promotion but instead lost her job. Prosecutors restrict themselves to very basic statements, as if they are only representing the "facts" (McConville et al., 2013, p. 199), again something that the author observed. The principal evidence against defendants are police reports and police witnesses, and they usually go unquestioned (Cownie et al., 2013; McConville et al., 2013). Because police are expert in giving evidence, their statements tend to be taken as "facts" (McConville et al., 2013, p. 228), leading defendants and critics to see magistrates as "pro-police" (p. 226). The burden of proof is thus reversed; it is shifted to the defendant (McConville et al., 2013). Poorly prepared lawyers sometimes drew attention to their client's character and personal situation, offering their client's statements about these matters as the only evidence. This tactic only worked if the lawyers briefed the client sufficiently in advance (McConville et al., 2013). Magistrates employ decision criteria such as offending circumstances, criminal history, and the defendant's reaction to the crime (Millie, Tombs, & Hough, 2007). An experienced lawyer knows that it is important to focus on these criteria in presenting a positive picture of the defendant and in forming effective arguments.

Due to the introduction of sentencing guidelines, a proliferation of laws, and the legally trained actors in the proceedings (prosecutors, defense attorneys, and the legal adviser), legal terminology is often used in an abbreviated form (Welsh, 2013). Even a small amount of legal language can alienate defendants, who are not in a position to understand it (Thomas et al., 2018). In contrast, the magistrates, with their background training, experience, and briefing by the legal adviser, receive the message.

The presiding magistrate routinely attempts to explain the decisions and asks defendants if they understood their sentence (own observation; Malsch, 2009). In the trials observed by the author, the defendants typically received an explanation for the outcome. If they were fined, the presiding magistrate or the legal adviser discussed modalities of payment with the convicted. However, increasing emphasis is placed on reading out prescribed pronouncements, which are hard for many defendants to grasp (Thomas et al., 2018). It is difficult to say if a defendant has really understood what was conveyed or may just acquiesce to what has been said.

But there is a further factor that can impede communication in court. It is the very layout of the courtroom.

COURT ARCHITECTURE AND ITS IMPACT

The buildings of magistrates' courts improved as many of the historic courthouses were replaced with new purpose-built architecture. Research points to the big distance between the dock where defendants sit and the elevated bench of the magistrates in old courtrooms. Often, defendants were simply unable to hear what went on (Thomas et al., 2018). There is some consistency in design among the newer courtrooms, but a variety of layouts can be found. Most conducive to an open atmosphere are those smaller courtrooms in which the seating approximates a circle and where the defendant can sit next to the lawyer at a table. Figure 7.1 shows the layout of a youth court in a newly built magistrates' court, but even here, there is a problem: the proximity of legal adviser and prosecutor, who may appear as one party to the defendant.

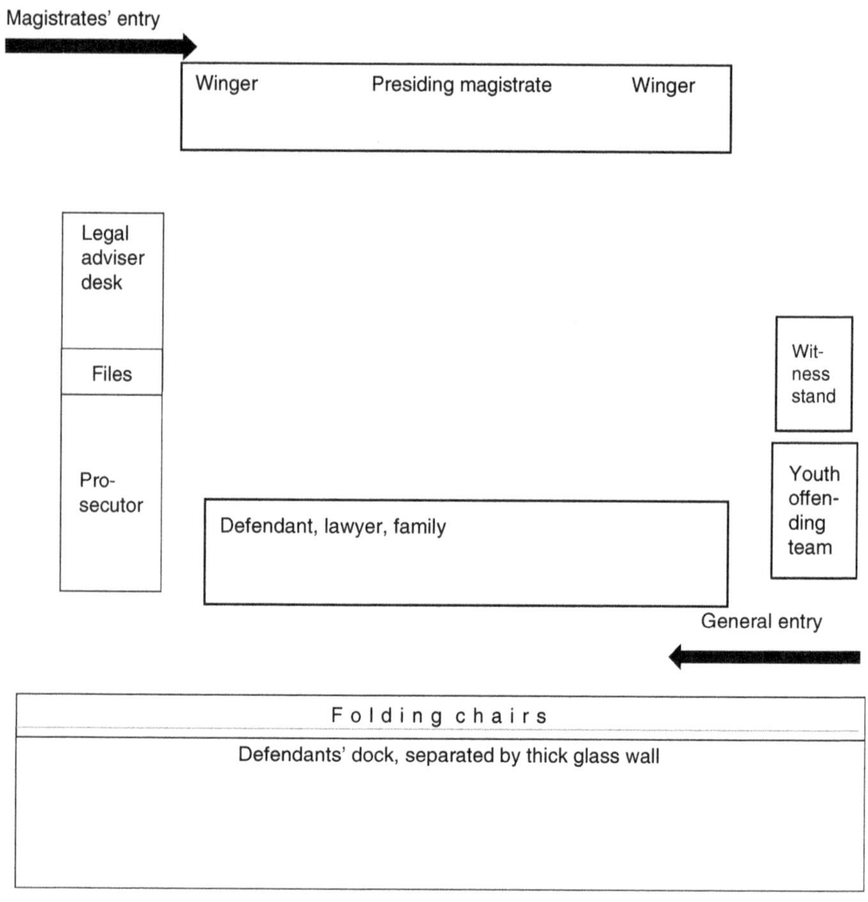

FIGURE 7.1 Example layout of a youth court

Most courtrooms seem to have a secure dock to which defendants in custody are led from holding cells by contracted private security guards. Surrounded by glass walls, they are clearly separated. Critics argue that the arrangement induces an assumption of dangerousness and guilt (Rossner, Tait, McKimmie, & Sarre, 2017).

Defendants have little access to their lawyers during the hearing and occasionally may be seen during breaks whispering through a small hole in the glass. Most stay silent.

Another issue is the appearance of defendants and witnesses via video link. Although courtrooms are equipped with technology, in practice, the quality of sight and sound is problematic. It often takes some time before a link is set up and works. Occasionally the technology fails, causing delays. For defendants who appear from a police station or a remand center, a video hearing must be a surreal experience that is not comparable to seeing the actors in the courtroom in flesh and blood. Screens make it more difficult to pick up on signs of emotion (Sherwin, 2000) or of mental health problems (Ward, 2015). Other issues include being under the control of the custody sergeant instead of having the case "heard against them in an open impartial court" and not being able to have a quick word with one's lawyer if the two are in different locations (Ward, 2015, pp. 352–353).

SOCIAL REPRESENTATIVENESS

Despite decades of debate, the magistrates are not fully representative of the citizenry. Members of many occupations simply cannot engage in a sustained honorary activity that regularly requires a large chunk of their time. Employers are often unsupportive (Magistrates Association, 2016; Transform Justice, 2016). There is a lack of candidates from nonmanagerial and nonprofessional backgrounds (Darbyshire, 2017). Morgan and Russell (n.d.) pointed out that magistrates are "disproportionally middle class, and almost certainly financially well-off" (p. 16). Although the basic criteria are broad – applicants can be between 18 and 65 years old and do not need to be UK citizens – the application window is just three weeks every two years, there is little advertisement, and often only the first 20 to 40 applications are considered (Darbyshire, 2017).

Older generations are overrepresented on the bench: in 2018, 31% were between 50 and 59 years of age and a full 55% were 60 years or over (Ministry of Justice, 2018b, p. 14). Women constitute a slight majority of magistrates, in contrast to their stark underrepresentation among professional judges (Table 7.2).

The percentage of minorities is again higher for magistrates than for professional judges (Table 7.2): 12% of the magistrates reported they were from a "Black, Asian and minority ethnic" (BAME) background. This approximates the percentage in the 2011 census for England and Wales (Office of National Statistics, 2012). The greater representativeness for BAME among magistrates as compared to professional judges has been attributed to targeted recruitment campaigns (Huxley-Binns & Martin, 2010).

The prestige of the office of a magistrate is high. It can be perceived as an appreciation of personal character and perhaps of service in local politics or charities. One magistrate described it as "the most exclusive club" (Ward,

TABLE 7.2 *Gender and ethnic background for court judges and magistrates in England and Wales*

	Female	Black, Asian, and minority ethnic
Professional judges, all courts	29%	7%
District Judges Magistrates' Courts	35%	7%
Deputy District Judges Magistrates' Courts	34%	7%
Magistrates	55%	12%

Note. "All courts" excludes administrative and employment tribunals.
Source: Ministry of Justice (2018b, pp. 1, 2, 5).

2017, p. 82). Being a magistrate offers more opportunities to develop role satisfaction than being a juror or a continental European lay assessor at criminal court.

Critics emphasize a lack of magistrates who know the living conditions of the typical defendants, who are suffering from multiple disadvantages such as racism, learning difficulties, poor mental health, and poverty, from their own experience (Raine, 1989). According to Millie et al. (2007), economically and socially disadvantaged defendants fared worse in magistrates' courts in England and Wales than defendants without those disadvantages.

Magistrates and the Magistrates' Association take pride in their perception that they are dispensing local justice. But the economically unrepresentative composition may be an obstacle. Ward (2017) takes a different view about the value of a representative magistry. She emphasizes the skill set required for magistrates, pointing out that lay judges with teaching and social-work backgrounds are likely to be especially insightful about their decisions, lessening concern about their overrepresentation on the bench. Still, an uneasiness about the composition remains.

DISTRICT JUDGES

Especially in big cities, professional judges, called District Judges Magistrates' Courts (DJMCs), hear a portion of the cases that go to magistrates' courts. DJMCs sit as single judges. They are recruited from lawyers who have served in a part-time function as deputies (Courts and Tribunals Judiciary, n.d.-a). There were 133 DJMCs and 101 deputies in 2016 (Darbyshire, 2017).

The professional judges, according to Diamond (1990), processed cases three times as quickly as the lay magistrates. She also found that they leaned toward more severe punishment than their lay colleagues, an effect partially attributable to their legal training and concern for crime control (Diamond, 1990). In contrast, "the lay magistrate is less concerned with the general sentencing of the court and focuses more on the individual offender than on the community at large" (Diamond, 1990, p. 215).

More recently, Darbyshire (2011) described the speed of proceedings led by DJMCs and their authoritative command of the courtroom. The lay magistrates in comparison were more methodical and took more time deliberating as well as seeking the view of their legal adviser. The author observed a DJMC at Monday court sessions, dealing primarily with people arrested over the weekend. The judge decided many custody cases expeditiously in a conveyer-belt fashion, sometimes in just three minutes. Guilty plea cases were sentenced equally quickly in his court.

Once they are to be tried by a magistrates' court, defendants cannot choose whether their case will be dealt with by a panel of lay magistrates or one professional judge (Darbyshire, 2017). Some authors note that courts often allocate presumably longer trials and more serious cases to a DJMC (Darbyshire, 2017; Ward, 2017). But the DJMC observed by the author dealt only with cases that allowed a rapid decision, while the time-consuming disputed cases, or cases in which the legally unrepresented client needed extensive help by the legal adviser, were heard by panels of lay magistrates.

MAGISTRATES AT THE CROWN COURT

Appeals against convictions and sentences by the magistrates' courts go to the Crown Court. These cases are heard by a mixed court: a presiding professional judge sitting with two lay magistrates. Similarly in Germany, mixed courts are involved in appeals (see Chapter 8, this volume). On Crown Court appeals panels, magistrates are instructed to "accept the judge's rulings on law" (Darbyshire, 2017, p. 309), a standard that is stricter than the German rules.

There has been little research on magistrates working at the Crown Court. Malsch (2009, p. 166) reports the opinion of two professional judges that decisions tend to be made consensually, and only "very rarely" is the professional judge outvoted. In the latter case, the professional judge can signal this in writing up the sentence. Once they have learned the case details, lay judges tend to be more lenient than professional judges. International research found that the influence of lay members in mixed courts largely depends on the attitude of the presiding professional judge (Kutnjak Ivković, 1999; Machura, 2016b).

THE SHRINKING REALM OF LAY MAGISTRATES?

Magistrates often say there is a plan to reduce their role and to replace them with professional district judges (Ward, 2017). Indeed, the number of magistrates fell from 25,155 in 2012 to 15,003 in 2018 (Ministry of Justice, 2018b, p. 13). According to the chairman of the Magistrates' Association, it has halved in the last 20 years, leading him to call for the recruitment of an additional 9,000 magistrates in the next 10 years just to keep the status quo (John Bache, cited in Gibb, 2018).

Although minor cases were taken out of the magistrates' courts and channeled to out-of-court mechanisms, serious crimes have been shifted toward them (Darbyshire, 2017; Ward, 2017). Magistrates' courts have also received more business from the prosecutors, who turned to indicting the lower of two possible charges against a defendant (Huxley-Binns & Martin, 2010).

Still, the overall effect of recent changes is a reduction of cases at the magistrates' courts (Ward, 2017). Disposed cases in the magistrates courts fell by 25% from 2 million to 1.5 million between 2008 and 2017 (Sturge, 2018). By comparison, disposed cases at the Crown Court dropped by 17% from 143,080 in 2008 to 118,605 in 2017 (Sturge, 2018). In stark contrast to both of these reductions, police-recorded crime rose during this period (Office of National Statistics, 2017). More of a threat to the institution has been the closure of 162 magistrates' courts out of 323 since 2010, with plans to close a further six in 2019 (Bowcott & Duncan, 2019), creating a challenge for the application of "local justice" (Magistrates Association, 2016). Magistrates are now unlikely to be aware of local contexts as court circuits have become larger (Ward, 2017). The extensive court closure program aimed at modernization, including the use of technology. These closures have made it difficult for some magistrates (Transform Justice, 2016) and many of the clients to travel to their courts. Magistrates and the Law Society, representing solicitors, have voiced concern about access to justice (Bowcott & Duncan, 2019).

THE YOUTH COURT

The youth court in England and Wales, a special section of magistrates' courts, offers an interesting contrast to proceedings in the general magistrates' courts. The youth court is closed to the public, and researchers are not allowed access. Consequently, there is very little published on the topic. In recent years, trials have been much reduced. The majority of cases are diverted into out-of-court settlements (Ministry of Justice, 2013). This follows from the received wisdom of academics and practitioners that any level of involvement with the criminal justice system easily leads to a young defendant adopting an unwelcome "offender identity." Today, only the worst cases, where other measures have failed, go to court (Ministry of Justice, 2016). Young defendants are often suffering from multiple disadvantages, for example a dysfunctional family, drug and alcohol addiction, or learning disabilities. Another consequence of dwindling case numbers is that youth magistrates outside of crime hotspot areas feel in danger of losing their qualifications due to infrequent trials (Magistrates Association, 2016).

Almost all defendants below the age of 18 have to stand trial at the youth court section of the magistrates' court (Stone, 2017). Sentences up to two years in prison can be imposed. To prepare them for their task, youth court magistrates receive special training. The style of the proceedings is intended to be more informal, using language that should be understandable to the child (Independent Commission, 2010). Defense lawyers' preparation may suffer from high caseloads, and they often lack the necessary training to work with young offenders (Carlile, 2014). The Carlile Report (2014) also found that the Crown Prosecution Service lacked training.

The trial at the youth court differs from the trial at an adult court: an initial adversarial procedure is followed by an investigative mode of trial. After the legal adviser, prosecutor, and defense lawyer have spoken, and any witnesses have been heard, the presiding magistrate takes over and asks the Youth Offending Team (YOT) representative for a report. YOT officers report circumstances that speak in favor of the juvenile, or that make his or her journey understandable. When youths are in breach of a court order, for example have stopped attending anti-aggression training, the YOT prosecutes them at the youth court. The presiding judge then questions the young defendants. The magistrates observed seemed to value the YOT report highly, as the YOT will have background information on the defendants, often from years of their involvement with social services. The presiding magistrate makes a special effort to engage the defendants, to find out about their perspective on their situation, and to determine their aspirations. When the sentence is announced, the chairperson takes care to explain it to the defendant. Typically, in the observed sessions, the chairperson pointed out how sanctions, for example a curfew, can be lifted if the youth faithfully engages with tailored training.

In the youth court, at least in semirural areas, there is a limited group of actors who have known each other for many years. Prosecutors, YOT representatives, and the legal advisers do not hide their acquaintance. Instead, they convey the impression that they are in a joint enterprise, subjugating the objective of punishment to the aim of bettering the defendant's life. Similar to adult criminal court, defense lawyers operate on the assumption that their juvenile clients are guilty and confine their efforts to suggesting more lenient treatment. Young defendants in some cases may not be ready to admit their part in the events leading to the indictment, but their lawyers will find words that sound as if the defendants are at a minimum about to repent. This then opens up the opportunity for the magistrates to arrive at a measured decision. It is the magistrates' court at its most paternalistic.

CONCLUSION

This discussion has shown why magistrates are so powerful even in comparison to US jurors and lay judges in a mixed court. They are both the judge and jury in the court that bears their name. Being a magistrate is a considerable commitment and also a highly prestigious role. In this, magistrates again differ from other forms of lay decision-makers, such as jurors and for the most part lay members in mixed courts, certainly those in lower criminal courts. In contrast to the US jurors and the German lay assessors, magistrates self-recruit to a degree, have more training, are regularly reappraised, and can call on a legal adviser if in doubt on the law. Magistrates do not share their powers with a professional judge in a trial at the magistrates' court, although the legal adviser may be highly influential.

Procedural fairness and justice of outcomes suffer severe blows when efficiency is treated as the paramount consideration, resources are inadequate, and proceedings are rushed. The magistrates' court is at the end of a chain of agencies and professionals involved in a criminal case. Shortcomings in the practices of police, prosecutors, and defense lawyers will affect the work of the courts. More than a decade of cuts has weakened public services in the United Kingdom, and the magistrates' courts reflect that loss. The recent closure of outlier courts endangers the very concept of "local justice," a pillar of magistrates' legitimation. Graham and Moore (2006) stated that the youth court cannot force local authorities and other agencies to provide adequate services to juveniles who find themselves in the criminal justice system. The same applies to the adult court. While crime control has a strong profile in public debates, it is not given the resources to work effectively with offenders. Ironically, if nothing else, this very constellation will secure the future of magistrates' courts as a cheaper alternative to employing a small army of professional judges.

Compared to their professional counterparts, the District Judges Magistrates' Court, lay magistrates take more time to hear a case, to learn more about the defendant, and to chart an appropriate response. If defendants were only aware of it, they indeed have a chance to be acquitted in the magistrates' court. Significantly, few defendants appeal the decisions reached in magistrates' courts, a fact that led Huxley-Binns and Martin (2010) to conclude: "despite their amateur status as lay magistrates, they do a remarkably good job" (p. 247).

The youth court presents a more positive picture than the adult court as more efforts are taken to engage with the juvenile and to tailor the court's response to the youth's needs. The fact that the youth magistrates are vetted and specially trained and that they are working with youth may supply an increased ability and intrinsic motivation. But it is also important that the trial mode differs: it begins as an adversarial proceeding, but then becomes more investigative, enabling the magistrates to play a more active role and providing them with an opportunity to engage more closely with the juvenile. Many adult offenders are also little over 18 years old and not fully mature (Pruin & Dünkel, 2015). One solution would be to expand the age bracket for defendants dealt with by the youth court. It might even be that a more investigative procedure at criminal courts generally, similar to the pattern at the youth court, could compensate for shortcomings of police, prosecutor, and defense lawyer work. An opportunity will be lost if the magistrates are employed only in a very restrictive way, confined to acting only as passive decision-makers.

Author's Note. The author wishes to thank Penny Darbyshire for arranging rare access to the youth court and one joint observation of trials at a youth court. Professor Darbyshire has also provided the author with a wealth of material on magistrates' courts, and we had many valuable discussions. For the chapter the author takes sole responsibility.

The author also thanks the postgraduate students of his "Social Science in Action" module at Bangor University, academic years 2017/18 and 2018/19. Thanks are also extended to magistrates, legal advisers, court staff, lawyers, prosecutors, and social workers for speaking about their work.

REFERENCES

Ames, A., Szyndler, R., Burston, K., Phillips, R. Keith, J., Gaunt, R., Davies, S., & Mottram, C. (2011). *The strengths and skills of the judiciary in the magistrates' courts*. London: Ministry of Justice/Ipsos Mori.

Bowcott, O., & Duncan, P. (2019, January 17). Half of magistrates' courts in England and Wales closed since 2010. *Guardian*. www.theguardian.com/law/2019/jan/27/half-of-magistrates-courts-in-england-and-wales-closed-since-tories-elected

Bundesamt für Justiz [Federal Office of Justice (Ger.)]. (2016). *Zahl der richter, richterinnen, staatsanwälte, staatsanwältinnen und vertreter, vertreterinnen des ffentlichen interesses in der Rechtspflege der Bundesrepublik Deutschland am 31. Dezember 2014* [Number of judges, public prosecutors, and representatives of public interest in the administration of justice in the Federal Republic of Germany on December 31, 2014]. www.bundesjustizamt.de/DE/SharedDocs/Publikationen/Justizstatistik/Gesamtstatistik.pdf?__blob=publicationFile

Burney, E. (1979). *Magistrate, court and community*. London: Hutchinson.

Cammiss, S., & Cunningham, S. K. (2015). Swift and sure justice? Mode of trial for causing death by driving offences. *Criminology and Criminal Justice*, 15, 321–339.

Carlile, Alex, Lord of Berriew (2014). *Independent parliamentarians' inquiry into the operation and effectiveness of the youth court*. http://michaelsieff-foundation.org.uk/content/inquiry_into_the_operation_and_effectiveness_of_the_youth_court-uk-carlile-inquiry.pdf

Courts and Tribunals Judiciary (UK). (n.d.-a). District judge (magistrates' courts). www.judiciary.gov.uk/about-the-judiciary/who-are-the-judiciary/judicial-roles/judges/district-judge-mags-ct/

(n.d.-b). Magistrates. www.judiciary.gov.uk/about-the-judiciary/who-are-the-judiciary/judicial-roles/magistrates/

Cownie, F., Bradney, A., & Burton, M. (2013). *English legal system in context*. 6th ed. London: Oxford University Press.

Darbyshire, P. (1999). A comment on the powers of magistrates' clerks. *Criminal Law Review*, May, 377–386.

(2011). *Sitting in judgment: The working lives of judges*. Oxford: Hart.

(2017). *Darbyshire on the English legal system*. 12th ed. London: Sweet and Maxwell.

Diamond, S. S. (1990). Revising images of public punitiveness: Sentencing by lay and professional English magistrates. *Law and Social Inquiry*, 15, 191–221.

Donoghue, J. C. (2014). Reforming the role of magistrates: Implications for summary justice in England and Wales. *Modern Law Review*, 77, 928–963.

Gibb, F. (2018, July 12). Dwindling number of magistrates. *Sunday Times*. www.thetimes.co.uk/article/dwindling-number-of-magistrates-sm9wr8tjz

Gov.UK. (2019). Work out who qualifies for criminal legal aid. www.gov.uk/guidance/work-out-who-qualifies-for-criminal-legal-aid

Graham, J., & Moore, C. (2006). Beyond welfare versus justice: Juvenile justice in England and Wales. In J. Junger-Tas & S. H. Decker (Eds.), *International handbook of juvenile justice* (pp. 65–92). Dordrecht: Springer.

Green, C., Sprott, J. B., Madon, N. S., & Jung, M. (2010). Punishing processes in youth court: Procedural justice, court atmosphere and youths' views of the legitimacy of the justice system. *Canadian Journal of Criminology and Criminal Justice*, 52, 527–544.

Haller, V., & Machura, S. (1995). Procedural justice at German courts as seen by defendants and juvenile prisoners. *Social Justice Research*, 8, 197–215.

Herbert, A. (2004). Mode of trial and the influence of local justice. *Howard Journal of Criminal Justice*, 43, 65–78.

Holvast, N. (2016). The power of the judicial assistant/law clerk: Looking behind the scenes at courts in the United States, England and Wales, and the Netherlands. *International Journal for Court Administration*, 7, 10–28.

Huxley-Binns, R., & Martin, J. (2010). *Unlocking the English legal system*. 3rd ed. London: Hodder Education.

Independent Commission on Youth Crime and Antisocial Behaviour. (2010). *Time for a new hearing. A comparative study of alternative criminal proceedings for children and young people*. London: Police Foundation.

Kutnjak Ivković, S. (1999). *Lay participation in criminal trials: The case of Croatia*. Lanham, MD: Austin & Winfield.

Lauermann, A. (1987). *Strafrechtspflege am englischen Magistrates' Court* [Administration of justice at the English magistrates' court]. Marburg: N. G. Elwert.

Machura, S. (2001). *Fairneß und legitimität* [Fairness and legitimacy]. Baden-Baden: Nomos.

(2016a). Civil justice: Lay judges in the EU countries. *Oñati Socio-Legal Series*, 6(2).

(2016b). Understanding the German mixed tribunal. *Zeitschrift für Rechtssoziologie*, 36, 273–302.

Magistrates Association. (2016). *Written evidence from the Magistrates Association*. http://data.parliament.uk/WrittenEvidence/CommitteeEvidence.svc/EvidenceDocument/Justice/Role%20of%20the%20magistracy/written/27965.html

Malsch, M. (2009). *Democracy in the courts*. Farnham, UK: Routledge.

McConville, M., Hodgson, J., Bridges, L., & Pavlovic, A. (2013). *Standing accused*. Reprint. Oxford: Clarendon.

Millie, A., Tombs, J., & Hough, M. (2007). Borderline sentencing. *Criminology and Criminal Justice*, 7, 243–267.

Ministry of Justice (UK). (2013). *Youth justice: Seventh report of session 2012–13 (Vol. 1)*. London: The Stationery Office.

(2016). *Review of the youth justice system. An interim report of emerging findings*. London: Ministry of Justice.

(2018a). *Criminal justice statistics quarterly, England and Wales, September 2016 to September 2017 (provisional)*. https://assets.publishing.service.gov.uk/government/uploads/system/uploads/attachment_data/file/681336/criminal-justice-statistics-quarterly-sept-2017.pdf

(2018b). *Judicial diversity statistics 2018*. www.judiciary.uk/wp-content/uploads/2018/07/judicial-diversity-statistics-2018–1.pdf

Morgan, R., & Russell, N. (n.d.). *The judiciary in the magistrates' courts*. http://citeseerx.ist.psu.edu/viewdoc/download?doi=10.1.1.629.5296&rep=rep1&type=pdf

Newman, D. (2012). Still standing accused: Addressing the gap between work and talk in firms of criminal justice lawyers. *International Journal of the Legal Profession*, 19, 3–27.

Office of National Statistics (UK). (2012). *Ethnicity and national identity in England and Wales: 2011*. www.ons.gov.uk/peoplepopulationandcommunity/culturalidentity/ethnicity/articles/ethnicityandnationalidentityinenglandandwales/2012-12-11

(2017). *Crime in England and Wales: Bulletin tables*. Year ending June 2017. Table 1. www.ons.gov.uk/peoplepopulationandcommunity/crimeandjustice/datasets/crimeinenglandandwalesbulletintables

(2018). *Population estimates*. www.ons.gov.uk/peoplepopulationandcommunity/populationandmigration/populationestimates

Pruin, I., & Dünkel, F. (2015). *Better in Europe?* London: Barrow Cadbury Trust.

Raine, J. W. (1989). *Local justice*. Edinburgh: T. & T. Clark.

Robin-D'Cruz, C., & Whitehead, S. (2019). *Pre-court diversion for adults: An evidence briefing*. London: Centre for Justice Innovation. https://justiceinnovation.org/sites/default/files/media/documents/2019-06/cji_pre-court_diversion_d.pdf

Rossner, M., Tait, D., McKimmie, B., & Sarre, R. (2017). The dock on trial: Courtroom design and the presumption of innocence. *Journal of Law and Society*, 44, 317–344.

Sherwin, R. K. (2000). *When the law goes pop: The vanishing line between law and popular culture*. Chicago: University of Chicago Press.

Statistisches Bundesamt [Federal Statistical Office (Ger.)]. (2019). *Bevölkerungsstand* [Population statistics]. www.destatis.de/DE/ZahlenFakten/GesellschaftStaat/Bevoelkerung/Bevoelkerungsstand/Bevoelkerungsstand.html

Stone, N. (2017). Sentencing children: Overarching principles revisited. *Youth Justice*, 17, 171–180.

Sturge, G. (2018). *Court statistics for England and Wales*. London: House of Commons Library. http://researchbriefings.files.parliament.uk/documents/CBP-8372/CBP-8372.pdf

Tarling, R. (2006). Sentencing practice in magistrates' courts revisited. *Howard Journal of Criminal Justice*, 45, 29–41.

Thomas, J., Ely, C., & Estep, B. (2018). *A fairer way: Procedural fairness for young adults in court*. London: Centre for Justice Innovation.

Transform Justice. (2016). *The role of the magistrate?* London: Transform Justice.

Tyler, T. R. (2006). *Why people obey the law*. 2nd ed. Princeton, NJ: Princeton University Press.

Ward, J. (2015). Transforming "summary justice" through police-led prosecution and virtual courts: Is procedural due process undermined? *British Journal of Criminology*, 55, 341–358.

(2017). *Transforming summary justice: Modernisation in the lower criminal courts*. London: Routledge.

Welsh, L. (2013). Are magistrates' courts really a "law free zone"? Participant observation and specialist use of language. *Papers from the British Criminology Conference*, 13, 3–16.

(2017). The effects of changes to legal aid on lawyers' professional identity and behaviour in summary criminal cases: A case study. *Journal of Law and Society*, 44, 559–585.

8

"In the Name of the People"

Lay Assessors in Germany

Stefan Machura and Christoph Rennig

Mixed tribunals are the typical form of lay participation in Germany. Mixed tribunals consist of professional judges and lay assessors, who work together to decide cases, and they serve on a variety of courts, including the criminal courts. German professional judges are career civil servants, who are independent in all matters related to judging. They have received extensive training in law by attending university and serving as legal apprentices. In contrast, lay assessors are not required to have studied law, and they receive only modest compensation for their service.

This chapter will focus on criminal courts because the largest contingent of the lay assessors serves on criminal courts. Even the formula for announcing court decisions, "*Im Namen des Volkes* (In the name of the people), the court finds the defendant . . . ," suggests that lay participation has a role to play in German courts. Indeed, the first paragraph of the Federal Law on Judges defines both professional judges and lay assessors as judges (Deutsches Richtergesetz [DRiG], 1972). We aim to show that, despite problems, lay assessors contribute to the work of the German criminal courts. In addition, unlike juries, which tend to be limited to certain types of cases in countries where juries exist, the German court of lay assessors is employed in a very wide range of cases.

This chapter mostly deals with the adult criminal courts. Lay assessors also serve on juvenile courts (Lennartz, 2016). They are recruited in a separate procedure, and the law requires relevant educational experience (Lieber, 2017). For example, teachers or youth workers qualify. One of the two lay assessors on the mixed tribunal in the youth court always has to be male and the other female.

Lay assessors make a variety of contributions to the criminal justice system (Machura, 2016; Rönnau, 2017). They bring common sense and a broader set of life experiences and views, rather than expert legal knowledge, to mixed tribunals. Lay assessors have not been socialized by a career in the judiciary. Their participation, in comparison to that of a single professional judge, or even a panel of professional judges, may lead to discussion or make professional judges think more carefully and present their arguments more persuasively. To employ a sufficient number of professional judges to create a debate is beyond the resources of the state, which is another reason for including lay assessors (Rennig, 1993).

Lay participation is also more "democratic" as it involves a wider segment of society in the work of the courts. "Lay" is of Greek origin and means "of the people." The term for lay assessors in criminal courts – *Schöffen* – points to another dimension. It comes from the German word for making things – *schaffen*. As members of a panel, lay assessors make law between the parties of a legal dispute (Battenberg, 1990). Parties might even trust the courts more if they see citizens represented on the bench as decision-makers. The involvement of lay assessors also requires lawyers to communicate in understandable language. For all these claims, there is some supportive empirical evidence in German and international sociolegal literature (Lempert, 2015; Machura, 2016).

Occasionally, legal scholars have expressed opposition to lay participation (for overviews, see Rennig 1993; Lennartz, 2016). They dispute that nonlawyers contribute anything to the work of the courts (Rönnau, 2017). The essence of these critiques is that only fully legally qualified judges can be relied on to deal with the complexity of the law. The brief history of lay participation presented in this chapter illustrates the extent to which lay participation was resented by some key players who formulate legal policy.

In contrast, professional judges tend to accept lay assessors. Theo Rasehorn (2016), a high-profile judge, observed that lay assessors are equally qualified when it comes to understanding the facts of a case and to deciding on a punishment within the parameters of the law. However, when it comes to interpreting the meaning of the law in relation to the case, the professional judge is superior (Rasehorn, 2016). In one study, most of the professional judges who presided over mixed tribunals viewed the lay assessors positively (Rennig, 1993). In the survey by Lennartz (2017, p. 3), almost three quarters of the professional judges at the juvenile court thought lay participation "made sense." In addition to an appreciation by judges, there is general political support for lay assessors.

HISTORY OF LAY PARTICIPATION IN GERMANY

From Introduction of Lay Participation to Its Abolition by the Nazis

In the Middle Ages, laypersons served as judges in Germany, but with the introduction of canonical law, professional judges, who had been educated in the newly founded law faculties, took over (Rennig, 1993). Criminal trials were inquisitorial (with judges investigating the case rather than lawyers preparing and presenting it to the court), were held in camera, and lacked an oral hearing. During the first half of the nineteenth century, liberals, opposed to authoritarian rule, called for independent judges, for public and oral trials, and for jury trials, especially in cases that raised issues of freedom of speech (so-called press offenses). The movement was temporarily successful with the revolution of 1848, which forced authorities to establish lay participation. After 1848, almost all the German states introduced either jury trials or mixed tribunals, or both. Some states had juries hear cases involving press offenses. The new codes of criminal procedure, which replaced the inquisitorial procedures, went hand in hand with the introduction of lay participation (for details, see Kern, 1954).

Since a nationwide unification of the judiciary code, beginning in 1869, lay participation in criminal trials has been widely accepted (Rennig, 1993). Everywhere in Germany, the courts of first instance had two forms of lay participation: not only mixed tribunals of two lay assessors and one professional judge, but also juries. However, in later years, critics called for a replacement of the jury by mixed tribunals and even the abolition of lay participation (Rennig, 1993). The debate focused on the alternatives: democratic representation of the people in the administration of courts or intellectual qualifications, namely, a requirement to have studied law and passed the state bar exams to judge criminal cases (Lennartz, 2016; Rennig, 1993). In 1924, an economically disastrous year, juries were abolished by an emergency decree. The government found that jury trials were too expensive (Rennig, 1993). Mixed tribunals, consisting of three professional judges and six lay assessors, replaced juries.

Soon after the National Socialist German Workers' Party (*Nationalsozialistische Deutsche Arbeiterpartei*, NSDAP) came into power in 1933, it began replacing professional judges and lay assessors. The party leadership aimed to turn over the criminal justice system to party members and supporters who were expected to decide cases based upon what they called "the sound sentiment of the people" (Casper & Zeisel, 1972), free from any legal restrictions (Rennig, 1993). On September 1, 1939, the day of the German attack on Poland that started World War II, a government decree abolished lay participation, except for the *Volksgerichtshof* ("People's Court"). The People's Court was a special instrument of Nazi terror. It was led by professional judges and included only laypersons selected from members of the party and the military.

Development in Postwar East and West Germany Until 1990

Four years passed between the end of World War II and the founding of the Federal Republic of Germany (FRG) in the western part of Germany. During this period, all the provinces set into force their own particular code of criminal procedure and established their judiciaries, all of which included lay participation. In 1950, the criminal justice system for all of West Germany was unified. In the courts that deal with minor and medium severe crimes, lay participation took the form of a mixed tribunal with one professional judge and two lay assessors. The high courts had a mixed tribunal with three professional judges and two lay assessors, and a mixed tribunal with three professional judges and six lay assessors

(*Schwurgerichtskammer*, "jury court chamber") with responsibility for capital crimes (Knittel, 1970).

In 1975, the composition of the *Schwurgerichtskammer* was changed, so that it consisted of three professional judges and only two lay assessors (Rennig, 1993). The reasons given by the legislature did not provide much explanation. The legislature found merit in the lay assessors, but concluded that "therefore" the number of lay assessors should be reduced (cf. Rennig, 1993, p. 81).

In the Soviet Zone east of the Elbe River, which later became the German Democratic Republic (GDR), mixed tribunals with two lay assessors and one professional judge were used for criminal trials and appeals (Mathes, 1999). These mixed tribunals were based on the idea that professional judges and lay assessors would control each other and in this way the Socialist Unity Party line would be put into effect more reliably. The professional judges had the opportunity to select the lay assessors who participated in a trial (Peller, 1999; Rottleuthner, 1994). Professional judges were subject to political influence, for example by receiving instructions from party authorities (Bundesministerium der Justiz, 1996).

The number of lay assessors in relation to the population was much higher in East Germany than in West Germany. East Germany had a population of about 17 million and about 59,500 lay assessors (Peller, 1999). West Germany in 1985 had a population more than three times larger, but only half the number of lay assessors in criminal courts (Rennig, 1993).

Since 1990: Germany After Reunification

After the peaceful revolution of 1989 and, while East Germany still existed, judges and prosecutors from the former GDR were evaluated as to past violations of human rights. Among the 1,899 judges and prosecutors who agreed to be evaluated, 1,094 remained as judges or prosecutors (Rennig & Strempel, 1996). After the unification, judges from the former West Germany, who were often young and inexperienced, worked in East Germany and it led to some conflicts with the locals. Cases often referred to the living conditions and laws of East Germany about which the newly arrived professional judges had no knowledge. Thus, the lay assessors were especially valuable (Lieber, 1994; Machura, 2006).

Reunified Germany, with a population of about 82.7 million (Kammholz, 2018), has an estimated 100,000 lay assessors in all branches of the courts together (DVS, 2016a). As of 2014, 36,997 lay assessors were in criminal courts, including 11,664 lay assessors in juvenile courts (Bundesamt für Justiz, n.d.). Additionally, there are lists of reserve candidates at each criminal court, bringing the total number of lay assessors in criminal courts up to 61,000 (Editors, 2019).

In 1993, the sentencing power of the single professional judge on the local court (*Amtsgericht*) was increased, as was the sentencing power of the mixed tribunal. On the one hand, the mixed tribunals lost a large segment of minor criminal cases; on the other hand, they were given more serious cases. In addition, the composition of the appellate courts with responsibility for appeals in matters of fact and law against the judgments of the local courts was changed from three professional judges and two lay assessors to one professional judge and two lay assessors. This move strengthened lay participation by increasing the proportion of lay assessors in mixed tribunals.

According to statistics for the year 2016, about 15% of the criminal cases for which public prosecutors opened investigations were passed on to the courts (Lieber, 2018b). In 2017, 18% of the 718,491 criminal cases decided in German courts were heard by mixed tribunals (Table 8.1). Yet, these cases with lay participation involve serious crimes and most were appeals from decisions of lower courts. In general terms and with respect to adults, prosecutors bring cases to mixed tribunals as courts of first instance when they expect a possible sentence of two years or more in prison.

LEGAL FRAMEWORK

German Legal Culture and Court Organization

Lay participation can best be understood in the context of both a country's legal system and legal culture, and the organization of its courts. For lay participation to work, lay judges should see their membership on the courts as a valuable addition. Thus, lay assessors should neither uncritically assume professional judges do everything well and the lay voice is superfluous, nor should the perception of the courts be so low that citizens (including lay judges) have given up on them. A majority of Germans trust the work of the courts (Köcher, 2014, Table A1). In a recent survey, for example, 68% indicated having respect for judges, placing judges at number three in a ranking of professions, right after general practitioners (75%) and professors (72%) ("Professorinnen und Professoren genießen hohes Ansehen," 2020). In another survey, 54% said that judges tell the truth, surpassed only by doctors at 66%, while police officers stood at 21% (Petersen, 2020). Confidence in the courts, but also lawyers, is a key feature of German legal culture (Machura, 2011). However, Germans think that courts do not punish convicted criminal defendants severely enough (Köcher, 2014, Table A1). This view can be challenged if people are confronted with the realities of particular cases. In a study, most *Schöffen* saw the outcomes of criminal cases as not harsh (Machura, 2001a). In an earlier study by Kronenberger (1989), few lay assessors found judgments too lenient or too harsh. In Lieber's (1994; 1997) research, lay assessors thought that the punishments provided by law were not harsh enough, and they saw punishments rendered by the courts similarly. Studies do not suggest that lay assessors face the courts with undue deference.

The proceedings and the trial are investigatory in nature. During the preparatory proceedings, the professional judge (or judges) decide(s) by reviewing the results of the investigations whether the charge should be admitted and the trial should be

TABLE 8.1 *Criminal cases decided with lay participation in Germany, 2017*

Court	Number of cases	Composition	% with lay participation
Local court (**Amtsgericht**)	654,537		11.3%
Single professional judge (*Strafeinzelrichter*)	438,711	1 professional judge	
Single professional youth judge (*Jugendrichter*)	142,013	1 professional judge	
Court of lay assessors (*Schöffengericht*)	36,554	1 professional judge, 2 lay assessors	
Extended court of lay assessors (*Erweitertes Schöffengericht*)	383	2 professional judges, 2 lay assessors	
Youth court (*Jugendschöffengericht*)	36,876	1 professional judge, 2 lay assessors	
	Σ 73,816		
District court (**Landgericht**)			
First instance	12,933		100%
Criminal division (*Große Strafkammer*)	8,465	2 (sometimes 3) professional judges, 2 lay assessors	
Jury court chamber (*Schwurgerichtskammer*)	1,348	3 professional judges, 2 lay assessors	
Criminal division for economic crime (*Wirtschaftsstrafkammer*)	966	2 (sometimes 3) professional judges, 2 lay assessors	
Grand youth division (*Große Jugendkammer*)	2,154	3 professional judges, 2 lay assessors	
Appeals	45,186		100%
Criminal division (*Kleine Strafkammer*)		1 professional judge, 2 lay assessors	
(a) Against single judge decision	32,293		
(b) Against court of lay assessor decision	7,227		
Criminal division for economic crime (*Wirtschaftsstrafkammer*)	540	2–3 professional judges, 2 lay assessors	
Grand youth division (*Große Jugendkammer*)	3,267		
Small youth division (*Kleine Jugendkammer*)	1,859	1 professional judge, 2 lay assessors	
High court			0%
First instance	46	5 professional judges	
Appeals	5,789		
All three courts	718,491		18.4%
First instance	667,516		13%
Appeals	51,605		87.8%

Source: Statistisches Bundesamt, 2018, pp. 14–15, 52–53, 102–103.
Note. Excludes trials at the highest court, the *Bundesgerichtshof*, where there are no lay judges.

held or not, and if the trial is held, what evidence will be used. In the main hearing, the professional judges and lay assessors have essentially equal rights and tasks, and they work together to decide the verdict and the sentence. The lay assessors participate only during the oral and public trial and in the deliberation that follows. Any conviction must be grounded only on the evidence presented in open court.

Trials at the courts of first instance can be heard by:

- the *Strafrichter* (criminal professional judge) at the *Amtsgericht* (local court)
- the *Schöffengericht* (lay assessor court) at the *Amtsgericht*
- the *Große Strafkammer* (criminal division) at the *Landgericht* (district court)
- the *Strafsenat* (criminal division) at the *Oberlandesgericht* (high court).

The high court consists of five professional judges, but no lay assessors, and is responsible for offenses such as genocide, terrorism, and espionage (Gerichtsverfassungsgesetz [GVG] 1877, §§ 122, 122(1)). The other three courts of first instance have responsibility for all other kinds of offenses, depending on the severity of the alleged crime, which increases from *Strafrichter* (least severe) to *Große Strafkammer* (most severe). The *Strafrichter* decides as a single judge (GVG 1877, §§ 24, 25). The *Schöffengericht* consists of one professional judge and two lay assessors (GVG 1877, § 29(1)). The prosecutor may request a second professional judge to be present. The constellation is called *Erweitertes Schöffengericht* – expanded court of lay assessors (GVG 1877, § 29(2)). Prosecutors use this rarely (Table 8.1) and mainly if they fear that the lay assessors may outvote the professional judge. The *Große Strafkammer* consists of two (sometimes three) professional judges and two lay assessors (GVG 1877, § 76).

In the mixed tribunals, the verdict and the sentence require a two-thirds majority among all participating judges (professional and lay assessors) (GVG 1877, § 196). Thus, the lay assessors at the *Schöffengericht* formally have the power to enforce any decision that they agree upon among themselves, even if the professional judge disagrees, while the lay assessors at the *Große Strafkammer* (with responsibility for the most severe crimes) have only a blocking minority in favor of the defendant.

Judgments rendered by the *Strafrichter* and the *Schöffengericht* may be appealed to the *Kleine Strafkammer* (criminal division) at the *Landgericht* by an appeal in matters of fact and law (*Berufung*) (GVG 1877, § 74(3)). In the *Berufung*, the legal issues and most of the facts are reviewed again. Like the *Schöffengericht*, the *Kleine Strafkammer* consists of one professional judge and two lay assessors (GVG 1877, § 76(1)). Thus, the judgments of first instance rendered by a single professional judge can always be appealed to a court staffed with two lay assessors and one professional judge. As members of the *Kleine Strafkammer*, *Schöffen* are involved in most of the cases heard by appeal courts (Table 8.1). The judgment of a *Berufung*, as well as the judgments of first instance rendered by a *Große Strafkammer* or a *Strafsenat*, may be appealed to the *Oberlandesgericht* or to the *Bundesgerichtshof* (BGH, the highest court in non-constitutional jurisdiction in civil and criminal cases) by an appeal in matters of law only (*Revision*) (GVG 1877, §§ 121(1), 133). The *Revision* addresses exclusively legal issues. The courts of *Revision* consist of professional judges only. In every case, guilty and not-guilty judgments may be appealed, and the prosecution may always bring an appeal also in favor of the defendant (which rarely happens, though). This is a consequence of the German investigative procedure in which the prosecution is obligated to investigate extenuating circumstances.

GERMAN LEGAL PROCEDURE

Germany uses an investigative procedure in the criminal courts. Before the main hearing, the judge reads the case dossier developed by the public prosecutor and has to be convinced that there is a *prima facie* case for a trial. The judge plans the trial, including the taking of evidence, based on the content of the dossier. In the main hearing, the judge tests his or her case theory (or theories) (Rennig & Machura, 1999). Only evidence heard in an open court can be part of the court decision. After the judges, including the lay judges, have finished their questioning of a witness, the presiding judge routinely invites additional questions by the prosecutor and defense. Cases in which the defendant has admitted guilt are still given a full trial, unless they are decided out of court. This happens if the defendant was offered and accepted a fine or a light suspended sentence by way of penal order (*Strafbefehl*), which is typical for misdemeanors. The judge decides on issuing a penal order; it does not involve plea bargaining. Indeed, most of the criminal cases are dealt with by penal order (Lieber, 2018a).

The German court culture values cooperation and consensus. The assumption is that judge, prosecution, and defense cooperate to establish the "truth" of the case or a "best possible approximation" (Pfister, 2010, p. 97). This is in contrast to the Anglo-American trial, in which two parties present two *different* versions of the case to the judge (Asimow, 2007). The culture of consensus, so typical in German courts, continues during the deliberations of the judges. The panel members tend to avoid confrontation, or even voting. Instead, they deliberate until they reach a mutually acceptable position (Machura, 2001a).

Typically, German judges avoid harsh sentencing (as perceived by the lay assessors, but also by the German public, as mentioned in the previous section). Even the prosecutors often change their position, as they are required to take into account all aspects that favor a defendant's cause (Machura, 2001a; Rüter, 1998). The Federal German Constitution (Grundgesetz für die Bundesrepublik Deutschland [GG, 1949], Art. 20(1)) defines a "social state of law" which, when combined with resource pressures, tends to translate into measured punishment for defendants. Contemporary penal philosophy stresses the idea of offender rehabilitation and not just retribution (Machura, 2001a). The death penalty is unconstitutional in Germany (GG, Art. 102).

In recent years, "deals" between prosecution and defense have become more common, sometimes encouraged by the professional judge, mainly to move cases more quickly. Still, the judge has to believe that a correct outcome has been reached. The practice of deals in court has come under increased scrutiny and has been partially curbed because some professional judges did not consult with the lay judges properly and permitted the lay judges to be effectively sidelined. According to § 257c Strafprozeßordnung (StPO, 1877), since August 4, 2009, no agreement can be approved without proper consultation with the lay assessors.

Selection, Rights, and Responsibilities of Lay Assessors

Lay assessors are chosen by a process of proposal and election (Lieber, 2017), which is dominated by the local parliaments and local authorities at both stages. Increasingly, there are campaigns inviting citizens to put themselves forward to serve as lay assessors (Lieber, 2017). Otherwise, there is a reliance on political parties and civic associations for proposals. The resulting parliamentary/council proposals are required to ensure that lay assessors will be representative of the community along the characteristics of gender, age, profession, and social status. To serve on the youth court, lay assessors need relevant educational experience, for example as school teachers, youth workers, or volunteers with a youth charity. Lay assessors are elected for a period of five years (GVG 1877, § 42). They hear several cases per year, and at least in the lower criminal court, several cases per day. Lay assessors can also be reelected, either to the same court or to another court.

Which lay assessor serves during which trial is determined randomly. The literature mentions ways for presiding judges to avoid lay assessors with whom they think they cannot cooperate, such as making up reasons to postpone the case to a day for which another set of lay assessors is allocated (Lieber, 1995). A lay assessor, like a professional judge, may be challenged by the defendant or the prosecution if there is a good reason to doubt the impartiality of the lay assessor.

Although lay assessors participate only in the oral and public trial, they have the same responsibilities and rights in those proceedings as the professional judges. They have to decide on factual as well as legal questions. During the trial, they also decide, together with the professional judge(s), on all of the important procedural questions that precede the final judgment. This arrangement follows from the investigative nature of the proceedings. If a decision, which may be made outside the oral and public trial, happens during the trial, then the lay assessors take part in this decision too. For example, lay assessors and professional judges participate in decisions pertaining to the prolongation of pretrial detention. The votes of professional and lay assessors have equal weight. More typically, however, a formal vote is not taken because the professional judges and lay assessors realize that they agree (own experience; Machura, 2001a). The lay assessors are instructed about the relevant legal issues by the professional judge(s). They are instructed not in open court, but in chambers during the preliminary deliberations (which means that the parties have no way of knowing).

During the taking of evidence, the lay assessors have the same rights as other participants in the trial to ask questions of the defendant, the witnesses, or the experts. The order in which participants can ask questions is as follows: presiding judge, other professional judges (present at the *Große Strafkammer*), lay assessors, prosecution, defense (or defendant). Here again, the investigative nature of the proceedings gives the lay assessors the chance to play an active role.

One of the hotly debated issues of German criminal procedure is lay assessors' access to the investigative dossiers (Lilie-Hutz, 2017). According to the long-standing position of the *Bundesgerichtshof*, which has been controversial among scholars (Schmitt, 2018), the lay assessors were not allowed to study the investigative dossiers. Lay assessors were not privy to the information in the dossiers unless it was made public during the oral and public trial. In 1997, however, the *Bundesgerichtshof* decided that professional judges could give lay assessors parts of the dossiers consisting of transcripts of wiretapped phone calls of the defendants when audio recordings were used as evidence in the trial (BGH 3 StR 42/96). This change helped lay assessors to understand the recordings. In the same year, the *Bundesgerichtshof* explained that lay assessors' knowledge of parts of the investigative dossiers did not bias them and did not violate key principles of criminal procedure (BGH 3 StR 250/97; Linkenheil, 2003).

SOCIAL SCIENCE FINDINGS

Over the past five decades, a number of empirical studies have been conducted on German mixed courts (Appendix A). Researchers varied the methodology ranging from quantitative to qualitative designs, covering courts of first and second instance, youth and adult courts, as well as different regions of Germany. For the most part, the results show a consistent picture.

The mixed tribunal is a task-related group, that is, a group formed for the purpose of fulfilling a specific task. According to status characteristics theory (Kutnjak Ivković, 1999), the status of members in such a group depends on their task-related contributions, or their perception of each other's contributions. For a mixed tribunal, the professional judge will be the authority in matters related to the law and procedure. The standing of the lay members will then depend on their input in other ways, such as their understanding of the evidence presented in court, or their contribution to finding the right sentence for a specific offender. This explains why lay assessors at the youth courts, who are selected for relevant educational experience, are held in high esteem by the professional judges (Lennartz, 2017). However, lay assessors are in a difficult position on the mixed tribunal because they lack the legal expertise of the professional judge. They often have to accept the word of the professional judge when it comes to matters of law.

The presiding professional judge will be the task group's leader. According to the relational model of authority in groups advanced by Tyler and Lind (1992), the group leader needs to treat the members fairly for them to have a good experience in the group. When this theory is applied to mixed tribunals, it means that the presiding judge should be unbiased, respect the rights of others as group members/citizens, treat them fairly, and give them the opportunity to express their views. Fairness is a paramount concern for people (Tyler, 1990). Indeed, German courts have introduced a "fair trial" as a principle of criminal procedure (Lemke, 1999), in accordance with the European Convention of Human Rights (1953), which guarantees a fair trial in a reasonable amount of time. The overall aim is the "just" disposition of cases. Given the widespread acceptance of fairness as a value, lay assessors care not only about how they are treated by the presiding judge, but also about how the parties in court are treated (Machura, 2001a). If the professional judges fall short of such expectations, a crisis of confidence will occur, perhaps triggering opposition by the lay assessors (Machura, 2001a).

Empirical research suggests that lay assessors can participate more during the deliberations than in any other phase of the proceedings. Because they cannot read the dossiers *in advance of the trial*, they must rely on the presiding judge's brief introduction before the trial for any information about the upcoming case. As a result, some find it difficult to ask questions during the main hearing (Machura, 2001a). Occasionally, *Schöffen* contribute questions perceived as helpful by the professional judges (Rennig, 1993). However, many professional judges discourage lay assessors from asking questions directly; instead, the professional judges suggest that the lay assessors submit their questions to the presiding judge who will, in turn, ask them (Machura, 2001a). This practice makes it difficult to know whether lay assessors are asking questions through the presiding judge or not asking questions at all.

To many lay assessors, the professional judge appears as an authority figure. The professional judges studied law and hear cases regularly. However, with the exception of very large courts, the lay assessors will often know their fellow judges and may be in a position to understand any preferences they have. Lay assessors work with a range of judges and over the years they will have seen many cases, including cases similar to the one at hand. Experience may work both ways, but certainly makes the lay assessors less reliant on the professional judge of the day. In general, *Schöffen* and professional judges find that lay assessors are able to follow the trial without problems (Lieber & Burchardt, 1989; Machura, 2001a; Rennig, 1993).

The introductory seminars for lay assessors are organized by the courts where they serve and tend to be brief. There are brochures describing the lay assessor's role. Lay assessors can also buy introductory books, or go to the website of the lay assessors' association *Bundesverband ehrenamtlicher Richterinnen und Richter – Deutsche Vereinigung der Schöffinnen und Schöffen (DVS)*, become a member, attend meetings and seminars, and receive the journal *Richter ohne Robe* (Judge without Robe).

After the professional judges and lay assessors hear the case, they deliberate together in the judges' chambers. The presiding professional judge leads the deliberations. Most lay assessors actively take part in the deliberations (Lennartz, 2017; Machura, 2001a). Lay assessors rarely advance extreme views (Rennig, 1993). Casper and Zeisel (1979) observed that professional judges and lay assessors tend to have a similar view of the case, particularly if the defendant has pleaded guilty. Also, mixed tribunals address offenses of serious and mid-level crimes, for which there is usually widespread condemnation in society and punishment is an appropriate response. In addition, ambiguous cases are commonly filtered out in the long decision-making process that leads up to a trial. In a study by Glöckner and Landsberg (2011), lay assessors would have favored a different judgment than the professional judge in 4% to 5% of cases. Lay assessors tend to be in their fifties and sixties, from the middle class, associated with political parties, and quite educated (Machura, 2001a). Hence, they may have views similar to those of the professional judges (Gerken, 1986; Rennig, 1993).

A key difference between the mixed tribunal and a trial by judge and jury is that the lay assessors can ask any type of question and receive an explanation from the professional judge, who is an expert in matters of law. Lay assessors are typically satisfied with the level of explanation provided by the professional judge (Machura, 2001a). Lay assessors have mentioned that they find it hard to question declarations by the presiding judge that a certain direction needs to be taken because it is standard practice in the courts (Machura, 2001a; Rennig, 1993). The same is true when the professional judge warns lay assessors that a decision they would like to make is likely to be overturned on appeal to a higher court (Struck, 2011). This is certainly part of the role of the professional judge on a mixed tribunal, but may occasionally be used as an easy way to avoid a discussion. To put it in perspective, fundamental disagreements between professional and lay assessors are rare. In Rennig's (1993) study, at least 38% of a large sample of lay assessors (n = 1,092) had at least once had the impression that a decision that the presiding judge said was compulsory was unjust. At least 20% of the entire sample thought this decision was too severe; at least 10% thought it was too lenient, and at least 7% thought the unfair outcome was linked to the defendant's wealth or lack of it. In another study (Lieber & Burchardt, 1989, p. 19), 18% of the lay assessors were of the opinion that "[p]rominent people are treated differently than little people."

In German courts, consensual decision-making is the norm rather than formal voting; not surprisingly, there is little evidence of lay assessors outvoting professional judges (Machura, 2001a). If the professional judge disagrees with the lay assessors, he or she can alter the announcement of the verdict from the traditional "The court has decided ..." to "The court of lay assessors has decided ..." (Klausa, 1972, p. 78). Alternatively, the professional judge can draft the written judgment so that it leads to an appeal (Rennig, 2001). However, professional judges do not usually take such steps because the professional judge and lay assessors tend to agree on the judgment (Machura, 2001a; Rennig, 1993).

Lay assessors might have a different view than the professional judge, and the lay assessors can influence the court decision through their deliberations with the professional judge. When more than one professional judge is part of the panel, any votes might be split in various ways. For example, the presiding judge outvotes the other professional judge with the help of the lay assessors, or the other way around, or one lay assessor's view is put aside by the rest of the panel.

In his early empirical study, Klausa (1972, p. 67) expressed concern that "authoritarian" presiding judges might silence the lay assessors. The same situation could arise with junior professional judges, who depend on the presiding judge for their careers (Lautmann, 1985; Rasehorn, 2016). Lay assessors should not shy away from necessary challenges and should not simply acquiesce to all that is said. Apart from seeking lay assessors with desirable qualities, including the willingness to express their views, there is no practical way to ensure that lay assessors will say what they think. However, lay assessors in Rennig's (1993) study voiced a different opinion than the presiding judge in at least 15% of the deliberations. In Machura's (2001a, pp. 228, 332) study of lay assessors at the lower criminal courts of Bochum and Frankfurt am Main, the majority of *Schöffen* reported that they participated in the deliberations and that they "occasionally" offered a different opinion than the presiding judge. Those who felt accepted by the presiding judge were more willing to assert dissenting opinions (Machura, 2001a).

Based on their empirical findings, Casper and Zeisel (1979; also Rennig, 1993) noted that for lay assessors to be influential and for the mixed tribunal to work most effectively, lay assessors need to be in the majority on the panel. Almost all German criminal courts with lay participation have this feature (of lay assessors in the majority), except for the *Erweitertes Schöffengericht* and the *Große Strafkammer*, courts that hear only a small number of criminal cases (Table 8.1).

In general, German lay assessors serving on mixed tribunals in criminal cases report having a good experience (Glöckner & Landsberg, 2011; Machura, 2001a). Lay assessors, as Machura's (2001a) study shows, feel respected and well treated by the professional judges, and this contributes to their positive experience, as does the perception that the mixed tribunals reached just decisions. In Kühne and Wolfe's study, lay assessors and professional judges state that the professional judges were "fair and friendly" to the lay assessors (Kühne, 1989, p. 180). Lay assessors also tend to view their fellow *Schöffen* as capable (Machura, 2001a). Most lay assessors are willing to serve again. Those who are not cite ill health or age as reasons for not serving again (Machura, 2001a). *Schöffen* were more likely to be open to an additional period of service when they also perceived that the defendants had been treated "very fairly" (Machura, 2001a, pp. 286–287, 311).

POSSIBLE REFORMS

One area in need of improvement is the recruitment of lay assessors. Under the current arrangements, citizens have no way of knowing if they will be comfortable serving as lay assessors. To address this, lay assessors could initially observe the work of a mixed tribunal. They would then be able to withdraw if they believe they are unsuited to the task (Gerken, 1986; Rennig, 1993). According to Rennig (1993), only about 8% of the lay assessors would have refused their election if they had the right to do so. Given the positive reaction that most lay assessors have to their experiences, it is unlikely that mixed tribunals would end up with too few lay assessors. On the contrary, the observation period might enhance the quality of lay assessors.

In addition, lay assessors could benefit from more training. One way is to provide an initial training period with follow-up training after the lay assessors have had some experience (Walter, 1992). Lay assessors could also benefit from learning about the contents of dossiers as well as the process of investigating a crime and the roles of the police, prosecution, defense lawyers, and judges. It would be useful for defense lawyers and prosecutors to describe their roles because some laypersons are suspicious of their work (Machura, 2001a).

In Machura's (2001a) view, improved training of lay assessors may also lead to lay assessors securing the right of access to the *full* dossier of a case and not just to parts of it as established by the ruling of the *Bundesgerichtshof* from 1997. It might help lay assessors understand the development and content of a dossier. This training would again highlight the importance for lay assessors to be present in open court and to hear arguments there. However, lay assessors' access to dossiers is a hotly contested issue (Lilie-Hutz, 2017). Rennig (1993, p. 586) argues that the "immediacy principle" has more importance and thus lay assessors should hear about the cases directly and exclusively in the main hearing. The German lay assessors' association DVS (2016b) suggests a middle way and only asks for lay assessors' access to key parts that are unlikely to lead to prejudice.

Professional judges need to respect and support their lay assessors. Empirical studies suggest that most professional judges treat lay assessors in this way (Lennartz, 2016; Machura, 2001a). Lay assessors need explanations, time for reflection, and the opportunity to express their views. Some professional judges are in the habit of setting too tight a schedule, and thus they curtail the opportunity of lay assessors to contribute as extensively as possible. Occasionally, the professional judges have misrepresented the voting rules to the lay assessors and sentenced defendants even though both lay assessors were against it. Training for lay assessors could go a long way to make them more assertive.

The practice by some professional judges of writing court decisions in a way that makes a successful appeal likely could be countered if the *Schöffen* see the final written text. This would be likely if the lay assessors had to sign the written verdict (Hillenkamp, 1998), or at least the main line of the judgment (Lieber, 1996).

CONCLUSION

The *Schöffen* and their brethren in other courts are part of the German legal culture. Without their presence, the courts would be more socially isolated from the general population. Lay assessors bring different experiences and views to mixed tribunals and they provide a counterweight to the professional judges and enhance the legitimacy of the courts through their contributions. German courts of lay assessors hear almost the whole spectrum of criminal cases above the category of minor crimes. In addition, lay assessor courts deal with appeals for minor crimes and crimes of medium level severity; they hear 88% of all appeals (Table 8.1). With this, they have an important function in the German legal system.

In the broader national context, the lay assessors at the adult criminal courts fall somewhere in the middle of a continuum of recognition running from lay assessors who are not selected for expertise to those who are. Like the case of the *Schöffen*, lay assessors on the financial and administrative courts are not required to have special knowledge or experience. They just represent the citizenry. In contrast to *Schöffen*, lay assessors on the financial and administrative courts deal with more abstract legal concepts and sometimes intricate conflicts (Baderschneider, 2010; Klausa, 1972; Machura, 2007), while typical cases at the criminal court are more understandable to a layperson. Thus, *Schöffen* find it easier to contribute to the mixed tribunal and enjoy a higher prestige among the professional judges than their colleagues in financial and administrative courts. Lay assessors at juvenile criminal court are selected for relevant educational experience and will often be social workers and teachers. Professional judges at juvenile courts draw on the experience of their lay assessors very much and their standing on juvenile criminal courts is somewhat higher than that of lay assessors on adult criminal courts.

In terms of broader lessons, the lay assessors' status on mixed tribunals is consistent with the application of status characteristics theory to lay assessors, which has been pioneered by Kutnjak Ivković (1999). In the task-related group of the mixed tribunal, individuals are assessed by their actual or perceived contributions to the work at hand. Juvenile lay assessors, with their statutory qualifications, are held in higher standing than other lay assessors. At the criminal court, lay assessors who speak their mind can at least bring in common sense and their moral understanding of the offense and circumstances. It is then the fairness of the presiding judge, opening up much needed space for real participation, that becomes crucial. In terms of theory, the relational model of authority in groups, as formulated by Tyler and Lind (1992), applies to situations like the mixed tribunals. People value having a good relationship with the authority figure in their group – in this case the professional judge presiding over the mixed tribunal – and their behavior depends on the fairness of this authority figure.

The positive contributions that lay assessors make to mixed tribunals and the positive experiences that they have in their role are not unique to Germany. For example, in labor courts in England and Wales, professional judges value the contribution of employee and employer lay judges, who bring experience from the world of work to the courtroom (Burgess, Corby, Höland, Michel, Willemez, Buchwald, & Krausbeck, 2017). The situation of lay judges in German criminal courts is similar to these employee and employer lay judges as evidenced by the way *Schöffen* experience their situation and the predominantly positive views held by German professional judges. The earliest studies on mixed tribunals already pointed out that the behavior of the presiding professional judge toward the lay assessors is crucial. The results by Klausa (1972) for a variety of German courts were preceded by those of the large Polish lay assessor study that included the observation of deliberations of mixed tribunals (Zawadzki & Kubicki, 1970). "The actual influence of the lay judge upon decision-making depends on particular relationships within the panel. The attitude of the professional judge toward the lay judge is highly relevant" (Borucka-Arctowa, 1976, p. 291). The influence of the Polish "*lawnicki*" (lay judges) was higher when the professional judges treated them as "equal partners" (Pomorski, 1975, pp. 204, 206).

German mixed tribunals are unique in some respects. They have a long-standing tradition in the German court system dating back to the nineteenth century. Lay assessors' deep roots on mixed tribunals in Germany are illustrated by the first paragraph of the judicial code defining judges as lay and professional judges (DRiG, 1972), by their presence throughout most parts of the court system (Machura, 2001a), and by their presence in courts of criminal appeals. What German mixed tribunals share with mixed tribunals in other countries is that their functioning is put to the test every day and their success depends on how well the individuals involved perform their roles.

REFERENCES

Asimow, M. (2007). Popular culture and the adversary system. *Loyola of Los Angeles Law Review*, 40(2), 653–685.

Baderschneider, M. M. S. (2010). *Der Bürger als Richter: Eine empirische Untersuchung des ehrenamtlichen Richters an den Verwaltungsgerichten* [The citizen as judge: An empirical study of lay assessors at administrative courts]. Frankfurt am Main: Lang.

Battenberg, F. (1990). Schöffen, Schöffengericht [Lay assessors, court of lay assessors]. In A. Erler & E. Kaufmann (Eds.), *Handwörterbuch zur deutschen Rechtsgeschichte* [Concise dictionary of German legal history], Vol. 4 (pp. 1463–1469). Berlin: E. Schmidt.

Borucka-Arctowa, M. (1976). Citizen participation in the administration of justice: Research and policy in Poland. In L. Friedman & M. Rehbinder (Eds.), *Zur Soziologie des Gerichtsverfahrens: Jahrbuch für Rechtssoziologie und Rechtstheorie* [On the sociology of legal proceedings: Yearbook for legal sociology and legal theory], Vol. 4 (pp. 286–299). Opladen: Westdeutscher Verlag.

Bundesamt für Justiz [Federal Office of Justice (Ger.)]. (n.d.). Ehrenamtliche Richterinnen und Richter zum 1. Januar 2014, Geschlechtsstruktur: Erwachsenen- und Jugendspruchkörper insgesamt [Lay assessors as of January 1, 2014. Gender structure:

Total of adult and youth panels]. www.bundesjustizamt.de/DE/SharedDocs/Publikationen/Justizstatistik/Schoeffenstatistik_2009.pdf?__blob=publicationFile

Bundesministerium der Justiz [Federal Ministry of Justice (Ger.)]. (1996). *Im Namen des Volkes? Über die Justiz im Staat der SED* [In the name of the people? On the legal system in the state of the SED]. Exhibition catalogue. 2nd ed. Leipzig: Forum.

Burgess, P., Corby, S., Höland, A., Michel, H., Willemez, L., Buchwald, C., & Krausbeck, E. (2017). *The roles, resources and competencies of employee lay judges: A cross-national study of Germany, France and Great Britain*. www.boeckler.de/pdf/p_fofoe_WP_051_2017.pdf

Casper, G., & Zeisel, H. (1972). Lay judges in the German criminal court. *Journal of Legal Studies*, 1(1), 135–191.

(1979). Bundesrepublik Deutschland [Federal Republic of Germany]. In G. Casper & H. Zeisel (Eds.), *Der Laienrichter im Strafprozeß* [The lay judge in the criminal case] (pp. 21–86). Heidelberg: C. F. Müller.

Deutsches Richtergesetz [German Law on Judges] (04/19/1972), § 1.

DVS. (2016a). *Lay judges in Germany*. www.schoeffen.de/ehrenamtliche-richter/lay-judges-in-germany.html

(2016b). Rechtspolitisches Programm des Bundesverbandes ehrenamtlicher Richterinnen und Richter e.V. [Legal-political program of the Federation of Lay Judges]. *Richter ohne Robe*, 28(1), 10–17.

Editors. (2019). Sidenote 3. *Richter ohne Robe*, 31(2), 62.

European Convention of Human Rights (09/03/1953), Art. 6(1).

Gerichtsverfassungsgesetz [Court Procedure Code (Ger.)] (01/27/1877), §§ 24, 25, 29(1), 29(2), 42, 74(3), 76, 76(1), 121(1), 122, 122(1), 133, 196.

Gerken, J. (1986). Bürger als Richter: Eine Studie über Einstellungen und Erfahrungen von Schöffen in Jugendstrafverfahren [The citizen as judge: A study on attitudes and experiences of youth court lay assessors in youth criminal trials]. Diploma thesis, Department of Psychology, University of Hamburg.

(1988). Bürger als Richter: Über Jugendschöffen und den Erziehungsanspruch des Jugendstrafrechts [The citizen as judge: On youth court lay assessors and the pretension of the youth criminal law to educate]. In J. Gerken & K. F. Schumann (Eds.), *Ein trojanisches Pferd im Rechtsstaat: Der Erziehungsgedanke in der Jugendgerichtspraxis* [A trojan horse in the rule of law: The educational concept in the practice of juvenile justice] (pp. 101–125). Pfaffenweiler: Centaurus.

Glöckner, A., & Landsberg, M. (2010). *Entscheidungsverhalten von Schöffen: Forschungsbericht* [Decision behavior of lay assessors at criminal courts: Research report]. Bonn: Max-Planck-Institut zur Erforschung von Gemeinschaftsgütern.

(2011). Der Schöffe entscheidet: Eine empirische Studie zum Entscheidungsverhalten von Schöffen [The lay assessor at criminal court decides: An empirical study on the decision behavior of lay assessors at criminal courts]. *Richter ohne Robe*, 23(2), 44–47.

Grundgesetz für die Bundesrepublik Deutschland [Basic Law of the Federal Republic of Germany] (05/23/1949), Art. 20(1), 102.

Hillenkamp, T. (1998). Zur Teilhabe des Laienrichters [On the participation of lay judges]. In H.-J. Albrecht, F. Dünkel, H.-J. Kerner, J. Kürzinger, H. Schöch, & K. Sessar (Eds.), *Internationale Perspektiven in Kriminologie und Strafrecht: Festschrift für Günther Kaiser zum 70. Geburtstag* [International perspectives in criminology and criminal law: Commemorative publication for Günther Kaiser on his seventieth birthday], Vol. 2 (pp. 1437–1459). Berlin: Duncker & Humblot.

Kammholz, K. (2018, June 29). Wieviele Einwohner hat Deutschland eigentlich? [How many inhabitants does Germany actually have?] *Berliner Morgenpost.* www.morgenpost.de/politik/article214716939/Wie-viele-Einwohner-hat-Deutschland-eigentlich.html

Kern, E. (1954). *Geschichte des Gerichtsverfassungsrechts* [History of the Court Procedure Code]. Munich: C. H. Beck.

Klausa, E. (1972). *Ehrenamtliche Richter: Ihre Auswahl und Funktion, empirisch untersucht* [Lay assessors: Their selection and function, empirically studied]. Frankfurt am Main: Athenäum.

Knittel, E. (1970). *Mitbestimmung in der Strafjustiz: Was soll aus dem deutschen Schwurgericht werden?* [Participation in criminal courts: What should become of the German jury court?] Marburg: N. G. Elwert.

Köcher, R. (2014, July 23). Großes Vertrauen in die deutsche Justiz [Great trust in German courts]. *Frankfurter Allgemeine Zeitung.* www.ifd-allensbach.de/uploads/tx_reportsndocs/FAZ_August_Justiz.pdf

Kronenberger, F. R. (1989). Laien in der Strafrechtspflege? [Laypersons in the administration of criminal law?] In H. Jung (Ed.), *Alternativen zur Strafjustiz und die Garantie individueller Rechte der Betroffenen* [Alternatives to criminal justice and guaranteeing individual rights of those affected] (pp. 185–191). Bonn: Forum.

Kühne, H.-H. (1989). Laienkompetenz gegen Expertenkompetenz im Strafrecht? [Lay competence versus expert competence in criminal law?] In H. Jung (Ed.), *Alternativen zur Strafjustiz und die Garantie individueller Rechte der Betroffenen* [Alternatives to criminal justice and guaranteeing individual rights of those affected] (pp. 175–183). Bonn: Forum.

Kutnjak Ivković, S. (1999). *Lay participation in criminal trials: The case of Croatia.* Lanham, MD: Austin & Winfield.

Lautmann, R. (1985). Rechtsfindung als Karriereberuf [Finding law as a professional career]. In *Festschrift für Rudolf Wassermann zum sechzigsten Geburtstag* [Commemorative publication for Rudolf Wassermann on his sixtieth birthday] (pp. 109–121). Neuwied: Luchterhand.

Lemke, M. (1999). Die grundlegenden Prinzipien des Strafverfahrens [The basic principles of criminal procedure]. In H. Lieber & U. Sens (Eds.), *Ehrenamtliche Richter: Demokratie oder Dekoration am Richtertisch?* [Lay assessors: Democracy or decoration at the judge's table?] (pp. 112–116). Wiesbaden: Kommunal- und Schulverlag.

Lempert, R. (2015). The American jury system: A synthetic overview. *Chicago-Kent Law Review*, 90, 825–859.

Lennartz, O. (2016). *Erziehung durch Jugendschöffen?* [Education by youth court lay assessors?] Baden-Baden: Nomos.

(2017). Erziehung durch Jugendschöffen? [Education by youth court lay assessors?] *Richter ohne Robe*, 17(1), 3–5.

Lieber, H. (1994). Umfrage zur Arbeit der Schöffen in Brandenburg [Survey on the work of lay assessors at criminal courts in Brandenburg]. *Richter ohne Robe*, 6(1), 1–13 (cited after the manuscript).

(1995). Das Fragerecht des Schöffen und seine Beschränkungen. Umfang, Verfahren, Konsequenzen [The right of lay assessors at criminal courts to ask questions and its limitations: Extent, procedure, consequences]. *Richter ohne Robe*, 7(3), 106–109.

(1996). *Handbuch für Schöffinnen und Schöffen* [Handbook for lay assessors at criminal courts]. Erfurt: Deutscher Kommunal-Verlag.

(1997). An der Wende zweier Schöffenperioden: Ergebnisse einer Umfrage [At the watershed of two periods of lay assessors at criminal courts: Results of a survey]. *Richter ohne Robe*, 9(4), 118–119.

(2017). *Die Verantwortung der Gemeinden und Kreise bei der Schöffenwahl 2018* [The responsibilities of municipalities and counties in the 2018 election of lay assessors at criminal courts]. Wiesbaden: Kommunal- und Schulverlag.

(2018a). 25 Jahre Rechtspflegeentlastungsgesetz: Eine Bilanz aus der Sicht der ehrenamtlichen Richter [25 years of the Law on the Relief of the Administration of Justice: A balance from the point of view of lay assessors]. *Richter ohne Robe*, 30(1), 14–17.

(2018b, October 10). Prozent der Strafverfahren in mündlicher Hauptverhandlung [Percent of criminal trials in oral hearing]. Email communication.

Lieber, H., & Burchardt, U. (1989). *Laienrichter: Dekoration oder Demokratie am Richtertisch?* [Lay judges: Decoration or democracy at the judge's table?] Dortmund: Pad-Verlag.

Lilie-Hutz, A. (2017). *Akteneinsicht für Schöffen* [Access to files by lay judges at criminal courts]. Frankfurt am Main: Peter Lang.

Linkenheil, B. (2003). *Laienbeteiligung an der Strafjustiz* [Lay participation at criminal courts]. Berlin: Berliner Wissenschaftsverlag.

Machura, S. (2001a). *Fairneß und Legitimität* [Fairness and legitimacy]. Baden-Baden: Nomos.

(2001b). Interaction between lay assessors and professional judges in German mixed courts. *International Review of Penal Law*, 72(1–2), 451–479.

(2006). *Ehrenamtliche Verwaltungsrichter* [Lay assessors at administrative courts]. Berlin: LIT.

(2007). Lay assessors of German administrative courts: Fairness, power distance orientation and deliberation activity. *Journal of Empirical Legal Studies*, 4(2), 331–362.

(2011). Media influence on the perception of the legal system. In K. Papendorf, S. Machura, & K. Andenaes (Eds.), *Understanding law in society* (pp. 239–283). Zurich: LIT.

(2016). Civil justice: Lay judges in the EU countries. *Oñati Socio-Legal Series*, 6(2), 235–254. http://opo.iisj.net/index.php/osls/article/viewFile/548/865

Mathes, R. (1999). *Volksrichter – Schöffen – Kollektive* [People's judges – Lay assessors – Collectives]. Frankfurt am Main: Peter Lang.

Pauli, H.-U. (1999). *Umfrage unter den ehrenamtlichen Richterinnen und Richtern bei dem Sozialgericht Münster* [Survey of lay assessors at the Munster Social Court]. Münster: Sozialgericht Münster. Az. M E 522–91.

Peller, W. (1999). Schöffen in der DDR [Lay assessors in the GDR]. In H. Lieber & U. Sens (Eds.), *Ehrenamtliche Richter: Demokratie oder Dekoration am Richtertisch?* [Lay assessors: Democracy or decoration at the judge's table?] (pp. 193–197). Wiesbaden: Kommunal- und Schulverlag.

Petersen, T. (2020, June 18). Die Stunde der Wissenschaft [The hour of science]. *Frankfurter Allgemeine Zeitung*.

Pfister, W. (2010). Die Verfahrensabsprache im Strafprozess: Welche Rolle haben die Schöffen? [The deal in criminal trials: What is the role of lay assessors in criminal court?] *Richter ohne Robe*, 22(2), 97–101.

Pomorski, S. (1975). Lay judges in the Polish criminal courts: A legal and empirical description. *Case Western Reserve Journal of International Law*, 7(2), 198–209.

Professorinnen und Professoren genießen hohes Ansehen [Professors enjoy high prestige]. (2020). *Forschung und Lehre*, 27(2), 7.

Rasehorn, T. (2016). Die Kompetenz des Schöffen in der Praxis [The competence of lay assessors in criminal court in practice]. *Richter ohne Robe*, 28(1), 17–18.

Rennig, C. (1993). *Die Entscheidungsfindung durch Schöffen und Berufsrichter in rechtlicher und psychologischer Sicht* [Decision-making by lay assessors in criminal court and professional judges from legal and psychological perspectives]. Marburg: N. G. Elwert.

(2001). Influence of lay assessors and giving reasons for the judgement in German mixed courts. *International Review of Penal Law*, 72(1–2), 481–494.

Rennig, C., & Machura, S. (1999). Die Zusammenarbeit zwischen Schöffen und Berufsrichtern [The cooperation between lay assessors at criminal court and professional judges]. In H. Lieber & U. Sens (Eds.), *Ehrenamtliche Richter: Demokratie oder Dekoration am Richtertisch?* [Lay assessors: Democracy or decoration at the judge's table?] (pp. 65–70). Wiesbaden: Kommunal- und Schul-Verlag.

Rennig, C., & Strempel, D. (1996). Einführung [Introduction]. In C. Rennig & D. Strempel (Eds.), *Justiz im Umbruch* [Justice in transition] (pp. 7–11). Cologne: Bundesanzeiger.

Rönnau, T. (2017). Lay judges in the German criminal justice system: A critical review. *Waseda Law School Review*, 2, 177–211.

Rottleuthner, H. (1994). *Steuerung der Justiz in der DDR* [Control of the justice system in the GDR]. Cologne: Bundesanzeiger.

Rüter, G. (1998). Wer bleibt im Netz der Strafverfolgung hängen? [Who does not get past the net of criminal persecution?] *Richter ohne Robe*, 10(1), 3–6.

Schmitt, B. (2018). *Strafprozessordnung* [Penal Procedure Code]. 61st ed. Munich: C. H. Beck.

Statistisches Bundesamt [Federal Statistical Office (Ger.)]. (2018). *Rechtspflege. Strafgerichte. 2017*. [Administration of justice. Criminal courts. 2017]. Fachserie 10, Reihe 2.3. www.destatis.de/DE/Publikationen/Thematisch/Rechtspflege/GerichtePersonal/Strafgerichte2100230177004.pdf?__blob=publicationFile

Strafprozeßordnung [Penal Procedure Code (Ger.)] (02/01/1877), § 257c.

Struck, G. (2011). *Rechtssoziologie* [Sociology of law]. Baden-Baden: Nomos UTB.

Tyler, T. R. (1990). *Why people obey the law*. New Haven, CT: Yale University Press.

Tyler, T. R., & Lind, E. A. (1992). A relational model of authority in groups. In M. Zanna (Ed.), *Advances in experimental social psychology*, Vol. 25 (pp. 115–191). New York: Academic Press.

Walter, A. (1992). Was müssen, was sollen Schöffen wissen? [What do lay assessors at criminal court have to and should know?] In Deutsche Vereinigung der Schöffinnen und Schöffen & Stiftung Mitarbeit (Eds.), *1. Deutscher Schöffentag: Mehr Demokratie am Richtertisch* [More democracy at the judge's table] (pp. 30–52). Bonn: Stiftung Mitarbeit.

Wolfe, N. (n.d.). Untitled research report. Manuscript.

Zawadzki, S., & Kubicki, L. (Eds.). (1970). *Udzial lawnikow w postepowaniu karnym* [Lay participation in criminal cases]. Warsaw: Wydawnictwo Prawnisze.

APPENDIX A STUDIES ON GERMAN MIXED TRIBUNALS (SELECTION)

Publication	Study, sample	Return rate	Notes
Casper & Zeisel, 1972, 1979	570 questionnaire reports of trials at a range of mixed tribunals, received from an unknown number of professional judges presiding over mixed tribunals in three provinces.	Unknown	Researchers had no information on participating judges due to concerns on the part of the court administration about the secrecy of deliberations.
Gerken, 1986, 1988	20 guided interviews and 25 nonstandardized questionnaires of juvenile lay assessors at local court and district court of Hamburg.	N/A	Qualitative study design.
Klausa, 1972	39 professional judges and 49 lay assessors in adult and juvenile courts in Berlin, face-to-face interviews.		Part of study involving professional judges and lay assessors at different branches of the courts.
Kronenberger, 1989	Standardized, face-to-face interviews with 114 lay assessors in Saarland province.	96%	119 lay assessors were approached to participate.
Kühne, 1989; Wolfe, n.d.	294 lay assessors and 108 professional judges in the area served by the district court of Freiburg.		Kühne, 1989 briefly mentions some results of the larger, presumably unpublished study.
Rennig, 1993	Study 1: questionnaire survey of 1,095 lay assessors and 229 professional judges at criminal courts and 307 public prosecutors in Hesse province.	Study 1: 67% (lay assessors), 59% (professional judges), 67% (prosecutors)	
	Study 2: presiding judges and lay assessors of 20 (out of 69) mixed tribunals (*Schöffengerichte*, 1 presiding judge, 2 lay assessors) answered standardized questionnaires on a particular trial in their court.	Study 2: 29%	

Lieber & Burchardt, 1989	113 participants in training seminars for lay assessors returned a mailed questionnaire, NW.**	34%	Respondents might have been especially motivated lay assessors as they attended training seminars in a political education institution.
Lieber, 1994	300 lay assessors in Brandenburg province, mailed questionnaire.	20%	DVS* sent out questionnaires to "approximately 1,500" lay assessors.
Lieber, 1997	136 lay assessors in the provinces of Brandenburg and Berlin, mailed questionnaire.	not stated	Survey by DVS* and a foundation close to the Social Democratic Party; number of people asked to participate not stated.
Machura, 2001a, 2001b	151 standardized, mailed questionnaires, lay assessors from Bochum local court: adult and juvenile court; additionally 51 face-to-face, guided interviews.	73%	
	417 questionnaires, lay assessors from Frankfurt am Main local court: adult and juvenile court.	74%	
Glöckner & Landsberg, 2010, 2011	67 lay assessors at local and district courts, questionnaire.	45%	150 lay assessors from Bavarian courts, plus 10 from Oldenburg district court invited to participate.
Lennartz, 2016, 2017	731 juvenile lay assessors and 54 professional youth court judges in NW,** questionnaire.	62%	Return rate seems to be for lay assessors and professional judges.

Note. *DVS = German lay judge association; **NW = North Rhine Westphalia province

9

The Jury in Canada

Testing the Comprehensibility of Styles of Jury Instructions and the Effectiveness of Aids

Marie Comiskey

As a young prosecutor conducting my second jury trial in Canada, I was taken aback when the defense lawyer began his closing argument by asking the jurors to shout out any questions that they had. I promptly leaped to my feet and objected to his unorthodox approach. Although the trial judge sustained my objection, I thought often about that experience over the next 15 years and wondered what I would have learned from having a face-to-face dialogue with jurors. I was curious about how effective the legal instructions read aloud by the judge were in teaching the jurors about the law. Did any of the aids that Canadian trial judges sometimes give to jurors enhance their comprehension of the law? Two aids that I was particularly interested in were: (1) written instructions that reduced to writing the oral instructions of the judge; and (2) a decision tree that summarized the judge's instructions visually in a one-page summary with a clear road map of the questions the jurors need to ask themselves in the deliberation room.

American jury instruction studies since the early 1970s had consistently found that jurors' overall understanding of legal concepts in both civil and criminal trials was poor (Ellsworth & Reifman, 2000; Goodman & Greene, 1989; Severance, Greene, & Loftus, 1984). While researchers have demonstrated that rewriting instructions to organize the material better, eliminate jargon, use plain language, and increase the use of the active voice is associated with significant improvements in comprehension, the overall comprehension scores are often far below optimum levels (Ellsworth, 1989; Ellsworth & Reifman, 2000). Although some trial judges are receptive to providing jurors with a toolbox of aids, more testing is needed on written instructions and decision trees because of studies' mixed results.

This chapter will canvass the early American studies on juror comprehension and the more recent work on how well death-qualified jurors understand instructions, and then will review the limited research on Canadian jurors' comprehension of jury instructions. I will then discuss how I designed my experiment to test and compare two styles of criminal jury instructions in Canada with the plain language instructions of California. In addition, I will also discuss how the study was designed to assess the effectiveness of two widely used aids in Canada: written instructions and decision trees.

EMERGENCE OF PATTERN JURY INSTRUCTIONS

Pattern or model jury instructions provide a template for trial judges to explain the law to jurors and enable trial judges to avoid having to reinvent the wheel each time they sit down to draft jury instructions. California was the first state in the United States to release pattern jury instructions with the publication of pattern civil jury instructions in 1938 by the Superior Court of Los Angeles County, which were then followed by pattern criminal jury instructions in 1946 (Nieland, 1979). By the late 1970s, almost all state courts in the United States had prepared pattern jury instructions (Nieland, 1979). Pattern jury instructions are sometimes criticized as being drafted to survive appellate scrutiny, rather than with the goal of communicating clearly to jurors (Diamond & Rose, 2005).

While Canada has a much shorter history of pattern jury instructions, Canadian trial judges have three sources to choose from in criminal jury trials. They are: (1) *CRIMJI: Canadian Criminal Jury Instructions* ("*CRIMJI*"); (2) *Watt's Manual of Criminal Jury Instructions* ("*WATT*"); and (3) *Canadian Judicial Council Model Jury Instructions* ("*CJC*") (Comiskey, 2010). The *CRIMJI* instructions were first published in 1987 as a joint collaboration between Justice John C. Bouck, a trial judge on the British Columbia Supreme Court, and Professor Gerald Ferguson of the University of Victoria Faculty of Law (Continuing Legal Education Society of British Columbia, 2017). Since Justice Bouck's death, *CRIMJI* is now authored by Professor Ferguson, Justice Michael R. Dambrot of the Ontario Superior Court, and Justice Elizabeth A. Bennett of the British Columbia Court of Appeal (Ferguson, Dambrot, & Bennett, 2005). The second Canadian source of instructions, *Watt's Manual of Criminal Jury Instructions*, was first published in 2003 by Justice David Watt while he was a trial judge on the Ontario Superior Court (Watt, 2005). Justice Watt was then appointed to the Ontario Court of Appeal in 2007, where he currently reviews the legal accuracy of jury instructions in criminal appeals. The third source, the *CJC* instructions, was published on the internet in 2004 by the National Judicial Council as part of an effort by former chief justice of the Supreme Court of Canada Antonio Lamer to ensure that model jury instructions are available in both French and English (Canadian Judicial Council [CJC], 2004). The preface to the instructions acknowledges that the *CJC* model instructions were heavily based on Justice Watt's instructions published one year earlier (CJC, 2004).

Canadian trial judges have discretion to choose which source of model instructions to rely on when drafting the instructions they will deliver to the jury at the end of the trial (Comiskey, 2010). Anecdotal data suggest that regional loyalties have affected trial judges' selection decisions in Canada so that reliance on *CRIMJI* predominates in the western provinces, whereas the *WATT* instructions predominate in central Canada and in eastern Canada (Comiskey, 2010). In light of these regional allegiances, it is worth testing empirically the relative comprehensibility of the various sources of pattern instructions for criminal jury trials in Canada to determine whether one is better understood by jurors. The results may encourage trial judges to be open to using a source other than the one to which they traditionally turn.

The object of this study was to compare the comprehensibility of two sources for criminal jury instructions in Canada. Since the *CRIMJI* and *WATT* instructions employ very different styles, this study was designed to test their relative comprehensibility to jurors. The *CJC* instructions were not included as they were modelled on the *WATT* instructions. When I analyzed the *CRIMJI* and *WATT* instructions in preparation for the empirical part of the study, I observed striking differences in how they communicated legal concepts. *CRIMJI* uses more traditional legal language to explain the law and quotes from the Criminal Code in Canada. Although the *CRIMJI* instructions use a more conservative approach, the authors have sought to improve the comprehensibility of the instructions by using the psycholinguistic principles recommended by American researchers in the 1970s, such as reducing sentence length, using the active voice, and avoiding complex clauses (G. Ferguson, personal communication, July 13, 2009). In contrast, the *WATT* instructions are framed as a series of logical questions to be answered by the jury. Each answer leads the jury either to the next question to be answered or to the final verdict. The *WATT* instructions are shorter than the *CRIMJI* instructions and do not contain excerpts from the Criminal Code.

I wanted to compare the *WATT* and *CRIMJI* instructions to California's plain language instructions for criminal trials, which are called the *California Criminal Jury Instructions* ("*CALCRIM*") (Judicial Council of California, 2005). I was intrigued that California's new plain language instructions were the result of a six-year complete overhaul in the 1990s and were not simply an update of a previous version of jury instructions (Tiersma & Curtis, 2008). The *CALCRIM* instructions were, in part, a response to a criticism made after the high-profile acquittal of O. J. Simpson that California's criminal pattern jury instructions, known as the *California Jury Instructions: Criminal* ("*CALJIC*"), were impenetrable and in need of complete revision (Judicial Council of California, 1996; Marder, 2006). I was impressed with how concise the *CALCRIM* instructions were, and I thought that Canada could learn from California on how to craft short and pithy jury instructions.

EARLIER STUDIES ON COMPREHENSIBILITY OF JURY INSTRUCTIONS

There have only been a handful of jury studies in Canada that have assessed the comprehensibility of jury instructions (Comiskey, 2010). One study conducted by the Canada Law Reform Commission in the late 1970s found that the comprehensibility of a sample set of instructions from one trial judge could be improved through rewriting the instructions using psycholinguistic principles (Jones & Myers, 1979). In addition, a series of studies on the comprehensibility of the *CRIMJI* pattern instructions found that the instructions were not well understood by mock jurors (Ogloff, 1991a, 1991b, 1998; Rose & Ogloff, 2001; Whittemore & Ogloff, 1995).

Since there were no published pattern jury instructions available to trial judges in the late 1970s, the Canada Law Reform Commission asked several judges to submit sample instructions for a murder case in which the defense of provocation was used (Jones & Myers, 1979). One judge's sample was chosen and then rewritten using psycholinguistic principles to simplify and clarify the instructions. The technique of rewriting using psycholinguistic principles was used by American jury researchers in the 1970s to improve the comprehensibility of pattern jury instructions (Elwork, Sales, & Alfini, 1977). The principles include eliminating the passive voice, avoiding double negatives, removing or simplifying embedded phrases, and improving the overall organization of the text (Charrow & Charrow, 1979). While researchers have found that rewriting the instructions does result in tangible gains in comprehension, a recent meta-analysis of 121 instructions from 63 articles found that using psycholinguistic strategies to simplify and clarify instructions is less effective as the complexity of legal concepts increases and alternative strategies may need to be developed for more complex legal instructions (Baguley, McKimmie, & Masser, 2017).

In the last 20 years, jury comprehension researchers have found that death-qualified juries in the United States have a poor understanding of the instructions they receive on weighing mitigating and aggravating factors (Diamond & Levi, 1996; Haney & Lynch, 1997; Wiener, Pritchard, & Weston, 1995). In a recent 2018 study, researchers found that a significant portion of white death-qualified jurors were erroneously using mitigating factors to justify their death penalty recommendation (Lynch & Haney, 2018). In a study on deliberations in Arizona civil cases, researchers found that the piecemeal approach of joining legally accurate descriptions of the law without regard to how the components fit together led to structural errors in almost a third of cases. Jurors sometimes mistakenly combined unrelated claims, liability standards, or damage instructions, or they made distinctions that were not supported by the law (Diamond, Murphy, & Rose, 2012). This suggests that a more holistic approach that integrates the instructions and considers the ways in which the individual pieces fit together is needed to improve juror comprehension.

Since my study design included the concise plain language criminal jury instructions from California, *CALCRIM*, I wanted to determine whether there were any US studies that compared the effectiveness of the previous California pattern jury instructions known as *CALJIC* with the newer *CALCRIM* instructions. Tiersma and Curtis (2008) found that mock jurors who received the newer *CALCRIM* instructions that explained the difference between direct and circumstantial evidence performed 11% better during testing than those who received the traditional *CALJIC* instructions. In a more recent study, Coleman, Espinoza, and Coons (2017) replicated this finding and found that mock jurors performed better on comprehension tests if they received the *CALCRIM* concise plain language instructions on reasonable doubt and the distinction between direct and circumstantial evidence. However, they did not find any significant difference in comprehension levels among the mock jurors between the *CALCRIM* or *CALJIC* instructions on murder aforethought, which explains the mental element required for murder in California (Coleman et al., 2017).

While there are no known studies comparing the relative comprehensibility of the *CRIMJI* and *WATT* instructions, there have been a series of jury simulation studies in Canada testing juror comprehension of some *CRIMJI* instructions and one study of the *CJC* instructions. Ogloff (1991a) tested juror comprehension of the attempted murder and aggravated assault instructions in *CRIMJI* and found that the mock jurors were able to recall less than a third of the key legal elements. Whittemore and Ogloff (1995) found that the *CRIMJI* instruction explaining the consequences of a not criminally responsible verdict to jurors was not well understood – only 20% of the mock jurors understood the instructions. Rose & Ogloff also found extremely low levels for the notoriously complex instructions on the co-conspirators' exception to the hearsay rule (2001; MacKinnon, 1977). Rose and Ogloff attempted to draft an improved "plain language" version of these instructions, but they did not find any significant comprehension differences between the two versions. A recent study by Bertrand and Jochelson (2018) examined how Canadian mock jurors self-reported their understanding of the *CJC* instructions on manslaughter, second-degree murder, and first-degree murder, but they did not objectively measure comprehension levels. Almost half of the jurors reported less than full comprehension of the *CJC* instructions, with the most common reason for lack of understanding being legal jargon. Since most studies have found that both actual and mock jurors tend to overestimate their level of comprehension (McKimmie, Antrobus, & Baguley, 2014; Thomas, 2010), this study raises the concern that the objective level of comprehension was even lower than the mock jurors self-reported.

Jury research in Canada on the comprehensibility of pattern jury instructions has been limited primarily to the *CRIMJI* instructions (Comiskey, 2010). Compared to the United States, there are far fewer empirical studies on the jury in Canada. This is due, in part, to fewer funding opportunities and in part to section 649 of the Canadian Criminal Code, which makes it a criminal offense for a juror to discuss the deliberation process, and which has had a chilling effect on field research. This prohibition remains despite numerous calls for its removal or amendment (Parliament of Canada, 2018; Department of Justice (Canada), 2009). The comprehensibility of jury instructions is only one aspect of jury research. Canadian researchers have conducted simulation studies on other aspects of juror decision making including the impact of pretrial publicity, photographic evidence, types of alibis, DNA evidence, and the gender of experts on juror decision-making (Douglas, Lyon, & Ogloff, 1997; Ewanation, Yamamoto, Monnink, & Maeder, 2017; Maeder & Dempsey, 2013; Ogloff & Vidmar, 1994; Schuller, Ryan, Krauss, & Jenkins, 2013; Schuller, Terry, & McKimmie, 2005).

A recent study conducted in both Australia and New Zealand found that jurors who received an integrated step style of instructions (called fact-based directions in Australia and New Zealand), similar to the *WATT* instructions in Canada, received the highest results on comprehension tests compared to the jurors who received other styles of instructions (Clough, Spivak, Ogloff, Tinsley, & Young, 2018). However, the differences were only statistically significant for the paraphrase questions and not for the multiple-choice questions (Clough et al., 2018). Among a subsample who were asked to deliberate and fill out one questionnaire per group, the researchers found that mock jurors who received the integrated step style of instructions had significantly higher scores than mock jurors who had received the standard pattern instructions, the plain language instructions, or a decision tree (Clough et al., 2018). This recent study suggests that there may be comprehension advantages to a style of instructions that integrates legal concepts into factual questions and that it is worth considering whether the same benefits observed in the joint Australia and New Zealand study might equally apply to the *WATT* integrated step style of instructions in Canada.

JURY AIDS THAT EMPLOY A VARIETY OF SENSES MAY ENHANCE COMPREHENSION

When trial judges use only the traditional method of reading their instructions aloud without providing any aids, jurors acquire their legal knowledge aurally through listening to the instructions. However, pedagogical studies have found that, when material is presented to adult learners through more than one sense (e.g., visually and aurally), the acquisition of knowledge is enhanced (Shams, Wozny, Kim, & Seitz, 2011; Shams & Seitz, 2008). By analogy, the ability of jurors to absorb legal concepts could be improved by taking a multisensory approach to juror learning. The two aids tested in this study were written instructions and decision trees because they are two low-cost and low-technology tools that are easily at the disposal of trial judges in Canada. Providing individual written instructions allows jurors to supplement listening to the judge's instructions with reading and visually seeing the instructions at the same time. A decision tree is a tool that reduces the instructions to a visual chart with a list of questions that guide the jury to the appropriate verdict in light of the jury's answers to the relevant legal questions. The chart clearly identifies how the jury's answer affects the next question for the jury to answer or the verdict that flows from the answer. In Canada, decision trees are readily available to trial judges as *WATT* contains sample decision trees for the most common serious criminal offenses. In this section, I examine the existing research on the efficacy of these aids.

Written instructions and decision trees are two aids that the Canadian Judicial Council recommends trial judges provide to jurors, although they are not mandatory (CJC, 1996–1997). There are no empirical studies on the frequency with which judges make these aids available in Canada. From my own experience as a trial and appellate lawyer, many Canadian judges do not provide the written instructions until after the oral instructions are delivered and the jury is about to enter into deliberations. Sometimes only one copy of the instructions is provided to the jury. This may dilute the efficacy of the tool as jurors are forced to rely on listening as the initial way to learn the legal concepts and can only refer to the written instructions as a resource later.

Written Instructions

Several field and jury simulation studies from the United States and the United Kingdom have found an association between written instructions and increased comprehension of legal concepts among individual jurors (Kramer & Koenig, 1990; Prager, Decklebaum, & Cutler, 1989; Thomas, 2010). In a large field study, Kramer and Koenig (1990) found that those jurors who received written instructions in addition to oral instructions during a criminal trial had an average overall comprehension score that was 9% higher than those who received only the oral instructions. Written instructions had a stronger impact than years of education and age on overall comprehension score, although all three factors were associated with higher comprehension levels. Similarly, in a study on intervening causation in civil trials, the comprehension levels of those who received a written transcript of the Florida model instructions, while listening to instructions delivered orally, were more than 10% higher than those who listened to the instructions without any aid (Prager et al., 1989). The impact of written instructions was even stronger in the same study for those who received the pattern instructions that the researchers had rewritten and had attempted to simplify. While these studies suggest that supplementing oral jury instructions with written instructions is associated with higher levels of comprehension, at least one large American field study was unable to find an association between written instructions and improved comprehension (e.g., Heuer & Penrod, 1989).

In the late 1980s, Heuer and Penrod (1989) studied the impact of written instructions on jurors' comprehension of criminal and civil instructions in a large field study with 550 jurors in Wisconsin. They found no significant comprehension difference between those who received a written version of the judge's instructions as a supplement to the oral instructions and those who received only the traditional oral instructions from the trial judge (Heuer & Penrod, 1989). However, some elements of the field-study design may have made it more difficult to detect an improvement effect. For example, researchers were not permitted to approach jurors in the courthouse; instead, they were required to mail them questionnaires after the trial (Heuer & Penrod, 1989). Furthermore, when the individual jurors completed the questionnaires an average of 2.1 days after the trial ended, they did not have the written instructions with them. The power of the tool may have been diluted by the passage of time and by the fact that the jurors did not have the written instructions available to them when they filled out the questionnaire.

Decision Trees

Research studies have yielded mixed results about the role of a decision tree in enhancing juror comprehension of legal instructions (Dann, Hans, & Kaye, 2004; Ede & Goodman-Delahunty, 2013; Ogloff, 1998). In some studies, the effect of the decision tree could not be measured either because it was not used by the jurors or because it was combined with another tool, such as an animation, to explain the legal concepts (Brewer, Harvey, & Semmler, 2004; Ogloff, 1991a). The research from Australia suggests that decision trees may enhance comprehension in complex trials, but they are less useful for a concept such as reasonable doubt.

In the only known Canadian study on decision trees and juror comprehension of criminal law, there was no difference detected between those who received a decision tree and those who received no aid in a trial simulation of an attempted murder and assault trial (Ogloff, 1998). However, Ogloff cautioned against drawing any negative conclusions about the efficacy of decision trees because he discovered that the mock jurors did not refer to or appear to rely on the decision trees when he reviewed the videotapes of the deliberations in his study.

There have been two American studies that suggest that a decision tree has the potential to improve juror comprehension. In a study on comprehension of mitochondrial DNA evidence, mock jurors who received a checklist summary of questions had higher comprehension scores than those who were given another aid, such as the opportunity to ask questions of an expert or the opportunity to use a juror notebook with a glossary of DNA terms, and a copy of the expert witness's slides (Dann et al., 2004). However, the differences were not statistically significant when compared to jurors who received no aid. In a more recent study on Virginia death penalty instructions, the mock jurors who received a summary list of questions along with pattern instructions rewritten in simplified language performed better on all the legal knowledge questions when compared with jurors who received no aid (Patry & Penrod, 2013). However, Patry and Penrod (2013) could not pinpoint whether the improved comprehension was associated with their revisions to the standard Virginia instructions or to the summary sheet that reduced the instructions to a decision tree list of questions because the mock jurors received both. Similarly, although Brewer, Harvey, and Semmler (2004) found that Australian mock jurors who received a decision tree performed substantially better on a comprehension test than those who received only oral instructions, they could not be sure whether the decision tree was the cause of the improved comprehension because these mock jurors had also been exposed to an animation explaining the law of self-defense. While these studies raise the possibility that a decision tree may improve juror comprehension, careful attention needs to be paid to the methodological design to ensure that if a benefit exists, it can be identified.

Recent studies in the United Kingdom and Australia have found that a decision tree may be more useful in complex cases (Ede & Goodman-Delahunty, 2013; Thomas, 2010). In a large study on jury instructions in England, the jurors from Winchester Crown Court who received a decision tree-style list of questions during the simulation were significantly better able to identify the two specific questions to be answered in determining whether the defendant had acted in self-defense in a case of assault causing bodily harm (Thomas, 2010). Australian mock jurors who received a decision tree during the recreation of an infanticide trial performed significantly better on four complex legal comprehension questions than those who received written instructions or no aid, but there were no significant differences for the six simple questions (Ede & Goodman-Delahunty, 2013). The results of another recent study in Australia and New Zealand suggest that a decision tree may assist jurors in structuring their deliberations more efficiently and focusing their discussion on the legal elements in dispute (Clough et al., 2018). This was determined by measuring whether the mock jurors were able to reach a unanimous verdict and by interviewing the mock jurors about which legal concepts were discussed during deliberations (Clough et al., 2018). Unanimity, however, is not a reliable indicator of comprehension as a deadlocked jury may have an accurate understanding of the law but nonetheless disagree on the verdict. The results were not significant and future studies are needed to determine whether a decision tree is likely to improve legal comprehension and the quality of jurors' deliberations.

THE NEW CANADIAN STUDY

The aims of this study were to assess two distinct styles of jury instructions available to Canadian trial judges (the traditional legal language style of the *CRIMJI* instructions and the integrated step style of the *WATT* instructions) and to compare them with the concise plain language style of the *CALCRIM* instructions from California, a state recognized as a leader in drafting plain language instructions in the United States (Diamond et al., 2012). The study also tested the role of two jury aids, written instructions and decision trees, in enhancing jurors' ability to absorb and to learn legal concepts.

I predicted that the *CALCRIM* concise plain language instructions would be associated with higher levels of comprehension than the other two types of instructions because the *CALCRIM* instructions were the result of a multiyear project to transform California criminal jury instructions into a plain language version that could be easily understood by jurors. The other two types of instructions, the *WATT* integrated step instructions and the *CRIMJI* traditional legal language instructions, were relatively new in Canada. Of the two Canadian styles, I predicted that the integrated step style of the *WATT* instructions would be better understood than the *CRIMJI* instructions. I theorized that the technique of breaking down legal concepts into a logical series of factual questions with an explanation of the law relevant to each question would be easier for jurors to understand when compared to the *CRIMJI* traditional legal language instructions that contained legal terminology and cited from the Canadian Criminal Code.

Next, I hypothesized that the mock jurors who were given one aid (the written instructions or decision tree) or both aids (written instructions and decision tree) would have higher overall comprehension scores than the group with no aid. I also hypothesized that the highest scores would be obtained by those who received both aids. My rationale was that having access to at least one of the aids would enable the mock jurors to learn in a variety of ways that would supplement the traditional method of aural learning. I also hypothesized that there would be a benefit to having access to both jury aids (written instructions and decision tree) and that mock jurors in this aid group would have the highest levels of comprehension.

Method of the Study

A total of 571 jury-eligible Canadian citizens with an average age of 40 participated in the jury simulation. Almost two-thirds of the mock jurors were female. English was the mother tongue for just over three-quarters of the mock jurors and almost three-quarters were born in Canada. Approximately one-third of the participants were recruited from the courthouse after being summoned for jury service, while the remainder were recruited by community advertisements such as Craig's List. The study was run in three cities in Ontario: Brampton, London, and Toronto. Participants received C$50 for their involvement in the study. The mock jurors were informed that they were participating in a study on jury instructions and that they would be asked to watch a filmed re-creation of a murder trial. They were told that they might be asked to deliberate for 45 minutes, but that everyone would be asked to fill out a questionnaire at the end of the experience. The mock jurors signed a consent form acknowledging that their participation was voluntary.

All mock jurors viewed a filmed recreation of a murder trial based on an actual case from Canada in which the defendant Norman Thibert was accused of murdering his wife's lover, Alan Sherren, in a parking lot (R. v. Thibert, 1996). While Thibert admitted shooting the victim, the key issue for the jurors to determine was whether he was guilty of manslaughter, second-degree murder, or first-degree murder (refer to Appendix A). Thibert relied on the defense of provocation and claimed that he had been provoked by taunting remarks made by the victim to "go ahead and shoot me" immediately before the shooting (R. v. Thibert, 1996). Thibert claimed that he had been in a fragile emotional state because of the breakup of his marriage and that the comments made by Alan Sherren, his wife's lover, had provoked him to discharge the gun (R. v. Thibert, 1996).

The trial simulation was filmed in the Old City Hall Courthouse in Toronto. The witness roles were played by professionally trained actors, while the legal roles were played by an actual prosecutor, defense attorney, and trial judge of the Ontario Superior Court. The evidence portion of the film lasted 70 minutes and closely mirrored the testimony given at trial. This was made possible because trial counsel, Peter J. Royal, QC, for Thibert, provided the trial transcripts to me.

The participants were assigned randomly to receive one of the three experimental *jury instructions* at the end of the filmed trial: (i) *CALCRIM*; (ii) *WATT*; or (iii) *CRIMJI*. The participants were also assigned randomly to one of four experimental *jury aid conditions:* (i) written instructions; (ii) a decision tree; (iii) a set of written instructions and a decision tree; and (iv) no aid. In Canadian trials, jurors usually have the option of taking notes, so note-taking was permitted in the experiment. Jurors could choose to take notes and were provided with a pen and paper. A sample of one of the decision trees used in the experiment is attached as Appendix A. The impact of accepting the defense of provocation is different in Canada and in California, so two different decision trees were necessary. In Canada, if the jury accepts the defense of provocation, the jury is instructed that the verdict should be manslaughter, whereas in California if the jury accepts the defense of provocation, the jury may reduce the murder to second degree and is told that the weight and significance of the defense is for the jury to decide.

After watching the filmed re-creation of the Thibert trial, half of the mock jurors were randomly assigned to deliberate in groups of 10–12 for 45 minutes to reach a verdict, while the balance of participants were asked individually to complete a questionnaire immediately after listening to the judge's legal instructions. The questionnaire contained 25 legal comprehension questions (24 true/false questions and 1 short-answer question on the elements of the defense of provocation worth four points) and a number of background questions, as well as questions about the verdict. The legal accuracy of the answers to be coded as correct were evaluated by lawyers from the relevant jurisdiction: two lawyers licensed in Ontario judged what the correct answers would be for jurors given the Canadian instructions, and a lawyer licensed in California judged what the correct answers would be for the California instructions. Most of the legal answers were the same. There were slight differences in the Canadian and California legal requirements for the defense of provocation, which should be kept in mind in evaluating the comparison.

The questionnaire tested the mock jurors' legal comprehension in five areas: (1) note-taking; (2) offense classification; (3) provocation; (4) burden of proof; and (5) types of evidence. The mock jurors needed to understand that jurors' notes were not evidence, the elements of the offenses of manslaughter, second-degree murder, and first-degree murder, the elements of the defense of provocation, the concept of proof beyond a reasonable doubt, and how to distinguish circumstantial evidence from direct evidence. After completing the questionnaire, mock jurors were given a debriefing sheet with additional information about the study.

After a one-hour training session, a newly licensed lawyer in Ontario independently scored all of the 571 participants' answers to the short-answer question on provocation using an answer grid developed by the author. There was a range of nine possible scores from 0 to 4 as half marks could be awarded. To verify reliability of the scoring, a second newly licensed lawyer scored 50 questionnaires that were randomly selected. The reliability was measured using Cohen's kappa (Cohen, 1960). The kappa was 0.75 ($p < .001$), suggesting a high level of agreement between coders (Landis & Koch, 1977).

Each mock juror earned an overall comprehension score out of 28 based on the legal comprehension test. To assess my hypotheses, a factorial analysis of variance (ANOVA) was conducted with mean overall comprehension score as the dependent variable and instruction style and aid type as the independent variables.

Findings and Their Implications

Those mock jurors who received the *WATT* integrated step style achieved the highest overall comprehension scores of the three instructions tested (Table 9.1). Their scores were 6% better than those in the *CRIMJI* traditional legal language group and 9% higher than those in the *CALCRIM* concise plain language group. The analysis of variance revealed that the overall comprehension scores were significantly different among the three instructions types. Put differently, mock jurors who received the *WATT* integrated step instructions had an overall comprehension score of 61%; those who received the *CRIMJI* traditional legal language instructions had an overall comprehension score of 55%; and those who received the *CALCRIM* concise plain language performed least well with an overall comprehension score of 52%.

Table 9.1 shows a breakdown of the mock jurors' performance on each of the five test subcategories by instruction type. Those mock jurors who received the *WATT* integrated step-style instructions achieved scores in each of the subcategories that were consistently higher than the other two instruction types and there were no significant interactions. Post-hoc Tukey HSD testing revealed that the differences were generally statistically significant except with *CRIMJI* on the provocation and burden of proof subscales and with *CALCRIM* on the evidence subscale. The largest effect size was in the provocation section, which included one short-answer question worth four points and six true/false questions worth one point each.

Mock jurors provided with both aids (written instructions and decision tree) had the highest comprehension levels of all four aid types (Table 9.2). The overall comprehension score of the mock jurors with both aids was 59%, which was 5% higher than those who received no aid. However, the effect size for type of aid was

TABLE 9.1 *Mean overall comprehension and subscale scores by instruction type*

Type of score	CALCRIM (N=194) M	SD	CRIMJI (N=184) M	SD	WATT (N=193) M	SD	F (2,568)	n^2
Overall comprehension score (out of 28)	14.50_a	(2.68)	15.43_b	(3.66)	17.16_c	(3.85)	29.91**	.10
Note-taking score (out of 2)	1.58_a	(.60)	1.45_a	(.75)	1.87_b	(.39)	24.90**	.08
Classification of offenses (out of 9)	5.07_a	(1.32)	5.40_a	(1.46)	5.90_b	(1.55)	15.90**	.06
Provocation (out of 10)	4.03_a	(1.27)	5.02_b	(1.82)	5.12_b	(2.10)	22.78**	.49
Burden of proof (out of 4)	2.00_a	(.91)	2.22_{ab}	(1.00)	2.33_b	(1.01)	5.68**	.02
Evidence (out of 3)	2.03_b	(.91)	1.73_a	(.89)	2.11_b	(.75)	10.03**	.04

** $p < .001$. Means in the same row with different subscripts were significantly different at $p < .05$.

small. There were no significant interactions. When a post-hoc Tukey test was conducted, the differences in overall comprehension scores were significant for the two-aid group (receiving both decision tree and written instructions) compared to decision tree and no aid but not when compared to written instructions. These results suggest that there is a benefit to having either written instructions or both aids, but that the decision tree may not be any more useful than no aid when given by itself to jurors.

I also considered the impact of deliberation on overall comprehension score. Deliberation was capped at 45 minutes. This time limit was a necessary logistical limitation in order to keep the total commitment to three to four hours in length for all participants. Mock jurors generally deliberated in groups of 12, but this number dropped to 10 or 11 on a few occasions when a mock juror did not show up or exited early. Those mock jurors who deliberated achieved overall comprehension scores of 54%, which were on average 4% less than those who did not deliberate, raising the possibility that the time spent deliberating may have impacted their ability to recall the instructions or that mock jurors who did not recall instructions correctly managed to convince others that their mistaken recollection of the instructions was correct.

CONCLUSION

The results of testing the comprehension of Canadian mock jurors using three distinct styles of jury instructions indicate that there is a significant advantage to integrating legal concepts into factual questions and presenting them in a logical

TABLE 9.2 *Mean overall comprehension and subscale scores by aid type*

Type of score	Decision tree and written instructions (N=147)		Written instructions (N=136)		Decision tree (N = 144)		No aid instructions (N=144)		F (3,567)	n^2
	M	SD	M	SD	M	SD	M	SD		
Overall comprehension score (out of 28)	16.57_a	(3.94)	15.54_{ab}	(3.22)	15.48_b	(3.63)	15.19_b	(3.43)	4.12^{**}	.02
Note-taking score (out of 2)	1.68_{ab}	(.57)	1.52_b	(.72)	1.60_{ab}	(.63)	1.72_a	(.52)	2.74^{*}	.01
Classification of offenses (out of 9)	5.68_a	(1.49)	5.22_b	(1.30)	5.60_{ab}	(1.64)	5.31_{ab}	(1.45)	3.22^{*}	.02
Provocation (out of 10)	5.30_a	(1.89)	4.89_{ab}	(1.81)	4.45_{bc}	(1.72)	4.24_c	(1.72)	10.12^{***}	.05
Burden of proof (out of 4)	2.28_a	(.99)	2.18_a	(1.02)	2.17_a	(.90)	2.09_a	(1.00)	.92	.01
Evidence (out of 3)	2.01_a	(.85)	1.97_a	(.81)	1.94_a	(.89)	1.92_a	(.92)	.27	.00

*** $p < .001$, ** $p < .01$, * $p < .05$. Means in the same row with different subscripts were significantly different at $p < .05$.

manner to jurors. However, the overall comprehension of the mock jurors was surprisingly low regardless of the style of instructions provided to them. The conundrum of how to improve the legal comprehension of jurors is one that confronts many countries, whether they employ the classical jury system or use lay assessors as Germany does in its mixed tribunal system. Arguably countries have a duty to ensure that jurors or lay assessors are adequately taught about the legal concepts on which they are expected to make a decision or give advice. Empirical studies that test the effectiveness of legal instructions provide a foundation on which future improvements can be made.

The results from the study on Canadian juror comprehension also suggest that aids have a role to play in enhancing and improving juror comprehension that should not be ignored. While watching a movie such as *12 Angry Men* may inspire viewers to take the civic responsibility of being a juror seriously, being provided with an effective aid may allow a juror to perform better by using a different learning strategy (such as by reading a set of written instructions or by looking at a decision tree) to acquire an accurate understanding of the law and to apply it correctly. The results suggest that it is most important to provide either written instructions or written instructions combined with a decision tree. The results also suggest that there may be a synergistic effect to providing two aids instead of one. Hence, it may be important for courts to think carefully about providing multiple aids to jurors.

Further study is needed to determine whether the style of instructions has broad implications for juror comprehension across a wide number of offenses beyond murder and whether the usefulness of written instructions and decision trees varies across offenses as well in Canada. While murder cases are the cases that often attract media attention and are higher profile, jury trials frequently occur for sexual assault, drug trafficking, and drug importing cases. In sexual assault, jurors are routinely asked to navigate complex issues of consent between two parties, which is an issue that rarely arises in a murder case. In drug importing cases, duress is frequently relied on as a defense by drug couriers who have been recruited to carry large quantities of drugs in their suitcases. It would be fruitful to explore how the *WATT*, *CRIMJI*, and *CJC* instructions explain concepts such as these and others that arise in nonmurder cases to determine whether there are significant comprehension differences among them.

There are also some lessons to be learned from conducting cross-jurisdictional research. There is the danger that there may be cultural linguistic differences that may affect comprehension and, unless the study is conducted in more than one country, it will not be possible to draw accurate inferences about the reasons for low comprehension levels. Of course, requirements even for very similar legal concepts may differ across countries, as we saw in the slightly different requirements for provocation in this cross-country comparison. What is more, determining whether there are linguistic differences in how jury-eligible citizens understand slightly different instructions requires running the study in two jurisdictions. In the study discussed in this chapter, the jury simulations occurred in three cities in Ontario, Canada. If the study occurred in at least one site in the United States, it would have been possible to determine whether the relatively poor comprehension of the experimental jurors who received the *CALCRIM* instructions would have been different in the United States. If the comprehension levels were higher in the United States for *CALCRIM*, then it would have been possible to conclude that there are linguistic differences that impeded comprehension among the Canadian subjects despite the fact that the two countries share a language and a similar criminal justice system. In order to be able to draw inferences that are applicable to both jurisdictions, it is important when designing a study to consider executing the study in all of the jurisdictions from which the jury instructions originate. Researchers also need to consider whether the benefits to be gleaned from cross-jurisdictional research outweigh the disadvantages that the research will be more complex and costly, and that it will be more difficult to interpret the results. It may be more prudent for researchers to use another jurisdiction's instruction style as an inspiration to create a revised version of their own country's instructions.

Regardless of the country in which the research is conducted, it is difficult to replicate the same level of stress and anxiety that a juror listening to instructions and then deliberating over a verdict experiences. However, jury simulation research into juror comprehension nonetheless can approximate many aspects of jury service by filming realistic reenactments of trials and having mock jurors deliberate before testing their comprehension of legal instructions. Jury simulation research can offer valuable lessons about how jurors acquire legal knowledge and how judges, lawyers, and jury instructions committees might make structural changes or offer a variety of aids that might result in real gains in comprehension. In the classical jury system, we place the lives of defendants in the hands of jurors every day. We ought to be committed to ensuring that they have an accurate understanding of the law by conducting rigorous research on how styles of instructions and jury aids can impact comprehension levels.

Acknowledgment: This research was funded by AP-LS Student Grant-in-Aid Award, SSHRC Doctoral Fellowship, Law Foundation of Ontario Grant, and a Canada–US Fulbright Award.

REFERENCES

Baguley, C. M., McKimmie, B. M., & Masser, B. M. (2017). Deconstructing the simplification of jury instructions: How simplifying the features of complexity affects jurors' application of instructions. *Law and Human Behavior, 41*(3), 284–304.

Bertrand, M. I., & Jochelson, R. (2018). Mock-jurors' self-reported understanding of Canadian judicial instructions (is not very good). *Criminal Law Quarterly, 66*, 137–161.

Brewer, N., Harvey, S., & Semmler, C. (2004). Improving comprehension of jury instructions with audio-visual presentations. *Applied Cognitive Psychology, 18*(6), 765–776.

Canadian Judicial Council. (1996–1997). *Annual report*. www.cjc-ccm.gc.ca/cmslib/general/news_pub_annualreport_1996–1997_en.pdf

Canadian Judicial Council model jury instructions. (2004). www.nji-inm.ca/index.cfm/publications/model-jury-instructions/?langSwitch=en

Continuing Legal Education Society of British Columbia. (2017). Celebrating 30 years of CRIMJI. www.cle.bc.ca/celebrating-30-years-of-crimji/

Charrow, R. P., & Charrow, V. R. (1979). Making legal language understandable: A psycholinguistic study of jury instructions. *Columbia Law Review*, 79(7), 1306–1374.

Clough, J., Spivak, B., Ogloff, J. R. P., Tinsley, Y., & Young, W. (2018). The judge as cartographer and guide: The role of fact-based directions in improving juror comprehension. *Criminal Law Journal*, 42(5), 278–295.

Cohen, J. (1960). A coefficient of agreement for nominal scales. *Educational and Psychological Measurement*, 20, 37–46.

Coleman, J., Espinoza, R. K. E., & Coons, J. V. (2017). An empirical comparison of the old and revised jury instructions of California: Do jurors comprehend legalese better or does bias still exist? *Open Access Library Journal*, 4, 1–15. https://doi:10.4236/oalib.1103164

Comiskey, M. (2010). Initiating dialogue about jury comprehension of legal concepts: Can the "stagnant pool" be revitalized? *Queen's Law Journal*, 35(2), 625–678.

Dann, B. M., Hans, V. P., & Kaye, D. H. (2004). *Testing the effects of selected jury trial innovations on juror comprehension of contested mtDNA evidence: Final technical report*. National Institute of Justice. www.ncjrs.gov/pdffiles1/nij/grants/211000.pdf

Department of Justice (Can.). (2009). *Report on jury reform*. Steering Committee on Justice Efficiencies and Access to the Justice System. www.justice.gc.ca/eng/rp-pr/csj-sjc/esc-cde/scje-cdej/toc-tdm.html

Diamond, S. S., & Levi, J. N. (1996). Improving decisions on death by revising and testing jury instructions. *Judicature*, 79(5), 224–232.

Diamond, S. S., Murphy, B., & Rose, M. R. (2012). The "kettleful of law" in real jury deliberations: Successes, failures, and next steps. *Northwestern University Law Review*, 106(4), 1537–1608.

Diamond, S. S., & Rose, M. R. (2005), Real juries. *Annual Review of Law and Social Science*, 1, 255–285.

Douglas, K. S., Lyon, D. R., & Ogloff, J. R. P. (1997). The impact of graphic photographic evidence on mock jurors' decisions in a murder trial. *Law and Human Behavior*, 21(5), 485–501.

Ede, T., & Goodman-Delahunty, J. (2013). Question trails in trials: Structured versus unstructured juror decision-making. *Criminal Law Journal*, 37(2), 114–136.

Ellsworth, P. C. (1989). Are twelve heads better than one? *Law and Contemporary Problems*, 52 (4), 205–224.

Ellsworth, P. C., & Reifman, A. (2000). Juror comprehension and public policy: Perceived problems and solutions. *Psychology, Public Policy and Law*, 6(3), 788–821.

Elwork, A., Sales, B. D., & Alfini, J. J. (1977). Juridic decisions: In ignorance of the law or in light of it? *Law and Human Behavior*, 1(2), 163–189.

Ewanation, L. A., Yamamoto, S., Monnink, J., & Maeder, E. M. (2017). Perceived realism and the CSI-effect. *Cogent Social Sciences*, 3, Article 129446.

Ferguson, G. A., Dambrot, M. A., & Bennett, E. (2005). *CRIMJI: Canadian criminal jury instructions*. 4th ed. Vancouver: Continuing Legal Education Society of British Columbia.

Goodman, J., & Greene, E. (1989). The use of the paraphrase analysis in the simplification of jury instructions. *Journal of Social Behavior and Personality*, 4(3), 237–251.

Haney, C., & Lynch, M. (1997). Clarifying life and death matters: An analysis of instructional comprehension and penalty phase closing arguments. *Law and Human Behavior, 21*(6), 575–595.

Heuer, L., & Penrod, S. D. (1989). Instructing jurors: A field experiment with written and preliminary instructions. *Law and Human Behavior*, 13(4), 409–430.

Jones, C. S., & Myers, E. R. (1979). Comprehension of jury instructions in a simulated Canadian court. *Studies on the jury*. Canada Law Reform Commission.

Judicial Council of California. (1996). *Blue ribbon commission on jury system improvement: Final report*. www.courts.ca.gov/documents/BlueRibbonFullReport.pdf

(2005). *California criminal jury instructions for judges and attorneys (CALCRIM)*. Advisory Committee on Criminal Jury Instructions. www.courts.ca.gov/partners/juryinstructions.htm

Kramer, G. P., & Koenig, D. M. (1990). Do jurors understand criminal jury instructions? Analyzing the results of the Michigan juror comprehension project. *University of Michigan Journal of Law Reform*, 23(3), 401–437.

Landis, J. R., & Koch, G. G. (1977). The measurement of observer agreement for categorical data. *Biometrics*, 33(1), 159–174.

Lynch, M., & Haney, C. (2018). Death qualification in black and white: Racialized decision making and death-qualified juries. *Law & Policy*, 40(2), 148–171.

MacKinnon, P. (1977). Conspiracy and sedition as Canadian political crimes. *McGill Law Journal*, 23, 622–643.

Maeder, E. M., & Dempsey J. L. (2013). A likely story? The influence of type of alibi and defendant gender on juror decision-making. *Psychiatry, Psychology and Law*, 20(4), 543–552.

Marder, N. (2006). Bringing jury instructions into the twenty-first century. *Notre Dame Law Review*, 81, 449–511.

McKimmie, B. M., Antrobus, E., & Baguley, C. (2014). Objective and subjective comprehension of jury instructions in criminal trials. *New Criminal Law Review*, 17(2), 163–183.

Nieland, R. (1979). *Pattern jury instructions: A critical look at a modern movement to improve the jury system*. Chicago: American Judicature Society.

Ogloff, J. R. P. (1991a). A comparison of insanity defense standards on juror decision making. *Law and Human Behavior*, 15(5), 509–531.

(1991b). *The use of the insanity defence in BC: A quantitative and qualitative analysis*. Ottawa: Department of Justice, Canada.

(1998). *Judicial instructions and the jury: A comparison of alternative strategies*. Vancouver: BC Law Foundation.

Ogloff, J. R. P., & Vidmar, N. (1994). The impact of pretrial publicity on jurors: A study to compare the relative effects of television and print media in a child sex abuse case. *Law and Human Behavior*, 18(5), 507–525.

Parliament of Canada. (2018). *Improving support for jurors in Canada*. House of Commons. Standing Committee on Justice and Human Rights. 42nd Parl., 1st Session. www.ourcommons.ca/Content/Committee/421/JUST/Reports/RP9871696/justrp20/justrp20-e.pdf

Patry, M.W., & Penrod, S. D. (2013). Death penalty decisions: Instruction comprehension, attitudes, and decision mediators. *Journal of Forensic Psychology Practice*, 13(3), 204–244.

Prager, I. G., Deckelbaum, G., & Cutler, B. L. (1989). Improving juror understanding for intervening causation instructions. *Forensic Reports*, 2(3), 187–193.

R. v. Thibert, [1996] 1 S.C.R. 37 (Can.).

Rose, G., & Ogloff, J. R. P. (2001). Evaluating the comprehensibility of jury instructions: A method and an example. *Law and Human Behavior*, 25(4), 409–431.

Schuller, R. A., Ryan, A., Krauss, D., & Jenkins, G. (2013). Mock juror sensitivity to forensic evidence in drug facilitated sexual assaults. *International Journal of Law and Psychiatry*, 36(2), 121–128.

Schuller, R. A., Terry, D. J., & McKimmie, B. M. (2005). The impact of expert testimony on jurors' decisions: Gender of the expert and testimony complexity. *Journal of Applied Social Psychology*, 35(6), 1266–1280.

Severance, L. J., Greene, E., & Loftus, E. F. (1984). Toward criminal jury instructions that jurors can understand. *Journal of Criminal Law & Criminology*, 75(1), 198–233.

Shams, L., & Seitz, A. R. (2008). Benefits of multisensory learning. *Trends in Cognitive Sciences*, 12(11), 411–417.

Shams, L., Wozny, D. R., Kim, R., & Seitz, A. (2011). Influences of multisensory experience on subsequent unisensory processing. *Frontiers in Psychology*, 2, Article 264, 1–9.

Thomas, C. (2010). *Are juries fair? Ministry of Justice research studies*. No. 1/10. London: HMSO. www.justice.gov.uk/publications/research.htm

Tiersma, P., & Curtis, M. (2008). Testing the comprehensibility of jury instructions: California's old and new instructions on circumstantial evidence. *Journal of Court Innovation*, 1(1), 231–262.

Watt, D. (2005). *Watt's manual of criminal jury instructions*. Toronto: Thomson Carswell.

Whittemore, K. R., & Ogloff, J. R. P. (1995). Factors that influence jury decision making: Disposition instructions and mental state at the time of trial. *Law and Human Behavior*, 19(3), 283–303.

Wiener, R. L., Pritchard, C. C., & Weston, M. (1995). Comprehensibility of approved jury instructions in capital murder cases. *Journal of Applied Psychology*, 80(4), 455–467.

APPENDIX A SAMPLE DECISION TREE

DECISION TREE: R. V. THIBERT

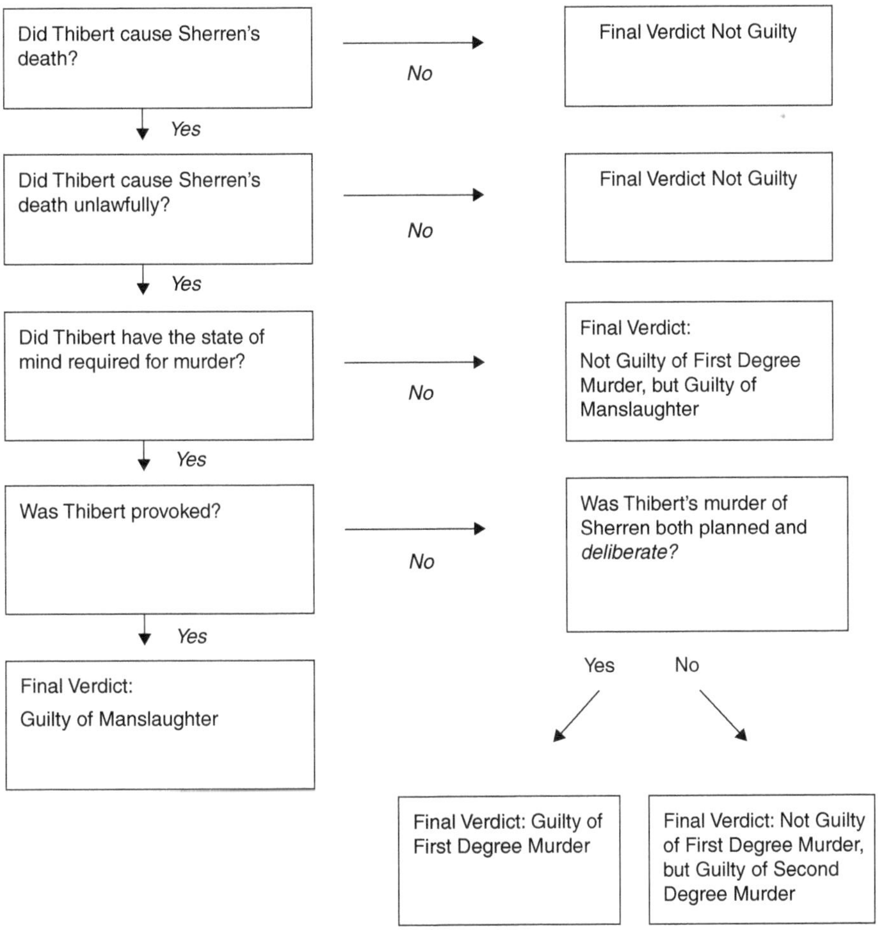

PART III

Challenges to Lay Participation in Law

10

Dismissing the Jury

Mixed Courts and Lay Participation in Norway

Anna Offit

The last decade has witnessed a resurgence of right-wing and populist sentiment in Europe and the United States, generating serious concern about the vulnerabilities of democracy (Edwards, Haugerud, & Parikh, 2017). While this concern has largely focused on the erosion of the rule of law, civil liberties, and electoral integrity, it is also critical to examine the openings for, and modes of, lay participation in justice systems. In this regard, one finds an ambivalent trend: amidst other forms of democratic backsliding, citizen participation appears to be rising in the aggregate, as countries including Japan, Argentina, South Korea, Georgia, Spain, and Russia, for example, have integrated (or reintegrated) laypersons into legal decision-making (Roudik, 2011; Scherr, 2015). It therefore seems strange that one country where things have moved in the opposite direction is one otherwise considered a bulwark of liberal democracy: Norway.

On January 19, 2017, after months of anticipation, Norwegian politicians reached an agreement to replace a system of all-layperson juries at the appellate level with mixed courts of lay and professional judges (Rundberget, 2017) – that is, the hybrid tribunals already used in the country's trial courts. Unlike their American counterparts, Norway's appellate courts provide defendants convicted of crimes that can result in a sentence exceeding six years of imprisonment with an automatic right to appeal guilty verdicts. In turn, they receive *de novo* review of their cases. The 2017 reform reflected the confidence of legal practitioners in Norway that lay and professional legal actors' deliberation as peers was more valuable than that of the all-layperson juries convened for appellate trials. They reasoned that abundant access to education, public-sector work, and advanced degrees in Norway have put more citizens on an equal intellectual footing with professional judges (M. T. Foss, 2011; Letvik, 2015). Further, they bet that, counter to what many scholars expect (Casper & Zeisel, 1972; Kutnjak Ivković, 2007), mixed courts would not necessarily lead to the domination of lay judges by their professional counterparts.

In this chapter, I argue that they were likely right, though for a reason that is often overlooked in empirical legal scholarship: culture. In her ethnographic research on relationships among Norwegian citizens, anthropologist Marianne Gullestad observed that Norwegian society is pervaded by nonhierarchical relationships characterized by an emphasis on – and desire for – "sameness" (*likhet*) and consensus rather than competition (Gullestad, 1992). When hundreds of Norwegian lay judges were anonymously surveyed between January and April of 2011 about their own experiences working with professional judges on mixed courts, they corroborated this finding (Norges offentlige utredninger [NOU], 2011:13). About 90% of respondents felt their perspectives were considered by professional judges and did not feel persuaded to change their minds.

Still, the interviews with lawyers, judges, and politicians discussed in this chapter suggest that an important qualification is needed. It appears that though lay and professional legal actors agree that ordinary citizens should participate in high-stakes criminal adjudication, they do not see eye to eye on whether lay participation should be extended equally to all criminal case types. In particular, my research reveals a pervasive view on the part of judges, prosecutors, and former lay decision-makers that with respect to cases involving violence against women, laypersons benefit from the intervention of professional judges in assessing evidence of alleged rape (Olsen, 2016).

Why are mixed courts in Norway generally viewed as better equipped than all-layperson juries to preside over criminal cases? Why do legal actors feel lay participation in mixed courts should be limited or guided in particular cases (e.g., rape prosecutions)? To address these questions, this chapter first offers an overview of the development and transformation of the jury system. It then examines aspects of (now abolished) all-layperson jury trials in Norway that prompted scrutiny of their authority vis-à-vis professional judges. After examining why the mixed court has been lauded as a fairer alternative to all-layperson juries, the chapter turns to the distinctive challenges posed by rape prosecutions that have led some lawyers and judges to criticize lay interventions in the legal system more generally. It pays particular attention to a high-profile rape prosecution known as *Hemsedalsaken* as a case that is illustrative of the still-contested place of laypersons in Norway's criminal justice system.

A BRIEF HISTORY OF LAY PARTICIPATION IN NORWAY

Although the demise of Norway's all-layperson jury system had long felt imminent to legal scholars and practitioners, it followed more than a century of debate about how laypersons ought to participate in the legal system. Drawing on the English system as a model, parliament-appointed commissions between 1853 and 1882 (referred to as "jury commissions") were tasked with evaluating lay participation in the legal system. After extensive negotiation and revision by the Ministry of Justice, the jury system became law on July 1, 1887, despite dissent by conservatives (Jordal, 2011). Proponents of the independent all-layperson jury during this period (including members of the jury commission) emphasized the importance of jurors' practical knowledge and life experience (*livserfaring*), which, they believed, counterbalanced and complemented the narrow expertise of professional judges (Jordal, 2011).

Until the official end of Norway's jury system, with the rendering of a final jury verdict in a corruption prosecution on January 28, 2019 (Olsson, 2019), Norway deployed a hybrid lay decision-making system. Two lay judges and one professional judge presided over most criminal cases before the court of first instance (Straffeprosessloven, 1981 Kap. 21 §275, Kap. 22 §276). In complex criminal matters, however, this panel was replaced by three lay judges and two professional judges who deliberated jointly (Straffeprosessloven, Kap. 22 §276). Cases with the potential to result in sentences that exceeded six years, in contrast, were decided by 10-member all-layperson juries and panels of three professional judges (Straffeprosessloven, 1981 Kap. 24 §§ 352–355). Unlike countries that deploy either juries (e.g., Russia, Spain, countries within the United Kingdom, and the United States) or mixed tribunals (e.g., Germany, Croatia, and China), the Norwegian legal system thus incorporated elements from both depending on the type of crime and phase of prosecution. In appellate criminal cases that utilized all-layperson juries, empaneled juries included five male and five female members. This feature distinguishes it from jury systems in which men or women can be disproportionately represented depending on the composition of the venire or attorneys' exercise of peremptory challenges (Straffeprosessloven, 1981 Kap. 24 § 356; Skeie, 1939).

Norway's all-layperson juries resembled US juries. And, as in American trials, judges in Norway instructed jurors not to conduct independent research or discuss their cases in advance of formal deliberations (Straffeprosessloven, 1981 Kap. 24 § 359). Juries rendered a single, collective verdict, though without the requirement of unanimity during voting; a finding of guilt required that 7 of the 10 jurors respond affirmatively to the yes-or-no questions outlined for them on a verdict form (Straffeprosessloven, Kap. 24 § 372). If the panel of professional judges accepted their verdict, three additional jurors would be selected – in addition to the foreperson and with consideration of gender parity – to determine the defendant's punishment (Straffeprosessloven, 1981 Kap. 24 § 376e).

During the century that followed, procedural changes affected the discretion and functioning of all-layperson juries. Most broadly, the question whether all-layperson juries were practical in light of Norway's culturally and politically specific milieu was revisited as part of the passage of the Criminal Procedure Act of 1981 (CPA). In place of all-layperson juries, a mixed court of one professional judge and two lay judges presided over cases tried in courts of first instance. In appellate criminal cases involving sentences with the potential to exceed six years in jail, three professional judges and 10-person juries were empaneled (NOU, 2011:6, 3.1.2).

Professional judges' power to disregard or "set aside" jury verdicts was also expanded. Section 376c of the CPA already permitted professional judges to supersede a jury's verdict when they found there was insufficient evidence of guilt (M. T. Foss, 2011; Jordal, 2011). On June 24, 1933, this discretion was extended to setting aside and retrying acquittals, a shift that was reinforced by the 1981 CPA. In both contexts, a mixed court of three professional judges and four lay judges would preside over retrials. In 1989, the all-layperson jury's mandate was further constricted: all cases involving allegations of bodily harm and assault were transferred to lower courts for trial before mixed courts of lay and professional judges (NOU, 2011:13, 5.3). These incremental reforms limiting the jury's reach and autonomy came in the wake of political debate weighing the risk of erroneous and unaccountable jury verdicts against the benefits of professional judges' direct contact with laypersons.

The process by which lay decision-makers are *selected* for service has also changed. Historically, lists of potential jurors and lay judges in Norway were solicited from political associations in municipalities (CPA § 355 (para. 1)). Some prosecutors thought a benefit of this system was the inclusion of lay decision-makers whose reputations were personally known to the public officials who endorsed them. Though jurors' employment differed, prosecutors commented on the prevalence of lay decision-makers who worked in the public sector and noted the racial homogeneity of this group (Offit, 2018). As the country's lay participation system became increasingly inclusive over time, some academic scholars and judges speculated that this shift compounded skepticism about an autonomous all-layperson jury (Offit, 2018).

NORWAY'S NEW *MEDDOMSRETT* (MIXED COURT)

In recent years, politicians in Norway moved to replace the all-layperson juries that presided over appellate criminal cases with mixed courts of lay and professional judges. After a 2014 proposal to repeal the jury system was submitted to parliament, Fremskrittspartiet (Progress Party) joined several political parties including Høyre (Conservative Party), Arbeiderpartiet (Labor Party), and Kristelig Folkeparti (Christian Democratic Party) in support of the jury system's elimination (A. B. Foss, 2015). On January 19, 2017, politicians reached an agreement that all-layperson juries in appellate trials would be abandoned (Rundberget, 2017). Parliament then passed a law on June 16, 2017, amending the CPA so that the default arrangement in such cases would be two professional and five lay judges who deliberated jointly (Lov om endringer i straffeprosessloven mv., § 332). Notably, this shift meant an increase in the number of lay judges, which had previously included two lay judges in appellate cases with potential prison sentences that fell below the six-year threshold required for a jury. This act came into force on January 1, 2018. After a phase-in period for cases already on the calendar, mixed courts have judged all subsequent criminal cases (Act 2017: 58: amendment to CPA).

Appeals courts in Norway hear testimony and evaluate the evidence anew, without reference to the proceedings below, before voting to convict or acquit a defendant. In order for the two professional and five lay members of the new appellate mixed court to convict a defendant of a crime, a five-person majority must agree on the guilty verdict (CPA, amended 2017: § 332). As we will see later in this chapter, this means it is possible for lay judges to overrule their professional counterparts in criminal cases. For those still skeptical of lay involvement in the criminal justice system, this can yield controversial outcomes that expose lay judges to public scrutiny, since – unlike American jurors – lay judges on mixed courts attach their names to majority or dissenting opinions they support. This development, however, does not affect the run of cases heard by the court of first instance, which have been – and will continue to be – jointly decided and sentenced by one professional judge and two lay judges.

A unique and enduring aspect of all mixed courts in Norway is the enforcement of gender parity among both lay and professional legal actors, which ensures (to the extent possible despite uneven numbers) that women's voices feature prominently in the justice system.

RESEARCH METHODS

Motivated by an interest in understanding the causes and consequences of Norway's impending abolition of its jury system, I conducted ethnographic research in Norway between July 2014 and July 2017. This chapter draws on the findings from this research. I interviewed 20 prosecutors, 12 professional judges, 5 defense attorneys, and 6 former lay decision-makers in the cities of Oslo, Bergen, Hamar, Tromsø, and Tønsberg. This study also benefited from conversations with journalists who covered the criminal cases, and politicians and legal academics who contributed to jury reform efforts (Offit, 2018). These interviews were not recorded. Instead, I generated typewritten, verbatim notes during interviews with my research subjects. I coded the transcripts from each interview to identify thematic patterns for later analysis (Bernard, 2011).

The open-ended questions asked of interviewees related to their experience with cases that involved lay judges and/or jurors and probed their attitudes toward lay decision-makers more generally. The inclusion of judges and prosecutors, in particular, offered a revealing window into distinctive features of Norway's adversarial legal system because they serve as impartial officers of the court (Lov om domstolene (Domstolloven) 3dje kapitel; § 55 and 6te kapitel; Kap. 6 Påtalemyndigheten § 55(4) and Kap. 9 Forsvareren § 100a).

Observations of two mixed court proceedings, eight jury trials, and discussions between lay and professional judges also contributed valuable data to this study. Though the legal proceedings I analyze were carried out in Norwegian, interpreters were used in proceedings that involved some non-Norwegian-speaking parties. My language training and residence in Norway allowed me to follow both public media discussions of the jury system and informal conversations beyond those cited here. Trial interpreters also served as key interlocutors who offered a window into their repeated participation in trial proceedings (Fiva, 2006).

LAWYERS' VIEWS ABOUT LAY PARTICIPATION

When sharing reflections on the jury system, a number of lawyers cited *Taxquet* v. *Belgium* (2010), in which the European Court of Human Rights (ECtHR) decided that Article 6 of the European Convention on Human Rights did not require that jurors provide reasons for their verdicts. However, the ECtHR explained that the accused and the public must nonetheless be able to understand the jury's verdict as a "vital safeguard against arbitrariness" in service of "public confidence in an objective and transparent justice system, one of the foundations of a democratic society" (*Taxquet* v. *Belgium*, 2010, p. 26). Though modifications of Norwegian law that narrowed the jury's purview in criminal cases preceded the *Taxquet* case, lawyers who cited it found it a helpful crystallization of jury concerns that had long circulated. Most significantly, prosecutors echoed the case's attention to the absence of written rationale for jury verdicts. "If the defendant is going to be sitting in jail for eight years he should at least know why the jury said 'yes'," a prosecutor argued (Prosecutor #16). Other prosecutors felt emphatic that individuals who were accused of crimes, like other citizens, should have access to the rationale behind decisions that would affect their lives and liberty. For example, one prosecutor decried the fact that in Norway "if you are convicted you do not know *why* they found you guilty" (Prosecutor #8, her emphasis). Several judges shared similar concerns about the jury system (Professional Judge #4; Professional Judge #5; Professional Judge #10).

NORWAY'S ALL-LAYPERSON JURY TRIALS IN PRACTICE

In Norway, as in the United States (Offit, 2016), all-layperson juries can inject uncertainty into legal proceedings. Despite the surface similarity of jury trials in the United States and Norway, research studies such as this reveal the diverse workings of such jury systems in practice, as prosecutors and judges manage them differently. In Norway, for example, my ethnographic research reveals that jurors' discretion is carefully circumscribed during trials. This is because prosecutors and judges: (1) adjust presentations of evidence based on questions posed by jurors and (2) incorporate explicit evaluations of witnesses' testimony in legal instructions. To examine how prosecutors and judges deploy these strategies and techniques to manage the uncertainty that jurors introduce into legal proceedings, I explore an illustrative case from the Borgarting Court of Appeal. It began as a dispute between two neighbors. Robert, who occupied an upstairs apartment, complained about the noisy renovation of the apartment below his and asked the neighbor who caused it to come upstairs. By Robert's account, the neighbor attacked him and Robert defended himself. The neighbor, however, testified that Robert stabbed him repeatedly. The neighbor testified that, as he lay on the ground bleeding, Robert put a knife in his hand to make it look as though he had acted in self-defense.

Prosecutorial Strategy

In an effort to persuade jurors to view guilty verdicts as just, some prosecutors tried to modify their presentations of evidence. One approach involved crafting rebuttals that made it clear that the government rejected defense counsel's arguments (Prosecutor #8). Others narrated the facts of their cases in hypothetical terms to amplify their arguments (e.g., Professional Judge #10). Here, again, the questions jurors posed during trial garnered special attention, since prosecutors believed such questions highlighted evidence that had either caused confusion or had inadvertently received undue emphasis (e.g., Legal Scholar #1; Prosecutor #9; Prosecutor #16).

The prosecutors I interviewed readily described the different approaches they took to narrating and presenting evidence to all-layperson jurors as opposed to professional judges. This attempted murder case was instructive in highlighting one prosecutor's attention to questions posed by jurors during his case. The prosecutor was particularly responsive to a juror's request to see the knife that Robert used to stab the defendant; the knife had broken in half and been covered in blood when he disposed of it. This request prompted the prosecutor to summon witnesses he would not otherwise have included in the case, including individuals who located, identified, and catalogued the knife. Based on the juror's question, the prosecutor was eager to demonstrate that the defendant's recollection of where he had put the bloody knife had been false, which undermined his credibility. Robert claimed when he testified that, after stabbing his neighbor, he put the bloody, broken knife into an empty box that he made no effort to conceal. Yet, the knife had been discovered under a pile of garbage outside his home. Out of concern that jurors' attention would be diverted by the defendant's emphatic insistence that the knife was in plain sight, the prosecutor described the investigation that uncovered the knife in detail.

Unfortunately, this plan was not as straightforward as the prosecutor had hoped. By the time Robert told police officers about the knife, he was already in custody, and the department was too short-staffed to dispatch someone to retrieve the weapon. The police therefore decided to call Robert's house and enlist the help of his wife. The prosecutor conceded that involving the defendant's spouse had the potential to distract jurors further, and he certainly would have preferred that the police officers had searched for the knife themselves. But clarifying potential misimpressions about the defendant's knife and credibility were a priority for him. With respect to the police's decision to turn the defendant's wife into a *de facto* informant, he commented:

> I think it wasn't very important in this case – though it affects one's impression of the police, I understand the reason. They didn't have enough people. Though this was an important case, they had other important cases – and this was the next day, so, new crimes. I don't like it, and I think they should have gone out there and taken a photo of the three bags before she picked them out and opened them. That would have been the right thing, I think. (Prosecutor #16)

His overriding concern was to demonstrate to his audience of lay decision-makers that the defendant could not be taken at his word. Though Robert's wife chose not to testify, and divorced her husband as the proceedings were underway, a police officer confirmed that the knife was found in a bag, not a box (Court observation, January 28, 2016).

The prosecutor remained attuned to his lay audience as he prepared to deliver his closing statement, which he sought to keep as straightforward as possible (Prosecutor #16). Rather than focus his comments on the legal issues the judge would later revisit in her own instructions, he again emphasized the defendant's lack of credibility (Court observation, January 28, 2016). Informed by his jurors' questions during the proceedings, he said that it was important to him to "explain the crucial points of decision for the jury, and what kind of evidence they should bear in mind" (Court observation, January 28, 2016). This meant "keeping away" from legal definitions when possible and focusing on the untruthful character of the accused.

Without the benefit of knowing whether questions were answered to jurors' satisfaction, or the extent to which misunderstandings might influence their verdicts, this prosecutor and his colleagues were attentive to points of ambiguity or confusion that *could* be rectified in their presentations of evidence. Another prosecutor likened presenting evidence to a panel of all-layperson juries as focused on persuasion, rather than offering pedagogical clarity to aid lay judges' authorship of opinions. She explained:

> [W]hen you have the lay judges – and most cases you have lay judges in the appeals court – you know you have to present the case so the judge will use your presentation to write the verdict afterwards, so you use a lot more effort to present this in a pedagogically correct way. But for the jury, you have to *convince* them, and that's a very different way of prosecuting a case. (Professional Judge #8, her emphasis)

Prosecuting cases in front of juries, by her account, required anticipating and responding to their intuitions about case outcomes; this audience presented a special narrative challenge.

Jury Instructions

In the interest of mitigating the uncertainty that all-layperson juries introduced to legal proceedings, judges could – and often did – offer their own commentaries on the credibility of witnesses and strength of evidence in criminal cases. Here, again, the attempted murder trial was instructive. Rather than defer the evaluation of the evidence in the case to jurors' later deliberation, the lead professional judge offered her own interpretation of Robert's behavior after the lawyers' closing statements:

> The defendant was not injured. He didn't have any injuries *at all* after the episode – he was just injured psychologically. He said he shouted to witnesses – that he was attacked on his balcony – but none of the witnesses observed anything that can support that. So there is the question of whether it is possible to get out of a fight with a knife without a single scratch. The victim, however, was seriously injured. If you were to arrive at the conclusion that he had done something to the defendant, one still has to consider the defendant's retaliation as disproportionate. (Professional Judge #4, her emphasis)

The first portion of this excerpt drew attention to the judge's perception of a gap in the evidence: though the defendant claimed self-defense, he offered no proof of having been attacked or injured himself. The judge went even further by noting that, even if the defendant *had* acted in self-defense, his reaction was excessive in light of the threat posed to him by his neighbor. The judge thus shared her own factual assessment of the inadequacy of the defense and, implicitly, the defendant's guilt.

The prosecutor who tried the case was particularly struck by the judge's characterization of Robert's behavior in her instructions as completely unjustifiable (*ubettinget utilbullgig*). In his view, this choice of language signaled the judge's perception that the defendant could not argue for acquittal based on self-defense. The subtext of this instruction, in his view, was that if jurors *did* choose to acquit the defendant, she might set their decision aside, a practice that had become increasingly common (e.g., Professional Judge #4; Supreme Court Justice #1). Though the prosecutor imagined this possibility would be lost on the all-layperson jury, his intuition was shared by the defense attorney with whom he chatted privately. Under the circumstances, however, the instruction did not surprise him. "In this case," he said, "I think it was right" (Prosecutor #16).

Here, as in other cases, a judge's concern about the discretion afforded to all-layperson juries prompted evaluative legal instructions that resulted in a new form of uncertainty. Some prosecutors worried, for example, that it was impossible to predict the tone judges would take when characterizing defendants and witnesses in their cases (e.g., Prosecutor #8). As one prosecutor put it, "It varies between judges and cases. Sometimes they're very careful to just present the law, and sometimes you feel like the judge is walking around and putting his arm on the defendant and saying '*this is the man*'" (Prosecutor #7). Although this particular attorney found the evaluative character of judges' instructions helpful, he thought judges sometimes went "too far" in injecting personal views.

Others emphasized the unpredictability of jurors' reactions to such instructions (see, e.g., Prosecutor #18; Prosecutor #20). An appellate judge commented, for example, that even after years of practice, it was impossible to predict case outcomes, which meant that analyses of the effects of legal instructions were "overrated" at best (Professional Judge #6).

Professional judges might also conceivably disagree about the instructions they wished to give to jurors (e.g., Lay Judge #2; Legal Scholar #7). To this end, a judge expressed concern that the efficacy of appellate judges' instructions to jurors varied greatly. His own starting point when formulating jury instructions was to be careful not to influence jurors' opinions of evidence (Supreme Court Justice #1). With an increased number of professional judges serving as chief presiding judges of jury trials, however, he worried that some of his colleagues lacked this sensitivity or delivered instructions that were unintelligible to nonlawyers. He was especially concerned about colleagues who read their instructions verbatim rather than gauge the receptiveness of their listeners by making eye contact with them, for example. The separation of lay and professional legal actors' deliberative processes and decision-making thus prompted concern about the bases of verdicts in cases with idiosyncratic or inexperienced professional judges.

With the benefit of open discussion, both professional and lay judges shared the conventional wisdom that professional judges could better reduce confusion about the law when deliberating as part of a mixed court (e.g., Professional Judge #6). A former lay judge, for example, would go out of her way to distinguish between legal clarifications appropriately offered by professional judges to lay counterparts and factual clarifications that might influence all-layperson juries' deliberations (Lay Judge #3). In sum, after observing all-layperson juries in practice and speaking to judges and lawyers, I found that professional judges often incorporated their own evaluations of the evidence into their legal instructions.

THE MIXED COURT

Interviews with attorneys, judges, and former lay decision-makers in Norway reveal a pervasive view that the mixed court (*meddomsrett*) is an egalitarian and transparent alternative to the practical reality of all-layperson jury trials. One of the reasons for this sentiment is that mixed courts invite collaboration among professional and lay judges that culminates in written and reasoned verdicts (Skjevestad, 2016). To this end, a number of prosecutors, judges, defense attorneys, and former lay decision-makers in Norway I interviewed articulated their belief that citizens can collaborate as peers, despite concern in other contexts, and countries, that judges who lack professional credentials are inferior or incompetent (e.g., Provine, 1986).

Thus, despite differences in lay and professional judges' training, the legal practitioners interviewed as part of this study evinced confidence that they could work together on an even footing (e.g., Professional Judge #4; Prosecutor #8; Prosecutor # 13). They thus characterized the mixed court system with emphasis on ordinary citizens' willingness to share their opinions with professional judges as equals. Some tied their confidence in lay judges to the breadth of life experience they brought to their adjudication of cases (e.g., Prosecutor #9; Prosecutor #11; Prosecutor #12). As one prosecutor put it, lay judges, were "very well educated. They can write and read and understand. And they are full of personal resources" (Prosecutor #13). A professional judge noted the high number of lay decision-makers with college degrees or other professional training (Professional Judge #4).

A common refrain in prosecutors' and judges' reflections was the extent to which professional legal actors could contribute useful expertise during deliberations. To the extent that a lay judge sought clarification of the law, for example, a prosecutor noted that professional judges could offer guidance. Others emphasized professional judges' ability to explain the significance of evidence to laypersons (Prosecutor #13), moving beyond the guidance jurors receive in the form of closing statements and legal instructions (see Straffeprosessloven, 1981 Kap. 24 § 368: "Rettens leder gjennomgår i et kort foredrag bevisene i saken og forklarer spørsmålene og de rettssetninger som skal legges til grunn"; Prosecutor #8). Lay judges, in turn, were willing to "speak up" and disagree with their professional counterparts (Lay Judge #4; Lay Judge #5). In some cases, they changed professional judges' perceptions of evidence. In one sexual assault trial, for instance, a judge recalled shifting her opinion of the behavior of a victim who lay judges believed had consented to the sexual activity in question (Professional Judge #9).

Judges' descriptions of their approaches to engaging lay judges in conversation during deliberations shed light on their rapport in mixed court contexts. In the interest of "ensur[ing] that the four lay judges feel free to – and are encouraged to – come up with their own view of the case," a chief judge explained, he and his colleagues invited lay judges' participation (Professional Judge #6). At times, he encouraged lay judges to share their perspectives first. On other occasions, he would invite lay and professional judges to alternately share their opinions during two "structured rounds" of comments. If lay and professional judges disagreed after a discussion of everyone's views, he would consider whether it would be appropriate for the mixed court to issue both a dissenting and majority opinion (Professional Judge #6).

Other professional judges emphasized their sense that regardless of the composition of juries or mixed courts, lay participation in legal decision-making was a valued part of the justice system because laypersons were capable and competent interlocutors (e.g., Professional Judge #4). In one judge's view, lay decision-makers were "prepared, interested and independent" and willing to "maintain their own points of view" during his deliberations with them (Professional Judge #6). Taking for granted the importance of incorporating laypersons into legal proceedings, one prosecutor said the key question was how the jury's deliberation would be moderated, which could affect the dynamics of their decision-making (Prosecutor #5). If professional judges were invited to share their opinions of the evidence first, for example, lay judges might be reluctant to disagree with them (Professional Judge #1).

According to a number of judges' and prosecutors' accounts, the high level of social equality among citizens in Norway was an essential component – if not a necessary condition – for the engaged and meaningful participation of lay decision-makers. One judge suggested that, at a time when laypersons have "university degrees and are able to think for themselves," it was inaccurate, and insulting, to assume that law degrees imbued professional judges and lawyers with special influence (Professional Judge #1; see also Prosecutor #14, Professional Judge #2, Professional Judge #4). Considering the effect that an increase in immigrant or refugee population might have on laypersons' confidence in the justice system, another professional judge argued that with the "integration of new arrivals" over time, confidence in all-layperson juries might again prevail (Professional Judge #6). The increasing number of defendants who were immigrants was a source of concern for some judges and lawyers who worried they might feel alienated during trials that did not feature relatable lay decision-makers (Professional Judge #8; Professional Judge #12).

Some scholars nonetheless worried that regardless of jurors' capabilities, judges' ability to moderate the deliberative process put them at an advantage (e.g., Mathisen, 2015; Sulland, 2016). One judge reflected:

> I have experience. I know the words – and I can argue. They can't. And that's a fact even if they are well educated and engineers and teachers and whatever – because this is what I work with every day and of course I will control the situation when I meet a lay judge. (Professional Judge #2)

He went on to explain how insufficient awareness of jurors' levels of comfort in participating in discussions could pose a problem; professional judges, in contrast, could play an active role facilitating lay judges' participation if they made a concerted effort.

Reasoned Verdicts

The legal practitioners and lay decision-makers I interviewed in Norway referred to verdicts that are supported by written rationales as "reasoned" verdicts, just as legal professionals do in countries such as Spain, Austria, and Russia (Burd & Hans, 2018, p. 323). This approach contrasts, for example, with the American practice of having the jury render a general verdict of "guilty" or "not guilty." The lawyers and judges I interviewed perceived jurors on all-layperson juries to focus their deliberations on which verdict each juror preferred, whereas the lay and professional judges on mixed courts engaged in a more collaborative decision-making process. Moreover, my interlocutors believed conversations among lay and professional judges avoided some of the pitfalls of secretive jury deliberations during which jury decisions could hinge on mistaken understandings of the law or fail to take different participants' perspectives into account. Jury decisions, which lack the benefit of written judicial opinions that are features of mixed courts, introduce an uncertain variable into the legal system that many viewed as antithetical to justice (e.g., Prosecutor #8).

In comparing the all-layperson jury to mixed courts, some judges described learning about jurors' mistakes firsthand during the sentencing phase of the proceedings. One professional judge, for example, recalled occasions on which jurors "described what their reasoning was" in support of their verdict leading the judge to believe that,

> they shouldn't have answered yes – but the verdict has been given already and perhaps it's just a slip of the tongue. But you get a slight feeling they didn't really understand. (Professional Judge #4)

He explained that this was particularly true of cases in which jurors convicted defendants for crimes that required intent yet said the accused "should have" known that his or her conduct was illegal (Prosecutor #14).

Though prosecutors conceded that jurors might steer deliberations away from relevant evidence, prosecutors nonetheless emphasized the value of jurors' fresh perspectives on cases. Rather than see their lack of legal training as a hindrance, some prosecutors praised jurors' abilities to approach evidence with a degree of open-mindedness that professional judges lacked (e.g., Prosecutor #8; Legal Scholar #1; Lay Judge #6). In describing an acquittal in a drug prosecution, one prosecutor commented on jurors' attentiveness to aspects of cases that professional judges seemed to overlook. He also speculated that jurors' ability to deliberate behind closed doors could lead them to verdicts that differed from those of mixed courts, where lay and professional judges could feel self-conscious about how decisions might reflect on their own character and reputations (e.g., Prosecutor #7; Defense Attorney #1).

Wholly apart from the question of whether professional and lay judges should deliberate jointly, several judges emphasized the value of written opinions to the decision-making process. One judge commented:

> For me, personally, I think that writing reasons is a tool to find out what the decision *should* be. It's a way of thinking – and I wouldn't make a decision without writing the main points down .... Sometimes when you try to write through the reasoning you see that something does not seem right, you may change your mind. (Professional Judge #4, his emphasis)

In this judge's view, outlining one's reasoning facilitated getting the "whole picture" of a case. He imagined jurors stood to gain from this same process (Professional Judge #4; Lay Judge #6). For a number of prosecutors and judges, the *absence* of a written rationale for jury verdicts was at odds with the broader cultural value of inviting citizens to understand and debate the bases of government decisions. By their accounts, this was a value that transcended legal contexts. As one prosecutor put it: "when the government enters your life to interfere, they have to give a reason –

an explanation. You get a list of all the things that contributed to the decision" (Prosecutor #14).

Another prosecutor expressed bewilderment that a decision as consequential as a person's conviction for a crime could be delivered as a "yes" or "no" without elaboration (Prosecutor #6). He considered this to be "shocking" (Prosecutor #6). Echoing this view, others pointed out that decision-making in the absence of a written rationale was contrary to the cultural value of transparency (e.g., Professional Judge #4). They described their distaste for exclusive organizations that carried out private discussions, such as social clubs or secret societies (Prosecutor #7). In workplace environments, including the prosecutors' office, other lawyers emphasized the importance of an "open door" culture in facilitating an open exchange of ideas (Prosecutor #9; Prosecutor #14). Explicit in lawyers' beliefs that verdicts should be written with the defendant and broader public in mind was also the underlying value that state decision-making should be accountable.

Another pattern in judges' and prosecutors' reflections on lay participation was their sense that professional judges' involvement in legal decision-making imbued the justice system with greater certainty (e.g., Nygard, 2010). Jurors, in contrast, injected uncertainty into legal proceedings (e.g., Defense Attorney #4). To this end, a common refrain among prosecutors, for example, was a feeling that jury acquittals could be demoralizing. One prosecutor recalled feeling so surprised by an acquittal that her "morale" was affected (Prosecutor #10). The experience led her to call the professional judge and ask whether she was "totally on another planet" (Prosecutor #10). Colleagues similarly emphasized their frustration that the jury's inconsistent responses on question-list verdict forms left them feeling that there was no "logic" to their verdicts. One prosecutor described exasperating situations in which jury verdicts suggested inconsistent readings of witnesses' credibility (Prosecutor #12). Other prosecutors pointed out that judges' decisions to set verdicts aside could feel erratic and unfounded, and that such a practice could cease with the elimination of autonomous all-layperson juries (Prosecutor #7; Prosecutor #11).

Interestingly, however, even prosecutors who recalled moments of surprise or shock did not fundamentally question the legitimacy or value of lay participation to the legal system. To this end, a prosecutor recalled feeling so stunned that a jury returned a "no" verdict that he began to question the defendant's guilt himself (Prosecutor #7). In his experience, and unlike his peers, the jury's unexpected decision unsettled his own certainty, leading him to feel only *more* confident in lay decision-makers' judgment. He recalled that, as he was packing his bags to leave the courtroom, the defendant approached him in the presence of his father and sister:

> [He] came and shook my hand ... he said he was very sorry about this and if I ever was in Amsterdam I was welcome to visit him. He wasn't mocking me. And I was thinking, what was that? Was he innocent? You get that. And that's probably in a sense the same thing the jurors had felt but I was too busy looking at arguments and shoving his face in lies and all the things that I thought he had lied about. (Prosecutor #7)

This prosecutor narrated the experience as a "wake up call" and took from it a sense of the importance of valuing jurors' perceptions and perspectives. Judges were sometimes caught off guard by verdicts, too; one judge described feeling "emotionally unprepared" by a jury's "no" decision (Professional Judge #1).

Lawyers' critiques of all-layperson juries in Norway often focused on the unpredictability and opacity of the reasoning behind their decisions. To the extent that legal professionals formally assessed lay decision-makers, this right was postponed until the end of trials. If professional judges agreed that the jury's verdict was incompatible with justice, they could "set it aside," leading to a retrial before a mixed court. This judicial prerogative is not unique to Norway. Judges' ability to overturn verdicts has recently been examined in the context of Spain's and Austria's legal systems as well (Jimeno-Bulnes, 2011; Murschetz, 2009).

Professional judges' ability to disregard jury verdicts was another understandable source of anxiety, because it meant that criminal defendants in Norway could be retried after all-layperson juries acquitted them (e.g., Professional Judge #8). Some judges emphasized the "strange" possibility that, even after an acquittal, a defendant could be ordered to compensate the victim's family due to the different burdens of proof in the criminal and civil phases of the trial (e.g., Professional Judge #6). To this end, judges highlighted the extent to which their discretion vis-à-vis all-layperson juries undermined the legitimacy that lay participation could confer on the legal process by keeping judicial power close to ordinary people.

Rape Prosecutions and Eroded Confidence in Lay Decision-Makers

Politicians and prosecutors expressed concern that in the particular context of rape prosecutions laypersons could not fairly assess the credibility of female victims (Member of Parliament #3; Prosecutor #9). For some prosecutors, this critique translated into broader condemnation of all-layperson juries. In such accounts, interviewees thought professional judges could productively intervene in distinguishing acceptable from impermissible grounds for assessing witnesses' credibility. One prosecutor commented, for example, that

> Judges see a lot of these cases, so they know – OK, this is a typical reaction [for a rape victim]. Not all rape victims behave the way laypeople believe they should. So they have more experience – and for the jury, maybe this is the only time they've heard someone testify about rape. (Prosecutor #9)

Prosecutors were particularly attentive to the special strain placed on victims of sexual assault by the jury system. As one prosecutor described it, victims first explained their assault to police officers, revisited the experience in district court, testified again if the case was appealed, and could testify a third time if the case was retried before a mixed court if a jury verdict was set aside (Prosecutor #8). As a result of this procedural reality, some felt that professional judges were well suited to interpret a victim's demeanor and tone in a manner that recognized the burden of testifying repeatedly, often without the benefit of a written transcript to refer to in the months between different proceedings (Prosecutor #7; Professional Judge #10).

To the extent that all-layperson juries did decide rape cases, several prosecutor interviewees expressed concern that, in the absence of a written verdict, it would be impossible to assess the basis of a conviction or acquittal (e.g., Prosecutor #8). "Most prosecutors here are skeptical about the jury," one commented, explaining that in rape cases they run the risk of "acquitting people for the wrong reasons" (Former Prosecutor #5). A Supreme Court justice I spoke with echoed the concern that male perpetrators found guilty of rape in the district court before lay and professional judges were later exonerated by all-layperson juries on appeal. In the absence of a reasoned verdict, he worried that jurors might fall prey to stereotypes about a victim perceived to be provocatively dressed or willing to accompany a stranger home (Supreme Court Justice #1). In the words of a prosecutor who worked in the city of Hamar, "what if you have jurors who feel a victim should not have worn a skirt, been drunk and showed an interest in the defendant earlier in the evening?" (Prosecutor #6). Lawyers' lack of clarity about the basis of all-layperson jury decisions thus translated into a pervasive concern that they might "focus on all the wrong things" (Prosecutor #10). One prosecutor, however, had her doubts. Older *professional* male judges, in her view, could be just as likely to harbor prejudicial attitudes toward female victims of sexual crimes (Prosecutor #9).

A professional judge who identified himself as an outspoken supporter of all-layperson juries was skeptical of prevailing political critiques of rape prosecutions involving lay decision-makers. Rather than focus on the evidentiary challenge of two individuals with different perceptions of a sexual encounter, he found it problematic that politicians appeared focused on sending a greater number of alleged assailants to prison (Professional Judge #2). He recalled discussions about the fact that, when all-layperson juries decided rape cases, a higher percentage of the cases resulted in an acquittal compared to other types of cases. "To me," he explained, "that's an argument *for* the jury but for most of the judges that was an argument against the jury" (Professional Judge #2, his emphasis). He found it particularly troubling that his colleagues felt a jury system should be evaluated on the basis of the number of guilty verdicts it reached. "The jury will often be skeptical about what is told to them," he explained. He viewed this as a broader feature of Norway's legal culture, and argued that skepticism was a healthy feature of any decision-making body.

In Oslo, in particular, rape cases occupied a significant part of any given prosecutor's docket. The prosecutors I interviewed largely embraced this emphasis, understanding it as the director of public prosecutions' interest in making women's rights a law enforcement priority. An unofficial survey that circulated around the office, however, revealed that over 50% of date-rape cases resulted in acquittal. This result could be demoralizing for prosecutors, including one who explained:

> [Y]ou yourself have been convinced of [the defendant's] guilt and the jury is not, and why should the judge then set the verdict aside? There is nothing tangible there – that's probably the most difficult kind of case. (Professional Judge #6)

Drawing on anecdotal evidence, the same prosecutor worried about cases in which Norwegian women accused minority or immigrant defendants of sexual crimes. Though judges could set aside the verdicts in rape cases, she worried that they lacked any "tangible" basis to question an all-layperson jury verdict (Professional Judge #6).

A recurrent theme in discussions of rape cases with prosecutors and judges was the challenge of evidentiary uncertainty. Had jurors filled in factual gaps with prejudicial assumptions about defendants' or victims' character? Could justice in such cases be served if verdicts could so easily be set aside or reversed? The high profile and highly controversial *Hemsedal* case appeared to bring the limitations of lay participation into relief on a public stage.

Hemsedal saken *(The* Hemsedal *Case)*

During the weekend of March 22–24, 2014, 18-year old Andrea Voll Voldum spent the weekend with her mother, younger sister, and a friend at a popular skiing destination called Hemsedal (Huuse, Røed, & Hansen, 2016). The defendants in the case were three friends who planned to spend the weekend snowboarding together. Andrea met one of the defendants and later joined him and his friends at an after-party. Over the course of the party, one of the defendants offered Andrea methylenedioxy-methamphetamine (also known as MDMA or ecstasy). Shortly after taking this drug, Andrea felt nauseated and gradually became numb. Her memories from that night then became spotty. She recalled being carried, face down, into a taxi, and waking up engaged in sexual acts in a bed. She did not remember – and did not remember consenting to – having intercourse and oral sex with the defendants during the hours that followed (Hemsedal saken, 2016).

After the three suspects in the case were arrested, they were prosecuted in a district court. Here, one professional judge and two lay judges presided over the case and convicted the defendants of jointly raping Andrea in the trailer they had taken her to by taxi. The defendants were sentenced to six years in prison. On appeal, a jury of 10 laypersons acquitted the defendants. However, the professional judges exercised their discretion to set the jury's verdict aside, remanding it for retrial by a new mixed court of three professional judges and four lay judges. A majority of five of the seven judges needed to vote for the defendants' conviction. Instead, only a four-person majority voted for conviction. This meant that, although a majority of the mixed court – including three professional judges and one lay judge – believed that the defendants were guilty, the votes of three lay judges won the day (Huuse et al., 2016). The prosecutor did not refer the case for reconsideration by the Supreme Court (Prosecutor #17) and, heeding this advice, the public prosecutor decided not to appeal the decision (Elden, 2017).

The defendants' acquittal by an all-layperson jury was an initial source of controversy. It confirmed, for some, that the interventions of professional judges were sorely needed. When three lay judges voted to acquit the defendants, however, the debate went in a different direction and questioned the role of lay participation in rape prosecutions more broadly (Sandvær, 2016). The lay judges who voted to acquit the defendants were the subject of scrutiny. Because their names were associated with their publicly disseminated opinion, they received harassing and threatening messages of protest (Sandvær, 2016).

Both the prosecutor and defense attorney in the case expressed surprise and alarm at the extent to which social media had been deployed to attack the laypersons involved in the decision (Defense Attorney #1; Prosecutor #17). The prosecutor noted the number of people who took to the internet with strong feelings about the lay judges and the verdict without having read the court decision or been privy to the evidentiary debates in the court. Members of the public were so incensed that the former mayor of one of Norway's largest cities expressed her outrage about the defendants, who were also named on Facebook, prompting condemnation that she had encouraged violence against them (Sigurd, 2016).

Though legal scholars are familiar with the sensitivity about all-layperson juries in rape cases documented in this chapter, the *Hemsedal* case highlighted the potential vulnerability of lay participants in Norway's legal system more broadly. To the extent that lay judges can be subject to personal scrutiny for decisions in cases, public coercion appeared to be an underappreciated risk in such a high-profile case – even more so than the pressure lay judges faced from professionals on the bench.

CONCLUSION

Ethnographic research offers unique insights into the extent to which lawyers in Norway view lay and professional legal actors as capable of effectively collaborating to resolve criminal cases. It demonstrates, further, that professional judges are not perceived as necessarily dominating lay counterparts in mixed court settings. Qualitative research and observation of some of the last all-layperson jury trials shed light on professional judges' and lawyers' special efforts to influence jurors' reception to and interpretation of evidence.

This perceived egalitarianism on mixed courts has been noted as a feature of lay participation systems elsewhere, too. In his study of Córdoba's mixed tribunal system, for example, Santiago Abel Amietta's interviews with lay decision-makers revealed a similar dynamic. Many of the lay judges he spoke with understood themselves as sharing the "attributes of a judge," and believed they could assert their opinions in cases of disagreement (Amietta, 2011). Similarly, while noting exceptions, María Inés Bergoglio's empirical work in the region revealed that most jurors felt respected and "able to take part in the tribunal's deliberation" without undue judicial influence (Bergoglio, 2017).

It is essential to bear in mind, however, that the distinctive cultural features of Norway's legal system make it difficult to generalize about the extent to which mixed courts might foster environments where laypersons contribute meaningfully – and *see themselves as contributing meaningfully* – to legal decision-making. "[I]nstitutional and legal–cultural differences" matter and distinguish the performance and practice of mixed courts in different countries (e.g., Machura, 2016, p. 283). This case study has sought to show that against a backdrop of broader anxiety about democracy, one seemingly anti-democratic move in the legal realm – eliminating all-lay person juries – has, for various reasons, limited the *quantity* of lay participation while enhancing its *quality*. There is perhaps a lesson here for democratic renewal more broadly: protecting the participatory nature of our justice system may require critical reflection on where we might amplify the value of participation by ordinary people, even if it means breaking with familiar but outmoded approaches that stress the sum and not the standard of that participation.

REFERENCES

Amietta, S. A. (2011). Governance in Córdoba's mixed tribunal: A study on microphysics of power. *Oñati Socio-Legal Series*, 1(1), 4–23. http://papers.ssrn.com/abstract=1735502

Bergoglio, M. I. (2017). Ten years of mixed tribunals in Argentina. https://papers.ssrn.com/abstract=2987942

Bernard, H. R. (2011). *Research methods in anthropology: qualitative and quantitative approaches*. 5th ed. Lanham, MD: AltaMira Press. https://bibdata.princeton.edu/bibliographic/6734220

Burd, K., & Hans, V. P. (2018). Reasoned verdicts: Oversold? *Cornell International Law Journal*, 51, 319–360.

Casper, G., & Zeisel, H. (1972). Lay judges in the German criminal courts. *Journal of Legal Studies*, 1, 135–191. www.jstor.org/stable/724014

Edwards, J., Haugerud, A., & Parikh, S. (2017). Introduction: The 2016 Brexit referendum and Trump election. *American Ethnologist*, 44, 195–200. https://doi.org/10.1111/amet.12467

Elden, J. C. (2017, May 7). Når Riksadvokaten svikter oss [When the attorney general fails us]. *Dagbladet*. www.dagbladet.no/kultur/nar-riksadvokaten-svikter-oss/61174889

Fiva, H. (2006). *In other words: A study of interpreting and power in Oslo*. [Master's thesis, University of Oslo]. www.duo.uio.no/handle/10852/16528

Foss, A. B. (2015, May 12). Stortinget fjerner juryen fra rettssalen [Parliament removes the jury from the courtroom]. *Aftenposten*. www.aftenposten.no/nyheter/iriks/Stortinget-fjerner-juryen-fra-rettssalen-8015604.html

Foss, M. T. (2011). *Juryordningen: Rollefordelingen mellom fagdommere og lekdommere* [The jury system: The distinction between the roles of professional judges and laymen]. [Master's thesis, University of Tromsø].

Gullestad, M. (1992). *The art of social relations: Essays on culture, social action and everyday life in modern Norway*. Oslo: Scandinavian University Press.

Hemsedal saken [Hemsedal case] (2016, July 7). No. LB-2015–85818, Borgarting lagmannsrett [Borgarting Court of Appeal].

Huuse, C., Røed, R., & Hansen, F. (2016, April 8). Tre menn frifunnet for gjengvoldtekt: Andrea Voll Voldum: De har tatt fra meg noe jeg aldri får tilbake [Three men acquitted of gang rape: Andrea Voll Voldum: "They have taken something from me that I'll never get back"]. *VG*. www.vg.no/nyheter/innenriks/i/K5lK6/tre-menn-frifunnet-for-gjengvoldtekt-andrea-voll-voldum-de-har-tatt-fra-meg-noe-jeg-aldri-faar-tilbake

Jimeno-Bulnes, M. (2011). Jury selection and jury trial in Spain: Between theory and practice. *Oñati Socio-Legal Series*, 1(9). http://opo.iisj.net/index.php/osls/article/viewFile/165/124

Jordal, P. (2011). *Juryutvalget* (Norges offentlige utredninger) [The Committee on Juries (Norwegian Official Reports)]. Departementenes servicesenter Informasjonsforvaltning. Oslo.

Kutnjak Ivković, S. (2007). Exploring lay participation in legal decision-making: Lessons from mixed tribunals. *Cornell International Law Journal*, 40, 429–454.

Letvik, T. (2015). Grunnloven kunne berget juryordningen [The Constitution could have saved the jury system]. *Juristkontakt* (5). www.juristkontakt.no/i/2015/5/juko-2015- 05-19

Lov om endringer i straffeprosessloven mv. [Law about changes in Criminal Procedure Act (Nor.)] (2017), § 332. https://lovdata.no/dokument/LTI/lov/2017-06-16-58

Machura, S. (2016). Understanding the German mixed tribunal. *Zeitschrift für Rechtssoziologie: The German Journal of Law and Society*, 36(2), 273–302. https://doi.org/10.1515/zfrs-2016-0022

Mathisen, G. (2015, July 30). Forsvarerne gir opp jurykampen [The defenders give up the jury fight]. *Advokaten*. www.advokatbladet.no/2015/07/forsvarerne-gir-opp-jurykampen/

Murschetz, V. (2009). The US jury system: An insight from a civil lawyer's perspective. In G. M. Grabher & A. Gamper, (Eds.), *Legal narratives* (pp. 159–174). Vienna: Springer. http://link.springer.com/chapter/10.1007/978–3-211–92818-9_8

Norges offentlige utredninger [Norwegian official report] NOU 2011:6, 3.1.2. www.regjeringen.no/contentassets/abb0967dae1146b5bc2912728bf2fa9d/no/pdfs/nou201120110006000dddpdfs.pdf

Norges offentlige utredninger [Norwegian official report] NOU 2011:13. www.regjeringen.no/contentassets/a1bdecfa47894a21b6ba66731cbd4017/no/pdfs/nou201120110013000dddpdfs.pdf

Nygard, L.-J. (2010). *Juryen for fall: Demokrati og rettssikkerhet* [The jury before a fall: Democracy and legal certainty]. Oslo: Unipub.

Offit, A. (2016). Peer review: Navigating uncertainty in the United States jury system. *UC Irvine Law Review*, 2(6), 169–206.

(2018). The jury is out: An ethnographic study of lay participation in the Norwegian legal system. *PoLAR: Political and Legal Anthropology Review*, 41, 231–246. https://doi.org/10.1111/plar.12268

Olsen, T. (2016, August 5). Derfor kunne voldtektssaken i Hemsedal ende med frifinnelse [Why the rape case in Hemsedal could end in acquittal]. *Aftenposten*. www.aftenposten.no/norge/Derfor-kunne-voldtektssaken-i-Hemsedal-ende-med-frifinnelse-601454b.html

Olsson, S. V. (2019, January 28). Fagdommerne avviste juryens kjennelse: Hele saken må opp på nytt [The professional judges rejected the jury's verdict: The whole case must be retried]. *NRK*. www.nrk.no/norge/fagdommerne-avviste-juryens-kjennelse-_-hele-saken-ma-opp-pa-nytt-1.14398128

Provine, D. M. (1986). *Judging credentials: Nonlawyer judges and the politics of professionalism*. Chicago: University of Chicago Press.

Roudik, P. (2011, November 9). Georgia: Courts with jurors established nationwide. *Global Legal Monitor, Library of Congress*. www.loc.gov/law/foreign-news/article/georgia-courts-with-jurors-established-nationwide

Rundberget, A. (2017, February 3). Juryordningen: En symbolsak står for fall [The jury system: A symbolic issue comes before the fall]. *Meninger*. www.adressa.no/meninger/2017/02/03/Juryordningen—en-symbolsak-står-for-fall-14156152.ece

Sandvær, H. (2016, August 8). Meddommere i Hemsedal-saken trues: Er bekymret for rettssikkerheten [Lay judges in Hemsedal case threatened: Are anxious about the rule of law]. *VG*. www.vg.no/nyheter/innenriks/i/Xy1GE/meddommere-i-hemsedal-saken-trues-er-bekymret-for-rettssikkerheten

Scherr, C. (2015). Chasing democracy: The development and acceptance of jury trials in Argentina. *University of Miami Inter-American Law Review*, 47, 316–353.

Sigurd, S. (2016, August 9). Tidligere ordfører anmeldt for voldstrusler i Hemsedal-saken [Former mayor reported for violent threats in Hemsedal case]. *NRK*. www.nrk.no/trondelag/tidligere-ordforer-anmeldt-for-voldstrusler-i-hemsedal-saken-1.13080448

Sulland, F. (2016). Juridiske tungvektere med forskjellig syn [Legal heavyweights with different views]. *Juristkontakt* 5.

Skeie, J. (1939). *Den norske straffeprosess [The Norwegian criminal procedure]*. Oslo: Olaf Norlisforlag.

Skjevestad, H. (2016). Vil ha to fagdommere og fem lekdommere [Will have two professional judges and five lay judges]. *Advokatforeningen Bladet*. www.advokatbladet.no/2016/10/gar-inn-for-to-fagdommere-og-fem-lekdommere

Straffeprosessloven [Criminal Procedure Act (Nor.)]. 1981 Kap. 21 § 275, Kap. 22 § 276. https://lovdata.no/dokument/NL/lov/1981-05-22-25/KAPITTEL_5-4#KAPITTEL_5-4

Taxquet v. Belgium, App. No. 926/05 (Eur. Ct. H.R., November 16, 2010). www.echr.coe.int/Pages/home.aspx?p=hearings&w=92605_21102009&language=lang

11

Trials by Peers

The Ebb and Flow of the Criminal Jury in France and Belgium

Claire M. Germain

The participation of lay jurors in criminal courts has experienced much ebb and flow in France and Belgium. These two countries belong to the civil law tradition, where juries are the exception rather than the rule in criminal trials, and they only exist in criminal, not civil, cases. In spite of some similarities, there are substantial differences between the two countries, and their systems are examined in turn.

In France, the *Cour d'assises* was inherited from the French Revolution. Originally, jurors sat alone, but the institution became a mixed court in 1941. Since then, lay citizens sit together with professional judges. The *Cour* adjudicates severe crimes only, mostly rapes and murders. A pilot program, begun in 2011, extended lay participation to criminal courts beyond the *Cour d'assises*, but was ended in 2013.

In Belgium, the institution of the criminal jury in the *Cour d'assises* is enshrined in the Belgian Constitution. Until 2016, the criminal jury functioned as a "true" jury in the sense that only lay citizens sat on the jury and reached a verdict on their own. A 2016 reform allowed for the reclassification of virtually all crimes to be judged by the criminal courts. As a result, most criminal cases are now decided by judges in the other criminal courts rather than in the *Cour d'assises*. In addition, since February 2016, in the *Cour d'assises*, judges deliberate with lay citizens on the guilt of the accused, although the professional judges do not have voting rights.

This chapter traces the history of the French criminal jury, its recent reforms, the short experiment, and the current situation, including a comparative note with the US legal system. It then turns to the history of the Belgian criminal jury, its recent reforms that almost abolished the *Cour d'assises*, and the current situation that may lead to a resurrection of the jury. It explores how political and economic struggles in both countries, combined with an underlying tension between professional judges and lay citizen judges, have influenced the ebb and flow of lay citizen participation. I close with a few remarks about the future for lay participation in these two countries, since there are several current proposals on the table, both in France and in Belgium.

FRANCE

Background

The French criminal jury system is embodied in the *Cour d'assises,* which adjudicates severe crimes only, mostly rapes and murders. Its composition has changed many times (Hans & Germain, 2011). The French *Cour d'assises* was inherited from the French Revolution as a reaction against the judges of the time who resisted any reform attempts (Sénat, 2011). At the same time, there was a change in the standard of proof; the concept of *intime conviction* (inward conviction) replaced the rigid system of legal proofs that had been used previously to convict people (Hans & Germain, 2011). The respective roles of judges and jurors also have evolved over the years. At first, lay jurors sat and decided cases independently. However, in the nineteenth and early twentieth centuries, jurors were perceived as too lenient; their acquittal rate rose to 40% because they were afraid that the sentence would be too severe (Salas, 2001). With the Law of November 25, 1941 (Loi du 25 novembre 1941 sur le jury), the jury became a mixed court system, consisting of professional judges sitting with lay citizens to determine guilt and sentencing (Hans & Germain, 2011). Nonetheless, it is still identified in France as a "jury" and its lay citizens as "jurors."

The *Cour d'assises* is not a permanent court, but sits at regular intervals (Redon, 2013). The procedure for a jury trial begins when the Chamber of Indictment sends an indictment (*mise en accusation*) to the *Cour d'assises* in the department or geographical location in which the offense occurred. The 102 *Cours d'assises* hold court sessions every three months (Redon, 2013). They can judge all offenses connected to the principal crimes. The *Cour* judges only the most severe crimes, principally rapes, thefts with violence, and murders. Terrorism and drug trafficking cases are excluded; there is a special *Cour d'assises,* consisting only of professional judges, for these crimes, because of the fear of threats that might be made by the accused against the jurors (Sénat, 2011). The *Cours d'assises* decide between 3,000 and 3,200 cases every year (Ministère de la Justice, 2011–2012, 2016). A common practice is the "correctionalization" or reclassification of crimes into lesser offenses that are heard by professional judges only in a criminal court (Hans & Germain, 2011).

The *Cour d'assises* consists of six jurors, randomly drawn from the general population, and three professional judges (one of whom is the president, who has special powers over the file and presides over the trial). Lay citizens and professional judges deliberate together on the facts and the law and decide the verdict of guilty or not guilty, as well as the sentence. A decision of guilt requires a two-thirds majority (six votes) by secret ballot; if five or fewer favor conviction, the defendant is acquitted, although the verdict is subject to appeal. The sentencing decision is made by an absolute majority of at least five votes, but the maximum sentence can only be given with a majority of six votes (Direction de l'information légale et administrative, 2018).

Unlike in the United States where criminal and civil proceedings are entirely separate, in France, the victim can join in the criminal trial as a civil party (*partie civile*) (Hans & Germain, 2011). After the *Cour d'assises* decides on criminal responsibility, the professional judges, without the jurors, rule on the request for civil damages, if they have been requested by the *partie civile* against the accused, or by the defendant against the *partie civile*.

Comparative Observations: Accusatorial vs. Inquisitorial Procedure

A comparative approach provides some useful perspective and contrast. The French and US juries are different institutions operating in different contexts (Garapon & Papadopoulos, 2003). The jury is embedded in the US Constitution and is part and parcel of the fabric of US law. The participation of jurors is circumscribed by specific procedures within the context of the adversarial trial. The American jury is used for both civil and criminal trials. The French jury is used only for the *Cour d'assises*.

In France, the role of the trial judge is much more active than the role of the trial judge in the United States, in keeping with the inquisitorial tradition. Even though the procedure at the *Cour d'assises* is oral and includes debates (*contradictoire*), the presiding judge (*Président*) has extraordinary powers. He or she is the only one with access to the file and performs much like the conductor of an orchestra. Unlike the accused in the United States, who has a right to remain silent at trial, a fundamental part of the trial in France is that the accused is interrogated by the presiding judge and is encouraged to speak freely about his or her background, circumstances, and views (Hans & Germain, 2011). The lawyers for each party have a much more limited role than their American counterparts.

The inquisitorial system with its distinctive criminal procedure changes the dynamic of the court and the roles of the key actors, including the lawyers for each side, the judge, and the jurors in jury trials. In the United States, the trial belongs to the parties. In contrast, in France, the trial belongs to the court. In the United States, the lawyers control the trial through adversarial techniques, which allow them to put forth evidence, question the other side's evidence, and make opening and closing arguments. The US judge is more like an "umpire" and plays a more neutral role.

In France, there is no grand jury or oversight of indictment by grand jurors. The *Juge d'instruction* (investigating judge) plays a major role in criminal and civil proceedings ("A quoi sert le juge d'instruction?," 2012). The investigating judge must seek evidence in a case brought to his or her attention by the prosecution or a victim, thus beginning a criminal investigation. He or she must determine whether there is sufficient evidence to bring a case to trial in either the *Cour d'assises* or the criminal court (*tribunal correctionnel*) staffed by professional judges only. The investigating judge assigned to the case collects evidence on behalf of both the prosecution and defense (*à charge et à décharge*) before determining if a trial is warranted. By way of comparison, in the United States, the investigation is led by the police and the prosecutor, and only on behalf of the prosecution.

French criminal law distinguishes three categories of offenses (Pradel, 2010). In broad terms, crimes are very serious offenses, such as murder and rape; *délits* are less serious offenses, such as theft, fraud, assault, and involuntary homicide. The last category, *contraventions*, includes a large range of regulatory offenses that often involve strict liability. The *tribunal de police* has jurisdiction over the *contraventions*, while the *tribunal correctionnel* deals with the *délits*. Appeals from judgments of both these tribunals are heard by the *chambre des appels correctionnels*. As noted above, the *Cours d'assises* have jurisdiction over crimes. The *Cour d'assises* consists of three judges and several lay citizens (Pradel, 2010).

Mixed Court/Echevinage

Echevinage refers to a panel consisting of nonprofessional and professional judges. The term comes from the Middle Ages. It is also used to describe the judges in commercial courts (Aubert & Savaux, 2012; Echevinage, 2014). The terms *échevinage*, *assesseurs*, and *jurés* seem to be used interchangeably to define lay assessors (*citoyens assesseurs*), lay jurors, or even *juges citoyens*. Some commentators distinguish between the lay juror who is selected at random from various lists and the *échevin* who is elected and chosen because of a particular specialty or expertise, for instance in commercial courts or the Tribunal for Children (Sénat, 2011). Adding to the confusion, the term *assesseur* can refer to a professional judge other than the president of the court.

2001 and 2011 Reforms

Several important, relatively recent reforms have changed the procedure of the *Cour d'assises*. One is an appeals process and the other is the need for the *Cour d'assises* to provide "reasoned verdicts" (*Taxquet v. Belgique*, 2010). In 2001, France, under pressure from the European Court of Human Rights (ECtHR) to meet European fair trial standards, instituted a court of appeals. The court of appeals does not provide an appeal in the sense of a review of the verdict given in the *Cour d'assises*; rather, it provides a new trial before an expanded appellate *Cour d'assises* (Loi 2000–516). For a long time, there was no second level of review for crimes because of the presumption of the infallibility of the jury. The jury was seen as infallible because it represented the will of the people. In the ratification of the Convention, France had declared that review by a higher court could be limited to applying the law correctly, like review by the *Cour de cassation* (Pradel, 2001; Redon, 2013). However, this gap seemed to be contrary to Protocol No. 7 of the European

Convention for the Protection of Human Rights and Fundamental Freedoms and its protocol on the right to appeal, which France had ratified in 1988. Article 2 of this Protocol provides: "Everyone convicted of a criminal offense by a tribunal shall have the right to have his conviction or sentence reviewed by a higher tribunal" (European Convention on Human Rights, 2010).

Pursuant to that reform, statistics show that, over a two-year period, some 1,262 appeals were heard. Of those appeals, 5% were successful and the criminal defendants were acquitted. However, when the prosecution appealed acquittals, 57% were overturned. Thus, prosecutors appear to benefit more from the "second chance" offered by the *Cour d'assises d'appel* than criminal defendants (Hans & Germain, 2011).

Again under the influence of the ECtHR, several cases raised the issue of "reasoned verdicts" (*Taxquet v. Belgique*, 2010). A reasoned verdict refers to a jury having to give written reasons for its verdict. A traditional jury in a criminal case only provides a verdict as to guilt or innocence without providing a written explanation of how it reached its verdict. The question raised by several cases before the ECtHR was whether a fair trial requires that a criminal defendant understand the reasons for his or her conviction. The Law of August 10, 2011 (Loi 2011–939), on the participation of lay citizens in criminal justice, modified the composition of the *Cour d'assises* and instituted the obligation to provide reasoned verdicts (Pradel, 2011a; Redon, 2013). Furthermore, a decision of March 2, 2018, of the Constitutional Council requires a reasoned decision for the sentence itself (Conseil constitutionnel, 2018).

The Law of 2011 added another change of note, in effect since 2012. The presiding judge now has to summarize the facts, the indictment, and the elements for the prosecution and the defense. This change in practice is designed to make it easier for jurors to understand the case because they no longer have to listen to the text of the decision that led to sending the case to the *Cour* (*décision de renvoi*); the decision can be a very long document with technical terms.

Under the influence of European human rights law, the *Cour d'assises* has professionalized its procedure in an attempt to make the trial more understandable, transparent, and responsive to international standards of fair trial and intelligible procedure (Conseil constitutionnel, 2018). It has also resulted in greater professional control over lay decision-making.

The number of lay citizens on the *Cour d'assises* has fluctuated over the years. The Law of 1941 lowered the number of lay citizens from 12 to 6, but other laws raised it to 9. Thus, until 2011, three professional judges along with nine jurors worked together to decide the facts and the law, as well as the sentence. The Law of 2011 then reduced the number of jurors in the first instance from 9 to 6, and on appeals courts from 12 to 9. The lay citizens and a three-judge panel deliberate together. Defendants must be found guilty by at least a six-vote majority at trial and eight votes on appeal. The aim of this measure was to expedite the judgment of these cases, and was taken in the context of increasing the use of lay citizens in criminal courts beyond the *Cour d'Assises* (Loi 2011–939).

Extension of Lay Participation to Criminal Courts beyond the Cour d'assises

In 2011, President Nicolas Sarkozy proposed extending lay participation to other French criminal courts beyond the *Cour d'assises* (Pradel, 2011b). This was done in the context of security concerns and a strong political will. President Sarkozy saw it as a way to bring citizens closer to the justice system and to remedy a perceived leniency of judges in the face of high-profile scandals, including several murders allegedly committed by criminal defendants who had been released by judges (Brafman, 2012). In August 2011, the French Parliament voted on a new law that was validated for the most part by the Constitutional Council. The new law provided for a pilot program that extended the participation of lay citizens to criminal courts beyond the *Cour d'assises* (Huyghe, 2011; Pradel, 2011b). This extension of lay citizens was limited to specific cases of serious thefts and violent assaults that were punishable by 5 to 10 years of imprisonment (De Charette, 2010). Lay citizens in the criminal courts could not judge drug crimes, pimping, or less serious thefts. The law provided that two lay citizens (*citoyens assesseurs*) would sit together with three professional judges in the criminal court (*tribunal correctionnel*) and the appeals criminal court. They were to participate in the determination of the facts, decide on the culpability of the defendant, and determine the sentence (Loi 2011–939). This extended use of lay citizens was significant because it would potentially involve 6,000 to 9,000 lay citizens, and apply to some 40,000 cases (out of 600,000 cases in criminal courts in any given year) (Huyghe, 2011).

In addition to introducing lay citizens in these other criminal courts, the Law of 2011 also introduced lay citizens in the Criminal Tribunal for Minors (*Tribunal correctionnel des mineurs*) and the Criminal Tribunal for Implementation of Sentences (*Tribunal d'application des peines*). In each, two lay citizens would deliberate with three professional judges to examine parole requests or their revocation for all sentences that exceed five years of imprisonment (Loi 2011–939). In the Court of Appeals for Implementation of Sentences (*Chambre d'application des peines de la cour d'appel*), lay citizens were to replace specialized jurors.

The main objective of the law was to involve French citizens in the judging of particular offenses. Sarkozy hoped that juries would be stricter than judges. The cost of this reform was estimated to be substantial, about 40 million euros. For that reason, the government decided to implement a pilot program in some jurisdictions before extending the practice throughout the entire French territory (Sénat, 2011). The experiment started in the regions of Dijon and Toulouse and was extended to include Angers and Béthune in January 2013.

The constitutionality of certain provisions of the law were challenged before the Constitutional Council, in particular some of the provisions that pertained to minors. There were concerns that these provisions violated the fundamental principles of juvenile justice, including the use of specialized courts, mitigated criminal responsibility due to age, and priority placed on educational rather than law enforcement measures. The council found four articles of the law unconstitutional, and those articles were deleted from the law (Conseil constitutionnel, 2011).

What were the reactions to the expanded role of lay citizens (*citoyens assesseurs*)? From a study I undertook of national and regional online newspapers and magazines that made references and comments (*Le Monde*, *Nouvel Observateur*, *Le Figaro*, and *Libération*, among others), the public was generally in favor of the program. Narratives from lay citizens showed that they were mostly satisfied with their experience, and that they took their responsibilities seriously. The legal profession, including judges and *avocats*, however, were mostly opposed to it (Rastello, 2012). The judges immediately reacted negatively to it and expressed their views through their unions; they saw the expansion of lay participation as evidence of public distrust of their profession (Neuer, 2012).

However, conditions changed after the election of the Socialist government in May 2012. The new minister of justice Christine Taubira requested a report from two prosecutors. The two prosecutors wrote a report that severely criticized the pilot program of lay citizens in criminal courts in two courts of appeals in the jurisdictions of Dijon and Toulouse (Ministère de la Justice, 2013; Salvat & Boccon-Gibod, 2013). They said that it was extremely burdensome and costly and did not involve citizens in a meaningful way in the justice system. Their arguments were that the program had caused numerous difficulties, including the heavy workload of selecting lay citizens, the length of the hearings, and their added cost. They felt that the one-day training was not enough, and that the lay citizens depended too much on the professional judges for technical guidance. What is more, the anticipated greater severity of sentences had not materialized. Following the report, the minister of justice put an end to the experiment and to the participation of lay citizens in criminal courts beyond the *Cour d'assises* (Arrêté du 18 mars, 2013).

The experimentation failed in large part because of bad relations between President Sarkozy and the judges who felt under attack. Christophe Régnard, the president of the Union Syndicale des Magistrats (USM), called the introduction of lay citizens in criminal courts a "mistrust of judges" (Neuer, 2012).

After that experiment ended, the minister of justice commissioned four different reports on justice reform. These reports were followed by the Law on the Modernization of Justice, which does not mention the participation of lay citizens in criminal courts (Loi de modernisation, 2018).

This raises an interesting question about the attitude of the Socialist party with respect to lay participation in the legal system. During the nineteenth century, the left fought in favor of lay participation in civil and criminal matters (Faure, 2011). But now, the left has lost so much contact with the *classes populaires*, "the people," that the left tends to mistrust them (Faure, 2011). Only a few socialists have expressed their support for the *jurés populaires*, in particular the politician Andre Vallini, who observed that

> the citizen does not know the procedure or fine points of the law. But the heart of the criminal trial rests on essential questions, such as "does the accused lie? Is the accused credible? What are the reasons [for] the crime? Are there extenuating circumstances?" It is not with a diploma that one can answer these questions, but with one's conscience. Of course, judging is a profession. But I only see advantages in having a citizen sit together with professional judges in the *Tribunal correctionnel* (Réju, 2012).

Another explanation for the reduced presence of lay citizens as legal decision-makers in France involves the role, attitudes, and culture of professional judges in France, particularly since the inception of a national school to train judges. The National Centre for Judicial Studies, which was created in 1959, became the French National School (*Ecole Nationale*) for the Judiciary in 1972. It is located in Bordeaux and has a presence in Paris. It instructs the corps of judges and public prosecutors who serve in all posts on the bench as well as in the public prosecution in first instance courts (first trial level). Judges are civil servants. They are paid during their studies and they form an *esprit de corps* during their careers. Beginning in 1968, they were permitted to unionize in order to represent their interests. The judges express a strong distrust of citizens interfering with what they perceive to be their functions.

Situation in 2019

In the spring of 2018, Justice Minister Nicole Belloubet introduced a legislative proposal that included taking a substantial number of cases away from the *Cour d'assises* and having them heard in an intermediate court, a new *cour criminelle départementale* (first called the *tribunal criminel*) (Jacquin, 2018). The justification for this was to judge these cases faster, particularly rape cases. A *Cour d'assises* proceeding can exceed 18 months, from the time the inquiry starts to the time the trial commences (Egré & Raisse, 2016). Previously, many rape cases had been reclassified as sexual assaults to get a quicker judgment by criminal courts. The law was passed as part of a comprehensive law on justice reform (Loi 2019–222). The new departmental criminal court decides crimes punishable from 15 to 20 years of prison, such as rape or theft with a weapon. These cases are adjudicated by five professional judges, without any lay citizens. The appeals still go to a *Cour d'assises* appeals court, thus preserving a role at the appeals stage for lay judges. The most severe crimes continue to be heard by the *Cour d'assises*.

Nonetheless, this experiment represents a substantial constriction of the role of the French jury. It is estimated that some 60% of the cases will be taken away from the *Cour d'assises* docket (Pradel, 2018). This new court has been functioning on an experimental basis since January 1, 2019, and will continue for three years in test departments, before being expanded to other departments. This seems to be a reasonable decision, especially if one considers that rape cases are not currently handled in the best way for the victim. The cases need to be heard by an appropriate court for the level of the offense and adjudicated in a timely manner.

BELGIUM

Background

The situation in Belgium is different from France and offers a useful contrast, particularly because the Belgian jury is protected in its Constitution. Belgium inherited the jury by way of Napoleon, the French emperor who wrote the French Civil Code with a team of lawyers, and who exported it to countries under his domination. The Belgian criminal jury was suppressed in 1814 by King William I of the Netherlands, but then, after Belgian independence, the Belgian Congress inscribed it into the Belgian Constitution in 1831 to make it harder to undo (Goffinon, 2011). Belgian judges and legislators have never liked the jury much (Goffinon, 2011), but the institution remains enshrined in the Belgian Constitution. Article 150 of the Belgian Constitution (2007) provides: "[T]he jury is established in all criminal matters and for political and press offenses, with the exception of those inspired by racism and xenophobia."

Beginning in the nineteenth century, Belgian courts, like courts in France, have reclassified serious crimes into less serious offenses (*délits*) to prevent the use of the *Cour d'assises* and to send these cases to the other criminal courts, which do not use juries. This practice, which began with a law in 1838, was extended over the years, and has sometimes been used for crimes punishable by life imprisonment, forced labor, or even the death penalty (Chambre des représentants de Belgique, 2015). At the same time, other laws lengthened the sentences allowed in these other criminal courts to 10, 20, and even more years of imprisonment (Chambre des représentants de Belgique, 2015). Broadening the range of criminal sentences was seen as allowing judges in the criminal courts more discretion to individualize sentences to suit the defendant and the crime (Chambre des représentants de Belgique, 2015).

With regard to the provision in Article 150 of "political and press offenses," the categories are so narrowly defined by case law that in practice hardly any political offenses or press offenses such as libel have been brought to the *Cour d'assises* (Bourlet, n.d., p. 3). Press offenses inspired by racism or xenophobia were removed from the competence of the *Cour d'assises* by a 1999 law; instead, these cases go to the criminal courts (Centre Permanent pour la Citoyenneté et la Participation, 2016; Loi du 7 mai 1999).

Until 2016, the criminal jury functioned as a traditional jury in the sense that 12 jurors participated and decided the verdict on their own and without the participation of professional judges. The judges only joined the jury for deliberation on the sentence. The number of criminal cases brought to the *Cour d'assises* is very low.

Between 2000 and 2013, the *Cour d'assises* heard 83 cases per year, in contrast with the other criminal courts, which held 50,000 to 55,000 criminal trials per year (Centre Permanent pour la Citoyenneté, 2016). However, the *Cours d'assises* cases are usually sensational cases that receive extensive media coverage.

The *Cour d'assises* in Belgium, like the *Cour d'assises* in France, is not a permanent court. The 11 *Cours d'assises* sit any time a criminal defendant is sent there by the chamber of indictment. The court normally sits in the provincial seat of the different provinces and in Brussels. The jury consists of 12 jurors randomly drawn from the community. A maximum of two-thirds of the jurors can be of the same sex. To be a juror, one must be between 28 and 65 years old, be able to read and write, and have had no criminal sentence longer than four months, and enjoy the restoration of civil and political rights (Bourlet, n.d.).

In the Belgian jury system, a simple majority is enough for a verdict, unlike in the French system where a two-thirds majority is necessary, but the judge in the Belgian *Cours d'assises* can send the case to another court if he or she feels that the jury erred (*Code d'Instruction Criminelle* (Code of Criminal Procedure)). With respect to the jury instructions, there is a major difference between French and Belgian practices. A 2009 reform in Belgium replaced the notion of "*intime conviction*" (inward conviction) with the standard of "beyond a reasonable doubt" (Goffinon, 2011). Article 327 of the Belgian *Code d'Instruction Criminelle* replaced the old Article 342, and is thus closer to the US standard of proof beyond a reasonable doubt.

Until 2016, the Belgian jury determined on its own the culpability of the criminal defendant. After the jury had delivered its verdict, it would work with the professional judges (of which there were three, including a president and two other professional judges) to decide the sentence (Bourlet, n.d., p. 19). The reasoned verdict is a recent development in Belgium (*Taxquet v. Belgique*, 2010). Although *Taxquet* did not require Belgium to take this step of providing a reasoned verdict, Belgium chose this way to provide more information to defendants about their conviction (Bourlet, n.d., p. 19). Belgium, unlike France, does not have an appeals court yet for the *Cour d'assises*.

2016 Reform

In 2016, Justice Minister Koens Geens orchestrated a transformative reform in Belgium, fundamentally changing the *Cour d'assises* and leading to its suppression in practical terms (Centre Permanent pour la Citoyenneté, 2016). The planned reform allows for the "correctionalization" of virtually all crimes with very few exceptions. This means that crimes would be heard only by professional judges in the criminal courts, unless the prosecutor or the chamber of indictment decided that because of the extreme gravity of the facts, the criminal defendant must go before a *Cour d'assises*. No criteria were specified for this choice of court.

Since February 2016, there has been another significant change in the Belgian jury. The three professional judges deliberate with the 12 lay citizens on culpability (Loi modifiant le droit pénal, 2016), thus making the traditional jury in Belgium into a mixed court as in France. The judges' participation is deemed to be passive, as they do not vote on the verdict, only the jurors do. This is an interesting contrast with France, where the judges deliberate and vote with the lay citizens on the criminal defendant's guilt. However, the Belgian judges deliberate and vote with the lay citizens on the sentence. Because Article 150 of the Belgian Constitution specifically provides for a jury, the Council of State was asked to advise on the matter. It concluded that it is up to the legislature to define criminal matters (Chambre des représentants de Belgique, 2015). The reform also lengthened the maximum sentences to be given by criminal courts to 40 years or life imprisonment. The rationale for this reform of the jury was the cost. The first legislative proposals reserved some cases for the *Cour d'assises*, such as crimes against the police or minors. However, the Council of State decided that assigning certain types of cases to the *Cours d'assises* would be discriminatory. In the end, Justice Minister Geens decided that all crimes should be within the jurisdiction of the criminal courts (Geens, 2016).

Not surprisingly, this reform was controversial, and as recent developments show, the situation is still fluid. There were some strong negative reactions to the announced suppression of the *Cour d'assises*, particularly from lawyers and others concerned about the potential unconstitutionality of this reform. Critics argued that Article 150 of the Belgian Constitution needed to be revised before these changes could occur. Critics also argued that the jury is a democratic institution and a protection against abuse by the powerful. They pointed out that it guarantees citizens' rights and that the public is in favor of the jury for serious crimes. However, the justice minister, the Judges' Union, and the High Council of Justice all supported the quasi-suppression of the *Cour d'assises*. Their reasons include the high cost of the *Cours d'assises* (five times more expensive than any other criminal court), the complexity of cases, and the difficulty that juries have in providing a reasoned verdict (Vansiliette, 2016).

In the summer of 2016, the Belgian Bar Francophone and Germanophone sections introduced an action before the Constitutional Court. They argued that the quasi-suppression of the *Cour d'assises* violated Article 150 of the Belgian Constitution (Ordre des barreaux, 2016). In September, 2016, Justice Minister Geens, faced with strong negative reactions, announced plans to end the *Cour d'assises* after December 2016 and to replace it with a new *Cour d'assises* model, called "*assises* 2.0," which would consist of a criminal court with 6 jurors (rather than 12), along with experts (psychologists and criminologists) who would sit next to the professional judges and assist them. The trial would be shorter, but would include open debates and testimony by witnesses and experts, similar to the current *Cour d'assises*. The decisions could be appealed, which is still not the case in Belgium for

Cour d'assises verdicts. This project was debated in commission during the legislative process, but then other events intervened (Wauters, 2016).

Situation in 2019

The Constitutional Court ruled in December 2017 on the request from the Bar and annulled several provisions of the new law as unconstitutional, notably those that provided for almost all crimes to be adjudicated by other criminal courts, rather than the *Cour d'assises* (Cour constitutionnelle, 2017). The Constitutional Court indicated that the government could not circumvent the Constitution. The Constitutional Court also annulled the creation of sentences up to 40 years in prison, as well as the practice of these other criminal courts sentencing criminal defendants to prison for more than 20 years (Cour constitutionnelle, 2017).

In the fall of 2017, Justice Minister Geens proposed a new form of the Belgian jury, consisting of three professional judges and four lay citizens drawn randomly (Geens, 2017). A major change would be that the members of the jury would serve for a set amount of time, such as one year. Thus, a panel of lay citizens would be drawn at random, and these would be one of the seven members of the jury, serving on one or more trials during the set time. This proposal sparked controversy again. Professor Benoit Frydman, president of the Perelman Center for Legal Philosophy at the Université Libre de Bruxelles, argued that the proposed jury would no longer be a jury, but a new form of jurisdiction, and a way to circumvent the Constitution, and it would probably be annulled by the Constitutional Council the following year ("Benoit Frydman sur la réforme," 2018).

ANALYSIS AND FUTURE PROSPECTS

As my coauthor and I wrote in *The Jury at a Crossroads*, historically the French and Belgian juries emerged as a product of the French Revolution (Hans & Germain, 2011). As such, they were seen as a way to fight arbitrary justice. In today's world, even though France and Belgium follow the rule of law and have professionally trained judges and an independent judiciary, the participation of lay citizens retains an important symbolic and practical value. It allows citizens to have a direct voice in the resolution of criminal trials. Public opinion largely favors the jury, and the public is attached to the institution; 73% of those polled in Belgium support the jury (Commission de réforme de la cour d'assises, 2005, p. 8) and 82% of those polled in France support it (Lederman, 1997). The jury provides a good way for citizens to be involved in the justice system so that they understand the issues better.

The various reform proposals and options presented in France and Belgium could lead to either the practical suppression of the *Cour d'assises* and its replacement with professional judges, or a modernization and simplification of the procedure, or even a reappearance of the jury, albeit in a different form.

The most significant obstacle to abandoning the jury in Belgium is that the jury is inscribed in the Belgian Constitution. The efforts of Justice Minister Geens to abolish the jury in almost all crimes led to a sanction by the Constitutional Court in December 2017, showing the difficulty of modifying the constitutional provision for jury trials without a constitutional amendment. It is very complex to modify the Belgian Constitution. This is not the situation in France, where the jury is not mentioned in the Constitution or even considered a fundamental principle of the Republic. However, the obstacle in France is that public opinion is largely in favor of the institution of the jury. In both countries, most people agree that the cost of a jury trial is very high and that the hearings are interminable because of the orality of the debates and the number of witnesses.

Some of the recent developments in France suggest that the participation of lay citizens has been manipulated by political parties both on the right and the left. There was also collateral damage as a result of the Law of 2011, in that jurors are now less well represented at the *Cour d'assises* because their number has been reduced.

The legislature in France has tweaked the *Cour d'assises* over the years. The legislature has taken several measures in France to improve the procedures and to conform to the European requirements for a fair trial. One change was to require a reasoned verdict both for the judgment and the sentence; another change was to include an appeals process to another *Cour d'assises*. In addition, the Law of May 2014 (Loi 2014–535) implemented a Directive of the European Union concerning the right to information in criminal proceedings. With that law, the defendant is allowed to remain silent during the trial (as well as to speak and to answer questions) and has a right to an interpreter; the parties now have the right to obtain documents from the file; and the proceedings have to be recorded (Loi 2016–731). All of these reforms make sense and are consistent with contemporary European standards of fair trial procedure and the rights of the defense.

In both countries, some practical steps might help modernize and streamline the proceedings in the *Cour d'assises*. These steps should include sharing more information with the lay citizens before the trial, permitting greater use of the written dossier (including written documents prepared ahead of the trial and testimony) by the lay citizens, and permitting fewer oral testimonies. In addition, the testimony by witnesses could be shortened and the number of witnesses could be reduced. The parties could rely on the written dossier, and lay citizens could have access to it. However, the current French government has curiously set aside this latter recommendation. The government argues that lay citizens do not have time to read the entire file after they are selected because the trial starts right away, and in any event, they may not have the competence to understand the legal arguments (Sénat, 2018).

Some French judges experienced in *Cour d'assises* cases provided some advice in a 2015 report (Durançon, 2015). They recommended less reliance on oral questioning, explaining that this emphasis on oral proceedings came about when lay citizens were illiterate in the past, but that is no longer the case today. They feel that access to the file would enable lay citizens to provide a verdict more readily. Currently, lay citizens must operate without access to the file (*dossier d'instruction*). Only the presiding judge can see the file; lay citizens and the other professional judges are unable to review it. Judges also recommend a "lighter" procedure, which, with the agreement of all parties, could lead to expedited proceedings. For example, limiting the testimony of witnesses and experts would result in some cases being decided in one-day hearings. In contrast, the current *Cour d'assises* proceedings (hearings) last a minimum of two days for simple cases due to oral questioning and witnesses' testimony.

The number of professional judges and lay citizens on a mixed court also matters, as do their respective roles. A larger number of lay citizens, for instance, is more costly, but a smaller number means that they have less influence. As mentioned earlier, another recommendation is for lay citizens to be appointed for a set amount of time, for example, a year, rather than just one session. Also, some lay citizens could be drawn from the general population, and others could be specialists, such as experts or criminologists. In Belgium, the proposal by Justice Minister Geens of four lay citizens and three professional judges is an example of this approach. Proposals in Belgium offer a potentially useful alternative, with a mix of lay citizens, experts, and professional judges who can benefit from each other's perspectives and experience (Geens, 2017).

The new French law proposal by French Justice Minister Nicole Belloubet does away with lay citizen participation in a substantial number of cases. Its presumed advantage is that it provides better and faster justice, particularly in cases of rape. Because of the delays at the *Cour d'assises*, many rape cases are currently downgraded to the regular criminal courts. The *cour criminelle départementale* is different from the *tribunal correctionnel* (criminal court) in its procedure and has more judges, five judges rather than three. It might be useful to permit the victim to choose between the *Cour d'assises* or the new *cour criminelle*. The new court's decisions can be appealed to a *Cour d'assises*, which includes lay citizens. The most serious crimes are still within the competence of the *Cour d'assises*. It is a reasonable proposal, particularly if it is tried as a pilot project (Pradel, 2018).

One potential source of controversy is the guilty plea (plea bargain) (*plaider coupable*), which was recently introduced in France and Belgium. In France, it can only be used for *délits*, and certain *délits* are excluded, specifically crimes of violence, threats, sexual aggressions, involuntary homicides, and press and political offenses. At least one commentator wrote about the fear that one day it might be applied to rapes and other violent crimes (Pradel, 2018). In the United States, most criminal cases end up with a plea bargain rather than a jury trial. In France, however, guilty pleas are not yet part of the French culture; there is a feeling that justice cannot be rendered properly without a full trial.

CONCLUSION

When doing comparative law research, it is important to consider the context in which the institution has arisen. In civil law countries such as France and Belgium, lay jurors are not ingrained in the legal culture. They do exist, but they are not a dominant factor. Everyone recognizes that the jury has certain benefits, but the perception has changed over time, driven by politics, economics, and scandals.

The two main considerations in reducing the role of lay citizen juries are cost and the underlying tension between professional judges and lay citizen judges. The latter is a strong obstacle in France in particular, with its corps of career judges, who do not look favorably at lay jurors.

In recent years, Belgium and France have struggled with questions about who should judge, and how much citizens should participate in the criminal justice system. In both countries, there is a consensus in the public that there is a need for lay citizen participation. The participation of lay citizens in the criminal justice system is costly and time consuming, yet it enhances deeply held values, such as checking the power of professional judges and permitting citizens to contribute their views to the criminal justice system.

Acknowledgments: I wish to thank Professors Sarah Lewis, Seth Brostoff, and Taryn Marks, my colleagues at the University of Florida College of Law, for reviewing this chapter and helping with citations. This chapter originated as a paper prepared for the Oñati Conference on Juries and Mixed Tribunals across the Globe: New Developments, Common Challenges and Future Directions (Germain, 2014) and a short article in the *RCSL Newsletter* (Germain, 2017). It was also presented in different venues, including the Law and Society Association meetings in Mexico City (2017) and Toronto (2018).

REFERENCES

A quoi sert le juge d'instruction? [What is the purpose of the investigating judge?] (2012, August 31). www.vie-publique.fr/decouverte-institutions/justice/fonctionnement/justice-penale/quoi-sert-juge-instruction.html

Arrêté du 18 mars 2013 mettant fin à l'expérimentation des dispositions prévoyant la participation de citoyens assesseurs au fonctionnement de la justice pénale [Order of 18 March 2013 ending the experimentation of the provisions providing for the participation of citizen assessors in the functioning of the criminal justice system], March. 22, 2013, *Journal Officiel de la République Française* [Official Gazette of France], p. 4897.

Aubert, J. L., & Savaux, E. (2012). *Introduction au droit* [Introduction to law]. 14th ed. Paris: Sirey.

Benoit Frydman sur la réforme de la cour d'assises [Benoit Frydman on the reform of the assises court]. (2018, January 10). *Vivreici.be*. www.vivreici.be/commune/5000/les-gens-d-ici/detail_benoit-frydman-sur-la-reforme-de-la-cour-d-039-assises-10-01-2018?videoId=90318

Bourlet, A. (Ed.). (n.d.). *La cour d'assises*. https://justice.belgium.be/sites/default/files/downloads/La%20cour%20d%27assises.pdf

Brafman, J. (2012, April 9). Justice: Nicolas Sarkozy table sur l'appel au peuple [Justice: Nicolas Sarkozy is counting on the call to the people]. *Slate*. www.slate.fr/story/52901/justice-sarkozy-programme

Centre Permanent pour la Citoyenneté et la Participation [Permanent Center for Citizenship and Participation (Belg.)]. (2016, June). *Vers la fin du jury d'assises?* [Toward the end of the assises jury?] www.cpcp.be/medias/pdfs/publications/cour_assise.pdf

Chambre des représentants de Belgique [Belgian House of Representatives]. (2015). *Projet de loi, modifiant le droit pénal et la procédure pénale et portant des dispositions diverses en matière de justice* [Legislative bill modifying criminal law and criminal procedure and carrying various provisions in justice matters]. www.dekamer.be/flwb/pdf/54/1418/54K1418001.pdf

Code de Procédure Pénale [Criminal Procedure Code], Art. 712–713, al. 2. (Fr.)

Code d' Instruction Criminelle [Criminal Procedure Code] (Belg.). www.ejustice.just.fgov.be/eli/loi/1808/11/17/1808111701/justel

Commission de réforme de la Cour d'assises [Commission on the Reform of the Assises Court (Belg.)]. (2005). *Rapport définitif de la « Commission de réforme de la Cour d'assises » remis à madame la Ministre de la Justice le 23 décembre 2005* [Final report of the reform Commission of the Cour d'assises presented to Madam Minister of Justice, December 23, 2005]. www.philodroit.be/IMG/pdf/B._FRYDMAN_R._VERSTRAETEN_-_Rapport_definitif_de_la_Commission_de_reforme_de_la_Cour_d_assises.pdf

Conseil constitutionnel [Constitutional Court] Decision No. 2011–625 DC, Mar. 10, 2011, Rec. 122 (Fr.).

Decision No. 2017–694 QPC, Mar. 2, 2018 (Fr.).

Constitution (Belg.) (2007).

Cour constitutionelle [Constitutional Court] decision no 148/2017, Dec. 21, 2017, www.const-court.be/public/f/2017/2017-148f.pdf (Belg.)

De Charette, L. (2010, December 2). Les jurés siégeront en cours d'appel [Jurors will sit on courts of appeal]. *Le Figaro*. www.lefigaro.fr/actualite-france/2010/12/02/01016-20101202ARTFIG00729-les-jures-siegeront-en-cours-d-appel.php

Direction de l'information légale et administrative (Premier ministre), Ministère chargé de la justice [Directorate of Legal and Administrative Information (Prime Minister), Ministry of Justice (Fr.)] (2018). Déroulement d'un procès devant la cour d'assises [Trial proceedings before the assises court]. www.service-public.fr/particuliers/vosdroits/F1487

Durançon, D. (2015). La Cour d'assises: Une juridiction séculaire et atypique en perpétuelle quête de renovation [The Assises Court: A secular and atypical jurisdiction, permanently looking for renovation]. Unpublished doctoral dissertation, University of Paris-Saclay.

Echevinage. Etudes Générales [Echevinage. General studies]. (2014). In *Bibliographie de l'Histoire de la Justice Francaise (1789–2011)* [Bibliography of the History of French Justice (1789–2011)]. https://criminocorpus.org/fr/outils/bibliographie/consultation/themes/13483

Egré, P., & Raisse, T. (2016, March 14). Délais d'audiencement: Les assises attendent le verdict [Court hearings delays: the assises courts are waiting for the verdict]. *Le Parisien*. www.leparisien.fr/espace-premium/actu/les-assises-attendent-le-verdict-14-03-2016-5623943.php

European Convention on Human Rights (2010). https://www.echr.coe.int/Documents/Convention_ENG.pdf

Faure, S. (2011, July 7). La loi sur les jurés populaires est paradoxale du point de vue de l'histoire [The law on popular juries is a paradox from the standpoint of history]. *Liberation*. www.liberation.fr/societe/2011/07/07/la-loi-sur-les-jures-populaires-est-paradoxale-du-point-de-vue-de-l-histoire_747679

Garapon, A., & Papadopoulos, I. (2003). *Juger en Amérique et en France* [To judge in America and in France]. Paris: Odile Jacobs.

Geens, K. (2016). Correctionnalisation [Correctionalization]. www.koengeens.be/fr/policy/1-correctionalisering

(2017, September 22). Assises « Trois juges et quatre jurés » [Assises courts: "Three judges and four jurors"]. https://jubel.be/fr/assises-trois-juges-et-quatre-jures

Germain, C. M. (2014, June). The rise and fall of lay participation in French criminal courts [Paper presentation]. 2014 Conference on Juries and Mixed Tribunals Across the Globe: New Developments, Common Challenges and Future Directions, Oñati, Spain.

(2017, Winter). Lay participation in the criminal jury: France and Belgium. *RCSL Newsletter*, 7–9. http://rcsl.iscte.pt/rcsl_nl_2017_1_.pdf

Goffinon, J. (2011). *Le jury populaire: Véritable juge ou simple expression de la démocratie* [The popular jury: Real judge or simple expression of democracy]. www.philodroit.be/IMG/pdf/colloqueliegetexte.pdf

Hans, V. P., & Germain, C. M. (2011). The French jury at a crossroads. *Chicago-Kent Law Review*, 86, 737–768.

Huyghe, M. S. (2011, June 15). *Rapport fait au nom de la commission des lois constitutionnelles, de la législation et de l'administration générale de la république sur le projet de loi (No. 3452), adopté par le sénat après engagement de la procédure accélérée sur la participation des citoyens au fonctionnement de la justice pénale et le jugement des mineurs* [Report written in the name of the commission of constitutional laws, of legislation and of the general administration of the republic on the legislative bill (No. 3452) adopted by the senate after the fast-track procedure on the participation of citizens to the functioning of criminal justice and judgment of minors]. Assemblée nationale. www.assemblee-nationale.fr/13/rapports/r3532.asp

Jacquin, J. B. (2018, March 9). Nicole Belloubet veut un « tribunal criminel » à la place des assises [Nicole Belloubet wants a "criminal tribunal," instead of the assises court]. *Le Monde*. www.lemonde.fr/police-justice/article/2018/03/09/un-tribunal-criminel-a-la-place-des-assises_5268210_1653578.html

Lederman, C. (1997). Jures d'assises et magistrats [Assises jurors and judges]. *Regards.fr*. http://www.regards.fr/archives/archives-web/jures-d-assises-et-magistrats,382

Loi 2000–516 du 15 juin 2000 renforçant la protection de la présomption d'innocence et les droits des victims [Law 2000–516 of June 15, 2000, on strengthening the protection of the presumption of innocence and the rights of victims]. *Journal Officiel de la République Française* [Official Gazette of France], June 16, 2000, p. 9038.

Loi 2011–939 du 10 août 2011 sur la participation des citoyens au fonctionnement de la justice pénale et le jugement des mineurs [Law 2011–939 of August 10, 2011, on the participation of citizens in the functioning of criminal justice and the adjudication of minors]. *Journal Officiel de la République Française* [Official Gazette of France], August 11, 2011, p. 13744.

Loi 2014–535 du 27 mai 2014 portant transposition de la directive 2012/13/UE du Parlement européen et du Conseil, du 22 mai 2012, relative au droit à l'information dans le cadre des procédures pénales [Law 2014–535 of May 27, 2014, transposing Directive 2012/13/EU of the European Parliament and of the Council of May 22, 2012, on the right to information in criminal proceedings]. *Journal Officiel de la République Française* [Official Gazette of France], May 28, 2014, p. 8864.

Loi 2016–731 du 3 juin 2016 renforçant la lutte contre le crime organisé, le terrorisme et leur financement, et améliorant l'efficacité et les garanties de la procédure pénale [Law 2016–731 of June 3, 2016, strengthening the fight against organized crime, terrorism and their financing, and improving the effectiveness and guarantees of criminal proceedings]. *Journal Officiel de la République Française* [Official Gazette of France], June 4, 2016. www.legifrance.gouv.fr/affichTexte.do?cidTexte=JORFTEXT000032627231&categorieLien=id

Loi 2019–222 du 23 mars 2019 de programmation 2018–2022 et de réforme pour la justice [Law No. 2019–222 of March 23, 2019, planning for 2018–2022 and justice reform]. *Journal Officiel de la République Française* [Official Gazette of France]. www.legifrance.gouv.fr/affichTexte.do?cidTexte=JORFTEXT000038261631&categorieLien=id

Loi du 7 mai 1999 modification à la constitution [Law of May 7, 1999, on modifying the Constitution]. *Moniteur Belge* [Official Gazette of Belgium], May 29, 1999, p. 19310.

Loi du 25 novembre 1941 sur le jury [Law of November 25, 1941, on the jury]. *Journal Officiel de la République Française* [Official Gazette of France], December 12, 1941, p. 5355.

Loi modifiant le droit pénal et la procédure pénale et portant des dispositions diverses en matière de justice [Law amending criminal law and criminal procedure and providing miscellaneous provisions on justice], February 5, 2016. *Moniteur Belge* [Official Gazette of Belgium], Feb. 19, 2016, p. 13130.

Ministère de la Justice [Ministry of Justice (Fr.)]. (2011–2012). Statistiques pénales [Criminal statistics]. Paris.

(2013, March 1). L'expérimentation des citoyens assesseurs évaluée [The experiment of citizen assessors as judges assessed]. www.justice.gouv.fr/la-garde-des-sceaux-10016/archives-2013-c-taubira-12869/lexperimentation-des-citoyens-assesseurs-evaluee-30038.html

(2016). *Les chiffres-clés de la Justice 2016* [Justice 2016 key numbers]. Secrétariat general, Service support et moyens du ministère, Sous-direction de la Statistique et des Études. www.justice.gouv.fr/art_pix/stat_CC%202016.pdf

Neuer, L. (2012, May 5). "Jurés Populaires" en correctionnelle: Premier bilan en demi teinte ["Popular juries" in the criminal tribunal: First mixed assessment]. *Le Point*. www.lepoint.fr/chroniqueurs-du-point/laurence neuer/jures-populaires-en-correctionnelle-premier-bilan-en-demi-teinte-05–05-2012–1458403_56.php

Ordre des barreaux Francophones et Germanophones de Belgique [Belgian Bar Association for French and German speakers]. Pot-Pourri II. (2016, September 8). *La Tribune*. http://us2.campaign-archive2.com/?u=d552fd66716b81b8fb8f922cc&id=c62332842c

Pradel, J. (2001). L'appel contre les arrêts d'assises: un apport heureux de la loi du 15 juin 2000 [Appeal against assises verdicts: A welcome contribution of the law of June 15, 2000]. *Recueil Dalloz*, 1964–1972.

(2010). Procédure pénale [Criminal procedure]. *Recueil Dalloz*, 34, 2254–2263.

(2011a). La Cour de Strasbourg n'impose finalement qu'une motivation minimale aux cours d'assises statuant avec des jurés [The Strasbourg Court finally only imposes a minimal ground for decision requirement to the assises court sitting with jurors]. *Recueil Dalloz*, 1, 48–50.

(2011b, September 5). Le citoyen comme juge pénal: A propos de la loi de 10 août 2011 [The citizen as criminal judge: About the law of August 10, 2011]. *La Semaine Juridique – Edition générale*, 1534.

(2018, April 2) Plaidoyer pour la création d'un tribunal criminel sans jurés [Plea for the creation of a criminal tribunal without any jurors]. *Semaine Juridique – Edition Générale*, 377.

Rastello, C. (2012, January 4). Jurés populaires en correctionnelle: une fausse bonne idée? [Popular juries in the criminal tribunal: a false good idea?] *L'Obs*. www.nouvelobs.com/societe/20120102.OBS7867/jures-populaires-en-correctionnelle-une-fausse-bonne-idee.html

Reasonable doubt (n.d.). In *Black's Law Dictionary*. 2nd ed. https://thelawdictionary.org/reasonable-doubt

Redon, M. (2013). *Cour d'assises: Un répertoire de droit pénal et procédure pénale* [The Assise Court: A directory of criminal law and criminal procedure]. Paris: Dalloz.

Réju, E. (2012, January 1). Associer les citoyens, c'est faire oeuvre de pédagogie [To involve the citizens is a pedagogical endeavor]. *La Croix*. www.la-croix.com/Actualite/S-informer/France/Associer-les-citoyens-c-est-faire-aeuvre-de-pedagogie-_EP_-2012-01-01-752937

Salas, D. (2001). Juger en démocratie [To judge in a democracy]. In *La Cour d'assises: Bilan d'un héritage démocratique* [The Assises Court: State of a democratic heritage] (pp. 7–21). Paris: La Documentation française.

Salvat, X., & Boccon-Gibod, D. (2013, February). *L'expérimentation des citoyens assesseurs dans les resorts des cours d'appel de Dijon et Toulouse* [The experiment of the citizen assessors in the courts of appeals of Dijon and Toulouse]. www.ladocumentationfrancaise.fr/var/storage/rapports-publics/134000144/0000.pdf

Sénat [Senate (Fr.)] (2011). *Etude d'Impact: Projet de loi sur la participation des citoyens au fonctionnement de la justice pénale et le jugement des mineurs* [Impact Study: Legislative bill on the participation of citizens in the functioning of criminal justice and the judgment of minors]. www.senat.fr/leg/etudes-impact/pjl10-438-ei/pjl10-438-ei.pdf

Taxquet v. Belgique [G.C.], 2010-VI Eur. Ct. H.R. 105.

Vansiliette, F. (2016, September 30). La Cour d'Assises: vers une lente agonie? [The Assises Court: Toward a slow agony?]. *Justice en Ligne*. www.justice-en-ligne.be/article919.html

Wauters, L. (2016, October 8). Koen Geens veut résusciter les Assises [Koen Geens wants to resurrect the assises courts]. www.koengeens.be/fr/news/2016/10/08/koen-geens-veut-ressusciter-les-assises

12

The Russian Jury Trial

An Ongoing Legal and Political Experiment

Nikolai Kovalev and Sergei Nasonov

Trial by jury (*sud prisiazhnykh*) was reintroduced by Vladimir Putin's predecessor, Boris Yeltsin, in 1994 as a pilot project in nine Russian provinces and underwent significant reforms when Putin served as President (2000–2008 and 2012–present) and Prime Minister (2008–2012). On the one hand, in 2003–2004, Putin expanded jury trials to the rest of the country, and in 2017–2018, he introduced jury trials in lower courts (Federal'nyi Zakon, 2016). On the other hand, in 2008, the government abolished jury trials for political offenses, and in 2017, it reduced the size of juries from 12 to 8 jurors (Kovalev & Smirnov, 2014). In spite of attacks on jury trials by politicians, legal scholars, and practitioners, this common-law institution has managed to survive in the hostile Russian inquisitorial criminal justice system. Observers might find it a paradox that the modern Russian form of trial by jury, which reveals defects of the Russian system of pretrial investigation and criminal courts, has been so resilient.

To explain this paradox, we look at the history of lay participation prior to the recent reforms. In this chapter, we recognize that the Russian trial by jury, as a form of lay participation, is a legal experiment, which was originally launched by the Great Reforms of the 1860s (Dzhanshiev, 2004). The institution went through various changes and was modified by several reforms in the Tsarist period. In the Soviet period, it was transformed into a mixed court and was revived again in the 1990s (Thaman, 1995). Today, the experiment continues. This chapter examines how jury trials endured over time, from the nineteenth century to the present day.

The main purpose of introducing and retaining jury trials in Russia was to legitimize judicial power in the eyes of citizens. In all historical periods, judges in Russia were dependent on the central and local governments (Kovalev, 2010). The Russian people did not trust professional judges and courts in the Tsarist period (Gessen, 1905), and they do not trust them now (Levada-Center, 2018). Lay participation in the form of juries provides the only independent and impartial tribunal that enables the government to justify a verdict in the eyes of the Russian people.

At the same time, the Russian government has never allowed trial by jury to function without supervision and restrictions, as demonstrated by three types of controlling mechanisms. First, as opposed to the US Founding Fathers, such as Alexander Hamilton, John Adams, and Thomas Jefferson, who regarded trial by jury as a political institution (Ferguson, 2014), the Russian government has always attempted to avoid the politicalization of this institution (Dzhanshiev, 2004; Kovalev & Smirnov, 2014). Although the Russian jury was and still is a political institution in the sense that it continues to participate in the administration of justice along with professional judges, the Russian government has always attempted to prevent it from becoming a political tool for the opposition, dissenters, and revolutionaries. Just like William Penn in England (Nager, 1964), John Peter Zenger in New York (Reed, 1996), or Joseph Howe in Nova Scotia (MacKay, 2016), Russian dissenters challenged the government by committing various political offenses, and, when they were tried by criminal courts, they appealed, often successfully, to the conscience of Russian jurors. As this chapter will explore, the government, in order to prevent the dissenters from transforming jury trials into a political struggle and to prevent potential jury nullification, took away the jury's right to hear cases pertaining to political or anti-government crimes and, thus, it weakened the role of the jury.

Second, the Russian government has tried to reduce the influence of defense attorneys on juries by curtailing their right to select jurors, to present evidence, and to make submissions to the jury (Kovalev, 2010). In other words, there has been no true equality between the criminal defendant and the prosecutor. The prosecution has always been in a more advantageous position during the trial than the defense, and this tendency is even more pronounced at the pretrial stage.

Third, the government has tried to exercise control over the composition of juries (Nemytina, 1995). In the Tsarist period, the government relied mostly on various qualifications for jurors (*tsenzy*), such as gender, residency, property, decency (*dobroporiadochnost'*), and religion (Vilkova & Nasonov, 2017). Instead of random selection of jurors, in the Tsarist period a special commission selected jurors based on its "discretion and through careful discussion" (Vilkova & Nasonov, 2017, p. 66). In the Republican period, despite the declared principle of random selection, executives and the judiciary manipulated jury lists to have an overrepresentation of people loyal to the prosecution in the jury pool (Jackson & Kovalev, 2016; Kovalev, 2010; Nikitinskii, 2019).

PRE-SOVIET JURY EXPERIMENT: RUSSIAN JURIES IN THE IMPERIAL PERIOD (1864–1917)

The history of trial by jury in Russia is often divided into two historical periods: the Imperial period (1864–1917) and the modern Russian period (1993–present time); there were no juries between 1917 and 1993. Some authors also interpose other historical periods between these two. For example, two additional periods include the time between the so-called counterreforms of the 1880s and the February Revolution of 1917, and then, a very short period between the February Revolution of 1917 and the establishment of the Bolshevik (Soviet) court system in November 1917, which abolished trial by jury (Demichev, 2001). Although the reforms of the 1880s and the reforms of the Provisional Government were very important historical events, they did not change the model of trial by jury originally adopted in 1864. Therefore, we will examine the role of the jury during these two main historical periods.

The first proposal to introduce trial by jury in Russia was made by legal scholar S. E. Desnitskii to Catherine II in 1767 (Afanas'ev, 2003). It appears that Desnitskii became interested in the institution while he was a doctoral student at the University of Glasgow and later translated Blackstone's *Commentaries on the Laws of England* (Istraty, 2015). He proposed a Scottish model of trial by jury (15-member juries reaching their verdicts by simple-majority rule), but his proposal was never adopted (Efremova, 2008; Surin, 2008). In 1809, a statesman, Count Mikhail Speranskii, recommended this form of lay participation to Tsar Alexander I, along with other principles of adversarial criminal procedure, such as equality between the parties, oral proceedings, and public trial (Korotkikh, 1989). Trial by jury was also an essential part of judicial reform by the revolutionary Decembrists and their political programs in the 1820s (Raeff, 1966).

Until the second half of the nineteenth century, these initiatives were futile because conservatives within the Russian intellectual elite and government advisors rejected trial by jury as a foreign, anti-Russian institution that threatened Orthodox Christianity and the absolute power of the Tsar (Cheltsov-Bebutov, 1995). The situation changed after Alexander II inherited the throne from his father, Nicholas I (1825–1855). Alexander II (1855–1881) went down in Russian history as the *Tsar Liberator* (Pereira, 1983) because he abolished serfdom and provided peasants (former serfs) with land. Following the emancipation of serfs, Alexander II carried out judicial reform. Both prerevolutionary and postrevolutionary (Soviet, Western, and contemporary Russian) historians and lawyers agree that the Emancipation of 1861 and the judicial reform of 1864 were interwoven (Dzhanshiev, 2004; Korotkikh, 1989; Mel'nik, 2003). The judicial reform of the 1860s, including the introduction of jury trials, was an integral part of the transformation from feudalism to capitalism, and from a despotic rule toward democracy (Kovalev, 2010).

In 1862, Alexander II approved the program of judicial reform called the *Fundamental Provisions of Transformation of the Judicial Part in Russia* (Korotkikh, 1989). The program was published to encourage public discussion of the reform. The *Fundamental Provisions* outlined judicial reforms, including separation of the judiciary from the executive, administrative, and legislative branches and the introduction of the jury system (Korotkikh, 1989). The principles were reflected in the Judicial Statutes (*Sudebnye ustavy*). The authors of the judicial reform adopted the jury court model consisting of two separate panels of three professional judges (*koronnye sud'i*) and 12 jurors (*prisiazhnye zasedateli*) (Foinitskii, 1996). The lay panel decided questions pertaining to the defendant's guilt or innocence or questions of fact (Ustav ugolovnogo sudoproizvodstva [Code of Criminal Procedure], 1864, Art. 754).

The jury system did not reach the provinces of the Russian Empire for more than 40 years and was not fully implemented even by 1917 (Bobrishchev-Pushkin, 1896; Kovalev, 2010; Sluchevskii, 1910). The jury system was limited to areas with a predominantly Slavic population, such as Russians, Ukrainians, and Belarussians. Thus, the jury system was not introduced in many territories of the Russian Empire, including the Caucasian provinces (current Georgia, Armenia, Azerbaijan, Dagestan, and Chechnya), the Polish Kingdom, the Baltic provinces (except Vil'no), Siberia (except Tomsk and Tobol'sk provinces), and Central Asia (except Akmolinsk, Semipalatinsk, and Uralsk) (Code of Criminal Procedure, 1864, Arts. 1256, 1309, 1338, 1423, 1461, and 1461[1]).

Originally, the subject jurisdiction of the jury covered one-fifth of the Criminal Code sections (a total of 410 articles of the Code), which was slightly more than the jurisdiction of the justices of the peace (384 articles of the Code) and much less than the jurisdiction of professional judges (a total of 775 articles of the Code) (Bobrishchev-Pushkin, 1896, p. 49). The laws of 1879 and 1889 decreased the authority of the jury by withdrawing from its jurisdiction crimes against administration, violent crimes against public officials, malfeasances, passport cases, a substantial number of house-breaking crimes, banking offenses, and crimes by press (e.g., lèse-majesté, proliferation of malicious news) (Bobrishchev-Pushkin, 1896; Dzhanshiev, 2004).

The first impulse to reduce the jurisdiction of juries was demonstrated with the acquittal of Vera Zasulich, who was charged with the attempted assassination of Fyodor Trepov, the general-governor of Saint Petersburg (Bhat, 1997; Gessen, 1905). In spite of the fact that the accused admitted that she had shot the victim and in spite of other evidence against her, the jury acquitted her and cheerful crowds of people greeted both the accused and her lawyer with ovations outside the courthouse (Gessen, 1905). A. F. Koni, a famous Russian jurist, who was the presiding judge at this trial, observed after the announcement of the verdict: "[T]his was the saddest day for the Russian justice system" (Gessen, 1905, p. 358). Indeed, public support for this jury nullification did not last long. Immediately after the verdict, the minister of justice proposed removal of crimes committed against public officials from the jurisdiction of juries in order to combat political criminality. As a Russian journalist of the time, Prince Vladimir Meshchersky, wrote in his memoirs: "When these new laws [reducing the jurisdiction of juries] were adopted, everybody understood that 'the government, not trusting the loyalty of not only the society supplying the jurors, but also the judicial department itself, has been placed in the position of self-defense, to transfer all political crimes to the court of special persons not involved in the judicial department'" (Gessen, 1905, p. 359). In 1878, many similar cases were transferred to military tribunals (Gessen, 1905).

In addition, other cases were transferred from juries to mixed courts, which consisted of professional judges and representatives from different classes, in accordance with the law of July 7, 1889 (Dzhanshiev, 2004). As opposed to jurors who were selected from all strata of society, class representatives were selected from the local leaders of each class: a provincial marshal of the nobility (*gubernskii predvoditel' dvorianstva*), a city mayor (*gorodskoi golova*), and a foreman of the administrative subdivision of the Russian province (*volostnoi starshina*) (Code of Criminal Procedure, 1864, Art. 1105). As indicated earlier, these legislative changes were examples of the tendency of the Russian government to "depoliticize" juries or, in other words, to remove from juries any cases that could have political implications.

The composition of Russian juries was representative of different classes of the Russian population. Moreover, in some regions the vast majority of jurors were formerly enslaved peasants (*krepostnye* or serfs). For example, the proportion of peasants among jurors in the Nizhii Novgorod and Kazan' provinces in the Imperial period in some courts reached about 80% (Afanas'ev, 1978). However, some categories of Russian subjects (poddannye Rossiiskoi Imperii) were excluded or restricted from jury service. For example, women were not eligible for jury service until 1917.

Although there was no specific religious qualification for jury candidates, in some areas of the Russian Empire the government used quotas for participation of non-Christian jurors in the administration of justice. For example, in provinces that are now part of modern Kazakhstan, the number of non-Christians, such as Muslims, could not exceed one-fourth of the jury panel (Code of Criminal Procedure, 1864, Art. 1461[1]). In nine western provinces, which are now territories of Ukraine and Moldova, the number of Jews on the jury panel was determined proportionately to the Jewish population of the *uezd* (region) (Code of Criminal Procedure, 1864, Art. 550). Moreover, non-Christian jurors could not be selected as jury forepersons in those provinces (Code of Criminal Procedure, 1864, Art. 670; Vilkova & Nasonov, 2017).

There were other jury qualifications, such as age (between 25 and 70 years old) and property qualifications, which varied among provinces and cities. For example, jurors were required to have an annual income of 500 rubles in capital cities and 200 rubles elsewhere. This was not a very high income threshold for some locations and even extremely poor people were able to serve on the jury (Vilkova & Nasonov, 2017). The legislation also disqualified people who belonged to certain professions and occupations, such as priests and monks, higher public officials, judges and prosecutors, police officers, teachers, and military men (Vilkova & Nasonov, 2017). The law also disqualified people who were expelled from their class or the estate of the realm (*soslovie*, e.g., nobility, clergy, urban dwellers, peasantry, and *inorodtsy* or aliens) by the judgments of these classes.

As mentioned earlier, preliminary general jury lists were compiled by special temporary jury commissions consisting of members elected by local legislatures. These commissions collected information about candidates from various officials, including chairmen of local government, town and city mayors, and heads of local police (Vilkova & Nasonov, 2017). The jury commissions used preliminary general lists for compiling regular jury lists and in the process used discretion after careful consideration and discussion of each candidate rather than random selection. In particular, commissions were looking for people who were not only eligible on the basis of legal qualifications (e.g., age, gender, property), but also those who would be able to perform jury duty because of their perceived moral qualities and other such reasons (Vilkova & Nasonov, 2017). In other words, jury commissions vetted the general lists and handpicked only those they viewed as the most trustworthy among them to be candidates for jury service. Hence the Russian government was able to regulate the jury system through its control of the composition of juries.

Once in court, candidates for every jury panel were selected randomly from regular lists (Code of Criminal Procedure, 1864, Art. 551). Candidates who showed up for the court session constituted the session jury panel. The entire jury panel took the oath before the jury for a particular case was selected (Code of Criminal Procedure, 1864, Arts. 645^7–645^8). Then, the prosecution and the defense could exercise their right to challenges. Russian Imperial legislation adopted the French model of jury challenges in court (Foinitskii, 1996), whereby neither *voir dire* nor challenges for cause were allowed. Peremptory challenges were made on the basis of information available in the jury lists given to the parties in court. The lists contained first names, last names, and patronimic (first name of the candidate's father), class or rank (e.g., merchant or state counselor), and religion (Vilkova & Nasonov, 2017), and were given to a public or private prosecutor (lawyer representing a victim) who crossed out the last names of the jurors he would like to challenge. Following this step, the defense counsel and the defendant could cross out the names of jurors they wanted to challenge. If the prosecutor refused to use his right to peremptory challenges, the defense could use its own peremptory challenges, plus the prosecutor's peremptory challenges, but no more than 12 peremptory challenges in total. Thus, the number of remaining jurors on the panel was 18 (Vilkova & Nasonov, 2017). Originally, the number of peremptory challenges was six for the prosecution and at least six for the defense, but the law of 1884 reduced the number to three for each side (Foinitskii, 1996). According to Ivan Foinitskii (1996, 1:425), one of the reasons for reducing the number of peremptory challenges was the claim that the defense "abused its right to peremptory challenges." This is another illustration of the government's intent to curtail the rights of the defense.

The final step in the selection of the jury was random selection of jurors from the remaining 18 prospective jurors. The first 12 names selected randomly constituted the jury for a particular case and the remaining names became alternates (Vilkova & Nasonov, 2017). Jurors selected a literate foreman, who was able to read and write in Russian (Code of Criminal Procedure, 1864, Art. 670). The Code required that for nine western provinces of Ukraine and Moldova with significant Jewish and Muslim populations, the foreman should be a Christian (Code of Criminal Procedure, 1864,

Art. 670[1]), including members of the Russian Orthodox Church, Catholics, Lutherans, and other Protestants.

Trial by jury in Imperial Russia reflected a peculiar combination of adversarial and inquisitorial models (Nasonov, 2016b). During the trial, jurors had the right to observe the exhibits (actual evidence), take notes, submit questions to witnesses, defendant, and victim via the presiding judge, and seek interpretations of the legal issues from the presiding judge (Code of Criminal Procedure, 1864, Arts. 672–677).

One of the distinctive features of the Russian jury trial in the Imperial period was that jurors were required to consider evidence in relation to the defendant's character. Authors of the Code of Criminal Procedure explained this requirement as follows: "Court always adjudicates not a separate act of the accused, but his whole personality, as far as it manifested in [...] an illegal act" (Shcheglovitov, 1887, p. 134). However, further judicial practice balanced the rights of the defense and the prosecution in the examination of such evidence. Thus, the Senate, the highest judicial body of the Russian Empire, in the case of *Bogdanov*, interpreted Article 687 of the Code of Criminal Procedure to provide that, upon request of the prosecutor, the court would examine the defendant's previous criminal record in the presence of the jury (Shcheglovitov, 1887). However, it was understood that the presiding judge would provide immediate instructions to the jury explaining the significance of the defendant's criminal record to the case. Moreover, the defendant had the right to provide his or her explanations as well.

Jurors could ask witnesses clarifying questions (Code of Criminal Procedure, 1864, Art. 724). Moreover, jurors were equal, at least in theory, to judges in terms of examining physical evidence, requesting to read protocols of inspections, identifications, searches, seizures, and examining expert witnesses (Code of Criminal Procedure, 1864 Arts. 672, 687, and 695).

There were other statutory and case-law rules that placed the defense in a less advantageous position than the prosecution when presenting evidence to the jury. For example, in his (there were no women jury lawyers in Imperial Russia) closing argument the defense counsel could not refer to his client's pretrial statement (Chebyshev-Dmitriev, 1875a). If the defendant pleaded not guilty, the law did not allow the defense counsel to examine his client, that is, to present the defendant's testimony in his or her own defense (Code of Criminal Procedure, 1864, Art. 683). These examples show that the Russian government and higher courts managed to restrict defense opportunities to influence the jury. As will be shown in the section on the modern jury, this practice continued.

Russian trial by jury adopted the continental system of a special verdict (Kovalev, 2010; Nasonov, 2016b), in which the jurors received specific questions instead of a general question about the defendant's guilt, as was the practice in common-law jurisdictions (Vidmar, 2000a). Question lists consisted of three mandatory questions: Was a criminal act committed? Did the defendant commit that act? Was the defendant guilty? The jury had to answer the first two factual questions in the affirmative before addressing the guilt question (Code of Criminal Procedure, 1864, Art. 754). All three questions were submitted to jurors with respect to each defendant and every alleged offense.

Before members of the jury retired to deliberate and to reach their verdict, the presiding judge gave jury instructions (*naputstvennoe slovo*, or "parting words"). According to Foinitskii (1996), jury instructions consisted of factual and legal parts. The factual part of jury instructions was a statement of material circumstances of the case or a summary of evidence. This element of Russian procedure was similar to the English procedure of summing up evidence (Lloyd-Bostock & Thomas, 2000). The only requirement for the factual part of the instructions was that the judge could not express his (there were no women judges in Imperial Russia) own opinions about the guilt or innocence of the defendant (Code of Criminal Procedure, 1864, Art. 802). This provision of the law was criticized by Russian scholars (Foinitskii, 1996) and practitioners (Ternovskii, 1901), who argued that judges would definitely express their prejudicial opinions through hints that would confuse the jurors. The Russian higher court recognized the right of the presiding judge in his jury instructions to "eliminate statements wrongly summarized by one of the parties," or in other words, the right to correct the submissions of the parties if either party had distorted the evidence (Chebyshev-Dmitriev, 1875b, p. 847). Judges often used this power against the defense (Chebyshev-Dmitriev, 1875b).

The presiding judge also instructed the jurors that they should reach their verdict based on their *intime conviction*, or inner or personal conviction (*vnutrenee ubezhdenie*), a principle of proof borrowed by Russian legislators from the French system. The French Constituent Assembly introduced the concept of personal or inner conviction, which belongs to the system of moral proofs, in the late eighteenth century (Esmein, 1913). It replaced the system of legal proofs that existed in Europe in the fifteenth through eighteenth centuries, in which the main proof was the confession of the accused obtained by torture (Esmein, 1913). At the same time, Russian legislators did not introduce the Anglo-American standard of proof *beyond a reasonable doubt*. Thus, jurors were left uncertain about the degree of proof that the prosecution had to establish in order for the jury to find the defendant guilty. If jury instructions were not impartial, that could be a ground for appeal. However, the parties had to object and the objection had to be recorded in the protocol of the court session (Shramchenko & Shirkov, 1913).

Similar to many civil-law jury systems, guilty verdicts in Russia required only a simple majority vote of 7 jurors out of 12. In the case of an equally split jury vote, the defendant was found not guilty (Code of Criminal Procedure, 1864, Art. 813). In addition to answering questions with regard to *corpus delicti* (essential elements of the crime) in cases when the defendant was found guilty, the jury could recommend leniency for the defendant. If the judge followed the recommendation, the sentence was reduced by a grade (Code of Criminal Procedure, 1864, Art. 828).

A jury's not-guilty verdict was binding on the court (Code of Criminal Procedure, 1864, Art. 819; Nasonov, 2016b). In some cases, a guilty verdict did not lead to a conviction. Specifically, if the court came to the conclusion that the jury convicted an innocent defendant, the court could refer the case to a new jury whose verdict would be final (Code of Criminal Procedure, 1864, Art. 818). Thus, if a professional panel of judges disagreed with the jury's guilty verdict, it could occur only one time in that case.

JURIES UNDER THE PROVISIONAL GOVERNMENT AND THEIR ABOLITION UNDER THE BOLSHEVIKS (1917)

The Provisional Government ruled in Russia between the abdication of Nicholas II on March 2, 1917, and the seizure of power by the Bolsheviks or Revolutionary Socialist Political Party of Russia (later renamed the Russian Communist Party) led by Vladimir Lenin in Petrograd on November 7, 1917. This short-lived government introduced some progressive changes in the Russian jury system. These reforms are noteworthy not only as part of the history of trial by jury in Russia, but also because they demonstrate that trial by jury as a legal and political experiment played a significant role in the political platform of liberal forces. These reforms went against the established legal culture and the government's controlling and restrictive policies toward the jury.

The Provisional Government resurrected some of the principles of the Judicial Reform of 1864, which had been altered in the 1870s and 1880s. The Provisional Government established the Commission for the Restoration of the Basic Provisions of the Judicial Charter of 1864 ("Commission for the Restoration") under the Ministry of Justice (Browder & Kerensky, 1961). Because the institution of the jury was a cornerstone of the judicial reform of Alexander II, the Commission for the Restoration drafted laws with a view to restoring the status of the jury, which had been reduced during the period of counterreforms in the 1880s.

The Provisional Government extended the jurisdiction of juries to all types of serious offenses, including state crimes that had never been tried by juries before (Demichev, 2003; Nasonov, 2016b). According to the drafts prepared by the Commission for the Restoration, the Provisional Government amended the Statute on Judicial Institutions of 1864 and expanded the eligibility for jury service by three democratic provisions: (1) women were granted the right to serve as jurors if they expressed an interest in having their name added to jury lists (Browder & Kerensky, 1961); (2) property qualifications for jurors were abolished (Browder & Kerensky, 1961); and (3) all restrictions and quotas for ethnic and religious minorities, discussed earlier, were also abolished (Nasonov, 2016b). These were progressive changes, especially compared to other countries at the time.

One of the reasons for these changes was that prior to the February Revolution, most political parties, including revolutionary parties that formed the Provisional

Government, supported the expansion of the jurisdiction of jury trials (Kovalev, 2010). The second reason was that the Provisional Government, which included several trial lawyers, was very enthusiastic about jury trials and considered this type of trial as the way to legitimize proceedings against former ministers of the Tsarist government in the eyes of the Russian people (Varfolomeev, 2011). In one of his speeches, Alexander Kerensky, the Minister of Justice of the Provisional Government, emphasized the importance of observing legal norms in the proceedings against top officials of the Tsarist regime. He explained: "I will not deviate from my principles based on faith in a person. My basic principle is a jury trial. Cases of former ministers will also be adjudicated by this court" (Varfolomeev, 2011). It is possible that Russian lawyer-revolutionaries were inspired by their French (Maximilien Robespierre and Georges Danton) and American predecessors (Thomas Jefferson, John Adams, and James Madison) who also advocated for jury trials after revolutions (Donovan, 2010). As opposed to the Tsarist regime, which attempted to depoliticize jury trials, the Provisional Government wanted to turn juries into a political institution.

Unfortunately, all the reforms introduced by the Russian Provisional Government were short-lived. In October 1917, the Bolsheviks, who were committed to the overthrow of all bourgeois institutions, eliminated the initiatives of the Provisional Government. Lenin wrote about the Bolshevik reforms (Kozhevnikov, 1957, p. 13):

> The indisputable obligation of the proletarian revolution was not to reform judicial institutions [...], but totally destroy, sweep away without a trace all old courts and their administration. This necessary task was fulfilled well by the October Revolution.

The destruction of the Imperial criminal justice system was "legalized" by the Council of People's Commissars' Decree "On Courts" on November 24, 1917. The decree abolished all judicial institutions, such as circuit courts, judicial chambers, and the Senate, including all departments, military and naval courts, all commercial courts, justices of the peace, the office of judicial investigators, the office of public prosecutor, and the bar (Golunskii, 1955). The decree did not indicate what type of judicial institutions were to replace juries and only mentioned that such provisions would be included in other legislative acts. At the same time, to resist counterrevolutionary forces, defend the gains of the revolution (*October coup d'etat*), and also control looting, sabotage, and other abuses, the decree introduced revolutionary tribunals consisting of a presiding judge and six lay assessors elected by local Soviets (Councils of Workers) (Vikova & Nasonov, 2017). It took the new government three months to promulgate the Second Decree "On Courts" on February 22, 1918. This decree replaced jury courts with circuit courts that included the participation of professional judges and lay assessors on mixed courts (Golusnkii, 1955).

The new institution was a hybrid model of the jury and mixed court. It consisted of a presiding judge and 12 people's assessors (*narodnye zasedateli*) elected by the

Soviets (Councils of Workers). In addition, the Second Decree abolished judge's instructions (*naputstvennoe slovo*) to people's assessors before deliberation. Similar to German *Schöffen*, or lay assessors forming a joint court with professional judges, people's assessors decided both questions of guilt and sentence (Jackson & Kovalev, 2016). The Bolsheviks' new model, however, had some unusual features, such as the right of lay assessors to challenge the presiding judge at any time during the trial and to impose a lesser punishment than provided by law or even release a convicted defendant without imposing any punishment at all (Vilkova & Nasonov, 2017).

The Decree "On Courts No. 3," adopted on July 20, 1918, limited the jurisdiction of the court of the judge and 12 people's assessors to crimes such as murder, rape, robbery, counterfeiting, bribery, and financial speculation. It also transferred other types of criminal cases to local courts with one permanent judge and two people's assessors (Golunskii, 1955).

In November 1918, the Bolshevik government reduced the number of people's assessors on mixed courts, which tried the most serious crimes, from 12 to 6. After four years, there was a further reduction to only two people's assessors (Golunskii, 1955). At the same time, the role of the professional judge increased in importance and complexity. From November 1918, the role of the presiding judge was no longer limited just to advisory functions, but the presiding judge also started participating in voting on both questions of guilt and sentencing. Consequently, during the first five years in power, the Bolshevik government transformed the independent jury of 12 people selected randomly from different classes of Russian society to the classical mixed court with the participation of one professional judge and two lay assessors appointed by Soviets, the only existing political party in the country.

The Bolsheviks gave various reasons to justify the abolition of trial by jury, which they had defended before the Revolution. Fourteen years before the Revolution, in 1903, the Bolsheviks' program provided for the "right of any person to prosecute any official before the jury" (Vasil'eva, 2013, p. 57). During the Tsarist times, Vladimir Lenin, the leader of the Bolshevik party, was a strong supporter of juries. Lenin clearly voiced his position while criticizing Mikhail Katkov, a well-known Russian publicist and editor of *Russkii Vestnik* (Russian Herald) and *Moskovskie Vedomosti* (Moscow Gazette), who called the jury the "street court" ("mob court"):

> The court of the street is valuable precisely because it breathes life into the bureaucratic formality which saturates our government in institutions through and through [...]. Aided by its flair, under the pressure of practical experience in social life and of the growth of political consciences, the street "is able" to grasp the truth toward which our official, academic judiciary, shackled by pedantry, is so laboriously and timidly groping (Kucherov, 1970, p. 341).

After the Revolution, however, Lenin proclaimed "any bourgeois court," including the jury trial, as a "ruthless and subtle instrument of repression of the exploited and defending the interests of money-bags" (Popova, 2016).

According to Bukov (1997, p. 203), Lenin's main goal was to replace trial by jury, which he perceived as the epitome of bourgeois false democracy, with proletarian democracy, which served to repress the exploiters and bourgeoisie by not granting them the freedoms and democracy it would give workers and peasants. In other words, Lenin believed that the new model of courts should not guarantee the right to an impartial tribunal to all Russian citizens, but should instead serve the Bolsheviks in repressing the upper classes.

The transformation of the jury to the mixed court, consisting of one professional judge and two lay judges, was gradual. This was mostly due to several years of strong opposition to the Bolsheviks' reforms by factions of leftist Socialist Revolutionaries (SR) and Men'sheviks within the coalition Soviet government. According to Kucherov (1970), leftist S. R. Steinberg, who was the People's Commissar of Justice from December 1917 to March 1918, believed that the new mixed courts were the final realization of the reform of 1864, which had been distorted by subsequent regimes. After Socialist Revolutionaries had voluntarily left the Council of People's Commissars and had been forced out of the government in July 1918, the Bolsheviks were able to reduce the number of lay assessors and to remove their privilege of deciding questions of guilt independently. Thus, a mixed court system, consisting of one professional judge and two lay assessors, was established by the Bolsheviks in 1918 and existed until 2004, when it was abolished by the new Code of Criminal Procedure adopted during the first presidential term of Vladimir Putin.

TRIAL BY JURY IN THE REPUBLICAN RUSSIA (1993 TO PRESENT)

Trial by Jury under President Yeltsin

In the modern period, the Russian trial by jury had two different models. The Law of July 16, 1993 introduced one model and the Criminal Procedure Code of 2001 introduced another model. Although in the 1960s and the late 1980s Soviet academics and politicians proposed different ways of reforming lay adjudication (Kovalev, 2010), there were no constitutional provisions or legislation introducing trial by jury in criminal proceedings until the collapse of the Soviet Union. In October 1991, the Supreme Council of the Russian Soviet Federative Socialist Republic (RSFSR) adopted the Concept of the Judicial Reform. The resurrection of jury trials was one of the key components of the Concept (Nasonov, 2016b). In the period between November 1991 and December 1992, the Supreme Council also amended the Constitution of the RSFSR with several jury clauses (Konstitutsiia (Osnovnoi Zakon) RSFSR [Constitution, RSFSR], 1992, Arts. 67.9, 164, 166, and 167). The new Russian Constitution, adopted in December 1993, also contained several jury clauses (Konstitutsiia Rossiiskoi Federatsii [Constitution, RF], 1993, Arts. 20, 47).

The government and President Yeltsin played a crucial role in the progress of jury reform. In September 1992, President Yeltsin ordered the State Legal Department by the President to draft a jury bill. Prior to presenting the bill to Parliament, the Legal Department submitted the draft for consultation to local government bodies in Russia, chairpersons of regional courts, and prosecutors in the regions (Nasonov, 2016b). In January 1993, the President introduced the bill to Parliament and, in June 1993, after it passed, he signed it into law ("Law of 1993"). The Office of the Prosecutor General tried to prevent its passage, but the Council of Judges and the Chairperson of the Supreme Court of Russia supported it (Nasonov, 2016b).

Although the defendant's right to trial by jury was recognized in the Constitution of the Russian Federation in 1993 (Constitution, RF, 1993, Arts. 20, 47), between 1993 and 2003 trial by jury was available to defendants in only 9 of 89 provinces of the Russian Federation, covering approximately 20% of the Russian population (Kovalev, 2010). The presidential administration identified nine "pilot" regions based on the consent of local administrations, courts, and departments of the Ministry of Justice in those nine provinces (Thaman, 1995). Initially, President Yeltsin decided to introduce jury trials as an experiment to test their performance in several regions. The Concept of the Judicial Reform stated that introduction of new institutions (jury trial) is possible in certain territories as an experiment to avoid significant mistakes in the redesign of the justice system (Dudko, 2013). However, in November–December 1992, the Ministry of Justice and the State Legal Department by the President refused to use the term "experiment" (Dudko, 2013). Instead, the staff of the presidential administration proposed, based on the experience of the Judicial Reform of 1864, a "phased introduction" of jury trials in Russia, starting in regions that were the most prepared, and most importantly, were willing to introduce them (Dudko, 2013). In other words, the introduction of jury trials in nine provinces of Russia in 1993–1994 was the first phase of the reform.

In May 1995, the Section for Judicial Reform of the State Legal Department by the President decided to extend trial by jury to 12 more provinces, but this step was postponed, ostensibly because of a federal budget deficit (Nasonov, 2016b; Stetsovskii, 1999). Moreover, the Section for Judicial Reform of the State Legal Department, which provided organizational and technical support for jury reform in Russia, was disbanded and its function was not transferred to any other state department (Karnozova, 2000). Shortly after trial by jury was introduced in 1994, the Russian government abandoned the reform until 2001, when the second President, Vladimir Putin, requested the government to introduce trial by jury in all regions of the Russian Federation before 2003 (Kozak, 2001).

Some researchers (Dudko, 2013) observed that jury reform was postponed for almost 10 years mainly due to lack of financial resources for renovation and preparation of courthouses, juror compensation, new court staff, and the protection and safety of jurors. However, Karnozova (2001) argued that bringing up financial constraints was only a cover-up for the real reasons. According to Karnozova (2001), the real issue was that jury trials turned out to be too radical. Jury trials required a transformation by professional judges and the government. Resistance to such a transformation created obstacles and constraints for the implementation of jury trials. Indeed, our research in Russia and other post-Soviet countries demonstrates that the judiciary and prosecutors commonly resist jury reforms.

Trial by jury, which was resurrected in 1993, mirrored in many respects the Imperial jury, with a few differences. According to the Code of Criminal Procedure of the RSFSR, the structure of the trial (the number, content, and sequence of stages) was consistent with the structure provided in the Code of Criminal Procedure of 1864. The Law of 1993 (Ugolovno-protsessual'nyi kodeks RSFSR [Code of Criminal Procedure, RSFSR], 1993, Art. 446(2)), like the Code of Criminal Procedure (1864, Art. 681), provided for the possibility of a summary examination of evidence during the jury trial if "all the defendants have fully pleaded guilty" and these confessions "are not disputed by any of the parties and do not cause the judge to doubt it." This meant that, in this case, the presiding judge could move directly to closing arguments or permit jurors to hear only those pieces of evidence that were submitted by the parties. According to Nemytina (1995), the summary examination of evidence in jury trials was very rare, at least in the first two years of practice.

One new feature of the Russian jury trial provided by the Law of 1993 (Code of Criminal Procedure, RSFSR, 1993, Art. 446) was that the defendant's prior criminal record could not be examined in the jury's presence. The law did not contain any other prohibitions regarding examination of other aspects of the defendant's personality, which was also similar to the approach of the Imperial jury model. However, the Supreme Court of the Russian Federation went further in interpreting this provision by prohibiting any consideration of the defendant's character evidence. The Supreme Court explained that, "within the meaning of the law and taking into account the competence of jurors, they [jurors] should not [...] examine evidence characterizing the defendant's medical record, his or her marital status, medical opinion on the need of the defendant in compulsory treatment for alcoholism or drug addiction, etc." (Nemytina, 1995).

The Law of 1993 (Code of Criminal Procedure, RSFSR, 1993, Art. 459) borrowed provisions from the Code of 1864 that the not-guilty verdict of jurors is binding on judges, but the rule of Article 818 of the Code of Criminal Procedure (1864), discussed in previous sections, on the onetime nature of the court's possible disagreement with the jury's guilty verdict was rejected. Furthermore, under the Law of 1993, the jury's jurisdiction over sentencing was expanded compared to the Tsarist jury model. The Law of 1993 provided juries with the power to recognize when the defendant deserved special leniency (*osoboe sniskhozhdenie*). In such a case, the presiding judge would impose a punishment below the mandatory minimum prescribed by the law for the crime or the judge would sentence the defendant to another, more lenient, type of punishment (e.g., a fine instead of incarceration) (Code of Criminal Procedure, RSFSR, 1993, Art. 460). This jury model existed in Russia for almost two decades before it was replaced by the first post-Soviet Criminal

Procedure Code adopted in 2001 during the first presidential term (2000–2004) of Vladimir Putin.

Trial by Jury under Putin (2000–present)

When Vladimir Putin was elected as President in 2000, the jury system existed in only 9 out of 89 provinces of the Russian Federation. The law did not provide any timeline for implementation of the jury system across the country. In 2001, the Russian Federation adopted the new Code of Criminal Procedure, which contained a new chapter on jury trials. This chapter came into force in July 2002, but only in nine pilot regions of Russia. The Federal Law of 2001 (Federal'nyi Zakon, 2001) provided that jury trials would be introduced on January 1, 2003, in all regions of the Russian Federation. However, a few days before that date, the Russian Parliament passed a law amending the statute according to which jury trials would be introduced in the remaining 80 regions of the federation in several phases depending on the degree of their readiness (Federal'nyi Zakon, 2002). In accordance with this law, trial by jury became available in the course of the next year in 78 regions. Jury trials were introduced in 60 regions on January 1, 2003, in 13 additional regions, including Moscow, on July 1, 2003, and in 5 regions, including Saint Petersburg, on January 1, 2004.

The same law (Federal'nyi Zakon, 2002) provided that jury trials in Chechnya would start on January 1, 2007. This starting date assumed that in war-torn Chechnya, government bodies would be created and would then select candidates for jury service. The Russian Parliament postponed the introduction of jury trials in Chechnya in 2006 by another amendment. Finally, in April 2010, Chechnya held its first jury trial, which marked the completion of the introduction of jury trials in Russia. When Crimea became a part of the Russian Federation in 2014, new legislation introduced jury trials in this region in January 2018 (Federal'nyi Zakon, 2014). The first jury trial in Crimea was held in March 2018 and resulted in a guilty verdict ("Pervyi sud prisiazhnykh v Krymu," 2018).

Against the backdrop of this expansion of the jury system in late 2008, the federal government excluded juries from considering nine categories of political offenses. They included terrorist acts, hostage-taking, organization of armed formation, mass riots, high treason, espionage, forcible seizure of power, armed rebellion, and sabotage (Federal'nyi Zakon, 2008). One of the main justifications for the abolition of jury trials in cases of terrorism was the claim of the bill's authors that there had been too many acquittals for these types of crimes in North Caucasus due to tribalism, anti-government bias, and jury intimidation (Kovalev & Smirnov, 2014). These changes in the jurisdiction of juries were very similar to the reforms of 1878 in the aftermath of the case of Vera Zasulich, discussed earlier. It is another example of the depoliticization of jury trials in modern Russia in which the government removes certain political crimes from consideration by juries.

The Code of 2001 (Ugolovno-protsessual'nyi kodeks Rossiiskoi Federatsii [Code of Criminal Procedure, RF], 2001) introduced new rules prohibiting the jury's examination of the defendant's character evidence. In addition, the Supreme Court prohibited consideration of other types of evidence before juries (Kovalev, 2010). In contrast to the Code of 1864 and the Law of 1993, the Code of 2001 (Code of Criminal Procedure, RF, 2001) prohibits the examination of defendant's character evidence, both positive and negative, before the jury, except for evidence necessary to establish certain elements of the crime.

The Supreme Court of the Russian Federation has said that the prosecution can examine even the information about the previous convictions of the defendant if this evidence allows it to establish certain elements of a crime (Sudebnaia kollegiia po ugolovnym delam Verkhovnogo Suda, 2013; Kovalev, 2010). At the same time, the Supreme Court interpreted the law as prohibiting the examination of evidence of the character of victims and witnesses before juries, without creating an exception as it did for the defendant's character evidence. The main argument for this position of the Supreme Court is that jurors are not authorized to establish facts concerning character evidence of witnesses and victims by their verdict (Verkhovnyi Sud Rossiiskoi Federatsii [Supreme Court, RF], 2011). The Supreme Court of Russia seems to take a more pro-prosecution position by controlling the type of evidence juries may hear and by restricting the rights of the defense. This is a common trend for both modern and Tsarist governments.

Overall, in contrast to both the Imperial jury model and the 1993 jury model, trial by jury under the Code of 2001 became more adversarial, which enabled the jury to choose between two narratives presented by the parties. The laws also gave the parties the right to make opening statements (Code of Criminal Procedure, RF, 2001), adversary proceedings were put in place for examination of evidence (Code of Criminal Procedure, RF, 2001), rights of the parties were equalized to the maximum extent (Code of Criminal Procedure, RF, 2001), and the prosecutor's refusal to support the charge was binding for the court, regardless of the victim's position (Code of Criminal Procedure, RF, 2001).

The Code of 2001 deprived jurors of the power to recognize a defendant who is found guilty as deserving special leniency (leaving the jurors only the power to recognize a guilty defendant as deserving leniency). If the jury decides that the defendant deserves leniency, the judge cannot impose a sentence of more than two-thirds of the maximum punishment for the crime the defendant was convicted of. Moreover, the accused who deserves leniency cannot be sentenced to life imprisonment or death (Code of Criminal Procedure, RF, 2001, Art. 349). In the case of *special leniency*, the judge is bound to impose a punishment less severe than the statutory minimum (Code of Criminal Procedure, RSFSR, 1993, Art. 460). This returned juries to the scope of their sentencing powers under the Code of 1864. In doing so, it appears that the government wanted to reduce juries' power in sentencing.

In 2016, the Russian Parliament passed the federal law amending the legal framework regulating jury trials in several ways (Federal'nyi Zakon, 2016). The law was called Amendments to the Code of Criminal Procedure with Regard to Expansion on Application of Jury Trial. This name only partially reflects the changes introduced by the government. Although the law introduced juries to lower trial courts (thus expanding the reach of juries), it restricted jury trials in numerous other ways, including reducing the size of the jury, restricting parties' role in *voir dire*, and reducing the number of peremptory challenges.

Expansion of juries to lower courts. Since the resurrection of jury trials in the 1990s, the ongoing jury reform in Russia has been ambitious with respect to the expansion of the jury's jurisdiction. Starting on June 1, 2018, in addition to participating in the adjudication of cases in the superior courts of each federal region of Russia (republic, region, federal city, autonomous region, province, and military district), juries began hearing criminal cases in the lower trial or district (*raionnye*) courts and garrison military courts, which consist of a panel of six jurors (Code of Criminal Procedure, RF, 2001). Prior to June 2018, there were 85 civilian and 12 military district and navy courts that tried cases with juries (Sudebnyi Departament, 2018). After June 2018, the number of courts with juries increased to 2,370: 85 regional superior courts, 2,166 lower trial (*raionnye*) courts, 12 district military and naval courts, and 107 garrison military courts (Sudebnyi Departament, 2019a). This reform also will increase the number of people who serve on juries and the number of cases tried by juries. For example, in 2017, the total number of defendants tried by juries was 578; in 2018, the total number of defendants tried by juries was 718 and in 2019 the total number of defendants tried by juries was 1,120 (Sudebnyi Departament, 2019b). Similarly, the total number of acquittals increased from 53 in 2017 to 90 in 2018, an increase in the acquittal rate from 9.2% to 12.5% (Sudebnyi Departament, 2019b). In 2019 juries acquitted 242 defendants, which constituted 21.6% acquittal rate.

The most significant obstacles to the effective expansion of jury trials will likely be as a result of internal problems in the system. One such problem is insufficient compliance with the rules regulating jury trials. Specifically, trial courts commonly interpret rules of evidence and other procedural issues differently. The Supreme Court provides no clear guidelines to trial courts.

Reduction in jury size. The Law of June 23, 2016 reduced the size of the jury in regional superior courts from 12 to 8 jurors, and in district courts the number of jurors was set at 6. This reform contradicts practices in most foreign jurisdictions (Jackson & Kovalev, 2016; Vidmar, 2000b). Although the number of jurors varies in other countries, where the number of jurors is fewer than 12, a two-thirds majority is always required for a guilty verdict (Jackson & Kovalev, 2016; Vidmar, 2000b).

Limitations on parties' *voir dire*. Prior to the adoption of the Federal Law of 2016 (Federal'nyi Zakon, 2016), legislation ostensibly allowed parties to question jurors freely during *voir dire* to ensure their impartiality. However, this opportunity existed more in theory than in practice. Trial judges used to reject the vast majority of questions submitted by the defense (Nasonov, 2014). Judges developed standards for the admissibility of questions, and many issues were inadmissible, such as questions about the prospective jurors' past or questions about their families or friends.

The amendment introduced by the Law of 2016 no longer enables parties to ask questions that in their opinion would help parties to identify impartial jurors or that they simply believe to be useful, as was the intent of the original legislation in the 1990s (Pashin & Karnozova, 1996). The amended Article 328(8) of the Code of Criminal Procedure restricts the subject area of *voir dire* to circumstances that prevent a person from participating as a juror. However, the Code does not provide a list of such circumstances. Thus, parties cannot use their own subjective criteria for questioning prospective jurors, while the legislation does not provide any objective criteria. Instead, the scope of *voir dire* questions is left to the discretion of the trial judge.

Judicial control over jury composition. Prior to the amendments of 2016, each party had a right to at least two peremptory challenges, depending on the size of the panel after challenges for cause and self-recusals (Code of Criminal Procedure, RF, 2001, Art. 328). According to the Federal Law of 2016, the number of peremptory challenges for each party was reduced to one. Although the explanatory note to the draft law indicated that the number of peremptory challenges had been reduced because of the smaller jury size, it provoked extensive debate in the academic and legal literature (Iasel'skaia & Grishchenko, 2018). The main criticism of this reduction in the number of peremptory challenges is that it gives the presiding judge control over jury composition. Moreover, there are also reported cases when the government manipulated jury lists and inserted pro-government candidates into juries. The most egregious example has been the *Igor Sutyagin* case, when a former KGB officer was intentionally included in the jury pool and selected as a juror for the trial of the Russian scientist charged with high treason (Jackson & Kovalev, 2016; Kovalev, 2014). There have been similar examples in nonpolitical criminal cases. The most recent reported case has been the third trial of Vil' Gareev, in which all jurors were selected from the city of Sterlitamak in the province of Bashkortostan, while the procedure requires that candidates be selected from the population of the entire province (Nikitinskii, 2019). Furthermore, in the same case the foreperson of the jury and the court clerk were friends who frequently socialized on Vkontakte (Russian version of Facebook) (Nikitinskii, 2019).

CONCLUSION

The Russian jury system has recently celebrated the twenty-fifth anniversary since its restoration in the post-Soviet period and the 155th anniversary from the moment this mode of trial was planted on Russian legal soil. Just like the Russian social and legal history, the story of the Russian jury is complex and unstable. The experiment with the institution of the jury has been going in cycles. The liberal reforms of 1864 (Alexander II), 1917 (reforms of the Provisional Government), 1993 (reforms of Boris Yeltsin), and 2004 (expansion of jury trials to the rest of the country), all of which granted the Russian people the right to be tried by juries and have criminal cases adjudicated independently from the government, were replaced by conservative counterreforms of 1878 (abolition of juries in some crimes against state officials), 1889 (creation of mixed courts and transfer of jurisdiction in some political cases from juries to mixed courts), 1917 (abolition of juries under the Bolsheviks), and 2008 (abolition of juries in political cases). The recent reforms of 2018 are somewhat unusual in this cycle. They appear to be the result of a compromise between the liberal and conservative forces within Russian legal and political elites. The liberal forces, which include defense lawyers, liberal academics, the younger generation of Russian businesspersons, and civil society, demanded the expansion of juries. The conservative forces, including law enforcement, prosecutors, and neo-Soviet academics (academics who defend Soviet political and legal tradition), demanded transformation of juries into mixed courts (Kovalev & Smirnov, 2014).

In this chapter, we have analyzed legislative changes and practices over time, and we have identified common trends in early and modern government policies pertaining to the jury trial, including depoliticizing juries, reducing the influence of the defense on juries, and controlling the composition of juries. These unique features of the Russian jury system demonstrate that trial by jury has always functioned within tight boundaries set by the Russian government. As a result, jury trials have failed to develop into a powerful political institution in Russia. The developments of the Russian jury over time also show that the Russian government learned how to restrain trial by jury without abolishing it.

It is uncertain how the jury experiment will develop in the future. There are two possible scenarios. The negative scenario is that the jury develops into a mixed court, even if it retains the name *trial by jury*, as has happened in France, Italy, Denmark, and recently, Norway (Jackson & Kovalev, 2016; Chapter 10, this volume). The positive scenario is that the jury develops by expanding the rights of the parties and the jurisdiction of juries, and perhaps even by expanding the size of the jury. The positive scenario, however, will only be possible if the balance between liberal and conservative forces in Russia shifts in favor of the former and away from the latter.

REFERENCES

Afanas'ev, A. K. (1978). Sostav suda prisiazhnykh v Rossii [Composition of juries in Russia]. *Voprosy istorii*, 6, 199–203.

(2003). Sud prisiazhnykh v Rossii [Trial by jury in Russia]. *Otechestvennye zapiski*, 2. https://magazines.gorky.media/oz/2003/2/sud-prisyazhnyh-v-rossii.html

Bhat, G. N. (1997). The moralization of guilt in late imperial Russian trial by jury: The early reform era. *Law and History Review*, 15(1), 77–114.

Bobrishchev-Pushkin, A. M. (1896). *Empiricheskie zakony deiatel'nosti russkago suda prisiazhnykh* [Empirical laws of the Russian jury trial]. Moscow: Pechatnia A. I. Snegirevoi.

Browder, R. P., & Kerensky, A. F. (Eds.). (1961). *The Russian Provisional Government, 1917: Documents. In three volumes*. Stanford, CA: Stanford University Press.

Bukov, V. A. (1997). *Ot rossiiskogo suda prisiazhnykh k proletarskomu pravosudiiu: u istokov totalitarizma* [From the Russian jury trial to the proletariat justice: At the origins of totalitarianism]. Moscow: Arkheograficheskii tsentr.

Chebyshev-Dmitriev, A. P. (1875a). *Russkoe ugolovnoe sudoproizvodstvo po sudebnym ustavam 20 noiabria 1864* g [Russian criminal procedure on the Judicial Codes of November 20, 1864]. Saint Petersburg: Izdatel'stvo V. P. Pechatkina.

(1875b). *Sistematicheskii svod reshenii kassatsionnykh departamentov Senata 1866–1875 gg. s podlinnym tekstov reshenii, izvlechennymi iz nikh tezisami i kriticheskim razborom ikh: v 3-kh tomakh, Tom III: Resheniia ugolovnovnogo Kassatsionnogo Departamenta, raz'iasniaiushchie Ustav ugolovnogo sudoproizvodstva* [A systematic collection of decisions of the cassation departments of the Senate 1866–1875 with the original text of the decisions, abstracts extracted from them and critical analysis of them, Volume 3: Decisions of the Criminal Court of Cassation explaining the Code of Criminal Procedure]. Saint Petersburg.

Cheltsov-Bebutov, M. A. (1995). *Kurs ugolovno-protsessual'nogo prava: Ocherki po istorii suda i ugolovnogo protsessa v rabovladel'cheskikh, feodal'nykh i burzhuaznykh gosudarstvakh* [The course of the Criminal Procedural Law: Essays on history of court and criminal procedure in slaveholding, feudal and bourgeois states]. Saint Petersburg: Alfa.

Demichev, A. A. (2001). Periodizatsiia istorii suda prisiazhnykh v Rossii [Periodization of the history of the jury trial in Russia]. *Zhurnal rossiiskogo prava*, 7, 137–150.

(2003). Sravnitel'no pravovoe issledovanie suda prisiazhnykh v Rossii (Istoriia i sovremennost) [Comparative legal analysis of the jury trial in Russia (History and modern period)]. Unpublished Doctoral of Jurisprudence dissertation, Nizhegorodskaia Academy of the Ministry of the Interior (MVD), Russia.

Donovan, J. M. (2010). *Juries and the transformation of criminal justice in France*. Chapel Hill: University of North Carolina Press.

Dudko, N. A. (2013). *Poetapnoe vvedenie suda prisiazhnykh v Rossii* [Phased introduction of the jury trial in Russia]. Barnaul: Izdatel'stvo Altaiskogo gosudarstvennogo universiteta.

Dzhanshiev, G. A. (2004). *Osnovy sudebnoi reform* [Judicial reform framework]. Moscow: Statut.

Efremova, N. N. (2008). Reorganizatsiia rossiiskoi iustitsii v epokhu prosveshcheniia [Reorganization of the Russian justice in the enlightenment era]. *Zhurnal rossiiskogo prava*, 3, 135–148.

Esmein, A. (1913). *A history of continental criminal procedure: With special reference to France*. Translated by J. Simpson. Boston: Little, Brown and Company.

Federal'nyi Zakon Rossiiskoi Federatsii o vvedenii v deistvie ugolovno-protsessual'nogo kodeksa Rossiiskoi Federatsii [Federal Law of the Russian Federation on the introduction of the Code of Criminal Procedure of the Russian Federation], No. 177-FZ, December 18, 2001.

Federal'nyi Zakon Rossiiskoi Federatsii o vnesenii izmenenii v Federal'nyi zakon o vvedenii v deistvie ugolovno-protsessual'nogo kodeksa Rossiiskoi Federatsii [Federal Law of the Russian Federation on amendments to the Federal Law on introduction of the Code of Criminal Procedure of the Russian Federation], No. 181–FZ, December 27, 2002.

Federal'nyi Zakon Rossiiskoi Federatsii o vnesenii izmenenii v otdel'nye zakonodatel'nye akty Rossiiskoi Federatsii po voprosam protivodeistviia terrorizmu [Federal Law of the Russian Federation on amendments to certain legislative acts of the Russian Federation counteractions against terrorism], No. 321–FZ, December 30, 2008.

Federal'nyi Zakon Rossiiskoi Federatsii o primenenii polozhenii Ugolovnogo kodeksa Rossiiskoi Federatsii i Ugolovno-portsessual'nogo kodeksa Rossiiskoi Federatsii na territoriiakh Respubliki Krym i goroda federal'nogo znacheniia Sevastopolia [Federal Law of the Russian Federation on the application of provisions of the Criminal Code and Code of the Criminal Procedure on the territory of Crimea and the city of federal importance Sebastopol], No. 91-FZ, May 5, 2014.

Federal'nyi Zakon Rossiiskoi Federatsii o vnesenii izmenenii v Ugolovno-protsessual'nyi kodeks Rossiiskoi Federatsii v sviazi s rasshireniem primeneniia institute prisiazhnykh zasedatelei [Federal Law of the Russian Federation on amendments to the Code of Criminal Procedure with regard to expansion of the application of jury trial], No. 190-FZ, June 23, 2016.

Ferguson, A. G. (2014). The jury as constitutional identity. *University of California Davis Law Review*, 47, 1105–1171.

Foinitskii. I. Ya. (1996). *Kurs ugolovnogo sudoproizvodstva* [Criminal procedure course]. 2 vols. Saint Petersburg: Alfa.

Gessen, I. V. (1905). *Sudebnaia reforma* [Judicial reform]. Saint Petersburg: Tipografiia F. Vaisberga & P. Gershunina.

Golunskii, S. A. (Ed.). (1955). *Istoriia zakonodatel'stva SSSR i RSFSR po ugolovnomu protsessu i organizatsii suda i prokuratury, 1917–1954 gg: Sbornik dokumentov* [History of legislation of the USSR and RSFSR on criminal procedure and organization of courts and prosecutors office, 1917–1954: Compilation of documents]. Moscow: Gos. izd. iurid. lit-ry.

Iasel'skaia, V. V., & Grishchenko, A. V. (2018). Sostiazatel'naia deiatel'nost' zashchitnika na etape formirovaniia kollegii prisiazhnykh zasedatelei [Adversarial advocacy of the defense counsel at the jury selection stage]. *Ugolovnaia iustitsiia, 11*, 119–123.

Istraty, V. V. (2015). Sotsial'naia terminologiia v russkom perevode traktata W. Blackstona "Istolkovaniia aglinskikh zakonov" [Social terminology in the Russian translation of W. Blackstone's "Commentaries on the Laws of England"]. *Acta Linguistica Petropolitana: Trudy Instituta lingvisticheskikh issledovanii, 11*(3), 635–659.

Jackson, J., & Kovalev, N. (2016). Lay adjudication in Europe: The rise and fall of the traditional jury. *Oñati Socio-Legal Series*, 6, 368–395.

Karnozova, L. M. (2000). *Vozrozhdennyi sud prisiazhnykh: Zamysel i problemy stanovleniia* [Resurrected jury trial: Design and problems of becoming]. Moscow: Nota Bene.

(2001). *Sudebnaia reforma: Problem i perspektivy* [Judicial reform: Problems and prospects]. Moscow: Institut gosudarstva i prava, RAN.

Konstitutsiia (Osnovkoi Zakon) RSFSR [Constitution of the RSFSR] (1978/1992), with amendments as of December 10, 1992. https://constitution.garant.ru/history/ussr-rsfsr/1978/red_1978/183126/

Konstitutsiia Rossiiskoi Federatsii [Constitution of the Russian Federation] (1993), adopted December 12, 1993. www.constitution.ru/en/10003000–02.htm

Korotkikh, M. G. (1989). *Samoderzhavie i sudebnaia reforma 1864 g. v Rossii* [Autocracy and judicial reform of 1864 in Russia]. Voronezh: Izdatel'stvo voronezhskogo universiteta.

Kovalev, N. (2010). *Criminal justice reform in Russia, Ukraine, and the Former Republics of the Soviet Union*. Lewiston, NY: Edwin Mellen Press.

(2014). Selection of jurors and lay assessors in comparative perspective. *Russian Law Journal*, 2, 9–62.

Kovalev, N., & Smirnov, A. (2014). The nature of the Russian trial by jury: "Jury patriae" or "raison d'état." *European Journal of Crime, Criminal Law and Criminal Justice*, 22, 115–133.

Kozak, D. (2001, May 17). Sud prosiazhnykh budet vveden [Jury trials will be introduced]. *Nezavisimaia gazeta*, No. 86 (2396). www.ng.ru/politics/2001–05-17/3_news.html

Kozhevnikov, M. V. (1957). *Istoriia sovetskogo suda 1917–1956 gody* [History of the Soviet court 1917–1956]. Moscow: Gosiurizdat.

Kucherov, S. (1970). *The organs of Soviet administration of justice: Their history and operation*. Leiden: E. J. Brill.

Levada-Center. (2018, October 22). *Institutional trust* [Press release]. www.levada.ru/en/2018/10/22/institutional-trust-4

Lloyd-Bostock, S., & Thomas, C. (2000). The continuing decline of the English jury. In N. Vidmar (Ed.), *World jury systems* (pp. 53–91). Oxford: Oxford University Press.

MacKay, R. (2016). Jury nullification: The quality of mercy is not strained. *Criminal Law Quarterly*, 63, 80–101.

Mel'nik, V. V. (2003). *Iskusstvo zashchity v sude prisiazhnykh* [The art of defense in jury trials]. Moscow: Delo.

Nager, B. R. (1964). The jury that tried William Penn. *American Bar Association Journal*, 50 (2), 168–170.

Nasonov, S. A. (2014). Jury selection: Problems of legal regulation and judicial practice. *Current Problems of the Russian Law*, 12(49), 2841–2846.

(Ed.). (2016a). *Sud prisiazhnykh i advokatura v Rossii, Tom I: Vvedenie i razvitie suda prisiazhnykh* [Jury trial and the bar in Russia, Volume 1: Introduction and development of the jury trial]. Moscow: Federal'naia palata advokatov Rossiiskoi Federatsii.

(2016b). *Istoricheskie modeli proizvodstva v sude prisiazhnykh* [Historical models of trial by jury]. Moscow: Bibliotechka grazhdanskogo obshchestva.

Nemytina, M. V. (1995). *Rossiiski sud prisiazhnykh* [Russian jury trial]. Moscow: BEK.

Nikitinskii, L. (2019, June 26). V usloviiakh neochevidnosti: Kak vidimost' v sude prisiazhnykh izmeniaetsia v zavisimosti ot togo, predstavliaet li svoi argumenty zashchita ili obvinenie [How the appearance in jury trial varies depending on whether the defense or the prosecution presents its arguments]. Novaia gazeta, No. 68. www.novayagazeta.ru/articles/2019/06/26/81033-v-usloviyah-neochevidnosti

Pashin, S. A., & Karnozova, L. M. (Eds.). (1996). *Sostiazatel'noe pravosudie* [Adversarial justice]. Moscow: Mezhdunarodnyi komitet sodeistviia pravosudiia.

Pereira, N. G. O. (1983). *Tsar-Liberator: Alexander II of Russia, 1818–1881*. Newtonville, MA: Oriental Research Partners.

Pervyi sud prisiazhnykh v Krymu: Vinovny v razboe i ubiistve [First jury trial in Crimea: Guilty of robbery and murder]. (2018, March 23). *ForPost*. https://sevastopol.su/news/pervyy-sud-prisyazhnyh-v-krymu-vinovny-v-razboe-i-ubiystve

Popova, A. D. (2016). *Demokratiia, pravosudie, grazhdanskoe obshchestvo: Stanovlenie i vzaimodeistvie* [Democracy, justice and civil society: Formation and interaction]. Moskva: Prospekt.

Raeff, M. (1966). *The Decembrist movement*. Englewood Cliffs, NJ: Prentice-Hall.

Reed, J. T. (1996). Penn, Zenger and O.J.: Jury nullification – Justice of the wacko fringe's attempt to further its anti-government agenda. *Duquesne Law Review*, 34, 1125–1140.

Shcheglovitov, S. G. (1887). *Sudebnye Ustavy imperatora Alexandra Vtorogo s zakonodatel'nymi motivami i raz'iasneniiami: Ustav ugolovnogo sudoproizvodstva*. Saint Petersburg: Tipografiia Stasiulevicha.

Shramchenko, M. V., & Shirkov, V. P. (Eds.). (1913). Ustav ugolovnogo sudoproizvodstva s pozdneishimi uzakoneniiami, zakonodatel'nymi motivami, raz'iasneniiami Pravitel'stvuiushchego Senata i tsirkuliarami Ministra iustitsii [Code of criminal procedure with the latest legalization, legislative motives, clarifications of the Governing Senate and circulars of the minister of justice]. Saint Petersburg: Izdanie Iuridicheskogo Knizhnogo Magazina N.K. Martynova.

Sluchevskii, V. (1910). *Uchebnik russkago ugolovnogo protsessa* [Textbook on criminal procedure]. 3rd ed. Saint Petersburg: Tipografiia M. M. Stasiulevicha.

Stetsovskii, Iu. I. (1999). *Sudebnaia vlast* [Judicial power]. Moscow: Delo.

Sudebnaia kollegiia po ugolovnym delam Verkhovnogo Suda [Criminal Chamber of the Supreme Court of the Russian Federation]. (2013). Apelliatsionnoe opredelenie [Appellate decision], July 9, No. 32-APU13-7sp. *Consultant Plus*. www.consultant.ru /cons/cgi/online.cgi?req=doc&base=ARB&n=347447 - 0023860874661191245

Sudebnyi Departament pri Verkhovnom Sude Rossiiskoi Federatsii [Judicial Department at the Supreme Court of the Russian Federation]. (2018). *Otchet ob itogakh deiatel'nosti Departamenta pri Verkhovnom Sude Rossiiskoi Federatsii za 2017 god* [2017 annual report of the activities of the Judicial Department at the Supreme Court of the Russian Federation]. www.cdep.ru/userimages/OTChYoT_2017.pdf

(2019a). *Otchet ob itogakh deiatel'nosti Departamenta pri Verkhovnom Sude Rossiiskoi Federatsii za 2018 god* [2018 annual report of the activities of the Judicial Department at the Supreme Court of the Russian Federation]. www.cdep.ru/userimages/ OTChYoT_2018.pdf

(2019b). *Sudebnaia statistika* [Judicial statistics]. www.cdep.ru/index.php?id=5

Surin, A. V. (Ed.). (2008). *Klassiki teorii gosudarstvennogo upravleniia: Upravlencheskie idei v Rossii* [Classics of theory of public administration: Governance ideas in Russia]. Moskow: Rosspen.

Ternovskii, N. A. (1901). *Iuridicheskie osnovaniia k suzhdeniiu o sile dokazatel'stv i mysli iz rechei predsedatel'stvuiushchego po ugolovnym delam* [Legal reasons for judgment on strength of evidence and opinions from the jury instructions of the presiding judge in criminal cases]. Tula: Tipografia V. N. Sokolova.

Thaman, S. C. (1995). The resurrection of trial by jury in Russia. *Stanford Journal of International Law*, *31*, 61–274.

Ugolovno-protsessual'nyi kodeks RSFSR v redaktsii zakona ot 1993 [Code of Criminal Procedure of the RSFSR] (1993).

Ugolovno-protsessual'nyi kodeks Rossiiskoi Federatsii [Code of Criminal Procedure of the Russian Federation] (2001).

Ustav ugolovnogo sudoproizvodstva [Code of Criminal Procedure of the Russian Empire] (1864), adopted November 20, 1864.

Varfolomeev, Yu. V. (2011). Advokaty vo vlasti: prisiazhnye poverennye – sotrudniki Chrezvychainoi sledstvennoi komissii Vremennogo pravitel'stva [Lawyers in the state power: Attorneys – employees of the Extraordinary Investigation Commission of Provisional Government]. *Advokat*, *6*, 60–70.

Vasil'ev, A., & Baranosvkii, A. (2017). *Sud prisiazhnykh: poslednii shans femidy* [Trial by jury: The last Themis' chance]. Moscow: Izdate'skie Reshenia.

Vasil'eva, E. V. (2013). *Programmy politicheskikh partii Rossii kontsa XIX-nachala XX vv* [Programs of political parties of Russia at the end of the nineteenth and beginning of the twentieth centuries]. Omsk: SibADI.

Verkhovnyi Sud Rossiiskoi Federatsii [Supreme Court of the Russian Federation], Postanovlenie Plenum: O nekotorykh voprosakh primeneniia sudami ugolovno-portsessual'nykh norm, reglamentiruiushchikh proizvodstvo v sude prisiazhnykh [Decision of the Plenum of the Supreme Court of the Russian Federation on issues of rules regulating jury trials], No. 9, December 20, 1994. www.consultant.ru/document/cons_doc_LAW_5676/

Kassatsionnoe opredelenie Verkhovnogo suda Rossiiskoi Federatsii [Cassational decision of the Supreme Court of the Russian Federation], No. 25-011-4SP, March 23, 2011. www.consultant.ru/cons/cgi/online.cgi?req=doc&base=ARB&n=189022 - 05617412749405002

Vidmar, N. (Ed.). (2000a). *World jury systems*. Oxford: Oxford University Press.

(2000b). The jury elsewhere in the world. In N. Vidmar (Ed.), *World jury systems* (pp. 421–447). Oxford: Oxford University Press.

Vilkova, T. Iu., & Nasonov, S. A. (2017). *Printsip uchastiia grazhdan v osushchestvlenii pravosudiia v ugolovnom sudoproizvodstve* [The principle of lay participation in criminal justice]. Moscow: Iurait.

Zakon ot 16 iulia 1993 g. No. 5451-I "O vnesenii izmenenii i dopolnenii v Zakon RSFSR 'O sudoustroistve RSFSR', Ugolovno-protsessual'nyi kodeks RSFSR, Ugolovnyi kodeks RSFSR i Kodeks ob administrativnykh pravonarusheniiakh" [Law of July 16, 1993 No. 5451-I "On amendments to the Law of the RSFSR" on the Judicial System of the RSFSR, Code of Criminal Procedure of the RSFSR, Criminal Code of the RSFSR and Code of Administrative Offences].

13

Trial by Jury in Georgia

A Catalyst for Evolving Independent Courts

Nikolai Kovalev and Giorgi Meladze

"Introduction of jury system – this promise has also been delivered. I am very proud that the first jury trial will be held this year in Georgia."

Ex-President Mikheil Saakashvili (2010)

"We have witnessed a complete failure of this institution [jury]. And we are obliged to overview it and fill in the gaps"

Prime Minister Irakli Garibashvili (2015)

Trial by jury in Georgia was part of a profound transformation in the criminal procedure and criminal justice system initiated and carried out by the government of former President Mikheil Saakashvili (Roudik, 2011). Introduction of the jury clause (Art. 82(5)) in the Constitution of Georgia (1995) in 2004 was one of the first constitutional reforms initiated by the government following the 2003 Rose Revolution, one of the "color" or "flower" movements that developed in post-Soviet societies in the early 2000s (Beachain & Polese, 2010; Kovalev, 2010). The revised Constitution, which went into effect in 2018 (Art. 59(3)), repeated the original clause stating that: "The cases shall be considered by juries before the courts of general jurisdiction in accordance with a procedure and in cases prescribed by law" (Sakartvelos k'onst'it'utsia [Constitution], 1995, Art. 59(3)). The Constitution contributed to the sense of self-determination among policy-makers; jury trials officially became part of the legal system and future reform agenda. In 2005, the Working Group established by Presidential Decree No. 914 (*Sakartvelos p'rezidentis gank'arguleba* No. 914) published a new strategy paper identifying the main directions for the reform and including reference to jury trials. However, the actual introduction of trial by jury had to wait nearly seven years before it was finally implemented by the Criminal Procedure Code (2009).

The reform of criminal procedure and introduction of juries were supported by civil society in Georgia. In the early 2000s, the Liberty Institute, one of the most vocal civil society non-governmental organizations (NGOs), together with political groups and international donors, lobbied for jury trials (Transparency International Georgia, 2010). In 2003, a proposal to introduce the jury system became part of "Ten Steps toward Democracy" – the declaration of the Rose Revolution, signed by opposition parties and presented to the public as a future reform agenda. Supporters of trial by jury viewed it as an effective way to improve public confidence in the criminal justice system and to increase citizens' participation in the administration of justice (Lomsadze, 2010). Leaders of the political party United National Movement (UNM) emphasized this objective during public debates and promoted the reform as an attempt to build bridges between the Georgian society and judiciary. Years of a totalitarian regime had left deep scars of distrust toward state agencies, where voices of ordinary citizens were effectively ignored by ruling elites and the communist party apparatus. The tradition of "telephone justice," the illegal practice in which officials from the executive branch contact a judge or chairman of the court in order to influence the outcome of a case (Solomon & Foglesong, 2000, p. 30), continued after independence was proclaimed in 1991 and throughout the 1990s. Therefore, the supporters of the reform advocated radical change in criminal justice legislation. The reformers expected that trial by jury could be a key radical change that would contribute to building trust (Transparency International Georgia, 2010).

The legislature adopted the new Criminal Procedure Code of Georgia (CPC) in 2009, which took effect in 2010. It introduced trial by jury, among other elements of the adversarial trial, in Tbilisi City Court, with plans for later expansion. At present, according to the Criminal Procedure Code of Georgia (Sakartvelos siskhlis samartlis sap'rotseso k'odeksi [CPC], 2009, Art. 21^1), jury trials exist in seven courts throughout Georgia. The first jury trial took place in Tbilisi City Court in November 2011 and received very broad news coverage (K'onstitutsiuri k'vlevebis tsentri, 2018).

As a new democracy and a relatively new member of the Council of Europe, Georgia positioned itself as a European nation striving to become a member of the European Union and NATO. The engagement and approval of foreign experts from the European Union and the United States were extremely important for Georgian reformers. However, experts varied in their opinions and advice regarding the jury reform: some experts supported the idea of juries while others opposed the reform (Lomsadze, 2010). As in other post-Soviet countries (Kovalev, 2010), most international experts critical of the jury system come from civil-law jurisdictions and supporters of the jury system are experts from the common-law tradition. Vogler (2009), who was more optimistic about trial by jury than some of his European colleagues, suggests that lack of experience with jury systems may explain the resistance from critical foreign experts. Criticism from this camp of foreign experts and advisors focused on two arguments: (1) the corrupt system would make jury trials ineffective; and (2) Georgia was too small to enable it to select impartial jurors. Thus, policy-makers in Georgia had to debate not only with jury skeptics within the country (mostly legal practitioners educated in the Soviet inquisitorial system), but also with jury skeptics from continental Europe.

While some Georgian law reforms, including police reform (Light, 2014), a crackdown on organized crime (Slade, 2013), and prison reform (Piacentini & Slade, 2015), have been well studied by Western researchers, trial by jury remained until recently a largely neglected research subject. There are just a few publications in English, which briefly mention the introduction of juries in Georgia (Jackson & Kovalev, 2016; Lomsadze, 2010; Thaman, 2011; Vogler, 2006). Only one article in Russian is dedicated to Georgian jury trials (Nasonov, 2015) and just a handful of reports and academic works exist in Georgian (Dolidze, 2015; Lekveishvili, 2013; Sakartvelos uzenaesi sasamartlo [Supreme Court of Georgia], 2012). The present chapter is the first attempt to examine more closely the seven years of the Georgian jury system.

THE HISTORY OF LAY PARTICIPATION IN GEORGIA

In the early feudal period, Georgia experienced various forms of lay participation in the justice system. Early texts dating back to the fifteenth century (King George V, 1913) describe legal proceedings in mountainous regions and the "council of elders" as a necessary institution for conducting just proceedings. The Procedural Code of Vakhtang VI (1716–1724) required as an option the participation of compurgators or co-swearers named by the accuser and the defendant (Davitashvili, 2003; Sofronenko, 1967). Compurgation is "a trial in which a defendant could have supporters (called *compurgators*), frequently 11 in number, testify that they thought the defendant was telling the truth" (Black's Law Dictionary, 2009, p. 327). The compurgators had the same social or political status as the accused and their number was determined by the significance of the particular case. Until recently, some forms of lay participation in dispute resolution, such as the "council of elders," were still in place in some communities (Javakhishvili, 1982).

In the early nineteenth century, the Georgian state was occupied by the Russian Empire, and so the laws of the empire applied. In 1801, the Russian Emperor Alexander I issued a decree that introduced an *uezd* (district) court in each of the five Georgian districts (Kavkazskaia Arkheograficheskaia Komissiia, 1866). These courts consisted of a Russian judge and two assessors (*msadzhuli*) selected from the Georgian nobles. In addition, when the defendant was a prince or a noble, a part of the Georgian government, a so-called *criminal expedition* (tribunal), conducted the trial. The tribunal consisted of a Russian chief judge and four native Georgian advisors (*mdivan-begi*) (Kavkazskaia Arkheograficheskaia Komissiia, 1866).

In the 1860s, judicial reform was introduced across the Russian Empire. The fundamental aspects of the reform included separation of the judicial branch from the executive branch, as well as the introduction of oral proceedings, the office of justices of the peace, the professional bar, and trial by jury. However, over the next

40 years, and, by the time of the Bolshevik Revolution of 1917, implementation of the jury system across the provinces of the Russian Empire had not been completed. The jury system had not been introduced in many territories of the empire: the Caucasus provinces such as Georgia and Armenia, the Polish Kingdom, Baltic provinces (except Vil'no), and Central Asia (except Akmolinsk, Semipalatinsk, and Ural'sk) (Kovalev, 2010). Some Soviet historians viewed the reluctance to implement trial by jury as a reflection of the distrust of the local Georgian community by the Russian government, as well as possible conflicts between the "law of people" with the laws of the empire (Kakabadze, 1997; Kikvadze, 1959). However, some pre-Soviet authors argued that it was due to the Russian government's fear that the jury system would encourage national self-recognition and independence movements in the border regions of the empire (Gruzenberg, 1917).

After the Bolshevik Revolution in 1917, the regime change in Russia caused the imperial institutions to crumble. Previously occupied states became independent; Georgia declared its independence on May 26, 1918 (Jones, 2005). Georgia's political elite gravitated toward Europe. The brief period of Georgian independence between 1918 and 1921, called the period of the First Georgian Republic, brought a remarkable set of legal reforms; a very progressive constitution was adopted, and the jury system was introduced by the Law of January 17, 1919 (Supreme Court of Georgia, 2020). A few sources in the national archives describe several jury trials. The first trial was held on March 8, 1919, and the jury was selected from a pool of 2,200 citizens (Sakhalkho Sakme, 1920). Short publications in the newspapers *Sakhalkho Sakme* and *Sakartvelo* from that time describe the concerns of lawyers; they worried primarily about lengthy procedures for the selection of jurors. The jury clause was included in the Constitution of 1921. Article 81 stated: "Grave crimes as well as crimes of political nature or relating to publishing work will be decided by jury trials" (Constitution, 1921; Papuashvili, 2012).

After a short period of independence, Georgia was occupied by the Soviet Union in 1921 (Jones, 1988). After the Bolshevik occupation, jury trials were abolished and resurrected only 90 years later after Georgia regained independence in 1991 and started a fundamental reform of the justice system (Lomsadze, 2010; Transparency International Georgia, 2010).

JURY REFORM IN GEORGIA: FIRST STEPS

In the early 1990s and during the first years of independence, Georgia was engulfed in conflict, violence, and a civil war as well as two wars with separatist regions (Wheatley, 2017). The weak political system left most of the state institutions neglected. This in turn provoked endemic corruption benefiting only small political elites, organized crime, and law enforcement institutions (World Bank, 1998). Georgia carried on with the legacy of Soviet judicial culture; the system of "telephone justice" (Solomon & Foglesong, 2000) remained strong during the first decade of independence.

The new constitution adopted in 1995 fuelled legislative activism; hundreds of new laws were adopted by Parliament in a very short time. In 1997, the Law on Judiciary was among the new initiatives (World Bank, 1998). With this new law, the government made the first attempt to reform the judiciary. However, the more comprehensive approach to reform the entire criminal justice system was abandoned and only the judiciary remained the "sandbox" for the reform (Meladze, 2007). The complex challenges within the judiciary included widespread corruption, complicated and lengthy trials, and the lack of enforcement of judicial decisions by executive authorities (American Bar Association/Central European and Eurasian Law Initiative, 2005).

This first attempt to reform the judiciary met resistance from criminal justice bodies. Even though new judges were appointed, the system in general did not respond positively (Supreme Court of Georgia, 2014). The judiciary was underfunded (Gupta, Kleinfeld, & Salinas, 2002) and isolated from the rest of the criminal justice system. The need for more comprehensive and thorough reform was obvious (Popjanevski, 2015; Transparency International, 2007).

Until 1998, Georgia retained the old Soviet Code of Criminal Procedure, which had been amended numerous times since 1961. In December 1998, the Georgian Parliament adopted a new Code of Criminal Procedure (CPC, 1998). Within the first three years of the new Code, hundreds of amendments were added. The Code was criticized by local NGOs as well as international organizations (Vogler, 2009). It violated the principle of equality of arms between the defense and the prosecution (i.e., did not provide equal access to the case file, disclosure of material to both sides, equal opportunity to do preliminary questioning of witnesses, ability to jointly attend investigative acts) (Cape, Namoradze, Smith, & Spronken, 2010). Because the Code had failed to provide a true adversarial proceeding, President Shevardnadze made a political decision to draft a new and fundamentally different law.

The Rose Revolution placed Georgia among other countries aspiring to accelerate reforms in many areas. For several years, between 2005 and 2007, Georgia was actively advancing freedom of entrepreneurship, combating corruption, and adopting advanced human rights legislation (World Bank, 2007). The introduction of jury trials in Georgia should be considered in the context of this wider reform agenda.

A group of reformers organized initially as Citizens' Union Georgia (CUG) formed a separate party – the United National Movement (UNM) – and took government office after the Rose Revolution. Led by President Mikheil Saakashvili, they continued to promote the idea of an adversarial trial to replace the Soviet inquisitorial model of criminal procedure. With Presidential Decree No. 914 (Sakartvelos p'rezidentis gank'arguleba No. 914, 2004) President Saakashvili created a temporary interagency commission to develop recommendations for further reform. The introduction of jury trials was seen by the UNM as a means to counter the wide distrust of the judiciary and to promote the principle of adversarial procedure. The group was active and reached out to the international community in an attempt to mobilize international support (Vogler, 2009). International donors such as the US Department of Justice Rule of Law program (USDOJ – ROL), Council of Europe, British Council, German Technical Cooperation Agency (GTZ), and Open Society Georgia Foundation (OSGF) supported several criminal justice reform initiatives (Kovalev, 2010). Funded activities included support of the joint working group on reform of the criminal justice system, international expertise, and conferences and working sessions with European and US experts. In addition, several internationally-recognized experts on criminal justice were invited to assess the draft code at various stages of its development (e.g., Herrmann, 2002; Leigh, 2002).

Before 2003, the legal reform did not place an emphasis on jury trials; the first draft of the Criminal Procedure Code presented to the public in 2002 referred to the Soviet institution of "lay assessors." This model was carried over from the Soviet system and was received with skepticism by Georgian civil society (Transparency International Georgia, 2010).

After several years, Georgia produced a new Criminal Procedure Code, which was adopted in 2009. The Code strengthened the principle of adversarial proceedings and introduced jury trials. However, Article 330 contained a clause postponing the implementation of the jury system until 2011 and providing that jury trials would initially be available only for murder cases, with the expectation that they would be used more widely at later stages of the reform. There were several reasons for this gradual approach. First, the number of murders with aggravating circumstances was relatively low in Georgia, so the expectation was that the new mode of trial would be used only occasionally for the small number of cases. Second, the prosecutor's office wanted to avoid the speedy implementation of juries in order to maintain control over proceedings. Third, most legal professionals assumed that Georgian society would need several years to become accustomed to jury trials (Korff, 2005).

THE GEORGIAN JURY MODEL

Right to a Jury Trial

The 2009 Georgian Criminal Procedure Code introduced the classical Anglo-American model of trial by jury. However, the Constitutional provision does not guarantee the accused the right to be tried by a jury in all criminal cases, or in any subset of cases, leaving it up to the government to identify which cases will result in jury trials. Therefore, the Constitution left open the possibility that the Georgian government could limit jury trials to a small fraction of cases, such as aggravated murder (CPC, 2009, Art. 109). The Constitution of Georgia simply declares that the jury is an alternative to a professional court, without stating clearly the role it should play in the Georgian criminal justice system. The CPC also fails to indicate when a jury trial is required or available.

The criminal procedure legislation initially stipulated that an accused was entitled to a jury trial in all cases where charges could result in a prison sentence (CPC, 2009, Art. 226(1) prior to 2016). This provision was never implemented and jury trials in the first few years were limited to cases involving murder. This limited jurisdiction of jury trials was intended to be a temporary measure. In 2016, however, amendments were introduced into the CPC that limited the jurisdiction of the jury to cases involving only fewer than two dozen specific Criminal Code offenses: murder, violent crimes, human-trafficking offenses, unlawful imprisonment, torture, malicious criminal prosecution of innocent persons, falsification, and explosion (Sakartvelos siskhlis samartlis k'odeksi [Criminal Code of Georgia], 1999; CPC, 2009, Art. 226(1)). These changes limiting the jurisdiction of juries seemed to be arbitrary and not based on a clear rationale.

An accused can waive his or her right to a jury trial and be tried by a district judge alone. The Georgian procedure allows for trials in absentia (CPC, 2009, Art. 22) and, if the accused fails to appear in court, the case will be tried without a jury.

Georgian juries are composed of 12 jurors and 2 alternates (CPC, 2009, Art. 27). However, the law permits smaller juries of at least 6 for less serious offenses (i.e., crimes punishable by a maximum of 5 years of imprisonment), of at least 8 jurors for serious offenses (i.e., crimes punishable by a maximum of 5 years of imprisonment), and of at least 10 for particularly serious offenses (i.e., crimes punishable by more than 10 years of imprisonment) (CPC, 2009, Art. 27(2)). When the jury system was originally initiated, it was limited to Tbilisi (the capital city) only. After two years, the reform was extended to the second major city, Kutaisi, and since 2017 it has been expanded to five more cities: Batumi, Zugdidi, Gori, Rustavi, and Telavi.

Jury Selection

In order to be eligible for jury service in Georgia, a person must be at least 18 years of age, a citizen of Georgia, and appear on the eligible voters' list (CPC, 2009, Art. 221). Georgian law, in addition, disqualifies persons from jury service if they are public officials, prosecutors, investigators, police officers, defense lawyers, members of the armed forces, the clergy, parties in the case in question, the accused, persons found responsible for an administrative (regulatory) offense, or persons with a previous criminal record (CPC, 2009, Art. 30). The Georgian CPC contains a provision prohibiting discrimination of juror candidates on many grounds (e.g., race, gender, financial status). However, a presiding judge does not have the power to (1) explore whether one of the parties used a peremptory challenge on the basis of one of the prohibited discriminatory grounds or (2) refuse to allow such a challenge even if the judge concludes that discrimination has taken place. In practice, because of their lack of familiarity with the official language, most citizens from several municipalities of Kvemo Kartli and Samtskhe-Javakheti are excluded from jury service.

The selection of prospective jurors starts with a list of 300 people randomly selected from the voters' list of either Eastern or Western Georgia, depending on the location of the court conducting the trial. After consultations with the parties, the judge approves the juror questionnaire, which is designed to collect information about candidates and will be used by the parties during *voir dire* (CPC, 2009, Art. 221(1)). The list of candidates is confidential, and parties are required not to disclose it.

The legislature granted trial judges the power to decide how to select candidates for jury service directly from the general lists of citizens. Although Article 221 states that the judge compiles a list of prospective candidates on the basis of random selection and after having consulted the parties, it is not clear whether this procedure is conducted in the presence of the parties.

Voir dire is conducted in open court unless there are grounds to close the courtroom to the public. A judge might close the courtroom if it is necessary to maintain order or to protect private matters of the parties. The judge has discretion to decide when to close the courtroom to the public. Parties must disclose to the judge the questions they want to ask jurors. They also have the right to request an unlimited number of challenges for cause, and the judge decides which ones to grant or deny. Parties also exercise a limited number of peremptory challenges. If the charge can carry a sentence of life imprisonment, parties have 10 peremptory challenges (CPC, 2009, Art. 223(10)); in all other cases, parties have 6 peremptory challenges (CPC, 2009, Art. 223(10)). If the jury is not selected during the first session, the judge summons candidates from the second half of the jury list. If a sufficient number of candidates is not selected from this pool, 100 more candidates are summoned. The time between the compilation of the list and the final selection day may not exceed 45 days (CPC, 2009, Art. 223).

The authors of this chapter observed prolonged selection proceedings, some of which lasted several months. The delays can be explained by the careful approach of judges to jury selection, the inexperience of judges, as well as the lack of public awareness and poor knowledge of the state language among minority populations. The most common problems that arise during *voir dire* and that delay the trial are refusals and self-recusals. A candidate may refuse to participate if he or she has already acted as a juror during the past year, if there are health reasons, if the candidate is over 70, if he or she resides in a foreign country, or if absence from work may cause substantial financial hardship (CPC, 2009, Art. 31). Candidates frequently use their work and inability to perform jury duties as the reason for excuses. Self-recusals present an even bigger problem as they are used by almost 80% of candidates. Examples of reasons for self-recusals provided by candidates in Georgian jury courts include inability to understand the law, inability to make a serious decision, and lack of interest in participating. Initially, candidates were frequently willing to offer such excuses and judges readily accepted them. However, the CPC amendments of 2016 now require prospective jurors to justify their claims and judges to substantiate their decisions (CPC, 2009, Art. 223).

Jury Instructions

The judge instructs the jury at the beginning of the trial and before the jury retires to the deliberation room (CPC, 2009, Art. 231). Brief instructions are also provided regarding the rules for evaluating evidence during the trial. Instructions defining legal principles and concepts cover various topics, including the presumption of innocence, elements of the alleged crime, and rights and duties of jurors.

Upon motion of a party, the presiding judge explains to the jury that the defendant may have committed a less grave crime consisting of certain elements of the crime the defendant is charged with. In this case, the jury is given an additional verdict form and the presiding judge instructs the jury on the difference between the charged crime and the second crime, the lesser included offense.

Jury Verdict Rule

Georgia's jury system allows qualified or special majority verdicts. The jury tries to reach a unanimous verdict first. If within four hours the jurors are unable to reach a unanimous verdict of guilty or not guilty with respect to each filed charge, they shall hold a vote and reach a decision through a majority of at least 8 votes within the next eight hours (CPC, 2009, Art. 261(4)). In the case of an equally divided final vote or if only 7 jurors vote for either conviction or acquittal, the judge dismisses the jury and sets a date for a new jury trial (CPC, 2009, Art. 261(6)). To date, there has been one high-profile trial that resulted in a hung jury, which provoked debate and legislative proposals to reform the jury system.

FURTHER JURY REFORMS IN GEORGIA

In June 2015, the jury in Tbilisi City Court failed to reach a verdict in the case of Giorgi Okropiridze, who was charged with the murder of Lasha Makharadze. The case attracted a great deal of attention as the investigation failed to produce consistent evidence during the pretrial coverage of the case in the media. Many different scenarios were discussed by state representatives in media interviews, and potential eyewitnesses refused to provide testimony (Netgazeti, 2017). This was the first case of a hung jury, provoking claims, including a statement from the Georgian prime minister, that the jury is not an effective institution (Gharibashvili, 2015). The prime minister of Georgia delivered a critical statement calling the outcome of the trial "a complete failure" and promising that the government would review the jury system and "fill the gaps" (Mchedlishvili, 2015). Almost immediately after this verdict, the

Ministry of Justice sponsored a bill proposing amendments aimed at making significant changes in qualifications, selection rules, verdict rules, and the scope of jury trials. The bill was criticized by both local and international experts, including the authors of this chapter (Kovalev, 2015).

Scope of Jurisdiction of Juries

The draft law proposed a significant reduction in the jurisdiction of juries (Kovalev, 2015). Presumably, the intent of the proposal was to reduce the financial burden on court budgets by limiting the use of juries to serious and very serious violent crimes, such as premeditated murder, intentional damage to health with aggravating circumstances, aggravated torture, sale of human organs, and racial discrimination. It appeared, however, that the proposal of the Georgian Ministry of Justice to limit the jurisdiction of juries was arbitrary and not based on clear criteria. While some 24 serious crimes were included in the jurisdiction of juries, more than 140 other serious offenses defined by the Criminal Code of Georgia as "grave crimes" punishable by seven or more years of imprisonment were not included. Many of the offenses excluded from the jurisdiction of juries were punishable by more than 10 years of imprisonment, for example, rape and sexual assault with violence, hostage taking, human trafficking, and torture. Some of these offenses were punishable by life imprisonment (e.g., drug trafficking committed by an organized group and terrorism offenses).

Assuming that a jury trial provides a benefit to a defendant, the government's proposal would have put many defendants charged with serious offenses punishable by periods of long incarceration in a disadvantaged position compared with those defendants charged with offenses with less severe penalties. If passed, the law would potentially violate the equality provision of the Georgian Constitution (Art. 14) as well as Article 14 of the UN International Covenant on Civil and Political Rights. A number of Georgian research centers released a joint statement expressing concerns regarding limitations of jury trial to only a few crimes (K'onstitutsiuri k'vlevebis tsent'ri, martlmsajulebis ganvitarebisa da samartlebrivi sts'avlebis cent'ri da adamianis uplebebis erovnuli inst'it'ut'i [Center for Constitutional Research et al., 2015]).

Professional Exclusions from Jury Service

The draft bill also would have made individuals with particular occupations, who were previously disqualified from serving as jurors, eligible for jury service (Kovalev, 2015). In particular, the bill proposed that police officers, investigators, lawyers, psychologists, and psychiatrists should be permitted to serve as jurors. In support of its proposal, the Ministry of Justice referred to the practice of Belgium and France, where these categories of professionals are not automatically disqualified (Kovalev,

2015). However, many other countries disqualify from jury service professionals associated with criminal justice, including lawyers and police officers. Many European jurisdictions, such as Austria, Denmark, Greece, Ireland, Italy, Poland, Portugal, Norway, Spain, and Sweden, exclude such professionals (Jackson & Kovalev, 2016). Many other countries also disqualify them from jury service, including Australia and Canada (Tanovich, Paciocco, & Skurka, 1997). It should be noted, however, that many US jurisdictions have removed these exclusions in recent years (Diamond, Rose, & Murphy, 2014).

Permitting professionals associated with the administration of criminal justice to serve as jurors may have adverse effects on juries in Georgia. It is difficult to agree with the argument of the authors of the draft law that there is a low risk of bias in cases where police officers or investigators serve as jurors (Kovalev, 2015). Since some Georgian investigators, police officers, and secret service agents have a strong bias against defendants, the participation of professionals involved in the administration of criminal justice may damage the impartiality of the jury. Moreover, jurors who are law enforcement agents may be influenced by their superiors or colleagues.

Some Georgian judges share the concern that police officers and investigators may exert undue influence as jurors. During the authors' meeting with Georgia's Supreme Court judges, we discussed whether police officers and lawyers should be excluded from jury service. Several of the judges noted that, since the general respect for the rule of law among the public in Georgia is weaker than in the United States, the presence of a lawyer or police officer in the deliberation room may intimidate and improperly influence jurors who are less qualified in law (Kovalev & Meladze, 2015). The amendment was nevertheless introduced in the final draft and adopted by Parliament.

Ensuring the Privacy, Safety, and Impartiality of Jurors

The current provision of the Criminal Procedure Code (CPC, 2009, Art. 222) permits the general public to attend and observe the *voir dire* procedure in open court. The bill of 2015 proposed an amendment that would have closed the selection process to the public. Advocates of the change argued that these measures were necessary to protect a juror's identity (Sakartvelos akhalgazrda iurist'ta asotsiatsia, 2016). Yet, this proposal would arguably violate the principle of open justice or publicity of court proceedings guaranteed by the Georgian Constitution (Art. 85(1)); CPC (2009, Art. 10(1)) and international treaties ratified by Georgia (Art. 14(1) of the International Covenant on Civil and Political Rights; Art. 6(1) of the European Convention of Human Rights and Fundamental Freedoms). Excluding the public from the *voir dire* proceeding would undermine public confidence in the jury selection process.

During the round table organized by the OSGF with Georgian and international criminal justice experts and legal professionals, including both authors and representatives of the UN Office on Drugs and Crime and the US Embassy in Georgia, the participants debated this proposed amendment (Pondi ghia sazogadoeba sakartvelo [OSGF], 2015). Some representatives of human rights organizations argued that closed hearings contradict "the essence of jury trials as the openness of such trials provides confidence towards the court and criminal justice." In opposition, some trial judges who presided over jury trials argued for closed hearings during *voir dire* proceedings. During the roundtable on jury trials, one of the Tbilisi court judges asserted that closed *voir dire* hearings are necessary to protect jurors' privacy rights (OSGF, 2015). According to the judge, jurors may be embarrassed to discuss their medical conditions and other delicate issues in public.

This concern is legitimate, but the privacy rights of prospective jurors can be protected without closing the *voir dire* hearing. In cases involving a sensitive issue, such as a medical condition, the discussion between the judge and the lawyers can be conducted in front of the judge's bench or at the sidebar, where the public or other prospective candidates cannot hear the conversation. The authors observed that sidebar conferences are already in use during *voir dire* hearings in Tbilisi City Court. This measure is sufficiently effective to protect the personal health information of prospective jurors.

At the experts' roundtable, another argument raised in favor of closed hearings was the personal safety of prospective jurors. Some Georgian officials expressed concerns about the safety of jurors and their protection from pressure. In particular, the representative from the Office of Public Defender (Ombudsman) of Georgia, raised the following issue: "Georgian law does not provide flexible and proper mechanisms for protection of jurors during the trial from any kind of influence by any person, including law enforcement officials" (OSGF, 2015). This position is worth considering. Instead of denying the defendant's right to a jury trial, the Georgian legislature may consider developing a mechanism for protecting jurors during the trial. The safety of jurors during the trial should be ensured by court personnel such as the court-marshal service, which is independent of the police and prosecution. However, a closed hearing cannot eliminate the risk of jury intimidation or tampering with the jury. According to one of the participants at the roundtable, Michael Grant, the resident legal advisor at the US Embassy in Georgia, closing the hearing would not protect the jurors (OSGF, 2015). In his opinion, a more effective safeguard against jury tampering would be prosecution of individuals who attempt to influence jurors. Moreover, parties who want to influence jurors during the trial can provide their relatives or accomplices who are not in custody with jurors' personal information that they learn from the closed *voir dire* hearing.

Form of the Jury Verdict

The Georgian legislature in 2009 adopted the general verdict rule, permitting jurors to answer the simple question of whether the defendant is guilty or not guilty of each count of the charges. The bill of 2015 proposed to replace this rule with a special verdict rule, under which jurors must answer four separate questions in the case of a not guilty verdict and five questions in the case of a guilty verdict. In support of their proposal, the authors of the bill referred to the decision of the European Court of Human Rights (ECtHR) in *Taxquet* v. *Belgium*. In particular, the authors noted that in that case the ECtHR found that laconic answers to vague and general questions coupled with a failure to provide the defendant with the jury's main reasons for a guilty verdict resulted in an unfair process of delivering the verdict by the jury (Kovalev, 2015).

This explanation mischaracterizes the *Taxquet* opinion. There are two decisions of the ECtHR in the *Taxquet* case. The first decision was delivered by the Second Section sitting as a chamber of seven judges on January 13, 2009. Later, however, following a request by the Belgian government, a panel of the Grand Chamber decided to refer the case to the Grand Chamber. The decision of the Grand Chamber of 17 judges was delivered on November 16, 2010. The authors of the Georgian draft law did not specify to which decision they referred in their explanatory letter, but it appears to have been to the earlier decision of the Second Section.

The Grand Chamber upheld the Second Section's ruling that the questions put to the jury did not enable the applicant to ascertain which of the items of evidence and factual circumstances discussed at the trial ultimately caused the jury to answer the questions put to it in the way that it did. However, the Grand Chamber differed significantly from the Second Section by stating that its case law "does *not* require jurors to give reasons for their decision and that Article 6 does *not* preclude a defendant from being tried by a lay jury even where reasons are *not* given for the verdict" (Taxquet v. Belgium, 2010, para. 90; emphasis added).

The Grand Chamber restated the principle that "for the requirements of a fair trial to be satisfied, the accused, and indeed the public, must be able to understand the verdict that has been given; this is a vital safeguard against arbitrariness" (Taxquet v. Belgium, 2010, para 90). At the same time, the Grand Chamber considered that this understanding could be met in a variety of ways:

> In proceedings conducted before professional judges, the accused's understanding of his conviction stems primarily from the reasons given in judicial decisions. [. . .] In the case of assize courts sitting with a lay jury [. . .] Article 6 requires an assessment of whether sufficient safeguards were in place to avoid any risk of arbitrariness [. . .]. Such procedural safeguards may include, for example, *directions or guidance provided by the presiding judge to the jurors on the legal issues arising or the evidence adduced*, and precise, unequivocal questions put to the jury by the judge, forming a framework on which the verdict is based or sufficiently offsetting the fact that no reasons are given for the jury's answers. (Taxquet v. Belgium, 2010, paras. 91–92; emphasis added)

The decision of the Grand Chamber provided reassurance that jury systems of the Council of Europe member states that employ a general verdict of guilty or not guilty, such as England and Wales, the Republic of Ireland, and Georgia, are compatible with the requirements of the European Convention for the Protection of Human Rights and Fundamental Freedoms and the jurisprudence of the European Court of Human Rights.

During the 2015 roundtable organized by the OSGF, Georgian legal practitioners expressed two different positions regarding the form of jury verdicts (OSGF, 2015). On the one hand, some practitioners supported the government's proposal to adopt special verdicts. These professionals cited the rationale provided by the government and did not contribute their own perspectives to the debate. In contrast, some of the practicing judges expressed opposition to the government's proposal. One of the judges stated that the current form of general verdicts was simple and easy to use by both judges and jurors. The same judge also suggested that jurors could probably answer special verdict questions, but doubted that those answers would be informative (OSGF, 2015). Another judge argued that "if we ask the types of questions" that the government is proposing, which require some degree of legal knowledge, "99% of jurors would not be able to answer them" (OSGF, 2015). Indeed, we argue that there is a substantial risk that jurors will be confused and unable to effectively answer cumbersome question lists consisting of dozens, if not hundreds, of technical questions.

The special verdict form was also criticized in the joint statement of the Constitutional Research Center at Ilia University, the Judicial Empowerment and Legal Education Center, and the National Human Rights Institute at Free University in October 2015 (Center for Constitutional Research et al., 2015):

> Since figuring out answers to these questions requires possession of a specialist professional knowledge, we believe the proposed way of making verdicts by jurors is unjustified. In making their verdict, jurors should be discussing the arguments adduced by the prosecution and the defense, which then serve as a ground for the jury verdict. However, the draft law proposes a process that will make it too difficult for jurors to make a decision due to excessively complicated issues on the questionnaire. If jurors decide on a person's guilt or innocence without clearly understanding the evaluation system they are using, the whole process would be contrary to the interests of justice.

As we have already described, the 2015 bill was adopted in part by the Law of June 2016. Some of the proposals were approved by the Georgian Parliament. For example, jury trials were limited to less than two dozen offenses, and some professionals, such as psychologists, became eligible to serve as jurors, and *voir dire* remained public. At the same time, the most controversial provision of the bill – the special verdict – was rejected.

SUPPORT OF THE JURY SYSTEM BY GEORGIAN SOCIETY

To support the legislative process in the early days of jury reform, the Georgian government invested in public opinion surveys. Two were undertaken by the

Institute of Social Researches in 2007 and 2009. The 2007 research showed that less than 40% of the population had a general understanding of the jury system (e.g., role in court, legal provisions concerning the jury, the reasons why it was introduced, and the way it functioned). Out of all respondents, 18% had positive expectations, 19% thought that it would be a positive change rather than a negative one, and only 3% had extremely negative views of the jury. The survey also revealed that the generally positive attitude was driven by distrust of the existing system (Nikolo, 2007).

The survey conducted in 2009 showed a significant increase, from nearly 40% to 66%, in public awareness, that is, in people who indicated that they had basic knowledge about the jury reform (Institute of Social Researches, 2009). Respondents on the 2009 survey were asked whether they believed that the jury system would make the courts independent and impartial. The question tested expectations in society as at that point no jury trials had yet taken place. Most respondents answered this question positively: 76.6% of respondents in Tbilisi, 89.1% of respondents in Kutaisi, 91.5% of respondents in Batumi, 94.9% of respondents in Zugdidi, 89.9% of respondents in Gori, and 70% of respondents in Telavi indicated that the statement was true or partially true (Institute of Social Researches, 2009).

At the same time, it appeared that the formal education system was not engaged in promoting the jury system. The failure has been addressed by the Ministry of Education only recently, and steps have been made to include mock jury trials in the public school curriculum. Still, the National Education Goals document (Minister of Education and Science of Georgia, 2016) has not been amended to mention courts and jury trials despite several updates on other subjects.

Problems persist in university education as well. As the jury trial is still very new, there are only a few publications about juries that can be used by law schools. Scholars of law have only recently started to renew and refresh their bookshelves, publishing new textbooks and academic articles (Mytton & Meladze, 2006). The lack of literature on jury trials remains problematic for professional lawyers as well.

CONCLUSION

One of the essential conditions for the effective functioning of the jury as suggested by Vidmar (2003, p. 405) is the "obvious fact that the government itself must be democratically inclined since the jury systems have not tended to be favored by authoritarian regimes." Indeed, the history of jury trials in Georgia clearly supports this thesis. Trial by jury, introduced by Georgian reformers in 1918, perished in the hands of Bolsheviks in 1921. Jury trials in modern Georgia are the product of the Rose Revolution in 2003. They demonstrated continuity in judicial reform and have been seen as a fresh start to complete reform and a way to build bridges between the judicial system and society, which deeply distrusted the post-Soviet judiciary.

However, the first steps in the implementation of jury reform were very timid, and the government was very cautious about the pace of change. After adoption of the new Criminal Procedure Code it took nearly two years to get to the first trial despite political support; reform was approached with reluctance from the legal community. The result is that by April 2020, only 46 jury trials had taken place, occurring in seven cities of Georgia against 59 defendants; 18 were acquitted and 41 were convicted between November of 2011 and April 2019. Thus, the number of crimes adjudicated by juries has been very limited.

There is evidence that jury trials have been subject to some attempts at influence through the media. Investigative materials are frequently published in the media by the prosecutor's office before jury selection, presumably in order to promote the prosecution's case. Media coverage of the *Smith Family* case once again highlighted the problem of pretrial media exposure, which led one of the coauthors of this chapter to file an ethics complaint against Imedi TV with the Ethics Charter NGO. The complaint was decided in favor of Mr. Meladze, supporting the view that pretrial exposure of evidence by the prosecutor's office violated ethical coverage rules (Meladze v. Imedi TV, 2019).

Due to the limited resources allocated to education and outreach, communities in rural areas are not receiving information on the functioning and procedures of the court, which makes it problematic to call citizens for jury duty and prolongs the selection process. Furthermore, the civic education curriculum in public schools ignores the subject of jury trials and even the textbook chapter dealing with the court system does not contain references to jury. Higher education institutions have been receiving more and more literature, however the study of jury trials still has gained little attention and only a few law schools teach the trial skills necessary for trial by jury. Similar observations can be made about continuing professional programs for lawyers. If it were not for international donors, local expertise would not be able to compensate for gaps in education and training.

Despite these difficulties, the jury system is evolving and the demand for trials is increasing. The acquittal of two defendants on November 6, 2018, in Tbilisi City Court once again proved that juries can withstand pressure from the executive. It gave an incentive to defense lawyers to use juries more frequently. This suggests that the system may gain greater support from members of society who can be convinced that juries are not unduly punitive or authoritarian. Eventually, the government may be pressed to expand the scope to a wider range of crimes in order to acknowledge fully the constitutional principle of an adversarial trial in the Georgian criminal justice system.

However, Georgian civil society and the legal community will need to pay closer attention to the government's proposals to reform the jury system. According to international organizations, global democracy indicators, such as the freedom rating, political rights, and civil liberties, have been declining over the last seven years (Freedom House, 2019). This is a matter of a great concern, as history shows that many anti-jury reforms took place when governments were not democratically inclined. Indeed, the institution of the jury suffered at the hand of authoritarian regimes in several European countries throughout the twentieth century: the Bolsheviks in Russia in 1917, Gomes da Costa in Portugal in 1927, Mussolini's fascist government in Italy in 1931, Franco in 1939, the Vichy government of Marshal Pétain in France in 1941, and the Junta in Greece in 1967 (Gleadow, 2000, pp. 30–38; Thaman, 2002a, p. 91; Vidmar, 2000, pp. 430–431). One of the most recent examples is Venezuela, where in 2001 the government headed by former President Hugo Chávez abolished trial by jury only two years after it had been introduced (Thaman, 2002b). Another example, which is more relevant in the post-Soviet context, is Russia, which abolished jury trials in political cases in 2008 (Kovalev & Smirnov, 2014). There is a possibility that Georgia may follow these examples. The proposals of 2015 and 2016 may be indicative of the course that, if pursued, will gradually eliminate trial by jury.

Until recently, scholars have conducted mostly theoretical and comparative research on jury trials in Georgia. This was due to the insignificant number of jury trials in the country. The authors of this chapter are currently engaged in the first empirical study of Georgian jury trials, which should help us to better understand jury trial practices in courts, identify major issues with jury trials, and potentially develop ways to address these issues. Also, further research is needed to examine the influence of legal education on the performance of lawyers in jury trials.

REFERENCES

American Bar Association/Central European and Eurasian Law Initiative. (2005). *Judicial reform index for Georgia*. Washington, DC: ABA.

Beachain, O. D., & Polese, A. (Eds). (2010). *The colour revolutions in the former Soviet republics: Successes and failures*. New York: Routledge.

Black's Law Dictionary (2009). 9th ed. St. Paul, MN: West.

Cape, E., Namoradze, Z., Smith, R., & Spronken, T. (2010). *Effective criminal defence in Europe*. Antwerp: Intersentia.

Davitashvili, G. (2003). *Sasamartlo mt'kicebulebani kartul chveulebit samartalshi* სასამართლო მტკიცებულებანი ქართულ ჩვეულებით სამართალში [The judicial evidences in Georgian customary law]. Tbilisi: Tbilisi State University.

Diamond, S. S., Rose, M. R., & Murphy, B. (2014). Embedded experts on real juries: A delicate balance. *William & Mary Law Review*, 55, 885–933.

Dolidze, A. (2015). Napits msajulta sasamartlo sakartveloshi da misi shesabamisoba adamianis uplebata evrop'ul k'onventsiastan ნაფიც მსაჯულთა სასამართლო საქართველოში და მისი შესაბამისობა ადამიანის უფლებათა ევროპულ კონვენციასთან [Jury trials in Georgia and their compatibility with the European Convention on Human Rights]. In K. Korkelia (Ed.), *Adamianis uplebebi da samartlis uzenaesoba* ადამიანის უფლებები და სამართლის უზენაესობა [European standards of human rights and their influence on Georgian legislation and practice] (pp. 43–59). Tbilisi: Tbilisi State University Press.

Freedom House. (2019). *Freedom in the world, Georgia*. https://freedomhouse.org/report/freedom-world/2019/georgia

Gharibashvili, I. (2015). P'remieri Gharibashvili: Napits msajulta inst'it'ut'ma sruli k'rakhi ganitsada პრემიერი ღარიბაშვილი: ნაფიც მსაჯულთა ინსტიტუტმა სრული კრახი განიცადა [A public statement by Prime Minister Gharibashvili: The jury institute has suffered a complete setback]. *Tabula*. www.tabula.ge/ge/story/96953-premieri-nafic-msajulta-institutma-sruli-kraxi-ganicada

Gleadow, C. (2000). *History of trial by jury in the Spanish legal system*. Lewiston, NY: Edwin Mellen Press.

Gruzenberg, M. O. (1917). *Sud prisiazhknykh v zakavkazie* [Jury trials in Transcaucasia]. Tiflis: Tipografia Kantseliarii Osobogo Zakavkazskogo Komiteta.

Gupta, P., Kleinfeld, R., & Salinas G. (2002). *Legal and judicial reform in Europe and Central Asia*. Washington, DC: World Bank, Operations Evaluation Department.

Herrmann, J. (2002). *Comments on the Code of Criminal Procedure of Georgia*. Strasbourg: Council of Europe.

Institute of Social Researches. (2009). *Sabaziso codnisa da aghkmis k'vleva sasamartlo sist'emis shesakheb* საბაზისო ცოდნისა და აღქმის კვლევა სასამართლო სისტემის შესახებ [Basic knowledge and perceptions concerning courts in Georgia]. www.msajuli.ge/uploads/2009.pdf

Jackson, J. D., and Kovalev, N. (2016). Lay adjudication in Europe: The rise and fall of the traditional jury. *Oñati Socio-Legal Series*, 6, 368–395.

Javakhishvili, I. (1982). *Sakartvelos ist'oria, t'omi 6* საქართველოს ისტორია, ტომი 6 [History of Georgia, Vol. 6]. Tbilisi: Mecniereba.

Jones, S. F. (1988). The establishment of Soviet power in Transcaucasia: The case of Georgia 1921–1928. *Soviet Studies*, 11(4), 616–639.

(2005). *Socialism in Georgian colors: The European road to social democracy, 1883–1917*. Cambridge, MA: Harvard University Press.

Kakabadze, S. (1997). *Kartveli khalkhis ist'oria 1783–1921 ts'lebshi* ქართველი ხალხის ისტორია 1783–1921 წლებში [History of the Georgian people 1783–1921]. Tbilisi: Nekeri.

Kavkazskaia Arkheograficheskaia Komissiia [Caucasus Archeological Commission]. (1866). *Akty sobrannye Kavkazskoi Arkheograficheskoi Komissieiu* [Documents collected by Caucasus Archeological Commission], Vol. 1. Edited by A. P. Berzhe. Tiflis: Tipografia Glavnogo Upravleniia Namestnika Kavkazkogo.

Kikvadze, A. (1959). *Sakartvelos ist'oria XIX–XX ss, ts'igni 2: 1861–1921* საქართველოს ისტორია : XIX–XX სს. : წიგნი 2 : 1861–1921 წწ [History of Georgia, XIX–XX centuries, Book 2]. Tbilisi: Tbilisi State University Press.

King George V (1913). *Dzeglis dadeba giorgi brts'q'invalis mier* ძეგლის დადება გიორგი ბრწყინვალის მიერ [Book of Law "Dzeglisdeba"]. Edited by S. Kakabadze. Tbilisi: S. M. Losaberidze.

K'onstitutsiuri k'vlevebis tsentri კონსტიტუციური კვლევების ცენტრი [Center for Constitutional Research]. (2018). *Mediis monitoringis angarishi* მედიის მონიტორინგის ანგარიში [Media monitoring report]. https://conlaw.iliauni.edu.ge/naphits-msajultha-sasamarthlo-mediashi-1998–2018

K'onstitutsiuri k'vlevebis tsent'ri, martlmsajulebis ganvitarebisa da samartlebrivi sts'avlebis cent'ri da adamianis uplebebis erovnuli inst'it'ut'i კონსტიტუციური კვლევების ცენტრი, მართლმსაჯულების განვითარებისა და სამართლებრივი სწავლების ცენტრი და ადამიანის უფლებების ეროვნული ინსტიტუტი [Center for Constitutional Research, the Judicial Empowerment and Legal Education Center & the National Human Rights Institute at Free University]. (2015). Gantskhadeba napits msajulta sasamartlostan dak'avshirebit dagegmili tsvlilebebis shesakheb

განცხადება ნაფიც მსაჯულთა სასამართლოსთან დაკავშირებით დაგეგმილი ცვლილებების შესახებ [Joint statement about the intended changes in the jury trial provisions]. http://nihr.freeuni.edu.ge/uploads/files/gantskhadeba_jury.pdf

Korff, D. (2005). *Comments on amendments to the Georgian Criminal Procedure Code and the draft New Georgian Criminal Procedure Code (as formulated in December 2005)*. Strasbourg: Council of Europe.

Kovalev, N. (2010). *Criminal justice reform in Russia, Ukraine, and the Former Republics of the Soviet Union: Trial by jury and mixed courts*. Lewiston, NY: Edwin Mellen Press.

(2015). *Analysis of the draft law of Georgia amending the Criminal Procedure Code of Georgia with regards to jury trials*. Report prepared for the Open Society Georgia Foundation, Tbilisi.

Kovalev, N., & Meladze, G. (2015, October 13). Authors' meeting with judges at the Supreme Court of Georgia.

Kovalev, N., & Smirnov, A. (2014). The nature of the Russian trial by jury: Jurata Patriae or Raison d'Etat. *European Journal of Crime, Criminal Law and Criminal Justice*, 22(2), 115–133.

Leigh, L. (2002). *Comments on the Code of Criminal Procedure of Georgia*. Strasbourg: Council of Europe.

Lekveishvili, M. (2013). Napits msajulta inst'it'ut'is sakmianoba tbilisis sakalako sasamartloshi ნაფიც მსაჯულთა ინსტიტუტის საქმიანობა თბილისის საქალაქო სასამართლოში [The operation of the jury trials in Tbilisi City Court]. In *Napits msajulta inst'it'ut'i sakartveloshi* ნაფიც მსაჯულთა ინსტიტუტი საქართველოში [The trial by jury in Georgia] (pp. 146–161; English translation, pp. 457–467). Tbilisi: Iverioni.

Light, M. (2014). Police reforms in the Republic of Georgia: The convergence of domestic and foreign policy in an anti-corruption drive. *Policing and Society*, 24(3), 318–345.

Lomsadze, G. (2010, October 1). Georgia: Jury trials aim to bolster public confidence in courts. *Eurasianet*. https://eurasianet.org/georgia-jury-trials-aim-to-bolster-public-confidence-in-courts

Mchedlishvili, Z. (2015, June 8). Sud prisiazhnykh razocharoval prem'er-ministra Gruzii [The jury trial disappointed prime minister of Georgia]. *Ekho Kavkaza*. www.ekhokavkaza.com/a/27060806.html

Meladze, G. (2007). Law and revolution: Formation of the new legal tradition in Georgia. *Turkish Policy Quarterly*, 6(3). www.esiweb.org/pdf/esi_turkey_tpq_id_115.pdf

Meladze v. Imedi TV, Case No. 244 (January 27, 2019). www.qartia.ge/ka/gadatsyvetilebebis-dzebna/article/67901-gadatsyvetileba-saqmeze-giorgi-meladze-irakli-chikhladzis-da-thamar-gogesashvilis-tsinaaghmdeg

Minister of Education and Science of Georgia. (2016). 2018–2024 ts'lebis erovnuli sasts'avlo gegma damt'k'itsebulia sakartvelos ganatlebisa da metsnierebis minist'ris 2016 ts'lis №40 brdzanebit 2018–2024 სასწავლო წლების ეროვნული სასწავლო გეგმა დამკიცებულია საქართველოს განათლებისა და მეცნიერების მინისტრის 2016 წლის №40/ნ ბრძანებით [National education goals document for 2018–24 (National educational goals, adopted by Minister of Education and Science Decree #40, 2016)]. http://ncp.ge/ge/curriculum/satesto-seqtsia/akhali-sastsavlo-gegmebi-2016-2021

Mytton, E., & Meladze, G. (2006). Legal education in transition: A study from Georgia. http://webjcli.ncl.ac.uk/2006/issue3/mytton-meladze3.html

Nasonov, S. A. (2015). Evropeiiskie modeli proizvodstva v sude prisiazhnykh v Gruzii (sravnitel'no-pravovoe issledovanie) [European models of the proceedings in the trial by jury in

Georgia (comparative legal studies)]. *Aktual'nye problem rossiskogo prava*, 6(55), 163–169.

Netgazeti (2017). Okrop'iridze sakartvelos ts'inaaghdeg ოქროპირიძე საქართველოს წინააღმდეგ [Okropiridze v. Georgia]. https://netgazeti.ge/news/202542/

Nikolo, M. (2007). *Napits msajulta mimart sazogadoebis inpormirebuloba da chartuloba* ნაფიც მსაჯულთა მიმართ საზოგადოების ინფორმირებულობა და ჩართულობა [Awareness of and participation in jury trial]. www.msajuli.ge/uploads/2007.pdf

Papuashvili, G. (2012). The 1921 Constitution of the Democratic Republic of Georgia: Looking back after ninety years. *European Public Law*, 18, 323–350.

Piacentini, L., & Slade, G. (2015). Architecture and attachment: Carceral collectivism and the problem of prison reform in Russia and Georgia. *Theoretical Criminology*, 19(2), 179–197.

Pondi ghia sazogadoeba sakartvelo ფონდი ღია საზოგადოება საქართველო) [Open Society Georgia Foundation]. (2015). Roundtable on jury trials. October 16, Tbilisi. Unpublished notes, on file with authors.

Popjanevski, J. (2015). Retribution and the rule of law: The politics of justice in Georgia. Silk Road Paper. Central Asia-Caucasus Institute & Silk Road Studies Program. https://silkroadstudies.org/resources/pdf/SilkRoadPapers/2015-popjanevski-retribution-and-the-rule-of-law-the-politics-of-justice-in-georgia.pdf

Roudik, P. (2011). Georgia: Courts with jurors established nationwide. *Global Legal Monitor*. www.loc.gov/law/foreign-news/article/georgia-courts-with-jurors-established-nationwide/

Sakartvelos akhalgazrda iurist'ta asotsiatsia საქართველოს ახალგაზრდა იურისტთა ასოციაცია) [Georgian Young Lawyers' Association]. (2016, June 22). The GYLA responds to legislative changes related to the jury system. https://gyla.ge/en/post/saia-nafic-msajulta-sasamartlotan-dakavshirebul-cvlilebebs-ekhmianeba#sthash.vChEOqA6.dpbs

Sakartvelos k'onst'it'utsia საქართველოს კონსტიტუცია [Constitution of the Democratic Republic of Georgia] (1921), adopted on February 21, 1921.

Sakartvelos k'onst'it'utsia საქართველოს კონსტიტუცია [Constitution of Georgia] (1995), adopted on August 24, 1995, with amendments as of March 23, 2018.

Sakartvelos p'rezidentis gank'arguleba No. 914 საქართველოს პრეზიდენტის განკარგულება No. 914 [Presidential Decree of Georgia No. 914] (2004).

Sakartvelos siskhlis samartlis k'odeksi საქართველოს სისხლის სამართლის კოდექსი [Criminal Code of Georgia] (1999), adopted on July 22, 1999, No. 2287. Arts. 108, 109, 117(2), (4), (6), and (8), 126(2), 135-1, 143(2-4), 143-1, 143-2, 143-3(2-4), 144-2, 146(2), 147, 149, 197(4), 198(3), 229.

Sakartvelos siskhlis samartlis sap'rotseso k'odeksi საქართველოს სისხლის სამართლის საპროცესო კოდექსი [Criminal Procedure Code of Georgia] (1998), adopted on February 20, 1998.

Sakartvelos siskhlis samartlis sap'rotseso k'odeksi საქართველოს სისხლის სამართლის საპროცესო კოდექსი [Criminal Procedure Code of Georgia] (2009), adopted on October 9, 2009, No. 1772.

Sakartvelos uzenaesi sasamartlo საქართველოს უზენაესი სასამართლო [Supreme Court of Georgia]. (2012). *Napits msajulta sasamartlo* ნაფიც მსაჯულთა სასამართლო [Jury trials]. www.supremecourt.ge/files/upload-file/pdf/12msajuli.pdf

(2014). *Sasamartlo sist'emis reporma sakartveloshi* სასამართლო სისტემის რეფორმა საქართველოში [Judiciary reform in Georgia]. www.supremecourt.ge/files/upload-file/pdf/broshura-2014.pdf

(2020). Napits msajulta sasamartlo damouk'idebel sakartveloshi ნაფიც მსაჯულთა სასამართლო დამოუკიდებელ საქართველოში (1917–1921 წწ) [Jury court in independent Georgia (1917–1921)]. www.msajuli.ge/index.php?m=796

Sakhalkho Sakme (1920, February 20). [Georgian newspaper].

Slade, G. (2013). *Reorganizing crime: Mafia and anti-Mafia in post-Soviet Georgia*. Oxford: Oxford University Press.

Sofronenko, K. A. (1967). *Istoriia gosudarstva i prava SSSR, Chast 1* [History of state and law of USSR, Vol. 1]. Moscow: Iuridicheskaia literatura.

Solomon, P. H., & Foglesong, T. S. (2000). *Courts and transition in Russia: The challenge of judicial reform*. Boulder, CO: Westview.

Tanovich, D. M., Paciocco, D. M., & Skurka, S. (1997). *Jury selection in criminal trials*. Toronto: Irwin Law.

Taxquet v. Belgium, Application No. 926/05 (January 13, 2009).

Taxquet v. Belgium, Application No. 926/05 (November 16, 2010).

Thaman, S. C. (2002a). Japan's new system of mixed courts: Some suggestions regarding their future form and procedures. *Saint Louis-Warsaw Transatlantic Law Journal, 2001–2002*, 89–117.

(2002b). Latin America's first modern system of lay participation: The reform of inquisitorial justice in Venezuela. In A. Donatsch, M. Forster, & C. Schwarzenegger (Eds.), *Strafrecht, Strafprozessrecht und Menschenrechte: Festschrift für Stefan Trechsel* [Criminal law, criminal procedure law and human rights: Commemorative for Stefan Trechsel] (pp. 765–780). Zürich: Schulthess Juristische Medien AG.

(2011). Should criminal juries give reasons for their verdicts? *Chicago-Kent Law Review*, 86, 613–668.

Transparency International. (2007). *Global corruption report: Corruption in judicial systems*. www.transparency.org/whatwedo/publication/global_corruption_report_2007_corruption_and_judicial_systems

Transparency International Georgia. (2010). *Refreshing Georgia's courts. Trial by jury: More democracy or a face-lift for the judiciary?* www.transparency.ge/sites/default/files/Trial by Jury.pdf

Vidmar, N. (2000). The jury elsewhere in the world. In N. Vidmar (Ed.), *World jury systems* (pp. 421–447). Oxford: Oxford University Press.

(2003). Juries and lay assessors in the Commonwealth: A contemporary survey. *Criminal Law Forum*, 13, 385–407.

Vogler, R. (2006, July 6–9). *Lay participation and the criminal justice revolutions in Eastern Europe: The cases of Georgia and Ukraine* [Paper presentation]. Law and Society Association Annual Meeting, Baltimore, MD. On file with authors.

(2009). *Report on the 2009 Draft of the Criminal Procedure Code of Georgia prepared on behalf of the Directorate General of Human Rights and Legal Affairs of the Council of Europe*.

Wheatley, J. (2017) *Georgia from national awakening to Rose Revolution: Delayed transition in the Former Soviet Union*. New York: Routledge.

World Bank. (1998, April 10). *Georgia judicial assessment* (Report No. 17356-GE). http://documents.worldbank.org/curated/en/293711468773997603/pdf/multi-page.pdf

(2007). *Doing business: How to reform* (Annual report). www.doingbusiness.org/content/dam/doingBusiness/media/Annual-Reports/English/DB07-FullReport.pdf

PART IV

Global Perspectives on Lay Participation

14

What Hollywood, USA, Teaches the World (Incorrectly and Correctly) about Juries

Nancy S. Marder

American jury films teach viewers in the United States and in countries around the world about the American jury system. These films, which focus on holdout jurors, portray juries incorrectly because holdout jurors occur infrequently in practice. However, *12 Angry Men* (1957), though it focuses on a holdout juror, does provide an accurate portrayal in its depiction of the jury as working hard to find the facts, as most actual juries try to do.

For dramatic purposes, jury films invariably rely on an individual juror who takes a minority view and holds onto it during deliberations. These "holdout jurors" often produce hung juries or convince other jurors to change their votes. In reality, holdout jurors are rare (Hannaford-Agor, Hans, Mott, & Munsterman, 2002), and those who change everyone else's views are exceptionally rare (Hans & Vidmar, 1986). Usually they join the majority to produce a unanimous verdict.

In spite of the unrealistic use of the holdout juror, *12 Angry Men* does accurately portray the way that a group of ordinary citizens, strangers to each other and to the parties, perform their role as jurors responsibly. The film powerfully portrays how disinterested individuals learn to work together as a jury to examine evidence carefully, resist bias, and overcome personality clashes.

Remarkably, *12 Angry Men* has gone from being a box office flop in 1957 to becoming an iconic film that has been remade in countries around the world, tailored to local audiences regardless of these countries' form of government or legal system. For viewers outside the United States who live in countries that do not have traditional juries, American jury films might be the only way they learn about juries. These foreign versions of *12 Angry Men* suggest to foreign audiences that they, too, can overcome prejudice and work together to make decisions of great consequence. This depiction of the jury, in which jurors ultimately learn to take their role seriously, does accurately portray how actual jurors perform.

THE WAYS IN WHICH HOLDOUT JURORS ARE PORTRAYED IN AMERICAN JURY FILMS

It is striking how often American jury films include a holdout juror. From *12 Angry Men* in 1957 to *Trial by Jury* in 1994 and a remake of it as *The Juror* in 1996 to *One Angry Juror* in 2010, the holdout juror figures prominently in American jury films. A viewer who watches American jury films might be forgiven for concluding that American juries always involve a holdout juror, when in reality they rarely do.

In cases with holdout jurors and no sign that the jury can reach agreement, the judge will conclude that the jury is a hung jury, declare a mistrial, and dismiss the jurors. In a criminal case, the prosecutor will decide whether to retry the criminal defendant before a new jury. In other cases, the holdouts manage to persuade the other jurors to change their votes so that the jury reaches a unanimous verdict consistent with the holdout jurors' position.

The Holdout Juror Who Turns Around All Other Jurors

The only example in films of the holdout juror who turns around 11 other jurors is *12 Angry Men*. The film involves a young man of Puerto Rican descent who is tried for the murder of his father. Juror #8, played by Henry Fonda, votes "not guilty," even though all of the other jurors vote "guilty" initially. Juror #8 explains that it is not easy to take a contrary position. However, he argues that a young man's life is at stake (in a jurisdiction that has a mandatory death penalty for murder) and the jury owes the defendant some "talk" before it sends him off to die (Rose, 1972, p. 177).

Juror #8 begins to break down the other jurors' resistance to his position by trying a risky gambit. He makes a deal: they will discuss the case for another hour, after which they will take a vote by secret ballot. If no other juror joins him, then he will capitulate, and the jury will be unanimous for guilt. However, if even one juror joins him, then they will continue to deliberate. When the jury takes a vote at the appointed time, another juror joins Juror #8, and so the jury continues to deliberate.

Different jurors contribute different recollections of the evidence. They call into question the credibility of some of the witnesses who had seemed so persuasive at first blush. With their discussion of each piece of evidence, more jurors have reasonable doubt and change their vote. In the end, only one juror remains convinced that the defendant is guilty, but he capitulates. He recognizes that his vote had been motivated by his anger toward his estranged son, who was about the same age as the defendant. Thus, Juror #8 managed to turn around the votes of the other 11 jurors.

A more recent jury film, *The Juror* (1996), involves a holdout juror named Annie (played by Demi Moore). She has been seated on a jury in a criminal case involving a Mafia boss. Initially, threats by the defendant's henchman, known as "The Teacher" (played by Alec Baldwin), compel her to do whatever he demands. As will be discussed in a later section, this portrayal of Mafia threats to jurors is a Hollywood depiction rather than a reflection of actual juror experience. In the film, The Teacher forces the juror's cooperation by bugging her house, threatening her and her son at home, and killing one of her close friends. Initially, The Teacher requires her to be a holdout juror and to produce a hung jury. Later, he demands a not-guilty verdict because the Mafia boss wants to be free. Annie and another coerced juror manage to convince the remaining 10 jurors, by wearing them down, to render a not-guilty verdict.

The prosecutor realizes that Annie had been coerced and offers her witness protection; however, Annie takes matters into her own hands to protect herself and her son.

The Holdout Juror Who Produces a Hung Jury

In some jury films, the holdout juror does not manage to convince the other jurors to adopt his or her position, but is able to maintain his or her stance and produce a hung jury. In *Trial by Jury* (1994), which was an earlier, but less compelling, version of *The Juror*, Valerie, the mother of a young boy, is called for jury duty in a case involving a Mafia boss. Valerie (played by Joanne Whalley-Kilmer) and her son are soon threatened by henchmen of the Mafia boss, including a former cop (played by William Hurt) who is now on the side of the Mafia boss, as well as the Mafia boss himself (played by Armand Assante).

During jury deliberations, Valerie votes not guilty, while the other 11 jurors vote guilty. She argues that the prosecutor has not established guilt beyond a reasonable doubt, but no other juror is persuaded, nor is the viewer. It is clear that the Mafia boss is guilty and that Valerie votes not guilty to protect her life and that of her son. Because Valerie maintains her stance as a holdout juror, the judge has no choice but to recognize the hung jury, declare a mistrial, and dismiss the jury. The prosecutor intends to retry the Mafia boss, but he wants to know why Valerie voted not guilty. She will not admit that she had been coerced because she does not believe the government can protect her. In the end, Valerie confronts the Mafia boss and each tries to kill the other, but Valerie prevails.

One Angry Juror (2010) also involves a holdout juror who maintains her stance and produces a hung jury. Sarah Walsh (played by Jessica Capshaw) is a lawyer who is selected to serve on a jury. The case involves an African-American defendant, Walter Byrd, who was charged with the murder of another African-American man. Byrd had been picked up by police because he wore clothing similar to that of the man seen leaving the crime scene. Later, the victim's sister identifies Byrd as the perpetrator. However, there is no physical evidence linking Byrd to the crime and he has no criminal record.

After some deliberation, the jury takes a vote: 11 jurors vote guilty and only Sarah Walsh votes not guilty. The jury continues to deliberate and Walsh manages to convince a few other jurors to see the case her way. She argues that the prosecutor has not established Byrd's guilt beyond a reasonable doubt. Although Walsh convinces some jurors, she does not convince all of them. The jury becomes a hung jury, and the government decides to retry Walter Byrd.

WHY DO AMERICAN JURY FILMS HAVE A HOLDOUT JUROR?

Although the foremost reason for jury films to have a holdout juror is to create tension that drives the story, there are other reasons as well. A holdout also pits the individual against the group. The holdout shows how hard it is to reach judgment and raises questions about the right answer. The trend in most modern American jury films is to provide viewers with certainty at the end; however, *12 Angry Men* leaves open the question of who is right, and such ambiguity has helped the film to endure (Marder, 2007a).

Holdout Jurors Create Tension

Although holdout jurors are rare in practice, they are common in American jury films because they are a powerful way to create simple and sustained dramatic tension. If all the jurors agreed, there would be no drama to watch. Mar Jimeno-Bulnes, a Spanish jury scholar, observed that, if *12 Angry Men* had been based on Spanish jury practice in which a majority verdict suffices, there would have been no film after the jurors took their initial vote. A vote of 11 to 1 in favor of guilt would mark the end of the story in Spain (Jimeno-Bulnes, 2007). The holdout juror on an American jury in which unanimity is required is the perfect storytelling device.

The holdout juror in *12 Angry Men* allows the story to progress and immediately creates tension between the holdout and the majority. After the initial vote in which Juror #8 votes not guilty and the other 11 jurors vote guilty, Juror #10 laments: "Boy-oh-boy. There's always one [who doesn't go along]" (Rose, 1972, p. 176). He views it as a bad development that one juror is standing in the way of a quick verdict, whereas Juror #8 understands that it is important to slow down the deliberations. Juror #8 recognizes that the jury needs to give careful consideration to the evidence and to assess whether the prosecution has proven its case beyond a reasonable doubt. Juror #8 believes that at the very least they owe the defendant some talk.

In *The Juror*, the holdout juror creates tension, but for a different reason than in *12 Angry Men*. The Teacher, who threatens Annie and her son with violence, creates the tension in *The Juror*. The tension shifts to the jury room, however, when The Teacher initially tells Annie that she, along with another juror, must become holdouts and produce a hung jury. The Teacher forces Annie to wear a device that allows him to breach the secrecy of the jury room and to listen to the deliberations. Even though Annie manages to be a holdout, The Teacher is not satisfied. He breaches the protections typically provided by sequestering a jury and goes to the hotel where Annie and the other jurors are required to stay. The Teacher tells her that the defendant wants an acquittal, not a hung jury. Annie and another juror manage to convince the others to go their way. However, the tension in this film does not end with the jury's acquittal. The Mafia boss decides that The Teacher must kill Annie and her son; they all end up in Guatemala, where Annie manages to set a trap to kill The Teacher, and that puts an end to his violence.

In *Trial by Jury*, which is quite similar to *The Juror*, the holdout juror creates tension, but not during deliberations. The film makes clear that the defendant is guilty and that the holdout will remain a holdout because her life is threatened. However, it is the threats and violence that create the tension in this film. In contrast, *12 Angry Men* focuses entirely on holdout Juror #8, and whether he will be able to stand his ground and then convince 11 other jurors to see the case his way and to change their vote.

Holdout Jurors Pit the Individual against the Majority

Jury films make use of the holdout juror to depict the struggle of the individual against the will of the majority. This is a recurring theme in American films, from *Mr. Smith Goes to Washington* (1939) (depicting one Senator's fight against corrupt politicians) to *It's a Wonderful Life* (1946) (showing the difference one individual can make to an entire town), and is not limited to jury films. A holdout juror can epitomize this struggle. In a jury deliberation, each juror is potentially placed in a difficult position. He or she is supposed to listen to fellow jurors and be open to their arguments, and yet, each juror is free to adhere to his or her own point of view. Thus, every juror has the potential to become a holdout, though few have the strength to remain a holdout. In American jury films, the holdout juror also needs to act from good intentions, unless, as in the Mafia films, the holdout juror was coerced.

12 Angry Men epitomizes the struggle of the individual against the majority, but the individual succeeds only if acting out of good intentions. Juror #8 votes not guilty when all the other jurors vote guilty. But he explains to his fellow jurors that he does not know if the defendant is guilty; he only knows that a young man's life is at stake. Juror #8 wants the jury to reach the correct verdict, and to do so, he understands that all the jurors need to contribute to the deliberations. As a cue to the viewer that Juror #8's motives are proper, he is dressed in a white linen suit; his demeanor remains calm and detached even while the other jurors suffer from the heat and close confines of the jury room; and he is guided by reason and evidence. He is able to maintain his position, even when he stands alone. In contrast, Juror #3 becomes the lone juror in opposition to the group at the end of the film. However, Juror #3 is unable to adhere to his stance, even though he says he has a right to do so. He succumbs to group pressure, not only because he is unable to give reasons to justify his position, but also because he acts out of bad purpose. He wants to punish the defendant because he is angry at his own son.

Holdout Jurors Can Show the Difficulty of Judgment

A holdout juror can highlight the difficulty of reaching a judgment in the face of uncertainty. If 11 jurors see the case one way and the holdout juror sees it another way, who is right? Some films, such as *12 Angry Men*, do not resolve that question. The ending leaves the viewer to decide, thus building upon an earlier tradition in jury films in which the viewer was the jury (Clover, 1998a). However, more recent American jury films such as *One Angry Juror* depart from this tradition and provide the viewer with a clear-cut answer.

12 *Angry Men*: Who Is Right? One reason why *12 Angry Men* has endured is that it is unclear whether the jury reaches the correct verdict by finding the defendant not guilty. When the jurors take an initial vote, they vote guilty, except for Juror #8. Even Juror #8 is uncertain, but he feels they owe the defendant some talk.

As the deliberation proceeds, Juror #8 succeeds in getting jurors to work together, even though these same jurors had initially voted to convict the defendant. As the jurors consider each piece of evidence, some jurors have doubts that they did not have initially. They are no longer certain that the defendant committed the crime, and they start to believe that the prosecutor has not met the "beyond a reasonable doubt" standard. Even as jurors adopt this view, some, such as Juror #12, the advertising executive, go back and forth depending on the piece of evidence under consideration. Juror #6, a laborer, worries that Juror #8 might persuade all of them to vote not guilty in the end, even though the defendant might actually have killed his father.

In a law review symposium in honor of the fiftieth anniversary of *12 Angry Men*, the contributors were almost as divided as the jurors in the film (Marder, 2007b). Some thought that the defendant had clearly committed the crime and that the jurors failed to consider all of the evidence together and required a standard that exceeded "beyond a reasonable doubt" (Asimow, 2007; Vidmar, Beale, Chemerinsky, & Coleman, 2007). Others thought that the jury engaged in misconduct that led it astray, such as bringing in extraneous material (e.g., the switchblade knife) and trying to reenact the scene in accordance with the testimony provided by the elderly witness (Weisselberg, 2007). Still others thought that the jury learned to play its role properly and to engage in a robust, albeit rancorous, deliberation that led it to reach the correct verdict of not guilty (Landsman, 2007; Marder, 2007c). The film continues to produce disagreement about whether the jury reached the right verdict, and this unresolved question contributes to *12 Angry Men*'s staying power.

Having each viewer decide the correct verdict builds upon an earlier jury film tradition. Carol Clover, a film professor who studied myriad early jury films, observed that they allow viewers to decide the case. In these early jury films, a jury is present in the courtroom, but sits silently and impassively. Clover explained that the jury is a placeholder for the viewer so that the viewer understands that he or she is to decide the case (Clover, 1998b). As Clover noted, *12 Angry Men* was an aberration because it focused entirely on the jury at work in the jury room. Jury films before *12 Angry Men* had not done this because the viewer was supposed to be the jury. Jury films after *12 Angry Men* did not do this, perhaps because *12 Angry Men* did not do well at the box office. *12 Angry Men* replicated the adversarial system but in the jury room. According to Clover, *12 Angry Men* is still a courtroom drama, even though it took place in the jury room (Clover, 1998b). Unlike early jury films, *12 Angry Men* provides the viewer with a verdict, but like early jury films, there is still room for the viewer of *12 Angry Men* to decide whether he or she agrees with the jury's verdict.

***One Angry Juror*: A Juror's Limited Information.** *One Angry Juror*, the television film involving a holdout juror who produces a hung jury, shows not only the difficulty of judgment that jurors face but also the limited information that is available to jurors. In *One Angry Juror*, the jury begins its deliberations with a vote. Eleven jurors vote guilty and Sarah Walsh votes not guilty. She argues that the prosecution has not established its case beyond a reasonable doubt. Although a few jurors eventually agree with Walsh, the jury reaches an impasse and the judge declares a mistrial. The defendant's grandmother asks Walsh, a lawyer, to represent the defendant when the prosecutor decides to try him before a new jury. Walsh agrees, and discovers the truth.

Walsh, as a juror, can only conclude that the prosecution has not established its case beyond a reasonable doubt, but Walsh, as the defendant's attorney and working alongside the public defender and his investigator, is able to learn the truth in this case. She obtains the police records, which had been mysteriously "misplaced" during the first trial; the records raise discrepancies between one witness's testimony in court and her earlier statements on the day of the murder. Walsh, as defense lawyer, is able to find evidence that her jury did not have before it during the trial or deliberations. Walsh's additional investigation establishes that the defendant is not guilty, as indeed the new jury so finds.

Walsh's role as juror is limited to deciding that the prosecution had not met its burden of proof, but in her role as lawyer she is able to uncover the truth. The holdout, as well as the other jurors, must reach a judgment even in the face of imperfect knowledge. When other actors in the criminal justice system, such as police in this case, fall short, then the role of juror is even more challenging (MacKillop & Vidmar, 2015). Under such conditions, the jury might reach an incorrect verdict or no verdict at all; the latter occurred in this film. Walsh's two roles highlight how limited her knowledge was as a juror and how extensive it became as a lawyer. Yet, jurors are asked to reach a verdict, even in the face of limited knowledge. The gap between the jurors' limited knowledge and the power of the jury's verdict on the parties' lives makes judging a particularly difficult task.

AMERICAN JURY FILMS' PORTRAYALS OF THE HOLDOUT JUROR DO NOT REFLECT JURY PRACTICE

American jury films frequently portray holdout jurors and hung juries, but this emphasis is misleading. It does not reflect what happens on actual juries. These films suggest that hung juries occur frequently, that holdout jurors pursue independent investigations afterward, that holdout jurors may often be coerced, and that members of hung juries do not feel bad about having failed to reach a verdict. These portrayals do not comport with actual practice.

Hung Juries Are Not a Frequent Occurrence

Although holdout jurors in *One Angry Juror* and *Trial by Jury* manage to stand their ground and to produce a hung jury, hung juries are infrequent in practice. Professors Kalven and Zeisel conducted a landmark study of criminal juries in the 1950s (Hans & Vidmar, 1991); they published their findings in *The American Jury* in 1966. They compared criminal jury verdicts with judges' assessment of the same cases and found that jurors and judges agreed in almost three-quarters of the cases (Kalven & Zeisel, 1966). When there was disagreement, it was in grey areas in which the jury tended to be more lenient than the judge. Kalven and Zeisel also found that 5.5% of the criminal juries ended as hung juries (Kalven & Zeisel, 1966). The figure of about 5% has been used ever since the publication of Kalven and Zeisel's study (Hannaford-Agor et al., 2002).

When Paula Hannaford-Agor and coauthors, under the auspices of the National Center for State Courts (NCSC), examined data from 30 jurisdictions, they found that 6.2% of the trials ended as hung juries (Hannaford-Agor et al., 2002). This percentage was close to the percentage that Kalven and Zeisel had observed decades earlier. In a second part of the NCSC study, the researchers looked at criminal cases in courts in four large urban areas, including Los Angeles County, CA; Washington, DC; Maricopa County, Arizona; and the Bronx, New York, and collected data from 358 cases in these courts. They looked at each jurisdiction separately because the percentage of hung juries varied from place to place. Juries in Los Angeles and Washington, DC, had a higher hung jury rate on all counts (11.7% and 12.8% respectively) than juries in Maricopa County and the Bronx (about 3%) (Hannaford-Agor et al., 2002). In the 46 hung jury cases in the researchers' sample, the predominant explanation was the weakness of the evidence (Hannaford-Agor et al., 2002).

Holdout Jurors Rarely Manage to Turn Around the Jury's Verdict

Although it is dramatic when Juror #8, the initial holdout in *12 Angry Men*, manages to win 11 jurors to his side during the deliberations, this turnabout rarely occurs on actual juries.

Social scientists have found that it is difficult for one holdout juror to remain a holdout without any other support, and it is exceedingly difficult for that one holdout to change the votes of 11 other jurors. Valerie Hans and Neil Vidmar noted that when there is only one holdout, or even two, it is difficult to withstand group pressure (Hans & Vidmar, 1986). The holdouts end up joining the majority. They rarely end up converting the majority to their point of view. For holdout jurors to succeed in turning around the jury, there usually must be three or four jurors taking that point of view. It is hard for one juror to withstand the group pressure, much less to convince 11 other jurors to change their minds (Simon, 1992). Saul Kassin and Lawrence Wrightsman observed that holdout jurors might go along with the majority because of two types of pressure: informational and normative (Kassin & Wrightsman, 1988). With informational pressure, the majority presents information or arguments that actually lead the holdouts to change their minds and agree with the majority. With normative pressure, however, the holdout jurors go along with the majority, not because they are persuaded by the merits of their position, but because they feel pressure to conform.

Holdout Jurors Rarely Pursue an Independent Investigation

In American jury films, the holdout juror might pursue an independent investigation during or after jury service, but on actual juries this rarely happens. During the trial, a juror is expected to decide the case solely on the evidence presented in the courtroom. An independent investigation during the trial or deliberations, if discovered, would be grounds for a juror's removal and even sanctions, and possible grounds for a mistrial. Following the trial's conclusion, actual jurors might appear in court when the defendant is sentenced, and they might even follow the case on appeal, but they rarely undertake their own independent investigation.

In the jury films *One Angry Juror* and *Trial by Jury*, the holdout juror undertakes her own independent investigation after the jury has been dismissed. In *One Angry Juror*, Sarah Walsh investigates the defendant's case when she becomes his lawyer in the second trial. In *Trial by Jury*, the holdout juror investigates further because she was coerced into being a holdout and must take matters into her own hands in order to survive after the jury trial. Even in *12 Angry Men*, the jury conducts its own investigation, albeit during the deliberations rather than afterward. Juror #8 brings a switchblade knife into the jury room and the jury discusses whether the exhibit knife is as distinctive as the prosecutor had argued.

The film scenario of the holdout juror who investigates the case after his or her jury service, while commonplace in American jury films and even in early British jury films (Marder, 2018), is highly unlikely in actual jury trials. At most, there are cases in which the jurors feel a sense of responsibility and decide to attend the sentencing (Marder, 2011). Other jurors might be interested in following the case on appeal, and some trial judges keep them informed by sending them a letter with an update about the appeal (Marder, 2001). However, there was one case in which a journalist who served as a juror investigated it afterward and wrote about his findings (Finnegan, 1994).

Holdout Jurors Are Not Usually Coerced to Be Holdouts

In American jury films such as *Trial by Jury* and *The Juror*, jury duty becomes a dangerous endeavor. Although true in jury films, this is not true in practice. There are a number of safeguards to protect jurors and to guard against jury tampering. In some American jury films, these protections prove ineffective, but in practice they usually prevent interference with the jury.

In *Trial by Jury* and *The Juror*, the main character approaches jury duty with civic pride and a willingness to serve. However, once Valerie in *Trial by Jury* and Annie in *The Juror* are seated, they are threatened by the Mafia and have no one to assist them.

Although there are a number of practices to help keep jurors safe, these work with actual juries, but not with film juries. For example, in both these films, the judge could have seated an anonymous jury, in which the jurors were identified by number rather than name (Mangat, 2018). This practice was used in the criminal trial of El Chapo, the Mexican kingpin drug dealer who kept escaping from Mexican prisons and was tried and convicted in federal court in New York (Hamilton, 2018). The goal is to prevent jury tampering and coercion of jurors by defendants who are willing to use force or the threat of force. Anonymous juries were not used in either *Trial by Jury* or *The Juror*. In some actual cases, jurors' identities are not released until sometime after the trial (*United States* v. *Doherty*, 1987). Appellate courts have upheld this practice as long as there is not unnecessary delay.

Another practice that courts use to protect jurors is to sequester them during the trial and deliberations. When they are not in court, they are in a hotel, where they stay overnight and have their meals. They are under the supervision of a marshal. Not only are they kept apart from family and friends, but also from anyone who might try to influence their vote through threats or bribes. In addition, the marshal has the task of ensuring that they are not exposed to media coverage of the trial. The jury in *Trial by Jury* was not sequestered, and the jury in *The Juror* was not sequestered until the deliberations. Moreover, The Teacher had no difficulty entering the hotel room where Annie stayed even though the jurors were guarded by a marshal.

When the jury deliberates, it does so in a jury room that no one else can enter. The bailiff takes the jurors to the jury room and makes sure that the jury is not disturbed.

In addition, the jury's deliberations are protected by the secrecy of the jury room. In *The Juror*, The Teacher was able to breach the secrecy of the jury room by insisting that Annie wear a device that allowed him to hear the deliberations. This might happen in film, but would be unlikely in real life. A federal statute prohibits jury deliberations from being recorded, taped, filmed, or transcribed. This statute, 18 U.S.C. § 1508, was passed after Kalven and Zeisel had recorded jury deliberations as part of their study, though they had obtained the permission of the parties, the trial judge, and the appellate court in advance. However, they did not have the permission of the jurors. Most important, some members of Congress viewed the breach as a "bugging" of the jury room ("Warning 'intruders,'" 1955), and Congress made sure, by passing a statute, that it could not happen again at the federal level, and many states followed suit. In two states, Wisconsin and Arizona, which permitted two television stations (WGBH and CBS, respectively) to film jury deliberations for two special television programs, all participants, including the jurors, had to consent. Although these statutes and practices protect most actual juries from jury tampering, they do not protect the juries in films when the defendant's henchmen are willing and able to violate the law.

Actual Hung Juries May Feel That They Have Failed

In the jury films in which there is a hung jury, the holdout juror acts based on principle (*One Angry Juror*) or coercion (*Trial by Jury*). In either situation, the jurors in the film who end up on a hung jury do not feel bad that they were unable to reach a verdict. Although the other jurors, as well as the prosecutor, do not understand how Valerie voted not guilty in *Trial by Jury*, they accept that the jury reached an impasse and was unable to render a verdict. Similarly, the jurors in *One Angry Juror* do not feel bad about the hung jury, nor does holdout Sarah Walsh, who was convinced that the prosecutor had not met his burden of proof.

In contrast, actual jurors express considerable disappointment if their jury does not reach a verdict. In one study, jurors on hung juries held more negative views of their jury deliberation than jurors on juries that reached verdicts (Hannaford-Agor et al., 2002). In one high-profile case, the first trial of former Illinois Governor Rod Blagojevich, which ended with a hung jury, the foreperson understood that hung juries are part of the American jury system, but he was still disappointed because he felt that his jury had failed in its task. The press portrayed the holdout juror as wrongheaded (St. Clair, 2010). However, the other jurors respected the holdout, but still were frustrated about being a hung jury. After all, the jury is charged with reaching a verdict. Indeed, when a jury reaches an impasse, the judge typically delivers an *Allen* charge in federal court or a similar charge in state court that tells the jurors to try to reach a verdict (*Allen* v. *United States*, 1896). The charge exhorts jurors to listen to each other, but also recognizes that they need not change their mind if they believe they are right. The charge is colloquially known as a "dynamite charge," based on the idea that it will act as dynamite and clear the logjam. The message is that jurors should do their best to reach a verdict. The message that the foreperson took away from the hung jury in the first Blagojevich trial was that the jury had failed because it did not reach a verdict (Davey & Saulny, 2010).

The hung jury performs an important and complicated role in the American jury system. Zeisel described the hung jury as "paradoxical" because it permits the holdout to act in accordance with his or her conscience, yet if there are too many hung juries, the system cannot function (Zeisel, 1971, p. 719). Even though the foreperson in the Blagojevich trial respected the holdout for voting her conscience, he was disappointed that the jury had not accomplished its task. Although actual jurors on a hung jury might have this response, this is not portrayed in American jury films, which tend to glorify the holdout and the hung jury.

LESSONS THAT VIEWERS MIGHT TAKE AWAY FROM AMERICAN JURY FILMS

Although viewers understand that films about juries do not necessarily depict how they function in real life, American jury films are widely watched in the United States and are available internationally. Thus, they can "inform" viewers about how American juries work. Many American viewers have never stepped inside a courtroom, much less served on a jury. A film about a jury might be their introduction to the jury system. For viewers outside the United States who live in countries that do not have traditional juries, American films might be the only way they learn about them. As described earlier, one lesson that viewers might take away from American jury films is the prevalence of holdout jurors and hung juries, and this is an incorrect view of what happens on actual juries.

However, viewers in the United States and other countries could take away another lesson from *12 Angry Men*, which is that ordinary citizens do ultimately learn to take their role as jurors seriously and to perform it responsibly, and this lesson reflects actual jurors' experiences as well. In *12 Angry Men*, the jurors eventually learn to proceed carefully and conscientiously when determining the facts that will decide a young man's fate. This empowering lesson might be one reason why *12 Angry Men* has endured for over 60 years in the United States and why the film has been remade in democracies such as Germany, Spain, India, Japan, and the Netherlands, as well as in authoritarian countries such as Russia and China.

American Jury Films Might Lead to Incorrect Views about the Prevalence of Holdout Jurors and Hung Juries

A viewer who watches American jury films might take away the lessons that all juries involve a holdout juror, and sometimes the holdout juror produces a hung jury and other times the holdout juror manages to persuade 11 other jurors to change their minds. The viewer who drew such lessons would be mistaken about what happens on most actual juries, but would be drawing a reasonable conclusion based on American jury films such as *12 Angry Men*, *Trial by Jury*, *The Juror*, and *One Angry Juror*.

It is hard to know whether other countries, such as Spain, which adopted the traditional jury in 1995, or some provinces in Argentina, which introduced the traditional jury in 2017, opted for majority verdicts because the jury proponents in these countries learned about juries from American films. It is interesting that in the United States all federal courts and all state courts now require unanimous verdicts in serious criminal cases (*Ramos* v. *Louisiana*, 2020). Yet, when countries or provinces that are new to traditional juries opt for traditional juries they often forgo the unanimity requirement even though there are compelling reasons to adopt it, such as encouraging more thorough deliberations, giving every juror an equal vote, listening to all jurors' views, and having to persuade jurors with different points of view (Diamond, Rose, & Murphy, 2006; Hastie, Penrod, & Pennington, 1983).

The Empowering Message of 12 Angry Men *in Other Countries*

Admittedly, viewers in other countries might not have seen many of the American jury films, such as *Trial by Jury*, *The Juror*, and *One Angry Juror*, but there is strong evidence that viewers in a surprising number of countries are familiar with *12 Angry Men* or at least its story line. In many countries, including Germany, Russia, China, Lebanon, India, Japan, Spain, and the Netherlands, there have been remakes of *12 Angry Men*. Most of these remakes follow the plot of *12 Angry Men* but are set in contexts that each country's viewers would understand. *12 Angry Men* might have widespread appeal, not only because it teaches viewers about the American jury, but also because it suggests how ordinary citizens anywhere can learn to work together as a jury and to take their fact-finding and decision-making responsibilities seriously, even if they did not do so initially.

Foreign Remakes of *12 Angry Men*. Foreign versions of *12 Angry Men* have been made in countries that do not have a traditional jury system as well as in countries that do, and in countries that are democratic as well as in countries that are authoritarian.

In Russia, which reinstated juries in 1993, though they remain limited in practice, well-known filmmaker Nikita Mikhalkov produced a Russian version of *12 Angry Men* called *12* (2007). The Russian version focuses on a young Chechen fighter charged with killing his foster father (Thaman, 2007). In *12*, the jury deliberates in a school gymnasium. This change in setting seems unnecessary except that the gymnasium is large, contains equipment that can be used to reenact some of the testimony, and allows for occasional references to shoddy workmanship. The lights go out intermittently, the heat is erratic, and birds fly in and out, perhaps symbolizing the jury's freedom to decide or presaging the defendant's ultimate freedom.

The Russian version maintains the basic evidence from *12 Angry Men*, including the knife, the testimony of the old man who claims to have seen the defendant fleeing, and the testimony of the female witness who is nearsighted. But this version also includes elements that would speak to a Russian audience, such as stereotypes held about a Jewish juror. The prejudice is directed toward Jews in this version, unlike the American version in which one of the jurors expresses prejudice toward Puerto Ricans.

The Russian *12* has an unusual twist at the end. After what appears to be the final unanimous not-guilty vote, the foreperson suddenly changes his vote to guilty. He worries that if the defendant goes free it will produce an endless cycle of violence, including the death of the defendant. In the end, the foreperson agrees to vote not guilty, but says that he will look after the defendant.

More recently, in 2015, Chinese theater director Xu Ang made his first foray into films and created a remake of *12 Angry Men* called *12 Citizens* (2015). Xu said he was drawn to the story because it examines people's biases. He explained: "'Every person wants fairness and justice. But to get rid of prejudices is very difficult [. . .] [E]fforts to pursue the truth need to be respected'" (Makinen, 2015). China does not have a traditional jury system, but it now has lay judges working with professional judges on people's courts. Xu tried to create a context that viewers would understand. He shows the jury trial as part of a law school exam about Western legal proceedings in which the parents of the students serve as mock jurors after observing a mock trial presented by the students. The defendant in *12 Citizens* is a rich young man from Henan province charged with killing his birth father. The film raises the issue of prejudice toward people from the provinces as well as prejudices that the rich hold about the poor and vice versa.

12 Citizens follows closely the story line of *12 Angry Men*, but makes some adjustments so that it resonates with Chinese viewers. For example, Juror #7 in the American version is a marmalade salesman, whereas Juror #7 in the Chinese version is a noodle salesman. Except for these small differences, the jurors in the Chinese version track the jurors in the American version, as does the evidence.

12 Citizens, like *12 Angry Men*, teaches that citizens need to take responsibility for a decision, especially one as important as whether the state has established that a young man committed a crime. The jurors in the Chinese version vote immediately and want a quick verdict. The responsibility falls to Juror #8, as in the American version, to slow down the deliberations and to ensure that they discuss the evidence carefully and with everyone's participation.

An Indian version of *12 Angry Men* called *Ek Ruka Hua Faisla* (1986) also follows the story line of *12 Angry Men* quite closely. There are few adjustments for an Indian audience, except that this version uses Indian actors speaking in Hindi. Other than several jokes at the expense of the Indian government, there is little Indian context provided.

One of the more interesting versions of *12 Angry Men* is *12 Angry Lebanese: The Documentary* (2009). The filmmaker, Zeina Daccache, went to Roumieh Prison in Beirut, Lebanon, and undertook a theater project with 45 prisoners. The 18-month project culminated in the performance of *12 Angry Men*, in which prisoners played the 12 jurors. They used the script from *12 Angry Men*, which had been translated into Arabic. The theater production included eight performances that spanned over two months. The prisoners' friends and families attended, as did Lebanese government officials.

Remarkably, in this version of *12 Angry Men*, the theater performance was the catalyst for the participating prisoners to reexamine their lives, feelings, and commitment to the theater group. The documentary does not explain why *12 Angry Men* was selected as the play. One reason could be that the subject matter was one that the prisoners could relate to on a personal level. The play focuses on jurors who must decide whether to convict or acquit a young man charged with the murder of his father. A number of prisoners were in prison for murder. Another reason is that some of the prisoners played jurors that they felt reflected their personalities. The men also understood the importance of the jury and the need for jurors to rely on evidence rather than intuition.

The viewer never sees *12 Angry Men* actually performed, but hears lines from the film as the men rehearse the play. The lines from *12 Angry Men* are familiar, and yet, this version is also different because of the context: it is a film of the prisoners preparing to perform the play in prison. The play proves to be transformative for the participants. For the first time, the prisoners feel connected to family and friends outside the prison and have newfound hope for the future. The theater performances also have practical consequences. The closing frames of the documentary indicate that Lebanon instituted a sentencing reform not long after the theater performances took place.

Aspirations Expressed in *12 Angry Men*. The spread of *12 Angry Men* to countries with and without juries and to democracies and authoritarian regimes alike makes it clear that *12 Angry Men* resonates with people in many countries. The film is not limited to a particular legal system, form of government, or generation of viewers. The film's spread to other countries and its endurance in the United States might be because it addresses such issues as fairness, responsibility, and the role of ordinary citizens in the careful search for truth.

Of course, the jury in *12 Angry Men*, though not diverse by gender or race, is diverse by background, profession, age, and experience (Ellsworth, 2003). It includes men who act out of prejudice, ignorance, and self-interest, as well as one man, Juror #8, who stands up to the group and takes an unpopular stance. He is uncertain of the correct verdict, but believes that the group must work together in the face of imperfect knowledge to understand the evidence as best it can. The jurors do not know the truth, but the best they can do is to put aside prejudice and personal animosities and assess the evidence as carefully and critically as they can.

The jurors' liabilities turn into assets as they draw from their experience to explain the evidence. For example, Juror #5 grew up in poverty and knows how to use a switchblade knife because it was prevalent in the neighborhood of his youth. Similarly, Juror #9, the elderly juror, understands why the elderly witness might have testified that he heard the defendant shout "I'm going to kill you" before he heard a thump on the floor above him, and thought he saw the defendant run down the stairs (Rose, 1972, pp. 238, 245). As Juror #9 explains, this elderly witness was a poor, meek man who needed to feel important just once in his life. However, the message to Juror #10, who is prejudiced against Puerto Ricans, is that prejudice will interfere with judgment. This point is made dramatically when one juror after another stands up and turns away from Juror #10 after he has delivered his tirade against Puerto Ricans.

The jurors in *12 Angry Men* did not have any legal training, but they performed their task with a greater sense of responsibility than any of the professionals in the trial. The judge delivered his instructions in a monotone, suggesting he was bored with the proceedings. The defense attorney did not challenge the prosecutor's version of events, perhaps, as Juror #8 suggests, because he viewed it as a lost cause and did not want to invest any more time in it than necessary. The message of Juror #8 to his fellow jurors is that each juror needs to act responsibly. They cannot depend on the work of others, even professionals, when the life of the defendant is at stake. The importance of personal responsibility is a message that could resonate with people in different countries, no matter the form of government or legal system.

The remakes of *12 Angry Men* in countries that do not have a jury system, such as China, India, Lebanon, and Germany, suggest that what resonates with audiences is the focus on a group of strangers who have to work together to make a critical decision. Human nature urges them to make quick work of their decision, but they learn to do the hard work of sifting through evidence to reach what they believe is the correct verdict.

Each foreign version of *12 Angry Men* uses the language and actors of the country in which that version was made. The remake is accessible to people in that country and ensures that the message of *12 Angry Men* reaches new viewers in countries across the globe. Each remake suggests that the lessons of *12 Angry Men* can take effect in viewers' own countries. The jurors in the American and foreign versions of *12 Angry Men* are ordinary citizens. They are no better or worse than any other group of citizens. Yet this group, after some urging by one of its members and a lot of give-and-take, eventually becomes a jury that tries to perform its task responsibly. The message is if it can happen to this ordinary group of men in the American version of *12 Angry Men*, it can happen to any group of citizens in any country anywhere in the world.

These foreign versions, almost all of which follow *12 Angry Men*'s story line closely, show that a group of ordinary citizens – whether from Russia, China, or India – can learn to work together as jurors. They might take a while to learn their role, but once they do, they proceed to examine the evidence carefully, to make use of everyone's recollections and experiences, and to identify and resist prejudice when it clouds different jurors' judgment.

This film portrayal of jurors as understanding their role and performing it responsibly accords with actual jurors' experiences in the United States. Actual jurors might be initially reluctant to embrace their role as jurors. They resist their summons and want to be excused (Boatright, 1998). However, once they are impaneled, they try to perform their role as ably as possible. They also leave their jury experience with a positive view of the jury (Diamond, 1993).

CONCLUSION

American jury films offer Americans and viewers in other countries a number of lessons about the jury. These films, including *12 Angry Men*, *Trial by Jury*, *The Juror*, and *One Angry Juror*, focus on the holdout juror. In some films, such as *Trial by Jury* and *One Angry Juror*, the holdout remains a holdout and produces a hung jury. In other films, such as *12 Angry Men* and *The Juror*, the holdout manages to persuade the other jurors to change their votes. These are unlikely outcomes on actual juries, but occur in American jury films. American jury films rely on holdouts to create dramatic tension, but this suggests incorrectly that holdouts and hung juries are prevalent in practice.

Although it is hard to know how much viewers learn about the jury from American jury films, the foreign versions of *12 Angry Men* suggest that this American jury film has reached a global audience. Filmmakers in countries that vary by form of government and legal system have remade this film, which suggests that it speaks to people around the world. Sidney Lumet's *12 Angry Men* offers the jury as the best way to counter prejudice, to provide fairness, and to undertake careful fact-finding when the facts are unclear. Although the jurors in *12 Angry Men* are just ordinary citizens, they eventually learn their role and perform it responsibly, as most actual jurors try to do. Although not all countries share *12 Angry Men*'s view of the jury as a panacea, several have moved in this direction.

Acknowledgment: I want to thank Mandy Lee, Research & Instructional Services Librarian at Chicago-Kent College of Law, for finding the foreign remakes of *12 Angry Men*. She not only discovered the different foreign remakes but also located copies with English subtitles so that I could watch them and understand them.

REFERENCES

Allen v. United States, 164 U.S. 492 (1896).

Asimow, M. (2007). *12 angry men*: A revisionist view. *Chicago-Kent Law Review*, *82*, 711–716.

Balashov, A., Gurevich, S. (Producers), & Mikhalkov, N. (Director). (2007). 12 [Motion picture]. Russia: Mosfilm Studios.

Boatright, R. G. (1998). *Improving citizen response to jury summonses: A report with recommendations*. Chicago: American Judicature Society.

Capra, F. (Producer), & Capra, F. (Director). (1939). Mr. Smith goes to Washington [Motion picture]. United States: Columbia Pictures.

(1946). It's a wonderful life [Motion picture]. United States: Liberty Films.

Chatterjee, B. (Producer), & Chatterjee, B. (Director). (1986). Ek ruka hua faisla [A pending decision] [Television film]. India: Eagle Home Entertainment.

Clover, C. J. (1998a). Movie juries. *DePaul Law Review*, *48*, 389–405.

(1998b). God bless juries! In N. Browne (Ed.), *Refiguring American film genres: History and theory* (pp. 255–277). Berkeley, CA: University of California Press.

Daccache, Z. (Producer), & Daccache, Z. (Director). (2009). 12 angry Lebanese: The documentary [Motion picture]. Lebanon: Catharsis-LCDT.

Davey, M., & Saulny, S. (2010, August 19). Jurors fault complexity of the Blagojevich trial. *New York Times*, p. A1.

Diamond, S. S. (1993). What jurors think: Expectations and reactions of citizens who serve as jurors. In R. E. Litan (Ed.), *Verdict: Assessing the civil jury system* (pp. 282–305). Washington, DC: The Brookings Institution.

Diamond, S. S., Rose, M. R., & Murphy, B. (2006). Revisiting the unanimity requirement: The behavior of the non-unanimous civil jury. *Northwestern University Law Review*, *100*, 201–230.

Ellsworth, P. C. (2003). One inspiring jury. *Michigan Law Review*, *101*, 1387–1407.

Finnegan, W. (1994, January 31). Doubt. *New Yorker*, pp. 48–67.

Fonda, H., Rose, R. (Producers), & Lumet, S. (Director). (1957). 12 angry men [Motion picture]. United States: Orion-Nova Productions.

Fufang, W. (Executive Producer), & Xu, A. (Director). (2015). 12 citizens [Motion picture]. China: Juben Production Company.

Hamilton, K. (2018, February 14). Can El Chapo get a fair trial? *Vice News*. https://news.vice.com/en_us/article/7x7x3a/can-el-chapo-get-a-fair-trial

Hannaford-Agor, P. L., Hans, V. P., Mott, N. L., & Munsterman, G. T. (2002). *Are hung juries a problem?* Williamsburg, VA: National Center for State Courts.

Hans, V. P., & Vidmar, N. (1986). *Judging the jury*. New York: Plenum Press.

(1991). *The American jury* at twenty-five years. *Law and Social Inquiry*, *16*, 323–351.

Hastie, R., Penrod, S. D., & Pennington, N. (1983). *Inside the jury*. Cambridge, MA: Harvard University Press.

Jimeno-Bulnes, M. (2007). A different story line for *12 angry men*: Verdicts reached by majority rule – The Spanish perspective. *Chicago-Kent Law Review*, *82*, 759–775.

Kahn, H. (Producer), & Kaufman, P. A. (Director). (2010). One angry juror [Television film]. United States: Front Street Pictures and Lifetime Television.

Kalven, H., Jr., & Zeisel, H. (1966). *The American jury*. New York: Little, Brown and Company.

Kassin, S. M., & Wrightsman, L. S. (1988). *The American jury on trial: Psychological perspectives*. New York: Hemisphere.

Landsman, S. (2007). Mad about *12 angry men*. *Chicago-Kent Law Review*, *82*, 749–758.

MacKillop, K., & Vidmar, N. (2015). Decision-making in the dark: How pre-trial errors change the narrative in criminal jury trials. *Chicago-Kent Law Review*, 90, 957–980.

Makinen, J. (2015, September 23). "12 angry men," 1 happy director; despite some dire predictions, Chinese filmmaker completes remake of US classic. *Los Angeles Times*, p. E1.

Mangat, L. (2018). A jury of your [redacted]: The rise and implications of anonymous juries. *Cornell Law Review*, 103, 1621–1649.

Marder, N. S. (2001). Juries and technology: Equipping jurors for the twenty-first century. *Brooklyn Law Review*, 66, 1257–1299.

(2007a). Introduction to the 50th anniversary of *12 angry men*. *Chicago-Kent Law Review*, 82, 557–576.

(Ed.). (2007b). Symposium: The 50th anniversary of *12 angry men*. *Chicago-Kent Law Review*, 82, 551–899.

(2007c). The banality of evil: A portrayal in *12 angry men*. *Chicago-Kent Law Review*, 82, 887–899.

(2011). Two weeks at the Old Bailey: Jury lessons from England. *Chicago-Kent Law Review*, 86, 537–583.

(2018). Juries in film and television. In H. N. Pontell (Ed.), *Oxford Research Encyclopedias: Criminology and Criminal Justice*. Oxford: Oxford University Press.

Ramos v. Louisiana, 140 S. Ct. 1390 (2020).

Robinson, J. G., Meledandri, C., & Gordon, M. (Producers), & Gould, H. (Director). (1994). Trial by jury [Motion picture]. United States: Morgan Creek Productions.

Rose, R. (1972). *Twelve angry men*. In G. P. Garrett, O. B. Hardison, & J. R. Gelfman (Eds.), *Film scripts two* (pp. 156–337). Milwaukee, WI: Applause Theatre & Cinema Books.

St. Clair, S. (2010, August 27). Blagojevich holdout explains vote. *Chicago Tribune*, p. 1.

Simon, R. J. (1992). Jury nullification, or prejudice and ignorance in the Marion Barry trial. *Journal of Criminal Justice*, 20, 261–266.

Thaman, S. C. (2007). The good, the bad, or the indifferent: *12 angry men* in Russia. *Chicago-Kent Law Review*, 82, 791–808.

United States v. Doherty, 675 F. Supp. 719 (D. Mass. 1987).

Vidmar, N., Beale, S. S., Chemerinsky, E., & Coleman, J. E. (2007). Was he guilty as charged? An alternative narrative based on the circumstantial evidence from *12 angry men*. *Chicago-Kent Law Review*, 82, 691–710.

Warning "intruders." (1955, October 24). *Newsweek*, p. 32.

Weisselberg, C. D. (2007). Good film, bad jury. *Chicago-Kent Law Review*, 82, 717–731.

Winkler, I., & Cowan, R. (Producers), & Gibson, B. (Director). (1996). The juror [Motion picture]. United States: Sony Pictures Entertainment.

Zeisel, H. (1971). . . . And then there were none: The diminution of the federal jury. *University of Chicago Law Review*, 38, 710–724.

15

The Case for a Hybrid Jury in Europe

John D. Jackson

This chapter considers the apparent declining health of the jury system in Europe and whether the institution has a future within the varied criminal justice systems across the continent. The civil jury has almost completely disappeared from the European scene, even in those common-law systems such as England and Wales where it was firmly embedded over a century ago. This chapter considers whether the criminal jury is destined to do likewise. One striking feature of the developments taking place in European criminal justice systems is that there is a great deal more cross-fertilization and policy transfer across the systems than used to be the case. The jury is not immune from this "cosmopolitanism," and this offers an opportunity for a new "hybrid" jury to emerge. This new jury can retain many of the features of the "traditional" jury, principally the fact that it consists entirely of laypersons who decide the verdict, but can also adopt certain other features that enable it to live up to modern demands for accountability, principally the need to provide some justification for such a verdict.

Before proceeding further, it is important to be clear about what is meant by the traditional jury. According to Jackson and Kovalev (2006), what distinguishes the jury model from other lay adjudication models in Europe is that it is a bifurcated system consisting of two separate panels, a judicial panel comprising one or sometimes more professional judges, and a lay panel (the jury), with the judicial panel directing the lay panel on the law but the lay panel having the sole responsibility of deciding the case. The European Court of Human Rights (ECtHR) has described this jury model as the traditional trial by jury (*Taxquet* v. *Belgium*, 2012, para. 43). This differentiates it from the French *cour d'assises* model, which has transformed from one where the jury was the sole deliberating body to one where the jurors now deliberate jointly with judges and is more aptly characterized as a collaborative or mixed court. On this mixed court, the professional judges and jurors collectively determine all questions of law and fact together, although they cast their votes secretly after the deliberation (Hans & Germain, 2011).

Other distinctive features of the traditional jury model are that (usually) 12 jurors are randomly selected; the jurors deliberate in secret; they deliver a general verdict (guilty or not guilty) without giving reasons; and the verdict has to be unanimous. Some of these traditional features have been diluted. Although in England and Wales, Northern Ireland, and Ireland, there are still 12 jurors who try the case, continental juries have fewer members. Austria has 8 jurors for example, and Spain and Sweden have 9 (Jackson & Kovalev, 2006). Scotland has always traditionally had 15 jurors (P. Duff, 1999). The unanimity rule no longer applies for European juries. A qualified majority verdict, constituting 10 out of 12 votes for conviction or acquittal, is accepted in England, Northern Ireland, and Ireland. In Malta, 6 out of 9 votes can qualify as a verdict, and in Spain, 7 out of 9 votes (Jackson & Kovalev, 2006). A simple majority verdict suffices in Scotland, Austria, Russia, and Belgium (Jackson & Kovalev, 2006; Leib, 2008). Until juries in Denmark and Norway were abolished recently, jurors in these countries were appointed rather than randomly selected (Jackson & Kovalev, 2006). Finally, certain continental juries such as those in Spain and Austria are also required to give reasons for their decisions (Taylor, 2011; Thaman, 2011).

The traditional jury owes its origins to the Anglo-Saxon jury that is often traced back to the Magna Carta in 1215. Clause 39 famously states that "no free man shall be taken or imprisoned or disseised or outlawed or exiled or in any way ruined [...] except by the lawful judgment of his peers or by the law of the land" (Arlidge & Judge, 2014, p. 189). One of the great strengths of the jury has been its ability to adapt to different legal and political cultures, at least in the common-law world. It has had less success in being transplanted onto continental European soil where inquisitorial procedures traditionally associated with civil-law systems have dominated the legal landscape, as opposed to the adversarial procedures associated with the common-law systems. A number of commentators have warned of the dangers of transplanting wholesale adversarial features into inquisitorial jurisdictions (e.g., Grande, 2016; Langer, 2004). This chapter traces the current state of the traditional jury in Europe today and goes on to attribute its decline in continental Europe to its difficulty in fitting in with the non-adversarial or inquisitorial tradition associated with the civil law. The chapter then describes changes in the way that juries are becoming more accountable for their verdicts in European common-law systems and argues that these changes provide a means of exploring the case for a hybrid jury able to appeal to both common-law and civil-law systems in the future.

TRADITIONAL JURY SYSTEMS IN EUROPEAN COUNTRIES

The traditional jury, whose chief characteristic is that it gives laypersons exclusive dominion over determining the defendant's guilt in the absence of professional judges, has waxed and waned over time in continental Europe (Sikich, 2013). In the eighteenth century, Enlightenment thinkers such as Beccaria, Montesquieu, and

Voltaire extolled its virtue as a practical example of the operation of moral proofs, in opposition to the system of legal proofs that relied upon the use of torture to extract confessions (Esmein, 1913). France adopted the jury after the French revolution as a "living incarnation" of French revolutionary and democratic ideals (Hans & Germain, 2011, p. 742). Following the turbulence of the revolution, the jury endured and was retained in the Napoleonic *Code d'instruction criminelle* (Criminal procedure code) of 1808 (Esmein, 1913).

When the code was exported to other parts of Europe, the jury was exported as part of it. During the course of the nineteenth century, all continental European countries introduced jury trials, with the exception of the Netherlands and Luxembourg (Vidmar, 2000). During the twentieth century, however, the system waned as authoritarian rule in Germany, Italy, Portugal, Russia, Spain, and elsewhere took hold over the continent (Lempert, 2001). Although certain countries reinstated the jury once democracy was restored – Spain and Austria are prominent examples (Taylor, 2011; Thaman, 2011) – in other countries, the jury has not returned.

A survey of European lay adjudication systems in 2004–2005 detected a resurgence of support for the jury in the late twentieth century within Eastern Europe as countries broke free from the Soviet Union (Jackson & Kovalev, 2006). Russia in particular introduced jury trials in 1993–1994, and a number of countries in the former Soviet bloc such as Azerbaijan, Georgia, and Ukraine expressed their intention to follow suit (Jackson & Kovalev, 2006). Altogether nine countries within the Council of Europe (besides the common-law jurisdictions of England and Wales, Scotland, Northern Ireland, and the Republic of Ireland) were counted as having traditional jury systems (Austria, Belgium, Denmark, Malta, Norway, Russia, Spain, Sweden, and some Swiss cantons), though some of these countries retained jury trials for a very limited number of offenses (such as violations of press laws in Sweden). A second survey in 2011–2012, however, found that the jury system had declined (Jackson & Kovalev, 2016). The former Soviet bloc countries that had expressed an intention to introduce jury trials had not done so (with the exception of Georgia). Within the Council of Europe (outside the UK and Ireland), the number of countries that continued to have a jury system was reduced from nine to eight. Although Georgia introduced the system in 2009, Denmark abolished it in 2008, and Switzerland did so in 2012. The figure of eight in the 2011–2012 survey has since been reduced to seven as legislation abolishing the jury trial in Norway came into operation on January 1, 2018 (see 16. Juni 2017 nr. 58 (Norway)).

In the common-law fringes of Europe, the traditional jury remains intact in serious criminal cases, although even here there are some signs of decline. In England and Wales, the traditional heartland of the jury system, a professional trial judge can replace the jury where there is a real and present danger of jury tampering (Criminal Justice Act, 2003, s. 44 (Eng.)). Although this professional alternative has been used sparingly, it is symbolic of a mindset that is prepared to sacrifice the principle of jury trial for a more expedient alternative (Jackson, 2002a; Thornton, 2004). In Northern Ireland, single judge "Diplock" trials have become the norm in terrorist cases due to the difficulty of preventing juror intimidation by terrorist organizations (Jackson, 2009). In the Republic of Ireland, the jurisdiction of the Special Criminal Court, which tries serious criminal cases without a jury, has expanded from hearing purely terrorist cases to hearing cases of organized crime as well (Campbell, 2014).

This prompts the question: Why the decline? The waxing and waning of juries has been commonly attributed to whether countries have embraced a system of democracy or not. Tocqueville (1835/1994, p. 283) famously said that throughout the history of trial by jury, "[a]ll the sovereigns who have chosen to govern by their own authority, and to direct society instead of obeying its directions, have destroyed or enfeebled the institution of the jury." There is some truth to the claim that authoritarian regimes would find it impossible to tolerate jury systems because the final verdict is entrusted to a body of laypersons rather than to state officials. Indeed, the jury in Russia has become a mere "decorative" institution in a criminal justice system that functions in much the same manner as it did before (Thaman, 2007, p. 428).

This does not, however, explain why some democracies such as the Netherlands have never resorted to a jury system and why others decided to jettison or marginalize it. The abolition of the jury in Germany in 1924 preceded any rise in authoritarianism and seems attributable to the practical difficulty in trying to find a workable system in which juries could give answers to questions of fact without addressing questions of law (Gorphe, 1937). There appears to be an increasing trend in recent years in which certain democracies (e.g., Denmark, Switzerland, and Norway) that once embraced the jury system have turned away from it. This suggests that democratic government may be a necessary, but not a sufficient, condition for a traditional jury system to function.

Apart from the link between democratic government and the traditional jury, Jackson & Kovalev (2016) have argued that one of the most important conditions from the standpoint of the traditional jury being able to exercise its functions effectively is the need for the legal culture within the state to be supportive of the idea of lay participation in the administration of justice. As the experience of countries in Eastern Europe, such as Russia, illustrates, without this support it is difficult to embed a properly functioning jury system into the administration of justice. But in the next section, it is argued that it is not just a question of the legal culture supporting the jury system. Rather, if the jury system is to endure, it must fit positively into the dominant procedural tradition in which it operates. While the jury system is underpinned by the adversarial tradition associated with the common law, there are a number of reasons why it has much more difficulty fitting in with the non-adversarial or inquisitorial tradition associated with the civil law.

THE JURY AND PROCEDURAL TRADITION

There has been an ongoing debate as to the main features of the adversarial and inquisitorial (or non-adversarial) traditions associated with common-law and civil-law jurisdictions respectively (Jackson & Summers, 2012). Damaška (1973) has argued that it is possible to locate common-law and civil-law jurisdictions along a spectrum between two ideals: the adversarial ideal involves a mode of proceeding that gives parties to a dispute considerable control over the way in which they wish to present their case, and the inquisitorial ideal arranges proceedings around the notion of an "official and thorough inquiry" driven by the court (p. 564). At first sight, it may seem that there is no reason why the mode of decision-maker need be tied necessarily to one tradition or the other. Adversarial proceedings could be determined by either a professional judge or a jury, and inquisitorial proceedings could be conducted by a lay jury, albeit with some degree of official assistance, as well as by a professional judge.

When the structural and ideological underpinnings of each tradition are probed, however, it becomes apparent why a lay jury is much more closely affiliated to the adversarial tradition than the inquisitorial tradition. Damaška (1986) drew a pair of insightful contrasts between the two dominant traditions. First of all, inquisitorial systems were drawn toward "top-down" hierarchical structures of authority, while adversarial systems were drawn toward coordinate structures of authority where different functions were allocated to independent bodies. Secondly, inquisitorial systems considered that the purpose of the administration of justice was to manage society by implementing the conception of the good life that the state embraces, while adversarial systems considered that the purpose of the administration of justice was to provide a framework for solving conflicts among citizens.

According to Damaška (1974, 1986), the hierarchical ideal, which is modeled on features of continental judicial organization in the inquisitorial tradition, is best pursued by assigning the administration of justice to professional decision-makers who are part of a hierarchical structure and who apply technical standards in their decisions, which can be reviewed by those higher up the hierarchy. Laypersons are unsuited to this role as they are "usually unable and often unwilling to look at criminal cases through the prism of general rules" (Damaška, 1974, p. 491). By contrast, the coordinate ideal, which is based on features that are within the Anglo-American adversarial tradition, is best pursued by assigning the administration of justice to lay decision-makers who are better able than professional decision-makers to apply local community standards rather than general rules.

The contrast between the hierarchical and coordinate ideals of officialdom feeds into different conceptions of the criminal law itself. Within the inquisitorial civil-law tradition the application of law is viewed as a science, whereas the adversarial common-law tradition is much more tolerant of the need for law to be mixed with value judgments and community standards (Lundmark, 2012; Taylor, 2011). When the standards are drawn from the community, there is less of a need for decision-makers from the community to justify their decisions. The largely inscrutable, general verdict (simply affirming whether the defendant is guilty or not guilty) is a crowning example of the jury's autonomous power. But when professional decision-makers are required to apply a centrally imposed criminal code, they must justify their decisions to be in accordance with the code and there must be a mechanism for appellate review so that those further up the legal hierarchy can correct any errors that have occurred.

The jury also fits into a model of administration of justice that views conflict resolution between two parties as the end of the administration of justice, with the two parties able to present their case before a neutral third party in a public oral trial. Back in the nineteenth century, the German jurist Carl Mittermaier saw this connection when he argued, against the tide of other jurists, in favor of a jury system rather than a mixed court consisting of professional judges and laypersons (Koch, 2000). He considered that any examination of the defendant and the witnesses by the judge based on the investigation file was an element of the old inquisitorial system that was incompatible with the new procedures of a public oral trial. In a mixed court, the lay assessors are expected to arrive at their decisions solely based on the evidence at the trial. But the trial is dominated by a judge who has access to the information in the investigation file, which can be used to influence the decision of the assessors. According to Mittermaier, only the jury court could adequately respect the principles of a public oral trial as the jury minimizes judicial interference and allows the parties to put their case directly to it. The jury then bases its decision purely on the evidence presented orally and publicly by the parties. Whatever the position of the mixed court, there is some empirical evidence that purely professional trials are less transparent than jury trials (Jackson & Doran, 1995). In a study carried out in the 1990s comparing jury trials in Northern Ireland with trials tried by judge alone, jury trials produced greater openness and transparency into court procedures by requiring parties to justify their case in open court (Jackson & Doran, 1995). The legal directions or instructions given to the jury also provide a way in which the values of the criminal law can be openly communicated to and reinforced by the public.

But if the jury acts as a driver toward greater openness and transparency, there are costs in terms of the implementation of policy based on a wide-ranging search for the truth. There has been much debate as to whether adversarial or inquisitorial systems are better able to find the truth (Jackson & Summers, 2012). Rather than trying to resolve this debate, some scholars have instead considered that the two systems approach truth-finding in different ways (Grande, 2008; Hodgson, 2006; Weigend, 2003). The adversarial system seeks the interpretive or procedural truth in which the truth emerges from the parties' opposing different views of reality. By contrast, the substantive or ontological truth sought in the inquisitorial tradition is based on a belief in the objective reconstruction of reality. These different approaches reflect the different ends of the administration of justice. In criminal cases, adversarial systems seek to resolve a conflict between two parties (prosecution and defense) as to whether the prosecution case in favor of guilt is satisfied, while inquisitorial systems seek to undertake a court-driven search for the substantive truth as to whether the defendant is guilty of the offense charged. The jury fits well into the former tradition as it will deliberate on the basis of which version of reality put forward by the parties is to be preferred in the course of a concentrated trial, given the limited time that juries can give to their forensic task. This mode of decision-making, however, is ill-equipped to carry out the kind of active investigation that must be undertaken by the decision-makers in the inquisitorial tradition if the decision-makers are to determine the substantive truth (Weigend, 2003).

Another cost to truth-finding from the inquisitorial perspective is the implementation of various exclusionary rules in the common-law trial that can prevent juries from seeing all the relevant evidence in the case, thereby impeding the fact-finder's freedom to pursue the inquiries they wish. The exclusionary rules of evidence have been rather extravagantly claimed to be the "child of the jury" (Thayer, 1898, p. 47). The argument is that exclusionary rules are needed in jury trials as juries are thought to be more susceptible than professional judges to placing more weight on certain kinds of evidence (e.g., hearsay or character evidence) than are really merited. A number of scholars have disputed this view as both an explanation and justification of the rules (Damaška, 2007; Schauer, 2006). Instead, they have argued that the adversary system of party control of the evidence creates its own dynamic for rules requiring that quality controls be put upon the admission of evidence and for evidentiary regulation to prevent information overload and unfair surprise (Damaška, 1997). But, even if the jury system has not *created* the common-law rules, the jury has played an important institutional role in *reinforcing* their exclusionary nature by enabling a bifurcated trial structure to be developed that effectively excludes the ultimate decision-maker from becoming privy to inadmissible evidence. In the unitary juryless trial, by contrast, the professional judge, who determines the admissibility of evidence cannot, as the ultimate decision-maker, be precluded from being privy to the items of evidence that he or she has excluded.

A final epistemic deficit that juries are said to bring to the truth-finding process from the inquisitorial perspective is their failure to give reasons for decisions. The claim here is not necessarily that providing reasons enhances truth finding per se. Reasons, especially when they are the result of collective deliberation, may be nothing other than ex post facto rationalizations of mental processes that do not improve the quality of decisions that are already made. The claim is rather that the absence of reasons inhibits appellate review and is an "anathema" to a system of justice committed to hierarchical control (Damaška, 1997, p. 45). An example of this inhibition is the way in which the English Court of Appeal has felt unable to reverse jury verdicts unless there is some fresh evidence in the case (S. Roberts, 2018). As the law stands, the Court of Appeal is unable to interfere with a verdict on the basis of perversity or inconsistency so long as "it is possible to postulate a rational line of reasoning in the verdicts given" (R. v. Mirza, 2004, p. 1133). The threshold that must be crossed before the Court of Appeal will interfere is a very high one. An appellant must persuade the court that any inconsistency between verdicts can only be explained on the basis that no reasonable jury could have arrived at the conclusions reached (R. v. Fanning, 2016). Even if the Court of Appeal were able to interfere, however, there is still a reluctance to do so because the jury verdict is seen as the only permissible constitutional verdict that can be entered in the case of those accused of serious offenses. As a consequence, any ground of appeal based on a lurking doubt about the verdict should be used only in exceptional circumstances (R. v. Pope, 2013).

All these factors would seem to provide ample justification for considering that the traditional jury is alien to the continental tradition of non-adversarial justice and why it has failed to take root in civil-law systems. In the next two sections of the chapter, however, I wish to take up the theme that one of the strengths of the jury system has been its ability to adapt to change. Certain pressures are moving the jury in a direction that is likely to make it appeal more to the civil-law tradition as it adapts toward greater adversarialism at the trial stage. Although crude transplants that attempt to impose features of one procedural tradition onto another without any regard to how they will be received are destined to fail, scholars such as Weigend (2011) have argued that each country's rules of criminal procedure not only are dependent on legal culture and procedural tradition, but also are shaped by political and pragmatic preferences that can change over time and are subject to transfers and transplants. Against this background, there is a case for what I will call a hybrid jury to emerge that is able to appeal to both traditions.

MAKING JURIES MORE ACCOUNTABLE

Over the past 30 years, periodic crises of confidence in the English jury system have led to concerns that jurors have not always been able or willing to take their responsibilities seriously (Jackson, 2016). The latest crisis has emerged from research highlighting incidences of jurors using the internet to access extraneous material about the case that has not been tested in court (Thomas, 2010, 2013). These revelations have been met by a spate of new offenses aimed at jurors who fail to behave properly (Criminal Justice and Courts Act, 2015, Part 3 (Eng.)). But I have argued that it is important to look beyond these individual instances of "unbecoming" behavior and consider whether the existing common-law framework for regulating the modern twenty-first century jury as a collective decision-making body is fit for its purpose. Damaška (1997) has commented on the paradoxical blend of the articulate and inarticulate, the transparent and the opaque, in Anglo-American jury trials. The jury system encourages the trial to be transparent by requiring parties to make their case orally in court and by requiring judges to describe the law through jury instructions. In contrast, the deliberation process is shrouded in mystery, and juries do not traditionally give reasons for their verdicts. Indeed, in England and Wales, it is an offense to "disclose information about statements made, opinions expressed, arguments advanced or votes cast by members of the jury in the course of their deliberations in proceedings before a court or to solicit such information" (Criminal Justice and Courts Act, 2015, s. 74(1)(Eng.)).

Whatever the justification for keeping jury deliberations secret (Jackson, 2002b; Jaconelli, 2002), such lack of transparency is becoming increasingly difficult to sustain. Just as the internet has made it more difficult to keep information about a case from the jury, so social media is making it increasingly difficult to keep information about how the jury deliberated from the wider public. In a recent high-profile rape trial in Northern Ireland, a juror posted comments online addressing the reasons the jury came to its decision (Gallagher, 2018). More importantly, it is becoming increasingly difficult to defend jury secrecy as pressure grows for jurors to be held more accountable for their actions, whether this pertains to their behavior in the jury room or to the decisions that result from it. Where allegations of bias are made by jurors against their fellow jurors before the jury returns its verdict, the ECtHR has held that the judge may be required to investigate them (Jackson, 2002b; Quinn, 2004; Sander v. UK, 2000). Jurors in England and Wales are now directed to report instances of juror misconduct by their fellow jurors to the trial judge (R. v. Thompson, 2011).

The duty to provide reasons has also emerged as a key principle in the context of any decisions that affect the lives of individuals caught up in the criminal justice system, from decisions by the police to arrest a suspect in the first place to decisions by the parole board to release convicted prisoners (Coen & Doak, 2017). Transparency helps to legitimize the exercise of political power (Coen & Doak, 2017; Lippke, 2009). Citizen jurors admittedly are not professionals like police officers, parole commissioners, or judges. However, Lippke (2009) has argued that jurors should be regarded as "quasi-state officials" during the time they serve, as they are entrusted with an important function by the state, and their verdicts are, by law and customary practice, treated as official state pronouncements.

The ECtHR took this position in its Second Section decision in *Taxquet v. Belgium* (2009) when it considered that the lay jury's laconic answers to vague and general questions as to whether the applicant was guilty of murder or attempted murder could have left him with "an impression of arbitrary justice lacking in transparency" (para. 48). In its Grand Chamber decision in *Taxquet* v. *Belgium* (2012), the court noted that a fair trial requires that "the accused, and indeed the public, must be able to understand the verdict that has been given; this is a vital safeguard against arbitrariness" (para. 90). The court, careful to respect each state's history, tradition, and legal culture, differentiated between professional judges, where the accused's understanding of his or her conviction stems primarily from the reasons given in judicial decisions, and lay juries, where the accused's understanding of the reasons for his or her conviction could be satisfied by assessing whether sufficient safeguards were in place, such as directions or guidance provided by the judge. The ECtHR nevertheless upheld the Second Section's decision in *Taxquet* v. *Belgium* that the questions put to the jury in the instant case were insufficient to meet the needs of the ECtHR. In particular, asking the jury questions such as whether the applicant was guilty of murder of a government minister and the attempted murder of the minister's partner and whether he acted with premeditation was not enough for the defendant to understand the court's decision and the part he played in the conspiracy, given that seven other defendants in the case were not convicted of premeditated murder.

Despite the assurance to member states who have retained the jury system that a suitable detailed judicial summation may compensate for the absence of a reasoned decision from the jury, there are a number of grounds for thinking that the system of judicial summation followed by a general verdict could be challenged in future cases. In cases such as *Taxquet*, however detailed and careful the judicial summation on the law may have been, a general verdict of guilty may not do enough to explain what the defendant's role in the conspiracy was, for example whether he was a principal or merely an accomplice. Besides complex cases such as this, proponents of reasoned verdicts have pointed out that, while judicial directions or guidance leading to a general verdict may enable a defendant to understand *how* the verdict could be justified, they do not provide insight into *why* this particular jury reached its verdict (Coen, 2014). It may be presumed that any general verdict of guilt that emerges has been reached in accordance with such a direction. But the difficulty is that defendants are still left in the dark as to whether the jury did indeed convict them on this basis or whether in fact it chose to convict them on some other arbitrary basis. If the criminal trial is considered a communicative enterprise in which defendants are held to account for a criminal offense, they are entitled in return to hold those who have convicted them to account for why they did so (A. Duff, Farmer, Marshall, & Tadros, 2007).

If giving reasons is now considered such a fundamental part of a fair trial, it may be asked why for generations, common-law juries have managed to escape from such an obligation. Notions of fairness change over time, as do rules of evidence and procedure. We have seen that the jury system enables parties to present their case and challenge the case against them, unhindered by a dominant judge. But the adversarial benefit that this instills can be undermined if juries are free at the end of the day to decide the case in any way they choose. Juries are tasked with judicial or quasi-judicial responsibilities to decide the case in accordance with the evidence and in a manner that is fair to the parties. As jurors have become more educated and literate, the value of the old restrictive rules of evidence is being reevaluated and many are being discarded or modified (R. v. H., 1995, p. 613, per Lord Griffiths cited in P. Roberts & Zuckerman, 2010). This has meant that juries are increasingly exposed to certain kinds of evidence such as hearsay and bad character that in previous times would have been regarded as too risky, misleading, or prejudicial to be admitted into the trial. On top of this, we have seen that there are increasing opportunities for juries to gain access through the internet to details about the case that are never subjected to adversarial scrutiny.

The point here is not that juries are necessarily acting irresponsibly in the vast bulk of cases. As juries become more educated and literate, it makes sense to trust them to deal responsibly with more evidence. But in these circumstances it seems all the more appropriate to ask them to explain their verdicts. This is not just a question of what is owed to defendants. In *Taxquet* v. *Belgium*, the ECtHR stressed that the public is also entitled to understand the reasons for the verdict. Similarly, in a recent decision, the Inter-American Court of Human Rights has considered that, in addition to the accused, the victim of the crime and the prosecutor need to understand the reasons for the decision of guilt or innocence, which the jury adopts through its verdict, as a guarantee against arbitrariness (*VRP, VPC and others* v. *Nicaragua*, 2018, para. 263). As juries are required to play a more demanding role in their deliberations on the evidence, affording full integrity to this process would seem to require some justification from them for the verdict (Jackson, 2016).

MOVING TOWARD A HYBRID JURY SYSTEM

If, as I have argued, there is a momentum triggered by the ECtHR toward making jurors more accountable individually for their behavior in the jury room and collectively for their decisions, juries then become more subject to the kind of hierarchical control that decision-makers are subjected to in continental civil-law systems. The question then is whether a hybrid jury – drawing upon common-law roots but more accountable than the traditional jury – could provide a means of giving the jury a more secure future across both common-law and civil-law jurisdictions in Europe. Scholars have noted an increasing hybridization of criminal procedure in general (Delmas-Marty, 2008). Although adversarial and inquisitorial procedures continue to exercise a "long shadow" on European procedural systems (Langer, 2014, p. 887), in recent years there has been so much intermingling between the two traditions, it is becoming more difficult to place systems in the inquisitorial or adversarial box (Weigend, 2011). Weigend (2011) has argued that over the past few decades we have seen a number of hybrid legal systems developing in countries that are traditionally associated with inquisitorial systems (e.g., Italy, Japan, and Spain). These countries are faithful to their inquisitorial roots, but also have distinct adversarial features. Weigend attributes these developments to the influence of human rights treaties such as, in Europe, the European Convention on Human Rights, and to regard for principles of individual autonomy and "equality of arms" or equal treatment between the prosecution and defense. These hybrid systems are also evident in the procedures of the international criminal courts and tribunals (Pocar & Carter, 2013). Typically, in these systems there exists a unilateral pretrial process, often conducted by the police under the guidance of the public prosecutor. But the trial is then marked by having the parties present evidence with the court retaining a right (and obligation) to ensure that relevant issues are covered. In this way, Weigend (2011, p. 408) argued that "an invisible hand" may be at work guiding the criminal process toward a more optimal cooperative model in which the parties and the court work together in an effort to determine the "true" facts.

Although Weigend (2011) did not see the traditional jury as contributing to this compromise model and considered a mixed court to be preferable from the perspective of truth-finding, the question is whether a hybrid jury system could provide a means of reinforcing such a model. Such a jury would retain the chief characteristic of the traditional jury – giving lay jurors exclusive dominion over making the final determination of guilt. This feature helps to encourage openness, transparency, and adversarial party participation during the trial at the expense of reliance on the case file and an overly dominant judge. At the same time, the judge would provide instruction to the jury on the law and how to handle certain types of evidence. To enhance the transparency of the outcome, the jury would provide some justification for its decision. In keeping with the hybridization of the procedures as a whole, the hybrid jury would retain its lay character and thereby enhance the adversarial potential of the trial, but would act more in the mode of the professional judge or the mixed court by providing a justification for its decision, which could be made the subject of greater appellate review.

There are at least three objections to making this hybrid jury a reality in both common-law and civil-law systems. Firstly, there is concern that it is not practical to expect a body of 12 lay jurors to give reasons for a decision. In his concurring judgment in *Taxquet* v. *Belgium*, Judge Jebens said that for the court to require juries to give reasons for their verdicts would undermine the very existence of the jury. It may indeed be unrealistic to expect a lay body of 12 persons to agree collectively on the weight to be given to all the items of proof that make up the evidence for each element of an offense and then to devise a detailed narrative justifying these conclusions. But this would not be necessary for the hybrid jury. All that would be required is that the jury indicates in some manner the primary considerations that led to its verdict.

The experience in those civil-law countries that have retained the jury is that this is possible, albeit that this experience has led to mixed views (Esmein, 1913; Mannheim, 1937; Taylor, 2011; Thaman, 2011). By and large, two procedural mechanisms have been adopted. The first is that the judge can provide juries with a series of questions to answer before they deliberate (leading to what common-law lawyers have called a "special verdict"). Secondly, the jury can be given free rein to explain its verdict within the parameters of the judge's directions (what is sometimes called a "narrative verdict"). Some jurisdictions, such as Spain, have vacillated between both approaches (Thaman, 2011). Depending on the particular panel of judges in a case, the Spanish Supreme Court has adopted both a "flexible" approach, which requires little more than giving answers to propositions in a question list, and a more "demanding" approach, which requires the jury actually to say why and how it arrived at its determination of the facts (Thaman, 2011, p. 634).

The civil-law experience of juries responding to a list of questions has not always been a happy one. It was one of the reasons why juries fell out of favor in Germany (Mannheim, 1937). The legal culture at that time was deeply suspicious of the ability of laypersons to apply the law, and as a result, the jury was required to answer numerous detailed questions in the hope that its task could be limited to the pure facts of the case. When the jury trial was reintroduced in Spain after the Franco era, professional judges at first had great difficulty in articulating the question list (Thaman, 1998). This has been attributable in part to "judges' antipathy toward trial by jury" and their unwillingness to adapt to the new system (Thaman, 2011, p. 631). But when the Spanish Supreme Court began to overturn jury verdicts, the trial courts, at least in part, began to pay more attention to how they directed juries. In Austria, the practice of requiring juries to answer questions has been commended as a means of guiding the jury helpfully through the issues to be determined and has been recommended for export to common-law systems (Taylor, 2011).

When the more demanding approach is taken of requiring that juries provide a fuller set of reasons in narrative form, the task for the jury is no doubt more arduous. Again, the experience has been uneven. In the first year or two of the reintroduced Spanish jury trials, the reasons given were often skeletal; they revealed little information as to why or how the jury reached its conclusions (Thaman, 2011). But other juries sometimes gave "admirably detailed reasons" (Thaman, 2011, p. 631). In Austria, jurors' reasons are reportedly not very enlightening ("with the occasional pleasing exception"), usually being confined to a few words, but there have been cases in which the statement of reasons has proved useful and has even assisted in the avoidance of injustice (Taylor, 2011, pp. 305–306, 325).

Over and above any directions that the judge may give on how to go about providing reasons, juries have been assisted in some European jurisdictions (such as Spain and, before juries were abolished in Switzerland, the canton of Geneva) by a legally qualified clerk or secretary to the court to help juries formulate their reasons (Thaman, 2011). But the danger in allowing any legally trained official to assist in drafting reasons after the jury has deliberated is that he or she may exert undue influence on the jury, which should have exclusive domain over the final decision whether to convict or acquit the accused. Another approach is to employ a trained lay facilitator or mediator to join jurors in their deliberations and assist in the process of providing reasons for the verdict at the end of the deliberation (Coen & Doak, 2017). The facilitator could also act as a conduit between the jurors and the court, helping to clarify any aspects of the written instructions given to them by the judge. Lay facilitators are widely used within "citizens' juries" outside the context of the criminal trial. They are used, for example, when stakeholders in a local community have assembled to deliberate on matters of public administration that affect them and they come up with conclusions and policy recommendations facilitated by a trained moderator (Coote & Lenaghan, 1997).

The broad conclusion from the experience of hybrid juries as they have operated on the European continent is that, with enough judicial guidance given in advance of the jury retiring and where, in particular, written instructions are provided, juries can provide a sufficiently reasoned decision (Thaman, 2011). The experience of inquest juries in the UK, which are required to issue special verdicts and sometimes narrative verdicts, is similarly that this is not an impossible task for juries (Jackson, 2016).

A second objection to the concept of the hybrid jury is that the requirement to give reasons would undermine the independence of juries in making decisions in criminal cases, as these could be scrutinized by judges and the parties and open up a route to more meaningful appellate review. Of course, it is this very prospect that might make juries more attractive in criminal jurisdictions that are used to a culture of hierarchical review. But it is important to distinguish between requiring juries to give reasons and the standard of review that should be applied to these reasons after they have been provided (Lippke, 2009). While the requirement to give reasons opens up the opportunity for a more meaningful review than when no reasons are given, the question of what the standard of review should be can vary according to the degree of hierarchical review that is considered appropriate. To take an example, there may be a consensus that reasoned convictions should be subject to some form of appellate review in order to safeguard against the possibility of a wrongful conviction, although even here there is scope for variation on what the intensity of the review should be. There may be much less consensus on the question whether reasoned acquittals should be subject to appeal. For some, the idea that acquittals should be appealable at all would move the jury away from one of the fundamental rationales for its existence, which is its political or constitutional role in acting as a check on unpopular laws, overzealous prosecutors, and biased professional judges. On this view, the requirement that the hybrid jury provides reasons that are then scrutinized by professional judges further up the legal hierarchy would undermine the jury's independent decision-making and in the case of acquittals would effectively obliterate its nullification function. Here we touch on an important fault line between the coordinate and hierarchical models of authority that underpin the common-law and civil-law systems respectively. But the hybrid jury, which in essence requires the jury to account for its verdict, need not entail any appellate review that would set aside verdicts of acquittal that were legally indefensible (Lippke, 2009).

The case for the hybrid jury can be made without taking a view about the degree to which the jury's nullification role remains important. Common-law systems that wish to preserve this role could do so simply by continuing to deny prosecutors the right to appeal directly from a jury acquittal. Civil-law systems could continue to give prosecutors a right to appeal. What is important is that the parties and the public are given insight into why the jury decided as it did and some avenue of redress is given to the parties when the jury appears to have acted in a wholly arbitrary manner. The hybrid jury's function is not only to issue a verdict but to issue a *reasoned* judgment on the merits of the case according to the evidence. Whatever stance one takes on the nullification function, it cannot be right for a jury to bring in a verdict, whether for conviction or acquittal, that is reached on a basis that is unrelated to the evidence or the merits of the case. We have seen that judges are required under human rights law to investigate allegations of bias in the jury room and, if need be, discharge the jury. When after its deliberation, the reasons given by the jury for the verdict reveal that the jury has reached its verdict in a totally arbitrary or biased manner, the judge should similarly have a duty to quash the verdict and the parties be given an opportunity to appeal against any failure to do so. The importance of upholding the jury's independence should not extend to permitting it to act in a manner that is wholly contrary to its legitimate function.

A final objection takes us back to a vital underpinning of any jury system, namely that there must be support for it within the legal culture in which it operates. It may be argued that a hybrid jury would be unable to secure sufficient support within the legal cultures of both common-law and civil-law systems. A hybrid jury, in which a jury must give reasons for its decision, appears to move juries closer to inquisitorial procedure by making their verdicts more susceptible to hierarchical review. This proposal is likely to meet strong opposition in common-law quarters on the ground that unreasoned jury verdicts are an essential part of the adversarial tradition. In reality, however, throughout the history of the common law, there have been various mechanisms to enable juries to provide a rationale for verdicts, whether in the form of special verdicts, jury riders (consisting of an addendum to the verdict), or simply questioning juries on the basis for their verdict (Coen & Doak, 2017).

Coen and Howlin (2018) have described a wide variety of contexts in which English and Irish juries in the nineteenth and twentieth centuries appended statements to their verdicts on a number of matters, including issues that influenced their reasoning, troubled them, or in their opinion required remediation by the authorities. A more recent mechanism for making the verdict more transparent has been for judges to provide juries with a "route to verdict" in the form of a series of written factual questions that lead logically to a verdict of guilty or not guilty (Leveson, 2015). Although juries are not yet required to answer these questions, providing a route to verdict may encourage greater interaction between the judge and the jury and help the parties to gain an insight into what the jury is thinking during the deliberation (Jackson, 2016). This kind of transparency is hardly incompatible with the adversarial tradition. On the contrary, it has the potential to enhance adversarialism by enabling parties to interact with the judge and jury at the deliberation stage of the verdict and to challenge more effectively any verdict that raises questions about fairness.

The hybrid jury is also likely to meet legal opposition in continental Europe. The notion that lay jurors should be solely responsible for bringing in verdicts of guilty or not guilty is not one that is easy for a legal culture steeped in an inquisitorial tradition to accept. The continental experiment with reasoned verdicts has yet to find a firm footing, but it has not been jettisoned altogether. In the aftermath of the Second Section decision in *Taxquet* v. *Belgium*, the easy solution for civil-law jurisdictions would have been to move toward a mixed court as Denmark and Norway have done. However, Belgium followed Spain in moving toward a reasoned jury verdict (Assize Court Reform Act, 2009 (Belg.)). A hybrid jury helps to move civil-law systems in the direction that many have been moving toward, namely in giving parties a greater role in the trial process. A lay jury that is able to bring in a verdict independently of the judge diminishes the ability of the judge to control the presentation of the evidence.

Time will tell whether the hybrid jury has a future. The inquisitorial tradition, with its demand that judges take the lead in eliciting the evidence and finding the truth, was unable to embrace the traditional jury easily. The adversarial tradition, on the other hand, found it difficult to embrace the notion of an all-powerful judge controlling the presentation and evaluation of evidence. But today's procedural systems in Europe do not divide neatly into inquisitorial or adversarial ideal-types and instead hybrid forms are emerging whereby the trial process facilitates both adversarial presentation and a collective commitment to truth finding. I have argued that within this process of hybridization, there is a role for a hybrid jury, which enhances both adversarialism and truth-finding. Such a hybrid jury would enable parties to present and challenge evidence at trial before an independent lay body guided but not dominated by a professional judge and would also, through a reasoned verdict at the end of trial, open up greater opportunities for scrutiny and challenge than has been the case with the traditional jury. True hybridization, as distinct from simple transplantation, requires a common grammar of guiding principles that gravitate toward meaningful party participation and a shared responsibility for truth-finding. A hybrid jury can play a role in promoting these principles.

Acknowledgment: This chapter is based on a lecture entitled "The Jury in Europe: Obsolete or the Future of the Criminal Justice System?" presented at the Faculty of Law, University of Göttingen, Germany, on January 23, 2018, as part of its Lecture Series on Anglo-American Criminal Law and Justice. I would like to thank the editors for their comments on earlier drafts.

REFERENCES

Arlidge, A., & Judge, I. (2014). *Magna Carta uncovered*. Oxford: Hart.

Campbell, L. (2014). The prosecution of organised crime: Removing the jury. *International Journal of Evidence & Proof*, 18, 83–100.

Coen, M. (2014). "With cat-like tread": Jury trial and the European Court of Human Rights. *Human Rights Law Review*, 14, 107–131.

Coen, M., & Doak, J. (2017). Embedding explained jury verdicts in the English criminal trial. *Legal Studies*, 37, 786–806.

Coen, M., & Howlin, N. (2018). The jury speaks: Jury riders in the nineteenth and twentieth centuries. *American Journal of Legal History*, 58, 505–534.

Coote, A., & Lenaghan, J. (1997). *Citizens' juries: Theory into practice*. London: Institute for Public Policy Research.

Damaška, M. (1973). Evidentiary barriers to conviction and two models of criminal procedure: A comparative study. *University of Pennsylvania Law Review*, 121, 506–589.

(1974). Structures of authority and comparative criminal procedure. *Yale Law Journal*, 84, 480–544.

(1986). *The faces of justice and state authority: A comparative approach to the legal process*. New Haven, CT: Yale University Press.

(1997). *Evidence law adrift*. New Haven, CT: Yale University Press.

(2007). The jury and the law of evidence: Real and imagined interconnections. *Law, Probability and Risk*, 5, 255–265.

Delmas-Marty, M. (2008). Reflections on the hybridisation of criminal procedure. In J. Jackson, M. Langer, & P. Tillers (Eds.), *Crime, procedure and evidence in a comparative and international context: Essays in honour of Mirjan Damaška*. Oxford: Hart.

Duff, A., Farmer, L., Marshall, S., & Tadros, V. (2007). *The trial on trial (3): Towards a normative theory of the criminal trial*. Oxford: Hart.

Duff, P. (1999). The Scottish criminal jury: A very peculiar institution. *Law and Contemporary Problems*, 62, 173–201.

Esmein, A. (1913). *A history of continental criminal procedure: With special reference to France*. Trans. J. Simpson. Boston, MA: Little, Brown and Company.

Gallagher, C. & Ferguson, A. (2018, March 30). Belfast rape trial juror's online comments are referred to AG. *Irish Times*. www.irishtimes.com/news/crime-and-law/belfast-rape-trial-juror-s-online-comments-are-referred-to-ag-1.3445059

Gorphe, F. (1937). Reforms of the jury-system in Europe: France and other continental countries. *American Institute of Criminal Law & Criminology*, 27, 155–168.

Grande, E. (2008). Dances of criminal justice: Thoughts on systemic differences and the search for truth. In J. Jackson, M. Langer, & P. Tillers (Eds.), *Crime, procedure and evidence in a comparative and international context: Essays in honour of Mirjan Damaška*. Oxford: Hart.

(2016). Legal transplants and the inoculation effect: How American criminal procedure has affected continental Europe. *American Journal of Comparative Law*, 6, 583–618.

Hans, V., & Germain, C. M. (2011). The French jury at a crossroads. *Chicago-Kent Law Review*, 86, 737–768.

Hodgson, J. (2006). Conceptions of the trial in inquisitorial and adversarial procedure. In A. Duff, L. Farmer, S. Marshall, & V. Tadros (Eds.), *The trial on trial (2): Judgment and calling to account*. Oxford: Hart.

Jackson, J. D. (2002a). Modes of trial: Shifting the balance towards the professional judge. *Criminal Law Review*, 4, 249–271.

(2002b). Making juries accountable. *American Journal of Comparative Law*, 50, 477–530.

(2009). Many years on in Northern Ireland: The Diplock legacy. *Northern Ireland Legal Quarterly*, 60, 213–229.

(2016). Unbecoming jurors and unreasoned verdicts: Realising integrity in the jury room. In D. Dixon, J. Hunter, P. Roberts, & S. Young (Eds.), *The integrity of criminal process: From theory into practice*. Oxford: Hart/Bloomsbury.

Jackson, J. D., & Doran, S. (1995). *Judge without jury: Diplock trials in the adversary system*. Oxford: Oxford University Press.

Jackson, J. D., & Kovalev, N. P. (2006). Lay adjudication and human rights in Europe. *Columbia Journal of European Law*, 13, 83–123.

(2016). Lay adjudication in Europe: The rise and fall of the traditional jury. *Oñati Socio-Legal Series*, 6. http://ssrn.com/abstract=2782413

Jackson, J. D., & Summers, S. J. (2012). *The internationalisation of criminal evidence: Beyond the common law and civil law traditions*. Cambridge: Cambridge University Press.

Jaconelli, J. (2002). *Open justice: A critique of the public trial*. Oxford: Oxford University Press.

Koch, A. (2000). CJA Mittermaier and the 19th century debate about juries and mixed courts. *Revue International de Droit Penal*, 72, 347–353.

Langer, M. (2004). From legal transplants to legal translations: The globalization of plea bargaining and the Americanization thesis in criminal procedure. *Harvard International Journal*, 45, 1–64.

(2014). The long shadow of the adversarial and inquisitorial categories. In M. D. Dubber & T. Höernle (Eds.), *The Oxford handbook of criminal law*. Oxford: Oxford University Press.

Leib, E. (2008). A comparison of criminal jury decision rules in democratic countries. *Ohio State Journal of Criminal Law*, 5, 629–644.

Lempert, R. O. (2001). Citizen participation in judicial decision making: Juries, lay judges and Japan. *Saint Louis-Warsaw Transatlantic Law Journal*, 1–14.

Leveson, B. (2015). *Review of efficiency in criminal proceedings*. London: Judiciary of England and Wales.

Lippke, R. L. (2009). The case for reasoned verdicts. *Canadian Journal of Law and Jurisprudence*, 22, 313–330.

Lundmark, T. (2012). *Charting the divide between the common and civil law*. Oxford: Oxford University Press.

Mannheim, H. (1937). Trial by jury in modern continental law. *Law Quarterly Review*, 53, 99–117, 388–412.

Pocar, F., & Carter, L. (2013). *International criminal procedure: The interface of civil law and common law legal systems*. Cheltenham, England: Edward Elgar.

Quinn, C. (2004). Jury bias and the European Convention on Human Rights: A well-kept secret? *Criminal Law Review*, 998–1014.

R. v. Fanning [2016] 1 WLR 4175 (Eng.).

R. v. H [1995] 2 AC 596 (Eng.).

R. v. Mirza [2004] 1 AC 1118 (Eng.).

R. v. Pope [2013] 1 Cr App R 214 (Eng.).

R v. Thompson [2011] 1 WLR 200 (Eng.).

Roberts, P., & Zuckerman, A. (2010). *Criminal evidence*. 2nd ed. Oxford: Oxford University Press.

Roberts, S. (2018). Post-conviction review in England and Wales: Perpetuating and rectifying miscarriages of justice. In G. Lennon, C. King, & C. McCartney (Eds.), *Counter-terrorism, constitutionalism and miscarriages of justice*. Oxford: Hart/Bloomsbury.

Sander v. UK, 31 EHRR 44 (2000).

Schauer, F. (2006). On the supposed jury-dependence of evidence law. *University of Pennsylvania Law Review*, 155, 165–202.

Sikich, K. W. (2013). Explaining the presence of the criminal jury in democratic political systems. Doctoral dissertation, American University, Washington, DC.

Taylor, G. (2011). Jury trial in Austria. *New Criminal Law Review*, 14, 281–325.

Taxquet v. Belgium, Application No. 926/05 (January 13, 2009).

Taxquet v. Belgium, 54 EHRR 26 (GC) (2012).

Thaman, S. C. (1998). Spain returns to trial by jury. *Hastings International & Comparative Law Review*, 21, 241–537.

(2007). The nullification of the Russian jury: Lessons for jury-inspired reform in Eurasia and beyond. *Cornell International Law Journal*, 40, 355–428.

(2011). Should criminal juries give reasons for their verdicts? *Chicago-Kent Law Review*, 86, 613–668.

Thayer, W. B. (1898). A *preliminary treatise on evidence at the common law*. Boston, MA: Little, Brown and Company.

Thomas, C. (2010). *Are juries fair?* London: Ministry of Justice.

(2013). Avoiding the perfect storm of juror contempt. *Criminal Law Review*, 483–503.

Thornton, P. (2004). Trial by jury: 50 years of change. *Criminal Law Review*, 119–137.

Tocqueville, A. de (1835/1994). *Democracy in America*. London: David Campbell.

Vidmar, N. (Ed.). (2000). *World jury systems*. Oxford: Oxford University Press.

VRP, VPC and others v. Nicaragua, Inter-American Court of Human Rights (ser. C) No. 350 (2018, March 8).

Weigend, T. (2003). Is the criminal process about truth?: A German perspective. *Harvard Journal of Law & Public Policy*, 26, 157–173.

(2011). Should we search for the truth, and who should do it? *North Carolina Journal of International Law and Commercial Regulation*, 36, 389–411.

16

A Worldwide Perspective on Lay Participation

Sanja Kutnjak Ivković and Valerie P. Hans

This chapter identifies which countries use lay citizens as legal decision-makers and how they use them. We know from past studies that many countries around the world use lay citizens as fact-finders in criminal cases (Vidmar, 2000). The prevalence of lay participation worldwide reflects the values that laypersons can bring to the decision-making process. They can incorporate community values into fact-finding, contribute to the transparency and legitimacy of the legal system, and offer some protection against biased or jaded legal professionals (Diamond & Rose, 2018; Kutnjak Ivković, 1999; Marder & Hans, 2015, 2016).

Lay participation promotes these values, but different countries use lay citizens in their legal systems in different ways. The four main ways in which countries use citizens as decision-makers in criminal proceedings are as jurors on juries, lay assessors on mixed tribunals, lay magistrates or justices of the peace, and lay judges on lay courts (Hans, Fukurai, Kutnjak Ivković, & Park, 2017). The *jury* consists of a group of citizens who decide together on the culpability of the criminal defendant (and, in some circumstances, on the punishment). In *mixed tribunals*, lay assessors (alternatively, lay judges) work alongside legally trained judges to decide questions of guilt and punishment. *Lay magistrates*, alternatively justices of the peace, are not formally trained in law, but decide criminal cases either individually or in small groups. Finally, on *lay courts*, which are not part of the official criminal justice system, laypersons conduct trials and reach decisions about criminal wrongdoing (e.g., popular courts in Cuba; Salas, 1983).

As this book illustrates, a substantial amount of research has been conducted on lay participation in these different forms in different countries. However, prior research has typically focused on a single form of lay participation in a specific country. Consider, for example, the compendium edited by Vidmar (2000), which includes specific chapters on the jury systems of England, the United States, Australia, New Zealand, and other countries. A number of chapters in this book take this same approach as well. For example, Vanoverbeke and Fukurai (Chapter 4) write about Japan, Park (Chapter 5) writes about South Korea, and Jimeno-Bulnes (Chapter 6) writes about Spain.

The single-country approach has a number of virtues. It often includes the historical development of lay participation in the specific country. It can offer an in-depth analysis of how that particular country uses lay citizens. The reader is able to get a detailed sense of a particular form of citizen participation in its political, social, and legal environment.

However, the study of lay participation thus far has been uneven across different forms of lay participation and in different parts of the world. Lay participation in some countries, such as the jury systems of the United States (Diamond & Rose, 2018; Marder, forthcoming; Vidmar & Hans, 2007) and the United Kingdom (Baldwin & McConville, 1979; Lloyd-Bostock & Thomas, 2000), have been the subject of extensive study, whereas other countries, such as the jury systems in Brazil, Ghana, and the Caribbean, have received only scant attention or have been ignored completely. The coverage of different forms of lay participation is also uneven, with juries and lay assessors receiving far more coverage than lay magistrates (Diamond, 1990), justices of the peace (Provine, 1986), and lay courts (Grant & Schwikkard, 1991).

A comprehensive, albeit snapshot, view of lay participation around the globe has substantial value (Hans, 2008). It would be useful to know which approaches countries have taken to involve their citizens in fact-finding in legal cases. It would also be useful to know which approaches are used most often. Do countries use one approach to the exclusion of others? Alternatively, do they adopt several ways to include lay citizens in different courts or for different purposes or in specific types of cases? A snapshot of worldwide lay participation in this era would also serve as a baseline for assessing future shifts and changes in lay participation.

In addition, a comprehensive picture of the global use of lay participation is an important first step in analyzing the antecedents, correlates, and consequences of lay participation in law. As for antecedents, developing a global picture of lay participation would allow us in future work to examine whether there are common experiences, such as a change in government or a decline in judicial legitimacy, that lead countries to adopt new forms of lay participation. Regarding correlates, it would help us to assess how lay participation is associated with legal traditions across countries and with particular types of social and political life. And having a comprehensive picture of lay participation would allow us to explore how variations in the use of lay fact-finding in law have consequences for citizens' legal consciousness and confidence in government. Identifying common problems and the variety of solutions adopted by different countries would also be worthwhile (Vidmar, 1999). In sum, a global picture of lay participation at this particular point in time would allow us to begin to undertake important theoretical and practical work on citizen participation in law.

PRIOR COMPARATIVE RESEARCH ON LAY PARTICIPATION

Although developing a full account of lay participation around the globe is very useful, only a handful of scholars have gone beyond the typical single-country approach or the comparative examination of a small number of countries. This shortcoming is understandable because any attempt to capture the details of lay participation in the world's countries is a massive task. We are fortunate to be able to build on the past research efforts, albeit limited in number and scope, because each has identified a different piece of the puzzle of lay participation.

The four broad comparative efforts that were most useful to us were projects by Thaman (2001), Vidmar (1999, 2000, 2002), Jackson and Kovalev (2006, 2016), and Voigt (2009). The comparative procedure scholar Stephen Thaman organized a groundbreaking international conference in Siracusa, Italy, in 1999, in which he brought together lawyers, judges, and scholars from around the globe to contribute to "Lay Participation in the Criminal Trial in the 21st Century." His conference resulted in several edited publications, most notably the *International Review of Penal Law (Revue Internationale de Droit Penal)* (Le jury dans le procès pénal au XXI siècle, 2001; Thaman, 2001). This publication included country reports on lay participation in 17 countries and 16 special reports that provided additional information.

Vidmar (1999, 2000, 2002) took two approaches to identifying and describing jury systems around the globe. First, he assembled experts from several countries (Australia, Canada, England, Japan, New Zealand, the Republic of Ireland, Northern Ireland, Russia, Scotland, Spain, and the United States) to write articles in which they described the jury system in their countries for a special issue of the journal *Law and Contemporary Problems* (Vidmar, 1999). Subsequently, he asked the authors to update their articles for his book *World Jury Systems* (2000). The book also included an introductory chapter providing historical and comparative perspectives and a concluding chapter on jury systems elsewhere in the world.

Second, Vidmar (2002) enlisted the aid of the Secretariat of the Commonwealth who surveyed member states for information about the laws regarding the use of juries and lay assessors in Commonwealth countries, dependencies, and associated states. Surveys included countries and other jurisdictions in the Channel Islands, the Irish Sea, the South Atlantic region, the Mediterranean, the South Pacific, the Caribbean, South and Central America, Africa, and Asia. Vidmar (2000, 2002) drew on these survey results to report on the use of juries and lay assessors in 46 Commonwealth jurisdictions. Although he noted that his project was descriptive in nature, and had not taken up important normative issues, Vidmar expressed the hope that the Commonwealth Survey would provide "a foundation for future comparative analysis" (Vidmar, 2002, p. 407).

Jackson and Kovalev (2006, 2016) conducted two surveys of experts in the field of lay participation in the 46 Council of Europe countries. Jackson and Kovalev were interested in assessing the connection between countries' use of lay participants in criminal proceedings and their commitment to human rights. In the first survey, conducted in 2004–2005, Jackson and Kovalev obtained information about lay participation in 38 countries and learned that almost three-quarters of these countries (74%) had some form of lay participation at the time of the survey (Jackson & Kovalev, 2006). The countries that used lay participants deployed them in different ways. Some countries used lay participants in only one way, while other countries used lay participants in two or more ways. Jackson and Kovalev determined that 11 Council of Europe countries used trial by jury (24%); 23 countries used mixed tribunals of lay citizens and professional judges (50%); five countries had tribunals in which professional judges worked with expert assessors to decide specific types of cases together (11%); and three countries used a pure lay judge approach (6%). Jackson and Kovalev (2006) noted a striking difference between Western European countries that were members of the European Union, and Eastern European countries that were at that time in transition from the Union of Soviet Socialist Republics (USSR). Western European countries showed a tendency to restrict or limit lay participation, whereas Eastern European countries were inclined to expand it.

In their second survey (Jackson & Kovalev, 2016), with data collected in 2011–2012, Jackson and Kovalev found evidence that the use of lay participation was declining. A few Western European countries had eliminated juries in the interim, whereas some Eastern and Western European countries had shifted from traditional juries to mixed tribunals or limited the jury's scope. Some countries imposed new requirements, such as asking juries to provide reasons for their verdicts (Chapter 11, this volume), after the European Court of Human Rights decided *Taxquet* v. *Belgium* (2010). That decision did not impose a requirement for reasoned verdicts by juries, but it nonetheless emphasized the importance of providing defendants with information about the basis for the verdicts in their cases. Movement toward reasoned verdict requirements effectively reduces jury independence because judges must rule on the adequacy of the reasons and could overturn reasoned jury decisions that seem to them to be inadequate (Burd & Hans, 2018; Chapter 6, this volume). In sum, the second survey revealed limitations or decline in the use of lay participation in both Western and Eastern European countries.

Finally, Voigt's (2009) survey was important because of his empirical approach and the large number of countries he included. He hypothesized that lay participation would be positively associated with judicial independence, less corruption in the judiciary, and more effective government. He sent questionnaires to ministries of justice and other country experts. Of the 80 countries for which he obtained survey information, Voigt determined that at the time of the survey, 53 countries used lay participation in their legal systems (66%), while 27 countries did not (34%). He reported that 27 countries used juries and 35 used lay assessors, with 13 of these countries using both juries and lay assessors. He determined that countries with a history of lay participation tended to have more independent and less corrupt judiciaries, but the effects were modest.

Several other research projects focused on a small number of countries, and these studies supplement the broad surveys of lay participation. For example, Vogler (2005) took a historical approach to trace the development of types of popular justice in countries that were once part of the British Empire. Malsch (2009) made use of courtroom observations and individual interviews to examine lay participation in five European countries. In one project, Kovalev (2010) compared lay participation systems in Russia, Ukraine, and the former Republics of the Soviet Union, with special attention to criminal justice reform in these countries. In another, he focused on selection procedures for jurors and lay assessors in Eurasian countries (Kovalev, 2014). Park (2010) examined new systems of lay participation in East Asia, and found a connection between lay participation and the post-Cold War spread of political democracies in the region. Colvin (2004) surveyed the criminal procedure codes of 12 jurisdictions in the South Pacific, and found that most included some form of lay participation, such as trial by jury or by lay assessors. These more narrowly focused projects are valuable as they offer deeper insights into historical developments as well as the functioning of lay participation in a smaller number of countries.

However, even when we combined the results from the broader empirical projects with the narrower, more focused studies, we still lacked a comprehensive picture of lay participation around the world. Prior research had captured only a subset of countries and had asked a limited range of questions. Our goal was to build on these earlier laudable, albeit limited, efforts to develop an empirical picture of lay participation around the globe.

OUR APPROACH TO CREATING A SNAPSHOT OF LAY PARTICIPATION WORLDWIDE

The aim of our project was to obtain information about the use of lay participation in criminal trials around the world. We were interested not only in whether a country uses any lay participation, but also in the form of lay participation that country uses, as well as other details that we could glean. We relied on the list of United Nations members as the definitive source of countries in the world. Ultimately, we obtained information on 195 countries, including 193 UN member nations and 2 other entities – Hong Kong and Taiwan. Hong Kong is officially a Special Administrative Region of the People's Republic of China, although it operates in many ways as an independent country. Important for our purposes is that it has an independent and distinctive legal system (Kritzer, 2002). Whether Taiwan (the Republic of China) is an independent country or part of China is the subject of considerable debate. Taiwan is recognized as a country by 19 UN member states, although it has no official status in the United Nations (Gilbert, 2018). For ease of reference, in this chapter we will refer to UN member nations and these two entities as countries.

Expert Surveys

We followed Vidmar (2002) and Jackson and Kovalev (2006, 2016) in developing a questionnaire for experts to complete so that we could obtain detailed empirical data about the use and form of lay participation in each country. We invited country experts from embassies and other sources as well as scholars who wrote about or researched lay participation in specific countries to complete our questionnaire. The survey included preliminary questions about the country's legal tradition and the educational requirements for professional judges, and then asked whether that country used lay participation in criminal trials and the form (or forms) it used: juries, lay assessors in mixed tribunals, lay magistrates/justices of the peace, and lay courts. The analyses we provide draw on basic information from the expert respondents. We developed both English and Spanish language versions of the questionnaire.

We drew on multiple sources to obtain lists of individuals who are knowledgeable about lay participation in their country. In our initial effort in the spring and summer of 2007, and a subsequent follow-up effort in the 2007–2008 academic year, we mailed a questionnaire to all foreign embassies in the United States and asked legal advisors working in these embassies to complete the questionnaire. Staff from 55 embassies returned completed questionnaires.

In the 2008–2009 academic year, we sent outreach emails to LLM and SJD students enrolled at Harvard Law School, and LLM and JSD graduates of Cornell Law School, asking them to complete a questionnaire about lay participation in their home countries. These students are foreign lawyers who are quite familiar with the legal systems in their home countries. Twenty-three students completed the online questionnaire. In 2011, we contacted members of different lay judges' associations in Europe when they met at the European Day of Lay Judges and asked them to participate in our online survey. Fourteen lay judges participated in the study.

We also relied on our own network of lawyers and research scholars working in the areas of comparative criminal procedure or lay participation, and we asked them to assist us in our project. We also searched Google Scholar to identify additional scholars who published papers on the judicial system in a specific country. In our first attempt in 2009, 26 experts responded. In our subsequent attempts in 2017–2019, experts from 68 countries responded to our invitation to participate in the surveys. These later attempts included a Spanish language version of our questionnaire that we sent to experts in countries in which Spanish is the main language.

Library and Legal Research

We used library and legal research to obtain basic information from countries not represented in any of our own questionnaires and to develop more details about forms of lay participation in different countries. We began with Vidmar's survey (2000), Voigt's survey (2009), and Jackson and Kovalev's surveys (2006, 2016) to add information about the countries they had studied. In this way, we were able to add 52 countries to our database (25 from Vidmar's study, 7 from Jackson and Kovalev's surveys, and 20 from Voigt's surveys).

In addition, we searched the internet for any information in English about a country's use of lay participation in criminal trials, by including phrases such as "jury," "lay assessors," "lay courts," "lay magistrates," and "judicial system." We particularly relied on Globalex, a program run by the Hauser Global Law School Program at New York University School of Law, as well as the *Nations' Encyclopedia* and *Wikipedia*. The combination of internet research with legal and library research (Kritzer, 2002) produced information from 60 additional countries.

Data Limitations

A challenge for any comparative study of lay participation is the different legal environments and court systems around the world. We instructed the respondents in our expert surveys to describe all forms of lay participation in criminal cases in their country or federation, regardless of whether they are used in their specific province, county, or state. For example, although the respondents in Argentina might be residing in a province that uses the jury, we instructed them to fill out the questionnaire for both juries (used in their province), and mixed tribunals (used in another province). If a country uses a particular form of lay participation, but this form varies across states or provinces (e.g., United States, Switzerland), we instructed respondents to describe either the federal system and/or the system in their state or province. Consequently, our strategy allowed us to collect information about all forms of lay participation used in that country, but it was limited in capturing the full range of types of lay participation in all the states or provinces in that country because the respondents answered about the country as a whole and not just about their own state or province.

Another challenge in comparative research is the diversity of world languages. Although English is the dominant language of business and professional communication in the twenty-first century, it is unrealistic to expect that all information about countries' legal systems can be recorded in English. In our expert surveys, we posted the questionnaire in English and Spanish. In our library research, we were limited to what was posted on the internet or written in published sources in English.

Another challenge is that lay participation might be established in a country's legal documents, such as its constitution or procedural criminal laws, but the country might not have actually put lay participation into effect. In other words, its lay participation exists on the books, but not in practice. For example, the Argentine Federal Constitution of 1853 provided for lay participation, but it was not until 2004 that the first province started implementing the law and creating opportunities for lay participation in the province of Córdoba (Chapter 3, this volume). Because we tried to find even the most basic information about each country, our data collection was more likely to include information about lay participation as it appears on the books and less likely to yield information about how it is actually put into effect.

Our data collection strategies resulted in data that spanned a period of about two decades, starting with Vidmar's 2000 survey. Whenever possible, we used the most recent information about a country. For example, we used Jackson and Kovalev's 2016 survey instead of their 2006 survey. Our dataset contained multiple entries for a handful of countries (e.g., United States, Israel, Italy, Germany, Spain, and Bolivia). In such cases, we used the most recent data source, and/or the most complete source, and created only one entry for each country.

The information that we developed about each country is based on the responses from the country experts or from the written information published in English. To that end, the facts about lay participation in each country are dependent upon the accuracy of the information provided to us either by our respondents or by written sources. Whenever possible, we used more than one source and double-checked the accuracy of information. In 43 out of 98 countries in which the respondents participated in the survey, we had two or more respondents from the same country filling out the questionnaire. We double-checked the accuracy of information before creating a single country record based on expert reports. In 32 out of 43 countries (74%), multiple respondents agreed in their answers. In 9 out of the 10 countries (90%) where they disagreed, we were able to select a more accurate set of answers by comparing their answers with the results from Vidmar's survey (2000), Voigt's survey (2009), and Jackson and Kovalev's surveys (2006, 2016). In one country with a disagreement on whether there is lay participation (Bulgaria), the respondents did not provide any answers about the form of lay participation used, so we supplemented the answers from Voigt's survey (2009) and Jackson and Kovalev's surveys (2006, 2016). Finally, in the library and legal research, we used more than one resource for 39 out of 80 countries. Whenever possible, we also compared the results of our surveys with the results from Vidmar's survey (2000), Voigt's survey (2009), and Jackson and Kovalev's surveys (2006, 2016).

Country-Level Characteristics

Continent: To classify countries/entities by continents, we used the online source *World Atlas* (2019). Although some countries could potentially be classified as belonging to two continents (e.g., Turkey, Russia), the *World Atlas* contains a single-continent designation for each country.

Legal Tradition: Legal tradition is defined as a set of "deeply rooted and historically conditioned attitudes about things such as the nature of law, the role of law in the society, organization of the legal system, and the way in which the laws should be made, applied, and changed" (Reichel, 2008, p. 100). Scholars have identified four modern legal traditions in the world today: civil, common, socialist, and religious/philosophical (Reichel, 2008).

Civil-law tradition, based on Roman law, is the oldest and most pervasive system of law. Approximately 140 countries have their legal systems built completely or partially on the civil-law tradition. It is built on an idea of organizing legal norms into systematic written codes (Reichel, 2008). Examples of countries that belong to the civil-law tradition include Germany, France, Spain, and Poland.

Common-law tradition is the second most frequently used legal tradition. Seventy-six countries have their legal systems built completely or partially on the common-law tradition. It originated in England and spread throughout the world as part of British colonization. It is built on the idea of a legal precedent (*stare decisis*) used in English courts. *Stare decisis* implies that judges are bound in their decision-making by earlier court decisions. Examples of countries that belong to the common-law tradition are the United Kingdom, Australia, and the United States.

Socialist-law tradition is the most recent legal tradition, and with the fall of the communist regimes across Eastern Europe in the 1990s, the least frequently used legal tradition. Only a handful of countries today have legal systems partly based on the socialist-law tradition. It is grounded in the civil-law tradition, modified to accommodate the basic tenets of Marxism–Leninism (Reichel, 2008). Examples of countries that belong to the socialist-law tradition are Cuba, North Korea, and Mongolia.

Religious-law tradition is based on the idea that religious writing is the foundation of the legal system. There are several such dominant religious-law traditions, including countries based on Islamic, Hindu, or Buddhist traditions (Reichel, 2008). With over 1 billion followers, Islam is the most pervasive religion in the world. Because of the large number of followers and the influence of the religious norms on legal rules in Islamic countries, we present the data separately for the countries that at least partly incorporate elements of the Islamic legal tradition. *Islamic-law tradition* is the legal tradition in which the origin of legal rules is divine and the primary sources are the Quran and Sunnah (Reichel, 2008). About 40 countries in the world include Islamic-law tradition as one of the legal traditions. Examples of countries that belong to the Islamic-law tradition are Afghanistan, Egypt, and Saudi Arabia.

In addition to the countries that belong to only one legal tradition, there are numerous countries whose legal systems are built on two or more legal traditions.

They might use a combination of the civil-law tradition and the common-law tradition or the civil-law tradition and the Islamic-legal tradition. Examples of such countries are Canada, Egypt, Japan, and South Africa.

The traditional classification of legal traditions does not incorporate customary law or indigenous traditions. The reason is simple: while all countries belonging to the same legal tradition share common features, and hence, can be classified into families of countries, indigenous systems do not share a mutual legal tradition. Reichel (2008, p. 105) argued that "they are, by definition, confined to a particular locale and are essentially independent of outside influences." Although no country today seems to rely only on customary law (Bracey, 2006), a country's legal system might be built not only on one or more of the four legal traditions, but also on the elements of customary laws. Because customary legal systems could incorporate lay courts, a form of lay participation of interest to this project, we also wanted to capture whether customary law plays a substantial role in a country's legal system.

We categorized legal traditions of each country according to the *CIA World Factbook* (2019), and supplemented it with the judgments of our own expert survey participants when those were available. In addition to the four legal traditions, we noted whether the country also relies on customary law.

Legal traditions not only influence substantive criminal law, such as definitions of crimes and associated punishments, but also procedural law such as processes used to collect evidence and to determine guilt. Lay participation in legal decision-making is part of criminal procedural law, and there are characteristic differences in criminal trial procedure across legal traditions. No countries today use a pure inquisitorial or adversarial procedure. Rather, modern countries have modified these pure models of criminal procedure (Reichel, 2008) as they borrow elements of the other type of procedure. Countries belonging to the *common-law tradition* rely on a modified version of adversarial procedure, in which the opposing sides present evidence before a passive judge who acts as a referee. Countries belonging to the *civil-law tradition* rely on a modified version of inquisitorial procedure, in which a judge takes an active role in developing and examining evidence during the investigatory and trial stages. Countries belonging to the *socialist-law tradition* typically utilize a modified version of inquisitorial procedure, while countries belonging to the *Islamic-law tradition* use a mixture of inquisitorial and adversarial procedures, with substantial variation from country to country.

OUR FINDINGS ON THE EXTENT OF LAY PARTICIPATION AROUND THE WORLD

Our initial aim was to quantify, for the first time, the extent and nature of lay participation in countries around the world. We can now report that a majority of countries use some form of lay participation in legal decision-making. Figure 16.1 is a map of the world's countries, illustrating the specific countries with and without

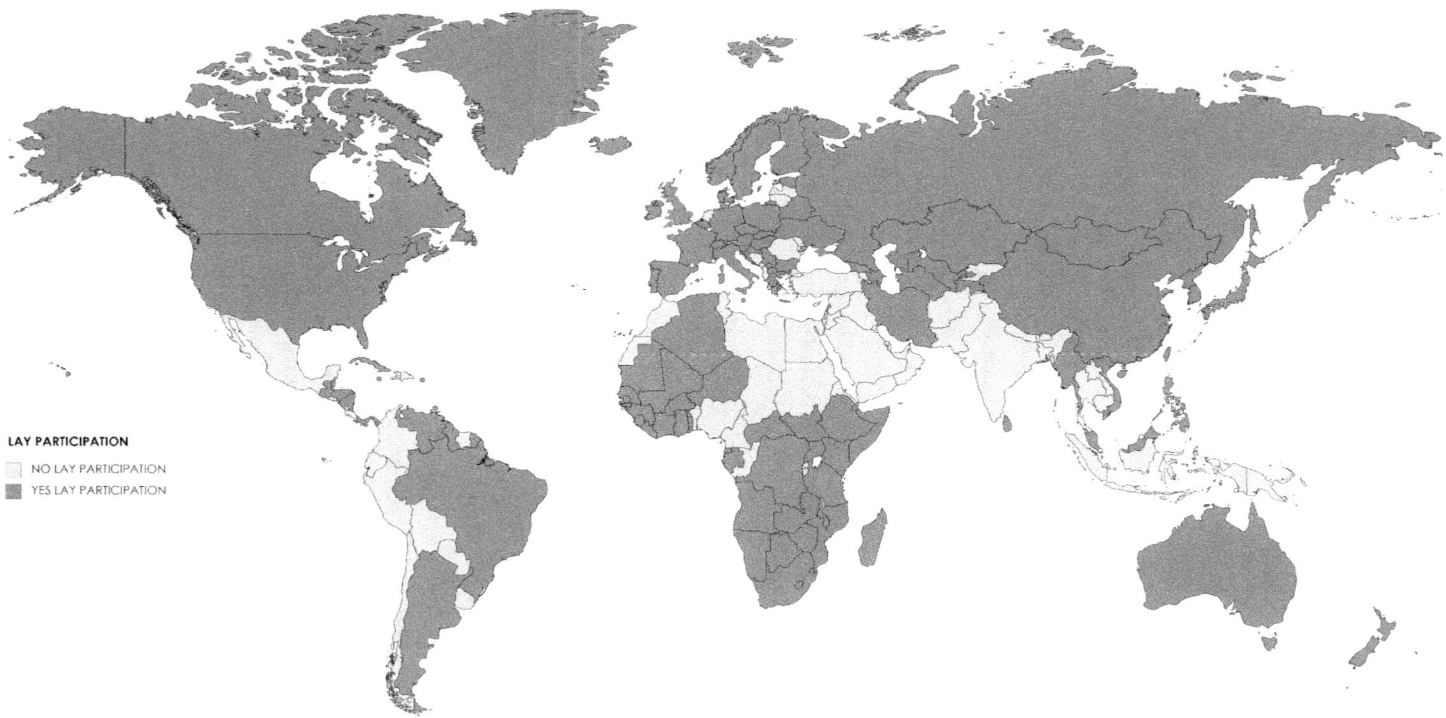

FIGURE 16.1 Map of lay participation

TABLE 16.1 *Lay participation by continent*

Continent	No lay participation		Some form of lay participation		Total
	N	Percent	N	Percent	
Africa	15	27.8%	39	72.2%	54 (100%)
Asia	27	58.7%	19	41.3%	46 (100%)
Australia & Oceania	1	7.1%	13	92.9%	14 (100%)
Europe	14	30.4%	32	69.6%	46 (100%)
North America	5	21.7%	18	78.3%	23 (100%)
South America	8	66.7%	4	33.3%	12 (100%)
Total	70	35.9%	125	64.1%	195 (100%)

lay participation. Table 16.1 shows that 125 of the 195 countries or about two-thirds (64%) of the countries use laypersons as legal decision-makers in criminal cases. On the continents of Africa, Australia and Oceania, Europe, and North America, the majority of countries incorporate laypersons into their legal procedures. The percentage of countries with lay participation on those continents ranges from a low of 70% in Europe to 93% in Australia and Oceania. In contrast, on the continents of Asia and South America, the majority of countries do not have lay participation, with just 41% of the countries in Asia and 33% of the countries in South America reporting some form of lay participation.

Legal Traditions and Lay Participation

The civil-law tradition is the most widespread across the world (Table 16.2); 140 countries or 72% of the world's countries have their legal systems either completely or partially based on the civil-law tradition (Table 16.2). The common-law tradition is the second most frequent, with 76 countries or 39% of the world's countries relying on it either completely or partially (Table 16.2). Although customary law is almost never used as the sole legal tradition, it is a part of the legal tradition of about one-third of the countries in the world (61 countries or 31% of the world's countries). The socialist-law tradition is never used as the sole legal tradition, and the Islamic-law tradition is very infrequently used as the only legal tradition. The Islamic-law tradition is combined with other legal traditions more frequently (37 countries or 19% of the world's countries) than is the socialist-law tradition (4 countries or 2% of the world's countries).

We first explore lay participation in the countries that belong to only one legal tradition. Although most of the countries that belong to either the common-law tradition or the civil-law tradition use lay participation, lay participation is somewhat more likely to be associated with the common-law tradition (73%) than the civil-law tradition (60%) (see Table 16.2). The number of countries belonging exclusively to

TABLE 16.2 *Lay participation by legal tradition*

Legal tradition	No LP		Yes LP		Total
	N	Percent	N	Percent	
Common	3	12.5%	21	87.5%	24 (100%)
Civil	29	37.7%	48	62.3%	77 (100%)
Socialist	0	0.0%	0	0.0%	0 (0.0%)
Islam	0	0.0%	1	100.0%	1 (100%)
Customary	0	0.0%	1	100.0%	1 (100%)
Common & civil	2	28.6%	5	71.4%	7 (100%)
Common & Islam	6	100.0%	0	0.0%	6 (100%)
Common & customary	1	5.9%	16	94.1%	17 (100%)
Common & religious	2	100.0%	0	0.0%	2 (100%)
Civil & socialist	1	33.3%	2	66.7%	3 (100%)
Civil & Islam	8	66.7%	4	33.3%	12 (100%)
Civil & customary	8	47.1%	9	52.9%	17 (100%)
Common, civil, & Islam	2	100.0%	0	0.0%	2 (100%)
Common, civil, & customary	1	11.1%	8	88.9%	9 (100%)
Common, Islam, & customary	1	25.0%	3	75.0%	4 (100%)
Civil, Islam, & customary	3	37.5%	5	62.5%	8 (100%)
Common, civil, socialist, & customary	1	100.0%	0	0.0%	1 (100%)
Common, civil, Islam, & customary	2	50.0%	2	50.0%	4 (100%)
Total	70	35.9%	125	64.1%	195 (100%)

either the Islamic-law tradition or customary law is too small to allow for broad conclusions.

We next explore countries by legal tradition, regardless of whether the country has only one legal tradition or has other legal traditions as well. Although the percentage varies depending on the combination of legal traditions, the majority of countries whose legal systems have at least some common-law DNA (Table 16.2) frequently incorporate lay participation into their decision-making in criminal courts. The only exception from this general rule is when the Islamic-law tradition is one of the legal traditions.

A very similar conclusion may be drawn about the countries in which the civil-law tradition is at least partly incorporated in their legal history (Table 16.2). Regardless of which legal traditions are mixed with the civil-law tradition, lay participation exists in most of these countries. The only exceptions are the countries in which the mixture of legal traditions includes Islamic law.

Having customary law incorporated into the legal DNA tends to be associated with an even higher chance of having lay participation (Table 16.2). This seems to be true even when one of the legal traditions included in the mix with the customary law is the Islamic-legal tradition.

When the Islamic legal tradition is combined with either the common-law tradition or the civil-law tradition, these countries are less likely to have lay participation than are countries with other combinations of legal traditions (Table 16.2). However, when customary law is added to the mix, the chances of having lay participation increase and at least one-half of these countries incorporate lay participation into their criminal courts (Table 16.2).

Only four countries have a socialist-law tradition as one of their legal traditions. Two of them have lay participation and two do not (Table 16.2).

When customary law is part of a country's legal DNA, it is most likely to have lay participation (Table 16.2). When customary law is combined with one or two legal traditions, even including the Islamic-law tradition, the overwhelming majority of the countries tend to have lay participation. In the five countries in which customary law is combined with three legal traditions, the chances of lay participation are lower (Table 16.2).

Number of Forms of Lay Participation

Among 125 countries that use lay participation, the overwhelming majority – 92 countries or 74% of the countries with lay participation – use just a single form of lay participation (e.g., Germany, Trinidad and Tobago, and Ukraine). Thirty-one countries or 25% of countries with lay participation include two forms of lay participation (e.g., Argentina, Austria, United Kingdom, and Zambia). Two countries (Angola and Belize) incorporate three forms of lay participation. No country uses all four forms of lay participation in their criminal courts (Table 16.3).

Although about three-quarters of the countries that use lay participation rely on only one form of lay participation (Table 16.3), the extent to which they do so varies across continents. Whereas countries in Asia and North America are most likely to use just one form of lay participation, countries in Africa and Australia and Oceania are most likely to use two forms of lay participation.

TABLE 16.3 *Number of forms of lay participation by continent*

Continent	One form		Two forms		Three forms		Total
	N	Percent	N	Percent	N	Percent	
Africa	24	61.5%	14	35.9%	1	2.6%	39 (100%)
Asia	17	89.5%	2	10.5%	0	0.0%	19 (100%)
Australia & Oceania	9	69.2%	4	30.8%	0	0.0%	13 (100%)
Europe	24	75.0%	8	25.0%	0	0.0%	32 (100%)
North America	15	83.3%	2	11.1%	1	5.6%	18 (100%)
South America	3	75.0%	1	25.0%	0	0.0%	4 (100%)
Total	92	73.6%	31	24.8%	2	1.6%	125 (100%)

TABLE 16.4 *Number of forms of lay participation by legal tradition*

Legal tradition	One form		Two forms		Three forms		Total
	N	Percent	N	Percent	N	Percent	
Common	16	76.2%	4	19.0%	1	4.8%	21 (100%)
Civil	37	77.1%	10	20.8%	1	2.1%	48 (100%)
Islam	0	0.0%	1	100.0%	0	0.0%	1 (100%)
Customary	0	0.0%	1	100.0%	0	0.0%	1 (100%)
Common & civil	4	80.0%	1	20.0%	0	0.0%	5 (100%)
Common & customary	10	62.5%	6	37.5%	0	0.0%	16 (100%)
Civil & socialist	1	50.0%	1	50.0%	0	0.0%	2 (100%)
Civil & Islam	2	50.0%	2	50.0%	0	0.0%	4 (100%)
Civil & customary	8	88.9%	1	11.1%	0	0.0%	9 (100%)
Common, civil, & customary	8	100.0%	0	0.0%	0	0.0%	8 (100%)
Common, Islam, & customary	2	66.7%	1	33.3%	0	0.0%	3 (100%)
Civil, Islam, & customary	2	40.0%	3	60.0%	0	0.0%	5 (100%)
Common, civil, Islam, & customary	2	100.0%	0	0.0%	0	0.0%	2 (100%)
Total	92	73.6%	31	24.8%	2	1.6%	125 (100%)

The number of forms of lay participation used in a country seems to depend upon the dominant legal tradition (Table 16.4). The common-law tradition, whether it is the only legal tradition in the country or just one of the legal traditions used in the country, typically leads to only one form of lay participation. About three-quarters (76%) of the countries that rely on the common-law tradition use only one form of lay participation. While countries with the common-law tradition, either exclusively or in combination with another legal tradition, account for about 44% of the countries with any lay participation, they account for only 39% of the countries that use two forms of lay participation.

Similarly, most (77%) civil-law countries also typically employ only one form of lay participation (Table 16.4). The countries that have civil law as their only legal tradition or as one of their legal traditions are proportionately represented among the countries with two forms of lay participation; they constitute about two-thirds (66%) of countries with any lay participation and, similarly, close to two-thirds (58%) of countries that use two forms of lay participation.

The number of countries that incorporate Islamic law into their legal systems is much smaller than the other legal traditions, making broad generalization difficult. For instance, just one country has Islamic law as its only legal tradition. It seems that the countries that have Islamic law as their only legal tradition or one of their legal traditions, particularly if combined with civil law, tend to be somewhat more inclined to incorporate two forms of lay participation (Table 16.4). Whereas countries with lay participation that have Islamic law in their legal systems account for about 12% of all countries with any lay participation, they account for about 23% of countries that have two forms of lay participation.

Similarly, countries that incorporate customary law into their legal systems also account for a larger percentage of countries with two forms of lay participation. Although countries that use customary law account for about 35% of all countries with any lay participation, their proportion in countries that use two forms of lay participation is somewhat higher at 39%.

Forms of Lay Participation

Table 16.5 reveals that mixed tribunals and juries are the two most frequently used forms of lay participation around the world, with juries present in 29% of the countries and mixed tribunals in 36% of the countries of the world. Lay magistrates (in 7% of the countries) and lay courts (in 10%) are found much less frequently. If we exclude countries that do not use any lay participation and compare the forms of lay participation across the countries that do use lay participation, mixed tribunals are the most frequently used (57%), followed by juries (45%). Magistrates and lay courts (10% and 16%, respectively) are used much less frequently (Table 16.5).

Countries with juries and mixed tribunals tend to rely solely on their own predominant approach to lay participation. Of 71 countries with mixed tribunals and 56 with juries, only 10 include both of these popular forms of lay participation. Countries relying on the less frequently used forms of lay participation (lay magistrates in 13 countries and lay courts in 20) are more likely to include another form of lay participation as well. All 13 of the countries with lay magistrates use another form of lay participation (100%), and 18 of the 20 countries with lay courts also use another form of lay participation (90%).

Table 16.6 and Figure 16.1 show the spread of different forms of lay participation across the continents. With the exception of magistrates and lay courts, other forms

TABLE 16.5 *Frequency and percentage of forms of lay participation*

	Countries with any LP form	Countries with juries	Countries with mixed tribunals	Countries with magistrates	Countries with lay courts
Number of countries with LP	125	56	71	13	20
Percentage of all countries	64.1%	28.7%	36.4%	6.7%	10.3%
Percentage of countries with any form of LP	100.0%	44.8%	56.8%	10.4%	16.0%

TABLE 16.6 *Forms of lay participation by continent*

Continent	Yes juries			Yes mixed tribunals		
	N	Percent of all countries on the continent	Percent of all countries with juries	N	Percent of all countries on the continent	Percent of all countries with MTs
Africa	16	29.6%	28.6%	23	42.6%	32.4%
Asia	6	13.0%	10.7%	12	26.1%	16.9%
Australia & Oceania	5	35.7%	8.9%	7	50.0%	9.9%
Europe	10	21.7%	17.9%	25	54.3%	35.2%
North America	16	69.6%	28.6%	2	8.7%	2.8%
South America	3	25.0%	5.3%	2	16.7%	2.8%
Total	56	28.7%	100.0%	71	36.4%	100.0%

Continent	Yes magistrates			Yes lay courts		
	N	Percent of all countries on the continent	Percent of all countries with magistrates	N	Percent of all countries on the continent	Percent of all countries with lay courts
Africa	4	7.4%	30.8%	12	22.2%	60.0%
Asia	0	0.0%	0.0%	3	6.5%	15.0%
Australia & Oceania	4	28.6%	30.8%	1	7.1%	5.0%
Europe	3	6.5%	23.1%	2	4.3%	10.0%
North America	2	8.7%	15.4%	2	8.7%	10.0%
South America	0	0.0%	0.0%	0	0.0%	0.0%
Total	13	6.7%	100.0%	20	10.3%	100.0%

of lay participation are used across all six continents. Furthermore, our data indicate that the highest proportion of countries that use juries on each continent are found in North America (70%), followed by Australia and Oceania (36%), and Africa (30%). The proportion of countries that use mixed tribunals on each continent also varies greatly (Table 16.6). The majority of the countries in Europe (54%) and Australia and Oceania (50%), and close to one-half of the countries in Africa (43%), use mixed tribunals (Table 16.6). However, only about 20% of the countries in Asia (26%), North America (9%), and South America (17%) rely on mixed tribunals (Table 16.6). Lay magistrates are less frequently represented overall; they are most likely to be selected as a form of lay participation in Australia and Oceania (29%), just as lay courts are most likely to be found as a form of lay participation in Africa (22%; Table 16.6).

Another way to explore the distribution of lay participation forms across the continents is to study all the countries that use the same form (Table 16.6). Juries are primarily used by countries in Africa (29% of all countries with juries) and North America (29% of the countries with juries). On the other hand, mixed tribunals seem to be primarily used in Europe (35% of countries with mixed tribunals) and Africa (32% of countries with mixed tribunals). Lay magistrates are spread across Africa (31%), Australia and Oceania (31%), and Europe (23%). Finally, lay courts are found almost exclusively in Africa (60%).

Table 16.7 describes the distribution of different forms of lay participation across legal traditions. While juries and lay magistrates are used in countries that follow the common-law tradition and the civil-law tradition, mixed tribunals appear to be more concentrated in countries that adhere to the civil-law tradition (Table 16.7).

Combining the countries in which the common-law tradition is one of the legal traditions with the countries in which the common-law tradition is the only legal tradition reveals that 33 countries or 59% of the countries that use the jury have the common-law tradition in their DNA (Table 16.7). Although the jury is not as widespread in civil-law countries, 27 countries or 48% of the countries that use juries have the civil-law tradition in their DNA as well.

Mixed tribunals are more concentrated in the civil-law tradition (Table 16.7). About one-half of the countries that use mixed tribunals adhere to the civil-law tradition as their only legal tradition (52%). When all the countries with mixed tribunals are examined, the overwhelming majority of them (59 countries or 83% of the countries with mixed tribunals) have the civil-law tradition in their DNA. The common-law tradition is not as frequent in countries with mixed tribunals (only 21 countries or about 30% of the countries with mixed tribunals have the common-law tradition in their DNA) and, in about one-half of these countries, the civil-law tradition is present as well.

Like juries, magistrates seem to be more concentrated in countries with a common-law tradition (10 countries or 77% of the countries with magistrates; Table 16.7). Although the civil-law tradition seems to be represented as well among countries with magistrates (3 countries or 23% of the countries with magistrates), it is not as dominant as the common-law tradition for magistrates.

Finally, lay courts tend to be associated with the civil-law tradition (Table 16.7). Fourteen countries or about 70% of the countries with lay courts tend to have the civil-law tradition as one of their legal traditions. Customary law is also well represented among the countries with lay courts. About one-half of the countries (10 countries or 50% of the countries with lay courts) have customary law (Table 16.7), while the common-law tradition (25%) and the Islamic-law tradition (25%) are not found as frequently in countries with lay courts.

TABLE 16.7 *Forms of lay participation by legal tradition*

	Yes juries		Yes mixed tribunals		Yes magistrates		Yes lay courts	
Legal tradition	N	Percent of all countries with juries	N	Percent of all countries with mixed tribunals	N	Percent of all countries with magistrates	N	Percent of all countries with lay courts
Common	19	33.9%	2	2.8%	5	38.5%	1	5.0%
Civil	14	25.0%	37	52.1%	3	23.1%	6	30.0%
Socialist	0	0.0%	0	0.0%	0	0.0%	0	0.0%
Islam	1	1.8%	0	0.0%	0	0.0%	1	5.0%
Customary	1	1.8%	0	0.0%	0	0.0%	1	5.0%
Common & civil	3	5.4%	3	4.2%	0	0.0%	0	0.0%
Common & Islam	0	0.0%	0	0.0%	0	0.0%	0	0.0%
Common & customary	7	12.5%	7	9.9%	5	38.5%	3	15.0%
Common & religious	0	0.0%	0	0.0%	0	0.0%	0	0.0%
Civil & socialist	0	0.0%	2	2.8%	0	0.0%	1	5.0%
Civil & Islam	1	1.8%	4	5.6%	0	0.0%	1	5.0%
Civil & customary	3	5.4%	4	5.6%	0	0.0%	3	15.0%
Common, civil, & Islam	0	0.0%	0	0.0%	0	0.0%	0	0.0%
Common, civil, & customary	2	3.6%	6	8.5%	0	0.0%	0	0.0%
Common, Islam, & customary	1	1.8%	3	4.2%	0	0.0%	0	0.0%
Civil, Islam, & customary	3	5.4%	3	4.2%	0	0.0%	2	10.0%
Common, civil, socialist, & customary	0	0.0%	0	0.0%	0	0.0%	0	0.0%
Common, civil, Islam, & customary	1	1.8%	0	0.0%	0	0.0%	1	5.0%
Total	56	100.0%	71	100.0%	13	100.0%	20	100.0%

CONCLUSION

Our goal in this chapter was to present a panoramic snapshot of the global spread of lay participation. Our analysis of these data is just beginning, but already some clear patterns have emerged.

First, the survey documents the strong prevalence of lay citizen decision-making in criminal courts around the world. Close to two-thirds of the countries in the world use some form of lay participation. This is a remarkable finding. From a historical perspective, in a world with few law-trained judges, it made sense to call on a community's members to decide legal disputes (Green, 1985; Langbein, Lerner, & Smith, 2009). Over the last century, and arguably even before that time, as the legal profession developed and the judiciary became increasingly professionalized, lawyers and legally trained judges increased in substantial numbers, reducing the need to rely on untrained citizens. Today, many if not most countries have more than a sufficient number of law-trained advocates and judges to staff their courts (Abel & Lewis, 1995). Nevertheless, the legal systems of close to two-thirds of the countries in our survey retain some element of lay citizen decision-making. Although prior research by Jackson and Kovalev, Thaman, Vidmar, and Voigt examined only a subset of the countries that are included in the present survey, we note with interest that our conclusion that approximately two-thirds of the world countries use lay participation aligns nicely with the 66% figure from Voigt's (2009) research. This strong presence of the citizenry may well reflect a political recognition of the legitimizing effects of public involvement in law, among other benefits.

Some scholars have documented declines in trials, including jury trials, over time (see, for example, Galanter, 2004; Lahav, 2017; Thomas, 2016). Jackson and Kovalev's (2006, 2016) surveys a decade apart also showed increasing restrictions on lay participation in legal decision-making. Our survey cannot speak to changes over time; its goal is to provide a current account of the presence of lay participation in different countries. Nonetheless, this contemporary snapshot can be used by future researchers to reveal continuity with or departure from the past. This snapshot can serve as a baseline measure of global lay participation should we or other researchers want to examine changes in the future.

Second, our survey confirms that countries adopt a diversity of approaches to lay participation in legal decision-making. The approaches are not random, but vary by the geographical region and the legal traditions of the countries. Countries that rely on the common-law tradition or customary law are more likely to have lay participation. The civil-law tradition does not have such a uniform effect: the civil-law tradition in a country's legal DNA tends to yield lay participation in countries in Africa, Europe, and Australia and Oceania, but not in Asia and South America. However, the Islamic-law tradition appears to have a more homogeneous effect: when the Islamic-law tradition is included in a country's mix of legal traditions, it is typically associated with no lay participation.

While the common-law tradition typically tends to be associated with juries, juries are to be found in countries that have the civil-law tradition in their legal DNA as well. However, mixed tribunals are almost exclusively associated with the civil-law tradition, mostly in Europe and Africa, just as magistrates are typically found in countries with a common-law tradition, mostly in Australia and Oceania. Lay courts are found in countries that use the civil-law tradition and/or customary law, typically in countries in Africa.

The global dissemination of the English common-law system (Vogler, 2005) and the French civil-law system (Hans & Germain, 2011) throughout the British and French empires respectively helps to explain both of these patterns. The predominance of juries and lay magistrates in common-law countries and mixed tribunals in civil-law countries also makes sense, considering this history.

Because the socialist-law tradition is closely linked with the civil-law tradition (e.g., Quigley, 1989; Reichel, 2008), it comes as no surprise that many of the now former communist countries used mixed tribunals during their period of socialist law, and that some of the countries that currently incorporate the socialist-law tradition use mixed tribunals. Once the communist regimes in Eastern Europe/Asia were toppled in the 1990s, the former communist countries mostly retained the same form of lay participation that is typical of civil-law countries – mixed tribunals (e.g., Belarus, Croatia, the Czech Republic, Hungary, Serbia, and the Slovak Republic) – or, less frequently, introduced a jury (e.g., Georgia, North Macedonia, and Russia) or abolished lay participation altogether (e.g., Bosnia and Herzegovina, Kazakhstan, and Montenegro).

Earlier, we observed that scholarship on lay participation has been uneven, focusing on jurors on juries and lay assessors on mixed tribunals to the relative exclusion of lay magistrates and lay courts. We now see that the former approaches (jurors and lay assessors) are much more common uses of lay participation, but now we are also able to identify the smaller number of countries that use lay magistrates and lay courts and can focus research attention on these distinctive forms.

Another way in which scholarship on lay participation has been uneven is in its geographical coverage. In particular, there is a relative dearth of research on lay participation in its multiple forms on the continent of Africa. Yet our survey reveals it is a continent with a substantial amount of lay participation, both in terms of its geographical spread and the number of forms of lay participation, which calls for further investigation. Our hope is that our survey findings will encourage scholars and policy-makers to recognize the importance of lay participation in legal decision-making. We also hope that they will undertake more systematic studies of how lay participation is implemented and used in countries around the world.

Acknowledgment: Valerie P. Hans is grateful to the Milton and Eleanor Gould Research Fund, the Eisenberg Empirical Legal Studies Memorial Fund, and

Cornell Law School for generously supporting the work on this chapter. Valerie P. Hans and Sanja Kutnjak Ivković are grateful to Eisenberg Research Scholar Alessandra Scalise for her contributions to the global survey of lay participation.

REFERENCES

Abel, R. L., & Lewis, P. S. C. (Eds.). (1995). *Lawyers in society: An overview*. Oakland: University of California Press.

Baldwin, J., & McConville, M. (1979). *Jury trials*. Oxford: Clarendon Press.

Bracey, D. (2006). *Exploring law and culture*. Long Grove, IL: Waveland Press.

Burd, K. A., & Hans, V. P. (2018). Reasoned verdicts: Oversold? *Cornell International Law Journal*, 51, 319–360.

CIA World Factbook. (2019). www.cia.gov/library/publications/the-world-factbook/geos/tt.html

Colvin, E. (2004). Criminal procedure in the South Pacific. *Journal of South Pacific Law*, 8(1). www.paclii.org/journals/fJSPL/vol08no1/1.shtml

Diamond, S. S. (1990). Revising images of public punitiveness: Sentencing by lay and professional English magistrates. *Law & Social Inquiry*, 15, 191–221.

Diamond, S. S., & Rose, M. R. (2018). The contemporary American jury. *Annual Review of Law and Social Science*, 14, 239–258.

Galanter, M. (2004). The vanishing trial: An examination of trials and related matters in federal and state courts. *Journal of Empirical Legal Studies*, 1, 459–570. https://doi.org/10.1111/j.1740–1461.2004.00014.x

Gilbert, K. (2018, May 29). Countries that recognize Taiwan. *WorldAtlas.com*. www.worldatlas.com/articles/which-countries-recognize-taiwan-as-a-country.html

Grant, B., & Schwikkard, P. (1991). People's courts? *South African Journal on Human Rights*, 7, 304–316.

Green, T. A. (1985). *Verdict according to conscience: Perspectives on the English criminal trial jury 1200–1800*. Chicago: University of Chicago Press.

Hans, V. P. (2008). Jury systems around the world. *Annual Review of Law & Social Science*, 4, 275–297.

Hans, V. P., Fukurai, H., Kutnjak Ivković, S., & Park, J. (2017). Global juries: A plan for research. In M. B. Kovera (Ed.), *The psychology of juries: Current knowledge and a research agenda for the future* (pp. 131–157). Washington, DC: APA Books.

Hans, V. P., & Germain, C. (2011). The French jury at a crossroads. *Chicago-Kent Law Review*, 86, 737–768.

Jackson, J. D., & Kovalev, N. P. (2006). Lay adjudication and human rights in Europe. *Columbia Journal of European Law*, 13, 83–123.

(2016). Lay adjudication in Europe: The rise and fall of the traditional jury. *Oñati Socio-Legal Series*, 6, 368–395. http://ssrn.com/abstract=2782413

Kovalev, N. P. (2010). *Criminal justice reform in Russia, Ukraine and the Former Republics of the Soviet Union: Trial by jury and mixed courts*. Lewiston, NY: Edwin Mellen Press.

(2014). Selection of jurors and lay assessors in comparative perspective: Eurasian context. *Russian Law Journal*, 11(2), 9–62.

Kritzer, H. M. (Ed.). (2002). *Legal systems of the world: A political, social, and cultural encyclopedia*. Santa Barbara, CA: ABC-CLIO.

Kutnjak Ivković, S. (1999). *Lay participation in criminal trials: The case of Croatia*. Lanham, MD: Austin & Winfield.

Lahav, A. (2017). *In praise of litigation*. New York: Oxford University Press.
Langbein, J. H., Lerner, R. L., & Smith, B. P. (2009). *History of the common law: The development of Anglo-American legal institutions*. New York: Aspen Publishers.
Le jury dans le procès pénal au XXI siècle [The lay participation in the criminal trial in the XXIst century]. (2001). *Revue Internationale de Droit Penal (International Review of Penal Law)*, 72, 1 & 2 trimesters.
Lloyd-Bostock, S., & Thomas, C. (2000). The continuing decline of the English jury. In N. Vidmar (Ed.), *World jury systems* (pp. 53–91). New York: Oxford University Press.
Malsch, M. (2009). *Democracy in the courts: Lay participation in European criminal justice systems*. Farnham, England: Ashgate.
Marder, N. S. (forthcoming). *The power of the jury: Transforming citizens into jurors*. Cambridge: Cambridge University Press.
Marder, N. S., & Hans, V. P. (2015). Introduction to juries and lay participation: American perspectives and global trends. *Chicago-Kent Law Review*, 90, 789–824.
(2016). Introduction to juries and mixed tribunals across the globe: New developments, common challenges and future directions. *Oñati Socio-Legal Series*, 6, 163–178. http://ssrn.com/abstract=2785708
Park, R. Y. (2010). The globalizing jury trial: Lessons and insights from Korea. *American Journal of Comparative Law*, 58, 525–582.
Provine, D. M. (1986). *Judging credentials: Nonlawyer judges and the politics of professionalism*. Chicago: University of Chicago Press.
Quigley, J. (1989). Socialist law and the civil law tradition. *American Journal of Comparative Law*, 37, 781–808.
Reichel, P. L. (2008). *Comparative criminal justice systems: A topical approach*. Upper Saddle River, NJ: Prentice Hall.
Salas, L. (1983). The emergence and decline of the Cuban popular courts. *Law & Society Review*, 17, 587–612.
Taxquet v. Belgium, Application No. 926/05 (2010). www.legal-tools.org/doc/a77480/pdf
Thaman, S. C. (2001). The idea of the conference. *International Review of Penal Law*, 72, 19–23.
Thomas, S. A. (2016). *The missing American jury*. New York: Cambridge University Press.
Vidmar, N. (1999). The common law jury. *Law and Contemporary Problems*, 62(2), 1–5.
(Ed.). (2000). *World jury systems*. New York: Oxford University Press.
(2002). Juries and lay assessors in the Commonwealth: A contemporary survey. *Criminal Law Forum*, 13, 385–407.
Vidmar, N., & Hans, V. P. (2007). *American juries: The verdict*. New York: Prometheus Books.
Vogler, R. (2005). *A world view of criminal justice*. Burlington, VT: Ashgate.
Voigt, S. (2009). The effects of lay participation in courts: A cross-country analysis. *European Journal of Political Economy*, 25, 327–339. doi:10.1016/j.ejpoleco.2009.02.005
World Atlas. (2019). www.worldatlas.com/cntycont.htm

Name Index

Subject Index

www.ingramcontent.com/pod-product-compliance
Lightning Source LLC
LaVergne TN
LVHW011702200926
848484LV00004B/1043
9781108483940